Spanish and Empire

HISPANIC ISSUES • VOLUME 34

Spanish and Empire

Nelsy Echávez-Solano

AND

Kenya C. Dworkin y Méndez

EDITORS

Vanderbilt University Press
NASHVILLE, TENNESSEE
2007

© 2007 Vanderbilt University Press
All rights reserved
First Edition 2007

The editors gratefully acknowledge assistance from the College of Liberal Arts and the Department of Spanish and Portuguese Studies at the University of Minnesota.

Frontispiece: *Americae sive quartae orbis partis nova et exactissima descriptio*, Diego Gutiérrez (1562). Library of Congress, Geography and Map Division.

The complete list of volumes in the Hispanic Issues series begins on page 273.

Library of Congress Cataloging-in-Publication Data

Spanish and empire / Nelsy Echavez-Solano and Kenya C. Dworkin y Mendez, editors.—1st ed.
  p. cm.—(Hispanic issues ; v. 34)
Includes bibliographical references and index.
ISBN 978-0-8265-1566-7 (cloth : alk. paper)
ISBN 978-0-8265-1567-4 (pbk. : alk. paper)
 1. Language and culture—Latin America.
2. Latin America—Civilization. 3. Imperialism—History.
4. Spanish language—Political aspects—Latin America.
5. English language—Political aspects—United States.
I. Echávez-Solano, Nelsy II. Dworkin y Méndez, Kenya.
F1408.3.S577 2007
980—dc22
2006038990

HISPANIC ISSUES

Nicholas Spadaccini
Editor-in-Chief

Antonio Ramos-Gascón and Jenaro Talens
General Editors

Nelsy Echávez-Solano and Luis Martín-Estudillo
Associate Editors

Fernando Ordóñez and Eric Dickey
Assistant Editors

*Advisory Board/Editorial Board
Rolena Adorno (Yale University)
Román de la Campa (Unversity of Pennsylvania)
David Castillo (University at Buffalo)
Jaime Concha (University of California, San Diego)
Tom Conley (Harvard University)
William Eggington (Johns Hopkins University)
Brad Epps (Harvard University)
Eduardo Forastieri-Braschi (Universidad de Puerto Rico, Río Piedras)
David W. Foster (Arizona State University)
Edward Friedman (Vanderbilt University)
Wlad Godzich (University of California, Santa Cruz)
Antonio Gómez-Moriana (Université de Montréal)
Hans Ulrich Gumbrecht (Stanford University)
*René Jara (University of Minnesota)
*Carol A. Klee (University of Minnesota)
Eukene Lacarra Lanz (Universidad del País Vasco)
Tom Lewis (University of Iowa)
Jorge Lozano (Universidad Complutense de Madrid)
Walter D. Mignolo (Duke University)
*Louise Mirrer (The New-York Historical Society)
Mabel Moraña (Washington University in St. Louis)
Alberto Moreiras (University of Aberdeen)
Bradley Nelson (Concordia University)
Michael Nerlich (Université Blaise Pascal)
Miguel Tamen (Universidade de Lisboa)
Teresa Vilarós (University of Aberdeen)
Iris M. Zavala (UNESCO, Barcelona)
Santos Zunzunegui (Universidad del País Vasco)

A la memoria de Juan R. Lodares (1959–2005)

Contents

Introduction:
Revisiting Spanish and Empire
Nelsy Echávez-Solano and Kenya C. Dworkin y Méndez — xi

PART I
Imperial Legacy—Language and Power in the Spanish Colonial Sphere

1. Languages, Catholicism, and Power in the Hispanic Empire (1500-1770)
   Juan R. Lodares — 3

2. Echoes of the Voiceless: Language in Jesuit Missions in Paraguay
   Fernando Ordóñez — 32

3. Languages and Imperial Designs in the Andes
   Juan C. Godenzzi — 48

PART II
Language and Resistance—The Fight for National and Individual Identities

4. Exploring the Problematics of Non-Castilian Emigration to the Americas through *la vida cuartizada* of Joan/Juan Torrendell
   Thomas Harrington — 69

5. *The Foxes* by José María Arguedas: A Death Warrant for Peru's Modern National Project
   José Antonio Giménez Micó — 97

6. Nuyorican Poetry, Tactics for Local Resistance
   Susan M. Campbell — 117

7   Latino, Latin American, Spanish American,
    North American, or All at the Same Time?
    Edmundo Paz-Soldán   139

PART III
Spanish in the Era of Multiculturalism and Globalization

8   Language Imperialism and the Spread of Global Spanish
    Clare Mar-Molinero   155

9   Signs of Empire in Mexican Graphic Narrative:
    A Research Agenda
    Bruce Campbell   173

10 Spanish, English, or Spanglish?
    Truth and Consequences of U.S. Latino Bilingualism
    John M. Lipski   197

11 Language and Empire: A Conversation with Ilan Stavans
    Ilan Stavans and Verónica Albin   219

    Afterword:
    Spanish among Empires
    Luis Martín-Estudillo and Nicholas Spadaccini   245

    Contributors   257

    Index   261

◆ Introduction:
Revisiting Spanish and Empire

Nelsy Echávez-Solano and Kenya C. Dworkin y Méndez

> [*Siempre*] *la lengua fue compañera del imperio; y de tal manera lo siguió,*
> *que junta mente començaron, crecieron y florecieron,*
> *y después junta fue la caida de entrambos.*
> —Antonio de Nebrija (*Gramática de la Lengua Castellana*). 1492 [1926] (5)
>
> (Language has always accompanied empire; and as such followed it,
> and together they began, grew and flourished, and later collapsed, together.)

The essays in this volume address the related issues of 'empire' and 'imperialism,' and the role that language plays with regard to them. From their varied disciplinary perspectives, the contributors describe and theorize the issue of Spanish (and to some extent, English) in relation to empire, imperialism, and globalization. As a result, they both clarify and challenge received notions of postcolonialism, language and culture, as well as certain sociocultural and linguistic manifestations associated with them at different moments in time. This discussion is particularly relevant at a time when the end of nation-states, national identities, and imperial formations are often invoked. 'Empire' and 'imperialism' are understood within the larger framework of historically situated, epistemic and/or sociopolitical crises; they are related concepts that can also be used in the description of certain social, cultural, and linguistic manifestations.

The notion of 'empire' and language's instrumental role in its creation and sustainability are questioned in these pages. In addition, by using the Spanish example, and contrasting it to that of English, particularly in the U.S., there is an attempt to clarify how the divergent language policies of the two powers with regard to their colonies brought about markedly different situations for the two languages. This Introduction also examines prevailing notions about the role of language in the creation of national and personal identities, in both the Spanish and English cases, and how in this contemporary age, advanced communications technologies and an increasingly globalized economy have made new forms of 'imperialism' possible in which the relationship between language and hegemony has been further complicated. To understand the imperial legacy in North and South America is to understand that one of the strongest 'weapons' "in building homogeneous imagined communities is and was language, which in its complicity with literature, culture, and nation [is] also related to geopolitical order and geopolitical frontiers" (Mignolo 218).

For the past thirty years, these formulations, and the concepts 'language' and 'empire,' have been examined by literary and cultural critics from various academic disciplines. More recently, postcolonial studies and subaltern studies have emerged as new modes of inquiry that have re-energized and re-oriented the debate regarding these concepts. This volume offers an interdisciplinary critique of the place of Spanish in the rise of the Spanish empire and in the independence movements of colonial Spanish America; it also examines the place of English *and* Spanish, later, in the changing demographic composition of the United States. An appraisal of the history of the Spanish empire and its linguistic policies, when compared to the spread of English throughout much of the world via colonization and settlement, will highlight the political and linguistic differences between the two imperial experiences and their legacies. It will also examine the political and linguistic histories that have lead to the current situation of Spanish in the context of globalization.

Rethinking Language and Empire

The notion of 'empire' is a very old one. It can be understood as a political structure comprised geographically of continuous and/or discontinuous lands (e.g., the Roman empire, the Ottoman empire, the French empire); the existence of a core (e.g., Rome, Istanbul, Paris); and, the existence of a periphery (e.g., Judea, the Maghreb, Haiti) (Ortiz 39). Thus, its spatial dimension is paramount to its definition, and both the Spanish and British empires had a core and peripheries. Shmuel Noah Eisenstadt sees empire as a social formation, involving vast areas, diverse and sometimes displaced peoples, and a relentless burocratic endeavor for its constant organization via military or faith-based means involving universalist religions (certainly the case in the Spanish example) (Eisenstadt 1969 [quoted in Ortiz 2005: 39]). In its European conceptualization, 'empire' is a product of modernity and can be identified with, among other things, the rise of the nation-state, industrialization, capitalism, and urbanization (e.g., as in the British empire, the home of the Industrial Revolution); the creation of the modern printing press; and, the promulgation of totalizing principles in the name of reason, as well as scientific and philosophical truths.

For Michael Hardt and Antonio Negri (2000), the concept 'empire' subsumes even contemporary changes in imperial/colonial modalities, i.e., transnationalism and globalization. Yet, their view tends to reproduce and perpetuate a master narrative of empire, a version of history that is purely Western and does not really fit contemporary reality or the case of contemporary Spanish and/or English. Their view of 'empire' (derived from Immanuel Wallerstein's 1976 'postmodern world-system' theory), attempts to offer a potential explanation for the current state of world capitalism that is so celebrated and justified by neoliberal ideology (the very same thinking that touts the demise of the nation-state, and so on). Notwithstanding, it is the idea of the 'network society' (as 'empire'), a term first coined by Jan van Dijk in 1991 and then by Manuel Castells in 1996, that captures much more precisely how more recent forms of imperialism should be seen as new, recycled and permutated forms of 'empire' (Castells 70–166). For our purposes, this model of 'empire,' unlike Hardt and Negri's (or Wallerstein's), allows for a more inclusive analysis of the history and legacy of Spanish not only in Spain and in the Spanish colonies of the Americas, but also in the United States.

In contrast to 'empire,' the word 'imperialism' is relatively recent; it came into use after the Industrial Revolution and was first coined in France in the mid-nineteenth century (Koebner and Schmidt 1964 [quoted in Ostler 2005]), at precisely the same moment that the Spanish empire was in a rapid and steady state of decline, largely though not entirely due to the loss of most of its colonies. Thus, while the concept 'imperialism' was never properly applied to Spain and its empire (because it had all but collapsed before the mid-nineteenth century, with the notable exception of Cuba, Puerto Rico, and Spain's Pacific possessions), it was and continues to be used to describe the relationship between Great Britain and all its colonies after 1870. The notion of Spain as 'empire' connoted, above all, an economic and religious enterprise that was attained, maintained, and defended through military might and a substantial, constantly replenished, Spanish-born, colonial and religious bureaucracy. The British model, on the other hand, was more of a socio-economic construct that held itself together through one, unitary political, moral, and linguistic ideology (Ostler 2005). Three centuries and different motives distinguish the differences that set the Spanish and British empires apart. Their linguistic strategies also played an important role in their differences and legacies.

In distinguishing 'empire' from 'imperialism,' particularly at the turn of the twentieth century, and within the context of old and new empires, as well as global capitalism, it is important to note that whereas an empire (the core, the original seat of power) traditionally has 'imperial' policies, i.e., the practice of extending its authority, its economic and political (and sometimes religious) hegemony over other nations (the periphery), it *does not* follow that imperialism is necessarily contingent upon the existence of a geographic empire. So, while both the Spanish and British empires held overseas and distant maritime and landlocked territories, it is only in the past sixty or so years that the economic and political trends that reconfigured the *mapamundi* during the post-World War II and Cold War period, have squarely positioned the United States in its self-appointed role as chief arbiter, negotiator, and enforcer of the West's economic and political will—as a transterritorial empire. This had not been challenged again (since the collapse of the Soviet Union), from without or even within the borders of the U.S., until very recently, over the past twenty years, and particularly in the post–9-11 era. Yet there is much more to understanding empires, past and present, than just geographical considerations. The contemporary struggle for political, religious, and economic hegemony by competing world or regional powers has changed all that. Moreover, just as in the case of some, old-style empires, the current situation is having important linguistic ramifications as well.

Rethinking nineteenth- and twentieth-century imperialism requires an accounting of the diachronic contradictions (Rivera Cusicanqui 1992) and the structural heterogeneity (Quijano 1997) that characterized colonial power since the sixteenth century, and that in the recent *fin-de-siècle* have become globalized. Hardt and Negri's conception of the history of 'empire' does not do this; instead, it ignores the spatial dimension of imperialism. A linear view of imperial history cannot explain modern, imperial history outside the direct, Eurocentric trajectory of Roman antiquity to European modernity. Castells' model of the 'network society,' on the other hand, does consider spatiality and involves the whole world (Asia, Africa, Australia, Oceania and the Americas). Regarding Spain and empire, an approach such as this successfully explains how a concept like the 'New World' (vis-à-vis the 'Old World') was constructed through a colonization of space *and* time. It also recognizes colonial difference and goes beyond the limits of Eurocentrism (Mignolo 2005). A spatial and temporal history of coloniality is history from the perspective of those who must contend with the consequence of others' global designs.

The concept 'colonialism,' as it relates to 'colony' (a non-self governing territory and people, i.e., the periphery) refers specifically to the condition of a territory and its people that have been absorbed by and are under the political control of an imperial state (e.g., Spain or English). A 'colony' is a subordinate political structure (e.g., *Nueva España* or New England). 'Colonialism,' as it relates to 'imperialism,' describes the impact of being a colony governed by imperial policies (e.g., the economic situation of colonial Mexico or Peru vis-à-vis Spain or of the thirteen British colonies in their relationship to Britain). The terms 'colony' and 'colonialism' aptly describe the political structure of both Spain and Britain's overseas territories and the condition of the people who lived therein, under their control, but that is where any similarity between the Spanish and British empires ends. Furthermore, even after the 'official' end of some empires, many of the conditions consistent with empire continue to exist in the newly independent territories.

This sort of 'neocolonial' situation is best examined from a 'postcolonial' perspective. 'Postcolonialism' (a quintessentially postmodern concept) essentially denies the existence of the kinds of universal truths, grand explanatory principles, and master narratives so characteristic of traditionally defined empires. It also highlights the subjective nature of all communication (pertinent to Castells' 'network society' theory), questions the validity of knowledges and identities organized and created under modernity, and acknowledges the pluralistic, non-centered, globalized nature of the contemporary world. Its perspective, in many ways, can actually be seen as a product of 'network societies,' whose domination by mass media facilitates their consumption of modern ideas and identities. In Hardt and Negri's conception though, 'postcoloniality' is not an essential characteristic of 'postmodernity' but rather derives from it; hence; they do not see 'postcoloniality' as the ominous underbelly of 'postmodernity.' Rather, they see it as signaling the end of coloniality reorganization of it (Mignolo 2005).

Postcolonial studies are concerned with the historical and contemporary legacy of colonialism: the struggle to develop national and personal identities, and address the imperial organization of history and knowledge about colonial subjects (designed to serve only imperial interests) and how peripheries began and continue to interact with their cores using colonially imposed languages (Prospero's language, if you will), in their own Calibanesque way, for their own purposes. In the current situation, this also means an examination of the transnational and militaristic corporatism that in many ways has extended beyond any one, economic and geographic center.[1] Thus, in this case, global leadership is not the result of territorial possession but rather of "the emergence of a process of decolonization, and global or transnational capitalism, which has had tremendous impact on contemporary connections between colonialisms and cultures" (King 5).

The emergence of the new political, economic and/or technological order has redrawn the map of modernity/coloniality. But this has in no way made the concept of imperialism obsolete, not in the context of the five-hundred-year legacy of Spanish and empire in Spain and Latin America, nor in the case of Britain and its colonies. This is also not the case for the United States (also an ex-colony of Britain), where the continued and growing presence of racialized ethnic minorities and immigrants, and liberal, multiculturalist policies in the United States beg for postcolonial understanding of U.S. minority groups as 'internal colonized nations' struggling through a decolonization process (Sharpe 111). Susan Campbell's contribution to this volume illustrates just that point, by analyzing how late twentieth-century Nuyorican poetry, with its purposeful subversion of both English and Spanish, serves as an example of 'the empire writing back to its internal colonizer,' so to speak. The works of the poets she examines represent a political and linguistic struggle to garner validation, a process akin to Jesús Martín-Barbero's notion of a form of cultural expression "that points to [a new] form of struggle" (209).

At the present moment, the issue of the linguistic threat posed by Spanish-speakers, both immigrant and native, in the United States, is even stickier. Immigrants and citizens alike are caught up in the contradiction of our nation's multiculturalist impulse, which pretends to celebrate and even encourage linguistic and cultural difference (e.g., through magnet, bilingual and International Baccalaureate programs) and the nativist, 'Official English,' 'English Only,' anti-immigrant response of recent decades that have come to a head in 2006.[2] It would seem, then, that an examination of the role of language in empire and in identity construction is in order, since language is only one of many possible markers of them, and because identities, national and personal, are not necessarily contingent upon it. The role of language in official histories and nation building, in both the Spanish and English context, is another matter entirely.

Empires and their Linguistic Legacies

In 1492, when the humanist Antonio de Nebrija presented Queen Isabel with his *Gramática de la Lengua Castellana* (from which the epigraph that heads this introduction is taken), he shared with her his thoughts on the historical role of languages in empire building, going so far as to trace a brief history of the linguistic rise *and* fall of three previous empires and their languages: King David's and his successor King Solomon's kingdom, and Hebrew; the Greek empire, and Greek; and the Roman empire, and Latin. Nebrija's concern seems to have been less connected to Spain's ensuing imperial project or to a standardized form of the language, per se, than to a desire that the written historical record of Spain's accomplishments during its imperial ascent be recorded in a language that would remain accessible to many generations of readers, for posterity:

> Por que si otro tanto en nuestra lengua no se haze como en aquéllas, en vano vuestros cronistas y estoriadores escriven y encomiendan a inmortalidad la memoria de vuestros loables hechos, y nos otros tentamos de passar en castellano las cosas peregrinas y estrañas, pues que aqueste no puede ser sino negocio de pocos años. I será necessaria una de dos cosas: o que la memoria de vuestras hazañas perezca con la lengua; o que ande peregrinando por las naciones estrangeras, pues que no tiene propria casa en que pueda morar. ("Prólogo," *Gramática de la Lengua Castellana* 5)

> (Because if we do not do the same in our language as was done with those [others], your chroniclers and historians are writing and commending to immortality the memory of your praiseworthy deeds and we attempt to write in Castilian [about] peregrine and strange things in vain, such that [this] endeavor cannot be but short-lived. And one of two things will be inevitable: or that the memory of your deeds will perish with the language; or that it will peregrinate through foreign nations, since it does not have its own proper home in which to live.) [our translation]

Through his assertion that language and the survival of memory are inextricably linked, it seems clear that Nebrija was ostensibly concerned with the endurance and resilience of Spanish to preserve and guarantee access to the empire's historical record. Moreover, he feared that if Spanish had no 'proper home' (i.e., *protection*), it would be threatened and, perhaps, forever changed in its journeys through the empire's newly acquired foreign lands, hence his *Gramática* was the first guide on how to preserve it. However, this should not be understood only as a linguistic concern; rather, his preoccupation with the language and accessibility of the historical record can be seen as an imperial one inasmuch as it is a projection of the empire's ensuing responsibility for organizing knowledge about its colonial subjects, in written form, which it could then use as just one of many tools to colonize them *and* their thinking.

At the onset of 1492, what existed in Spain was essentially a linguistic alliance of the peninsula's three major Romance languages, Galician (*gallego*) to the west, Castilian (*castellano*) in the center, and Catalan (*català*) to the east (Ostler 2005). When the marriage of Isabel and Ferdinand in 1469 united the kingdoms of Castile and Aragon, the language of Castile took prominence in the whole of Spain, just prior to the end of the *Reconquista* and the first of the Columbus voyages (1492), and the meteoric rise of literature in the early seventeenth century. Even today, despite the fact that *gallego* and *català* have remained linguistically independent from Castilian, it is *castellano* that has become synonymous with *español,* or the Spanish language. In the Americas it is referred to by both names indistinguishably; in this volume, only the term 'Spanish' is used. Despite the prominence of Spanish at the dawn of the age of European discovery, conquest, and colonization, and the fact that ruling circles in Spain believed in a total unity of purpose between the Church and State with regard to the 'New World,' there was a dramatic and contradictory difference between the linguistic priorities of the two. Colonial authorities did not envision Spanish as a compulsory tool of empire, a *sine qua non.* This is an erroneous idea that is often repeated and sustained by a narrow reading of Antonio de Nebrija's *Gramática de la Lengua Castellana* (see Lodares in this volume).

Juan R. Lodares, who traces the rise to prominence of Spanish that took place in Spain during the empire's early years, explains that in its earlier stages, the Spanish empire actually found it more useful to learn and employ the indigenous languages of its new subjects, and thereby have more efficient communication with, and control over, them. Fernando Ordóñez further explains that it was the Spanish empire's desire to create an *Universitas Christiana,* a universal transnational Catholic community throughout its newly acquired territories and Europe, via local and vernacular languages, despite the objection of numerous clergymen who argued that, contrary to Latin, indigenous languages could not convey the subtleties of Christian dogma and thought. The success of the Jesuits in Paraguay is an excellent example of how efficient the use of indigenous languages could be in Spain's Christianizing mission. In fact, the survival of Guaraní, one of only two indigenous American languages to achieve the status of an official national language, is due primarily to the Jesuit missions of Paraguay between 1609 and 1767.

The effect of the Jesuit enterprise, when seen in combination with the low penetration of Spanish in extremely remote Guaraní-speaking areas and the lack of Spanish-speaking women, explains the problematic but privileged status of this one, native language next to Spanish in contemporary Paraguay.

This, however, is an exceptional case; it is not illustrative of the fate of the many other indigenous languages caught up in Spain's imperial enterprise (estimated to be between one thousand five hundred and two thousand prior to the arrival of Europeans in the New World). This is indicative, though, of how an imperial policy that was lax about linguistic hegemony could result in empowering languages other than the colonial one, which, itself, can inspire indigenous, linguistic nationalism in other areas of the empire and its former colonies where a viable bilingual model survived (e.g., Peru).

Keeping in mind the importance of language to imperial documentation and organization, the *flexible* linguistic policy that the Spanish empire chose to employ in the conquest and colonization of its territories made it imperative for it to devise some other strategy by which to maintain control—which it did. In keeping with Nebrija's concern for 'protecting' Spanish and access to the historical record for future generations, the empire attempted to control, what was written, what was omitted, and what was published and circulated. The vast Atlantic (and Pacific) empire was, indeed, ruled by Spain, a place that became the geographical center of a seemingly limitless empire, and Spanish was the *only* historical, 'official' language associated with it (Mignolo 1992b; 1992c [quoted in Mignolo 2000: 257]). This does not mean, however, that Spain's linguistic policy between the fifteenth and eighteenth centuries would not have serious implications for the position of Spanish, globally, after the fall of the empire.

If one compares the spread of Spanish to that of English, it becomes evident that the fact that Spanish was not used as a single, solitary (linguistic) instrument for the expansion of its power, territory, religion, and culture, contributed to past and present use of both Spanish and English around the world. In Spain, there continues to be 'competitor' languages (particularly *català* and Basque), despite the dominance of Castilian. Similarly, in Spanish America many indigenous languages persist, and two in particular, Guaraní and Quechua, have become state-sponsored, official languages. English, on the other hand, which took shape from the fifth to the sixteenth centuries, on the island of Britain, and has been propagated since the seventeenth century, was the only official language introduced for any and all purposes by the English in their colonial enterprise (Ostler 2005).[4] Since the mid-twentieth century, English, and its influence, have continued to spread far beyond the national boundaries of the original British Empire, particularly due to the economic and political success of its most powerful ex-colony, the United States.

Language, Territory, and Identity

Since by the middle of the eighteenth century, almost three hundred years into its colonial endeavor, Spain had not universally spread its language throughout its empire, now it attempted to do so proactively, by decree (1770, 1782) and through Spanish-language education. Ironically, however, real success in this area was to come about much more through a deliberate abandonment of instruction or evangelization in Spanish (even the Paraguayan Jesuits were expelled from South American in 1767) then through a sustained, funded educational campaign. By 1830, the majority of the Spanish colonies had already achieved their independence from Spain (except Cuba, Puerto Rico, and the Pacific territories), marking the beginning of the end for the Spanish empire—an end that finally came in 1898 at the hands of the United States—in Cuba (and around the globe). As late as 1810, when the first of the Spanish colonies fought for independence from Spain, the ratio of speakers of indigenous language versus Spanish was three to one (Rosenblat 189–216 [quoted in Ostler 2005]). There was one fact, however, that would contribute mightily to changing this ratio: the Spanish American nationalist movements had been driven almost exclusively by *criollos*, i.e., Spanish-speaking, American-born, Europeanized descendants of Spaniards and other Europeans (and some *mestizos*), and this was also the case in the remaining colonial territories. This played a major role in the survival of the Spanish language far beyond the collapse of the Spanish empire. Furthermore, as biological and cultural descendants of Spain, the *criollos* used Spanish to retain a cultural and economic link with its colonial parent. It was Spanish that the leadership of the former colonies used to maintain coherence with each other, as well. Thus, what began as a colonial language became a multifaceted tool by which the empire's *criollo* descendants simultaneously achieved their political, economic, and cultural independence *and* maintained their connections to the 'Old World.'

The American Revolution (1775–1783), on the other hand, which won the independence of the thirteen English-speaking colonies from Britain, firmly established an English-speaking power in North America, a place that at the time seemed to have limitless, far-reaching geographic possibilities. English became the *de facto* common language of almost every settlement in eastern North America (including Canada) into two centuries; in fact, by 1853, nearly seventy years after the initial independence of the thirteen colonies from Britain, areas that eventually became the continental U.S. (the lower 48), had come under English-speaking control. By 1890, even the intensely Spanish-speaking areas of the southwestern United States were populated by overwhelming numbers of English-speaking settlers (Ostler 2005).

The generally accepted one language-one nation model came to be problematic throughout Latin America's post-independence, nation-building period precisely because twenty countries shared the same national language. Nation building "required an intellectual tradition detached from Spain that frustrated the question of national language; the struggle to find linguistic autonomy in Spanish America turned again and again to the problematic legacy of Spanish" (Morse 16). In the Andean case, for example, particularly in Peru, the contributions of both Juan Carlos Godenzzi and José Giménez Micó maintain that Spanish was and continues to be an 'imperfect' but important code for communication and that Quechua and Quechua-inflected or 'cholified' Spanish are used as a resistance strategy and serve in the construction of intranational selfhood and, perhaps, nationhood, as well. Mignolo's concept of 'languaging' which focuses not so much on the use of language for communication but rather as a social force, is helpful here as is viewed Spanish not just as representative of a colonial language that has taken on properties of American (indigenous or African) languages but, more importantly, of 'border thinking' (2000).

Conversely, in his essay about the quintuple multipositionality of a Mallorcan born man who emigrates from the Balearic islands to Uruguay in 1888, Thomas Harrington (in this volume) points out how at least one individual (surely representative of many more) found a multiple, 'proto-nationality' in keeping with his multipositional rather than strictly geographically and politically defined identity, which was facilitated by the fact that Spanish was (and is) the language of more than just one country. This was certainly not the case in the linguistically hegemonic, British empire, or in its ex-colonies (including the U.S.), where colonials and ex-colonials everywhere were united by the use of English. Interestingly, regarding the U.S. specifically, mainstream public opinion rejects the notion that there have ever been any colonial practices in the United States and expresses disbelief at the notion that imperialism has played any role at all in the construction and sustainability of American hegemony, the 'American' way, the American standard of living, and so on (King 3). Yet, the fall of the Spanish empire, which was ultimately brought about by U.S., intervention in the Cuban War of Independence (1895–1898), contributed mightily to the rise of American dominance; and, with it, to the spread of English and the demotion of Spanish from the language of a world power to that of ethnic minorities and a significant portion of the 'Third World' (Mignolo 2000: 260).

Spanish—From Imperial to Postcolonial to Global

By the turn of the nineteenth century, after the final collapse of the Spanish empire, Latin America *and* Spain were undergoing multiple political transformations that, to some extent, relied on language-based cultural notions and on citizenship projects in which language education was central. Therefore, the establishment of a coherent language policy, the shaping of public discourse about language, and the exercise of control over the institutions that produce and re-produce them became a political necessity, particularly while Spain strove to regain national and international prestige. Thus, Spanish capitalized on the fact it was a multicentered language. Now, at the turn of the twentieth century, the various hubs of power in the Hispanic world—as well as within Spain—were competing within the organization of a new postcolonial order. Regarding the contemporary situation of Spanish in Spain (where it is the language of the central government), vis-à-vis the nation's other major languages (*català*, Basque, and *gallego*), there is an ongoing monolinguistic, or centralist, versus pro-multilinguistic or federalist debate.

Complicating this is the fact that there is a very rooted notion among Spain's regional citizens that, historically, the successful expansion of Spanish throughout the peninsula has come at the expense of all the other languages of Spain. In fact, Spain's regions are actively engaged in somewhat conflictive educational and hiring campaigns that are sometimes counterproductive in their efforts to rescue the regional languages and promote bilingualism, and at the same time combat the reality that it might actually be more efficient and beneficial for the nation's people to express themselves in a common, unifying language, particularly in governmental and business matters (Lodares 5). Many Spaniards are at least bilingual; yet Spanish *is* the official language of the central government. Depending on whether a Spaniard is a regionalist or a centralist, he or she might or might not agree that Spain is truly a multilingual country (rather than just a country in which there are multiple languages) because *all* Spaniards can communicate in Spanish. In matters of intraregional international governance or business though, many see it is less a question of choice and more as a situation that demands practicality. Therein lies the difference between actual, state-sponsored and real multilingualism and simply protected linguistic pluralism—an important difference for the construction of personal, regional, and national identities.

In Latin America, for example, there are two countries that have an indigenous language as second official language besides Spanish—Peru, with

Quechua (spoken by around eight and a half million people), and Paraguay, with Guaraní (spoken by about three million people). Paraguay, and to a lesser degree, Peru, practice official bilingualism and support it through education. Since the mid-nineties, bilingual-bicultural education programs have also cropped up in other countries with large indigenous populations, but their quality is not consistent and there is a persistent correlation between being indigenous *and* poor and under- or uneducated. Yet, the official bilingualism of Peru or Paraguay, or all Latin American bilingual education programs cannot change the fact that this situation is really just a rearticulation of some of Spanish America's indigenous languages vis-à-vis Spanish, not by Spanish colonial authorities, as happened in the past, but by a system of Spanish American, postcolonial education (Mignolo 2000: 268). There are also nearly four million speakers of at least eight more languages from large linguistic families, yet there are somewhere between five to seven hundred indigenous languages still existence in contemporary Latin America (an estimated 1000 fewer than in the pre-Colombian era). Thus, bilingual programs in Spanish America do not really change the hegemonic position of Spanish at all.[5]

In addition, it is not just the total number of speakers of Spanish that matters but rather the role of Spanish in the interdependence of the Spanish-speaking world and in technology-enhanced communication. The language's 'standardization' and commodification are also crucial to our understanding of Spanish in a globalized context. With Madrid at the center of this phenomenon, Spain seeks a triumphant reentry into its former colonies in the name of business and intercultural relations (Moraña xix). Moreover, Spain is extremely cognizant of the increasing Latinoamericanization of the U.S. with more than thirty five million Latinos, eighty percent of whom consider Spanish their native tongue. Given Spain's cultural linguistic designs in the twenty-first century, it would be foolish to ignore these demographics (Ostler 2005). Apropos this, Clare Mar-Molinero's contribution examines the role of institutions like the *Real Academia Española* (RAE) and the *Instituto Cervantes* in promoting and selling global Spanish. Complicating this exportable, normalizing force regarding Spanish on a contemporary, global scale, are the boundaries between Spanish in Latin America and its 'others,' and its "tense coexistence [with] English . . . in the United States . . . ." (Moraña xvii). Rama, as well as McClennon, reminds us that in Latin America foreign cultural intervention is not simply absorbed but "often manipulated, transformed and hybridized . . ." (McClennon 19). Bruce Campbell's contribution to this volume on recent Mexican graphic narrative production illustrates just this point. Campbell examines the effects of transnational experiences on the Mexican graphic novel, and, particularly, how U.S. modernizing norms circulate among Mexico's popular sectors and how these norms are negotiated in relation to Mexican national values.

This situation is, perhaps, akin to that of the United States, where the minority population, which speaks multiple languages, is also subject to the decentering effects of globalization. Furthermore, there is division between those in the U.S. who want more protection and promotion of linguistic pluralism in the U.S. and others who see that as a total anathema. Any similarity between the issue in Spain or Latin America and the United States ends here though. Unlike the situation in Spain, where Spanish and three other regional languages are officially recognized, and in Spanish-speaking Latin America, where it is the official language of twenty countries, English has been the U.S.'s *de facto* language (in 2006 it was also voted the 'nation's common and unifying language' and may yet be made the 'official' language, as well).

Yet, for many (Spanish-speaking citizens, residents, and others), Spanish remains at the core of Latino identity; this does not necessarily conflict in any way with their political allegiance to the U.S. or their national identity as 'Americans.' After all, it has been continually present in what became the United States of America for nearly five hundred years and the number of its speakers has increased over time not just through ongoing immigration (as many people think) but also through U.S. territorial expansion and acquisition.[6] Some might even say that because of this long, uninterrupted presence (longer than English, by at least a hundred years), it should be considered as 'American' a language as English (in the U.S. sense of the word 'American'). Apropos this Edmundo Paz-Soldán critiques the received notion that language and literature have an inheritent, 'natural' link with a nation-state (particularly in the context of the U.S.) and of what is termed 'American' literature vs. the literature of the countries of Spanish America. For him, this cultural, linguistic anxiety works in the other direction, too. It is important not to forget that in the part of America that became the United States, Spanish began as a colonizing language, which it remained, without competition, for well over a hundred years. It is only in the past one hundred fifty years that it slowly lost its prior status.

Regardless, as the world bears witness to the Latinization of this mostly English-speaking country, the U.S. mainstream, whose foundational myth is primarily English monolingual and Anglo Saxon monocultural, cannot help but view this phenomenon with suspicion and trepidation. Furthermore, Spanish is not a prestige language in the U.S. Instead, it is frequently associated with racialized immigrants, illegals, and uneducated people. Not even in the U.S.

academy is Spanish taken seriously, as a language of intellectual exchange (Molloy 195). Thus, there is a problem with just how Spanish is seen internally or worldwide and how Spanish or Spanish-language cultural production (particularly literature) is seen within and outside the United States. This is further complicated by the forces of globalization, with their contradictory linguistic tendencies, both promoting the use of multiple languages *and* reducing the actual number of them that have any real power. This renders it even more difficult to unpack the relationship between languages and identity, and national, politico-economic and cultural hegemony.

Just as there are many different kinds of English spoken around the world, there are numerous varieties of Spanish in the U.S. and around the Spanish-speaking world, even in countries in very close proximity to each other, e.g., Chile and Argentina. In some areas of New Mexico and Colorado, for example, there are people who speak a rather archaic form of the language that preserves many of the characteristics of the Spanish that was spoken during the early days of Spanish settlement in the Southwest. Yet, most contemporary varieties of U.S. Spanish have been enriched in a two-fold manner. The language has either undergone lexical and/or syntactic changes, due to its prolonged contact with English for over one hundred and fifty years (mostly in the Southwest) or is constantly revived and invigorated by the steady arrival and establishment of what Ilán Stavans calls 'national subgroups' (e.g., Mexican, Cuban, Puerto Rican and, later, other *caribeño,* and Central and South American native speakers of Spanish) to the Southeast. More recently, these immigrants have come to the country's heartland, the South, and urban centers nationwide. Thus, in different U.S. locations there are speakers of a form of 'old' Spanish, or Cuban or Dominican-inspired Spanish, or Mexican-Central American Spanish, as well as of varieties that can be identified with other countries of origin. In some places, these different varieties have come into contact with each other *and* English, which has resulted in even more potential subvarieties.

John Lipski makes certain in his contribution to clarify these multiple possibilities for U.S. Spanish and explains yet another language strategy employed by many Spanish-English bilinguals in the U.S.—'Spanglish'—providing a brief review of anti- and pro-Spanglish sentiments. In his contribution, Ilán Stavans, too, offers his own understanding of the history and dynamics behind Spanglish, and the source of some of the negative attitudes towards it. Regarding language and Latino identity, Mignolo reminds us that as an issue, it may not be specific to Spanish American countries, per se, but remains relevant to them because it involves Spanish and, often, the influence of Spanish American immigration from those countries to the U.S. Ultimately, the problem stems from the historico-political transition between two empires—one defunct, the other operational—and their political, economic and linguistic contributions to contemporary forms of transnational, imperialism made possible by globalization (2000: 235). In fact, what is decidedly new or different about 'language and empire' today is its postcoloniality, according to current globalization theory, with its focus on transnationalism, and on culture and *mestizaje* (Krishnaswamy 69). Nevertheless, whether discussing Spain and its later defunct empire, the problems of postcolonialism and languages in Latin America, or the current moment in the United States, the issue of monolingualism or linguistic pluralism is still inextricably connected to knowledge management and hegemony. This is particularly true in the context of totally new forms of empire ('network societies') that are possible only through an increasingly globalized economy and advanced communications technology.

Conclusion

At the beginning of the third millennium CE, there are compelling reasons to examine the multilayered legacy of Spanish and empire on three continents (Europe, and North and South America) insofar as they concern individual, national, and transnational identities. It is also important to reexamine the traditional, one language-one nation paradigm that persists and the kinds of individual and (trans)territorial identities that are actually emerging (Mignolo 2000: 235–36). The following observations about Spanish in the territory north and south of the Río Bravo, and globally, are offered to bring our discussion of 'Spanish and empire' to a close.

It is hardly necessary to discuss the contemporary position of Spanish in Spain relative to other regional languages (which are protected by the Spanish constitution). But in the 'New World,' the persistence of Spanish today can primarily be attributed to a number of factors, among them its historical connection to the Catholic Church (which still predominates in twenty-first century Spanish America, despite the inroads of Protestantism). The linguistic legacy of Spanish Catholicism is an undeniable result of the conquest and colonization of the 'New World,' despite the empire's delay in seeking to establish an aggressive monolingual-Spanish policy. Another reason for the survival of Spanish is the exponential growth in the population of Spanish-speakers in North, Central, and South America.

Ultimately, the reach and persistence of a world language may not depend so much on the power behind it but rather on the size of the community that speaks it. By the year 2050, the U.S. could well increase its population by fifty percent, approximately thirty two percent of it due to immigration by Spanish speakers.[7] A century and a half after the U.S. obtained northern Mexico (the Southwest), Texas, and Florida, and English spread there, many of its Spanish-speaking residents still call Spanish their first language, and this is not taking into account the Spanish-speaking population of the Midwest, South, and Northeast. The lesson seems to be that migration rather than conquest is what fuels language spread.

Increasing erosion of the traditional distinctions made between concepts like 'formal empire,' imperialism, colonialism, and postcolonialism, between 'classic empire' and the 'new imperialism,' *and* the role of English, Spanish, or Spanglish in all of them, is causing these concepts to lose their conceptual clarity and interpretative usefulness in a world that is moving rapidly into a situation of increasing globalization. Terms such as these seem evermore unable to describe or represent present-day reality, in which economic and social inequality become even more pronounced. Any real attempt to understand this situation entails an appreciation of the predicaments associated with living through the conflicted aftermath of this reality; and this is what the essays on this volume, from varied disciplinary perspectives, try to address.

In closing, we would be remiss if we did not thank the contributors to this volume. We would like to express our heartfelt gratitude to the *Hispanic Issues* series editor, Nicholas Spadaccini, for his support, warm encouragement, and feedback, and for writing with, Luis Martín-Estudillo, the words that in closing our book, continue a stimulating, constructive debate in our disciplines.

Notes

1. Despite any perceived lack of a traditional center, or core, vis-à-vis the periphery of this transnational model, the flow of profits, labor and consumption in this era of globalization are remarkably yet predictably similar to those of earlier forms of capitalism. More on the economic makeup of late, twentieth-century capitalism and globalization can be found at see Cooppan, "W(h)ither Post-colonial Studies? Towards the Transnational Study of Race and Nation," 17–18, in Chrisman and Benita Parry (Eds). *Postcolonial Theory and Criticism.* Cambridge: The English Association, 2000.
2. Regarding the United States, it is also no coincidence that four interrelated, critical issues related to Hispanics in the U.S. *and* Spanish dominated the U.S. mainstream media for over a month between April and May of 2006, and that all four are relevant to the greater project of Spanish, 'language and empire.' Just a cursory review of the

media's focus on the Anglo American reaction to the nearly simultaneous release of the Latino-styled "Nuestro Himno," a Spanish-language version of the "Star Spangled Banner," the May 1, 2006 boycott and marches carried out by over one million Hispanics and their supporters, and the emotion with which the mainstream American public followed the ensuing congressional debates about immigration reform and resulting legislation that would contain a provision to establish English as the 'national' or 'common and unifying' language of the country is quite revelatory.
3. The issue of the Spanish empire's linguistic policies and the fact that its initial conquest and colonization of the 'New World' was carried out through a series of financially independent initiatives (sometimes in the name of the king of Spain, but often in the spirit of free enterprise) is also significant. In contrast, the British empire's early opportunism and later linguistic and cultural industriousness will become a significant difference and contribute to our discussion of the situation of Spanish and English as global languages at the turn of the twentieth century.
4. For a thorough discussion of the evolution of empire building and the place of language within it, see Ostler, *Empires of the Word: A Language History of the World*. New York: Harper Collins, 2005.
5. For information about indigenous languages in Spanish America, see <www.ailla.utexas.org/site/la_langs.html>.
6. U.S. acquisition of territories with Spanish-speaking populations (sometimes constituting a majority) include the Louisiana Purchase (in 1803 from France), West Florida (in 1810 from Spain), East Florida and the Sabine Free State (in 1819 from Spain), the Texas Annexation (in 1845, from Mexico, which caused the Mexican-American War from 1846–1848), the Mexican Cession lands (parts of Texas, Colorado, Arizona, New Mexico, and Wyoming, and all of California, Nevada, and Utah), through the Treaty of Guadalupe Hidalgo (in 1848 from Mexico), the Gadsden Purchase (in 1853 from Mexico), Puerto Rico, Guam and the Philippines (in 1898 from Spain), and the Boundary Treaty land (in 1970 from Mexico, in exchange for over two thousand acres of U.S. land).
7. For more information about current U.S. population data and projection, visit <www.npg.org/facts/us_pop_projections.htm>.

Works Cited

Boone, Elizabeth, and Walter Mignolo, eds. *Writing without Words: Alternative Literacies in Mesoamerica and the Andes*. Durham, N.C.: Duke University Press, 1994.

Castells, Manuel. *The Rise of the Network Society*. Ames & Boston: Blackwell Publishing, 1996.

Cooppan, Vilashini. "W(h)ither Post-colonial Studies? Towards the Transnational Study of Race and Nation." *Postcolonial Theory and Criticism*. Ed. Laura Chrisman and Benita Parry. Cambridge: The English Association, 2000.

Eisenstadt, Shmuel Noah. *The Political Systems of Empires: The Rise and Fall of the Historical Bureaucracies.* New York: Free Press, 1969.

Escobar, Alberto. *Arguedas o la utopía de la lengua.* Lima: Instituto de Estudios Peruanos, 1984.

Harth, Michael, and Antonio Negri. *Empire.* Cambridge, Mass: Harvard University Press, 2000.

King, C. Richard, ed. *Postcolonial America.* Urbana and Chicago: University of Illinois Press, 2000.

Krishnaswamy, Revathi. "Globalization and its Postcolonial (Dis)contents. Reading Dalit Writing." *Journal of Postcolonial Writing* 41. 1 (May 2006): 69.

Lodares, Juan R. "La comunidad lingüística en la España de hoy. (Temas y problemas de la diferenciación cultural)." *Bulletin of Hispanic Studies* 82: 1. Liverpool University Press, 2005. 1–15.

Martín-Barbero, Jesús. *Communication, Culture and Hegemony: From the Media to Mediation.* Trans. Elizabeth Fox and Robert A. White. Newbury, CA: Sage Publications, 1993.

McClennen, Sophia. "Comparative Cultural Studies and Latin America." Ed. Sophia A. McClennen and Earl E. Fitz. Thematic Issue. *CLCWeb: Comparative Literature and Culture: A WWWeb Journal* 4. 2 (June 2002). <http://clcwebjournal.lib.purdue.edu/clcweb02-2/mcclennen02.html>.

Mignolo, Walter D. "Colonialidad global, capitalismo y hegemonía epistémica." *Culturas imperiales. Experiencia y representación en América, Asia y África.* Comp. Ricardo Salvatore. Rosario: Argentina, 2005. 55–87.

———. *Local Histories/Global Designs: Coloniality, Subaltern Knowledges, and Border Thinking.* Princeton, N.J: Princeton University Press, 2000.

———. "Orientalización, imperialismo, globalización: herencias colonials y teorías postcoloniales." *Revista Iberoamericana* 61.170–71 (1992a): 26–39.

———. "Nebrija in the New World: The Question of the Letter, the Colonization of the Amerindian Languages, and the Discontinuity of the Classical Tradition." *L'Homme* 122–24 (1992b): 185–209.

———. "On the Colonization of Amerindian Languages and Memories. Renaissance Theories of Writing and the Discontinuity of the Classical Tradition." *Comparative Studies in Society and History* 34.2 (1992c): 301–35.

———. "Literacy and Colonization: The New World Experience." *1492–1992: Re/Discovering Colonial Writing.* Ed. Rene Jara and Nicholas Spadaccini. *Hispanic Issues 4.* Minneapolis, MN: University of Minnesota Press, 1989. 51–96.

Molloy, Sylvia. "Postcolonial Latin America and the Magic Realist Imperative: A Report to an Academy." *Nation, Language, and the Ethics of Translation.* Ed. Sandra Bermann and Michael Wood. Princeton, NJ: Princeton University Press, 2005.

Moraña, Mabel. "Introduction: Mapping Hispanism." *Ideologies of Hispanism.* Ed. Mabel Moraña. *Hispanic Issues 30.* Nashville, TN: Vanderbilt University Press, 2005.

Morse, Richard M. *New World Soundings: Culture and Ideology in the Americas*. Baltimore: Johns Hopkins University Press, 1989.
Nebrija, Antonio de. *Gramática de la Lengua Castellana*. London: Oxford University Press, 1926 [Salamanca, 1492].
Ortiz, Renato. "Revisitando la noción de imperialismo cultural." *Culturas imperiales. Experiencia y representación en América, Asia y Africa*. Comp. Ricardo Salvatore. Rosario: Argentina, 2005. 37–53.
Ostler, Nicholas. *Empires of the Word: A Language History of the World*. N.Y.: Harper Collins, 2005.
Quijano, Aníbal. "Colonialidad del poder, cultura y conocimiento en América Latina." *Anuario Mariateguiano* 9–9 (1997): 113–21.
Rama, Ángel. *Transculturación narrativa en América Latina*. Montevideo: Fundación Ángel Rama, 1989.
Rivera Cusicanqui, Silvia. "La raíz: colonizadores y colonizados." *Violencias encubiertas en Bolivia*. Ed. Xavier Albó et. al. La Paz: Hisbol, 1992. 10–86.
Rosenblat, Angel. "La hispanización de América: el castellano y las lenguas indígenas desde 1492." *Presente y futuro de la lengua española: Actas de la Asamblea de Folología del I Congreso de Instituciones Hispánicas*. Madrid, 1964. 189–216.
Salvatore, Ricardo. *Culturas imperiales. Experiencia y representación en América, Asia y Africa*. Rosario: Argentina, 2005.
Sharpe, Jenny. "Is the United States Postcolonial? Transnationalism, Immigration, and Race." *Postcolonial America*. Ed. C. Richard King. Urbana and Chicago: University of Illinois Press, 2000.
Wallerstein, Immanuel. "Dependence in an Interdependent World: The Limited Possibilities of Transformation within the Capitalist World-economy." *The Capitalist World-Economy*. Ed. Immanuel Wallerstein. Cambridge: Cambridge University Press, 1979. 49–65.

Part I
Imperial Legacy—
Language and Power in the Spanish Colonial Sphere

◆ 1

Languages, Catholicism, and Power in the Hispanic Empire (1500–1770)

Juan R. Lodares

(Translated by Gerardo Garza and Kenya C. Dworkin y Méndez)

In his book *El político* (The Politician) (1646), Baltasar Gracián made the following description of the Imperial orb: "In the realm of the Spanish monarchy, where the provinces are many, the nations different, *the languages varied in number*, inclinations oppositional and climates contradictory, it is just as important to preserve as to unite." In fact, the multiplicity of languages within the Spanish Empire was accepted as a most natural thing. Even Ferdinand the Catholic monarch himself, went to his grave convinced that in a few short years there would be sufficient people in Spain proficient enough in Amerindian languages to be able to communicate with the indigenous peoples of America without need of interpreters, sign language or Latin, methods that had already proven quite unreliable.

The idea that the Spanish language today is one of the world's great languages due to Spain's many years of Imperial domination is reasonable, yet perhaps at first glance only. It is also reasonable to think that the Spanish concerned themselves considerably with spreading their language or that they thought of it as one of their most useful weapons in unifying their dominions. Nevertheless, the factual reality of the Imperial epilogue is enough to refute these ideas, or at least cast doubt upon them. There is the account of Alexander von Humboldt, who having traveled throughout America, was surprised to discover that the vast majority of the Indigenous masses did not know Spanish. In fact, eight out of ten natives in the Viceroyalty of New Spain, during the reign of Charles II, did not speak Spanish. Mexican liberal Juan Bautista Ladrón del Niño de Guevara, who at the beginning of the nineteenth century journeyed through what is now Texas, recounted that in that vast territory he had encountered at most eighteen inhabitants who knew how to write in Spanish with some degree of accuracy.

Leaving aside any possible exaggeration on his part, there are numerous similar reports that could be cited, whose gist can be summarized in a paradoxical quip by Lázaro de Rivera, Governor of the Rio de la Plata Viceroyalty at the end of the eighteenth century: "We have gotten to the point where the language of the conquered peoples may ultimately dominate!" Opinions like these, easy to find in that period's documentation, have cast uncertainty on the possibly misleading premise of the equivalency of Imperial hegemony and linguistic hegemony, doubts that are not entirely new to American historiography. These doubts have also brought about an examination of the relationship between a state's power and its ability to disseminate a language, the difficulty a state encounters in spreading a language throughout its colonial territories, and the limited or nonexistent awareness, beyond that of ancient Rome-inspired rhetoric, of the political value of that language.

I believe that our penchant for philology has caused us to imbue the opinions of Antonio de Nebrija and Bernardo de Aldrete about the link between empires and languages with an importance they never actually had for the truly influential, authoritative and important people who actually controlled the strings of the Empire's projects. Furthermore, the word 'empire' has also been imbued with meanings it did not have three or four centuries earlier, when it basically meant 'monarchy' or 'government,' in which case expressions like "to speak the language of the Empire" were more descriptive than anything else.

In time, three considerations will gain acceptance in both academe and the public sphere, where this controversial matter of an imperial language, at least in Spain, keeps resurfacing. The first is the linguistic heterogeneity of the Imperial domain: in effect, Spanish was the most common—but not the only—language of administrative activity. It was used by (but was not hegemonic) among influential groups in the Imperial domain, due to literary, political or demographic factors. In many areas, few people spoke it and there was no function that could not be filled by other languages. Many seemed to acknowledge this quite openly, as was the case with Miguel de Cervantes: "All ancient poets wrote in their native language, and that being the case, the custom spread through all the nations, so that the German poet would not be less esteemed because he writes in his native tongue, nor the Castilian, nor even the Biscayan citizen who writes in his own language" (*Don Quixote*, II, XVI).

The second consideration regards doubts about the Empire's efforts to actually spread Spanish throughout its domain for almost three centuries, from the time of Charles I to Charles III, during which time the panorama somewhat changed. There was, of course, a legislative body responsible for momentous linguistic issues, but it was often the case that the state was also monumentally incapable of executing whatever related legislation was created or of even issuing information about it through a mail service that took many, many months to reach its destinations. Besides, that linguistic legislation did not always reflect the monarchy's political intention to spread Spanish throughout governing structures: it was the reflection of a struggle between Spanish and American social groups for whom arguing about language served as an excuse to obscure issues of another ilk. This all serves to help us understand the dizzying challenges American Spanish has faced.

The third consideration is that if Spanish has become one of the most prominently spoken languages in the world, on the international level, it is not because of the power of the Imperial era, i.e., from the end of the eighteenth century to the first half of the twentieth, but rather its decline. No doubt, this seems contradictory, because it seems more in keeping with a logic that dictates that there is a direct relationship between greater political hegemony and economic weight, and greater linguistic expansion. This can be said of French or English in our times, but it is not true for the Spanish language of the sixteenth to eighteenth centuries. In that sense, it seems a paradoxical language: it spread when imperial power waned. As strange as this seems, it is what happened. Once the imperial era had concluded, republican ideals for America and the abundant immigration that populated Spanish America in the nineteenth century did much more for the fate of Spanish than three centuries of colonial rule.

Almost the same thing could be said of Spain. Never in our history—nor in the history of the Spanish language—was Spanish more appreciated as a common, national, egalitarian language of *de rigeur* status among scholars and of inevitable adoption by institutions, as occurred during the intitial stages of the War of Independence. This continued to be the case through the time of the *Cortes de Cádiz* (Legislative Assembly of Cadiz). As a result of the 1813 *Junta de Instrucción Pública* (Congress for Public Instruction), it achieved a level of importance for study conceived by Laureano Figuerola, creator of the Spanish peseta coin, or Claudio Moyano—during a time we have come to know as the "Bourgeois" or "Liberal" revolution. One must not forget that the Spanish Empire existed during a pre-industrial time, a period of enormously difficult communications and a rigidly stratified society. Thus, while the *ancien régime* could not see the usefulness of a common language for civil matters, an enlightened middle class and nineteenth-century bourgeosie did.

This is also applicable, *mutatis mutandis,* to the case of Portuguese, another language favored in imperial rhetoric during the sixteenth and seventeenth centuries. Nevertheless, Portuguese begins to take root in America in the nineteenth century, not precisely due to an intervention by the Portuguese but, rather, as a result of a flow of people to Brazil that provoked Napoleon's troops to advance on the Lisboan aristocracy.

Language in the Rhetoric of the Empire

It cannot be denied that the Castilian mentality of the sixteenth and seventeenth centuries was a reflection of the Roman Empire. Castilians considered themselves the worthy successors of Rome and rightful masters of an even more extensive empire that they would govern with fairness. In some intellectual circles, e.g., the humanists who surrounded Charles I adopted the imperial motives with devotion and saw themselves as pioneers in the construction of a universal empire comprised of only one shepherd and one flock. The question was, then, what role the Spanish language played in such a project? Was the assumption that political and religious unity was also paired with linguistic unity? These questions deserve our consideration.

A strict interpretation of what Nebrija writes in the prologue to his *Gramática Castellana* (Castilian Grammar) might give one the impression that Castile really dreamed of having an empire and considered language a tool through which to create political unity. Yet, we also know that Nebrija was referring to a topic that was not unique to the Romance tradition as: Ibn Hazm from Córdova had already said as much in the eleventh century, in referring to the Arabic tradition. Furthermore, the idea of "one language for one Empire" fits much more comfortably, ideologically, within Islam than within Christianity.

When compared to the genuine bestseller *Instituciones Latinas* (Latin Institutions), on the other hand, Nebrija's *Gramática* had hardly any success at all. The comment that Nebrija included in the well-known prologue about language and empire seems more like an afterthought about a general theory of empire which he had already expressed in his *Historia de los Reyes Católicos* (History of the Catholic Monarchs), in which he makes no reference to language. Nebrija's theory of empire was not groundbreaking. It was traditional, and though it was not antiquated, it did not carry much weight with the influential and the powerful, who after the discovery of America, began to pose theoretical questions—for which the Roman imperial model, whose mirror image the Spanish Empire purportedly was, did not have satisfactory answers.

If one reads the linguistic *apologias* of the sixteenth and seventeenth centuries, a curious contradiction among literary genres become evident. The linguistic *apologias* of the sixteenth and seventeenth centuries reveal imperial arguments such as: "the Castilian language is universal and known everywhere the sun shines," "it is the envy of Greek and Latin," [and] "it moves victoriously forward with our flags." Those were statements that the apologists themselves knew were not true. Thus, it is understood that the works of Bernardo de Aldrete, Castillo Solórzano or Luis Cabrera de Córdoba were not addressing the precise geopolitical reality of the language but rather creating propaganda for it. Yet, if one reads the political literature of the time, in which empire theory was debated by men like Fernando Vázquez de Menchaca, Arias Montano, Baltasar Ayala, Alonso de Castrillo, and Juan López de Palacios, one can see that the issue of language was not a major concern. It can be said that it did not appear to be a matter of theoretical discussion: there were much more important issues to debate.

Occasionally, when it did appear, as in a letter from Arias Montano to the Duke of Alba on May 18, 1570, it was approached like a practical matter as Montano seldom employed rhetoric about language and empire. In fact, mutual communication in a language, or languages, was necessary for the governance of such a vast domain, and it seemed that Spanish was gaining ground where it had heretofore been unknown. Such was the case among the Dutch, to whose use of Spanish Arias Montano expressly referred: "[it is] due to their need of the language, for their public matters, as well as for their commerce."

In Spain, García de Loaysa suggested to Philip II the convenience of a unifying norm, specifically for the written form, because the vast majority of teachers taught writing in their own way. Having an army of linguistically ill-trained clerks to handle the complex administration of varied affairs could vastly undercut the essential role of language in schooling and bureaucratic matters and the creation of standards to promote general understanding as well as efficient archiving and record-keeping. In the context of Phillip II and his governing style, when writing became widespread (unlike during his father's reign) it was reasonable for Loaysa to believe that without a unified linguistic standard the administration of the empire would become more difficult. Nevertheless, Loaysa's recommendation was not generally accepted.

At that time in fact, Spanish enjoyed some measure of success as an interesting foreign language, and its popularity also increased within Spain in areas of linguistic contact. Yet, one cannot assume that its ascent was unstoppable to the point of erasing other languages, nor that this phenomenon was due specifically to any policy destined to make Spanish the Empire's mother tongue. When compared to the legitimate problems of the political process, everything seems to indicate that the language issue was never more than a secondary or practical matter. It was practical and not problematic because four out of five Spaniards understood one another in Castilian, given the demographically disproportionate number of kingdoms on Castile's side.

I regret having to disagree with Ramón Menéndez Pidal's theory in *La idea imperial de Carlos V* (The Imperial Idea of Charles V) about the Emperor's intention to elevate Spanish to an extremely high level of international esteem. His theory about the Emperor's linguistic ideas is based on a well-known speech that the monarch gave in Spanish to a French delegation in Rome headed by Bishop Maçon who, claiming that he did not understand a thing, received from Charles V this legendary reply: "Your Excellency, understand me if you wish, and do not expect from me words in anything else but my Spanish language, which is so noble that it deserves to be known and understood by all Christian people."

It is true that Charles V made a speech in Spanish at the Vatican on April 17, 1536. He had his reasons: on the one hand, he did not want to do it in French, his native tongue, because of his anger with the French people and, on the other, because Spanish was perhaps the most diplomatically neutral language for the occasion. Even so, it is likely that the apocryphal, oft quoted, and linguistically patriotic reply to the Bishop, was the invention of the fantasy-prone French writer Brantôme. What does appear to be historical, in any case, is that the use of Spanish did not draw much attention from anyone. All the same, the following day, the Emperor did resume his speech to the French delegation in private, in perfect Italian.

It would be hard to conclude from the linguistic arguments that were issued during the time of the Hapsburg reign that the state had any reason to make Spanish the general language of the Empire's domains. The only case of a policy being established specifically for the eradication of a language was that of Arabic. This was not due to the language itself but to reasons of religious assimilation. In America, in 1534, Juan de Charchoaga, a Basque whose religious orthodoxy was not sullied by not speaking Spanish, was able to try and condemn to death by hanging three countrymen of Antonio Nebrija in Biscayan, a language which they would not have understood despite the extremely public and legal nature of the proceeding! Despite religious prejudices, this was not the case with Hispano-Arabic speakers, whose language ultimately became an important code for understanding the Turkish spies of the Mediterranean coast.

Practical Uses of Languages

During this time period, Spanish was to be favorably positioned in the area of bureaucratic activity due to the fact that Philip II's Spain was the most advanced state. Spain had a highly organized and reasonably efficient communications network that was not entirely free of corruption (nor was it always fast and unencumbered), but it did unite the central government with the farthest reaches of its Empire. This network required a well-trained body of officials to keep it functioning, and it depended upon the educational system's expansion and, linguistically speaking, upon an increase in utilitarian prose in Spanish, a genre that made languages more important and attractive than other forms of literature.

Thus, Spanish is associated with the exercise of political power, government and other relevant matters. It seems reasonable that in those areas of linguistic contact—like Catalonia, where the bonanza of American trade and suitability of Spanish for its role in it were foreseen—Spanish became strongly entrenched and a diglossic situation favorable to Spanish established itself with a vengeance, a state of affairs that would last for centuries and, in 1557, would cause writers like Cristobal Despuig, author of *Colloquis de la insigne ciutat de Tortosa,* to exclaim: "It is scandalous for me to see the ease with which those Catalonian lords and respected gentlemen in Barcelona turn to the Castilian language. In years past, the magnificent Monarchs of Aragon did not tolerate such abuses. While I am not saying that the Castilian language is not noble, nor that important people do not need to know it, since in Europe it is the best known of all Spanish languages, I do believe that the ease with which we express ourselves in it everyday is worthy of censure, because little by little that will cause us to lose our homeland and it will seem as though the Castilians have conquered it all." His countryman Juan Gómez Andrín was even more critical: "The Monarchy's language has always been more respectable among wealthy men."

In areas such as Valencia or Catalonia, the Empire's rhetoric intensified to a degree possibly even greater than in Castille, so much so that yet another imperial linguistic pronouncement clearer than even Nebrija's can be attributed to important figures like the Bishop of Orihuela, Josep Esteve in Castille: "When [different] peoples are subject to the [very] same empire, the subjects have the obligation to learn their ruler's language." All this happened when the monarchy had neither made any declaration regarding an official language nor proposed any directives in linguistic matters that could be interpreted as unifying. There was extensive linguistic legislation, of which most could be interpreted as economic or mercantile in nature. Yet, this is often forgotten because the attractiveness of Spanish exerted much more force than any standardizing legislation.

That aside, activity in the highest circles of government was reasonably multilingual as it could not be any different to imagine how the Castilians, not known for multiple language proficiency, managed so many matters in such a highly complex context of their own creation: Philip II married an English princess, although it is not known if anyone else in the Spanish Court other than the second Duke of Feria knew English. Hardly anyone spoke either Dutch or German. However, the Italian ambassadors could express themselves in their language, which Philip II understood well, as he did French. Portuguese was never an unknown language in the environment of the court. Philip II understood it (after all, it was his mother's native tongue) and recommended to his children that they learn it along with French. The Portuguese used it occasionally to address the Count Duke.

During debates in the Spanish *Cortes*, Catalonians expressed themselves in Catalan with absolute naturalness, but not only in these cases: in 1627, at the audience that Philip III conceded to Joan Francesc Rossell, a *Consell* representative [councilman] from Barcelona, Rossell followed a deep-rooted custom by addressing the King in Catalan although the King was also given a copy of the speech in Spanish in case he wanted to read it and understand it better. Don Hernando de Cardona never stopped speaking in Catalan at the Court because it was easier for him to do so. There was little Latin proficiency among government officials: the Castilian aristocracy spoke little Latin and no Greek at all. It seems that Philip II expressed himself in Latin "with greater superiority than was habitual among the princes," although one should take into account that the comment comes from a Venetian ambassador who was just passing through Madrid.

Written documentation, regardless of which language it was in, was commonly translated into Spanish, sometimes pitifully, yet this did not resolve the problems of direct diplomatic communication. No Spanish envoy sent to negotiate the Westphalian Peace Treaty knew the language of his counterparts, so they met halfway by turning to French negotiators. This practice was quite common for Spanish diplomats of the period and even more so during the reign of Philip V; in fact, essentially more than half of the high-ranking diplomats during his reign were Italians.

Practical reasons aside, one should be mindful when considering this matter that the Spanish monarchy's deference towards the compositional diversity of its territories made it difficult to push for linguistic unification. The organized fora of the different kingdoms upon which the King and all his privileges, rights and liberties lay, made it possible for Spanish to become progressively established from within, in areas of linguistic contact. This was not brought about by the Spanish-speaking central government using laws or mandates because it wanted everyone else to use its language, but because of interest among the educated classes of said areas who wanted to master it. As a result, a diglossic model in which Spanish occupied the public space and the space of social ascension was established. However, this process did not eliminate the use of other languages. For instance, in 1610, when Francesc Calça asked: "Why do we Catalans abandon our own language?" the answer was always: "Because we all know it is more profitable to write in Castilian."

Considerations regarding the social and political need to institutionalize this diglossic process in Spain, with the promotion of only one language for state, official and public matters would not come until much later. Although they started in the second half of the eighteenth century, these ideas became more clearly manifested in the first third of the nineteenth century, as one can appreciate in the following statement by Catalan jurist Ignacio Dou, in 1801: "All states must establish a dominant language in their countries, for teaching, dispatching orders and for all other functions in matters relevant to public law. A dominant language offers many advantages in any nation, the first of which is the easing of internal trade, because there is no doubt that the difficulties that people from different kingdoms and provinces encounter in trying to speak to and understand each other have hindered and continue to encumber commerce in many places."

The liberalization of trade that occurred toward the latter part of the eighteenth century, particularly in the America ports, underscored for areas of language contact the advantages of a common language for reasons that were essentially economic rather than cultural or political. In Dou's time, it did not take much persuasion for people to become convinced of this matter.

Since the circumstances just discussed were well known, it would be useful to consider another situation that has received less attention, yet is of great importance for understanding how the concept of linguistic unification was perceived in the Spanish Empire: the extreme importance of the Catholic religion and its spread throughout the Empire.

Language and Religious Issues

The ideological underpinnings of the Empire rested on religious rather than linguistic unity. Furthermore, the linguistic strategies used from the very beginning for the propagation of the faith were precisely contrary to Nebrija's unifying imperial rhetoric. In addition they conflicted with the ideas of Juan de Barros or Duarte Nunes (both Portuguese), who felt that the Portuguese language had been called to become the language of the newly spreading Christianity. Similarly, these strategies also contradicted the ideas expressed by Bernardo de Aldrete, who deserves particular attention.

Bernardo de Aldrete's publication, *Del Origen y principio de la lengua castellana o romance que oi se usa en España* (Roma 1606) (Of the Origin and Beginning of the Castilian or Romance Language that is used today in Spain), is notable because it summarizes many of the ideas that were expressed on the imperial mission of Spanish throughout the previous century by such writers as Cristóbal de Castillejo, Domingo de Valtanás and Francisco de Medina. However, the emblem that appears in the prologue of the text, in reality serves to summarize or allegorize it in its entirety and is perhaps just as interesting—a triumphal arch with a medallion bearing the figure of the Crucified one on its angled section. The pillars that support the arch represent, on the left, the Militant Church on an earthly globe upon which the lands of the ancient Roman Empire can be seen; the pillar on the right symbolizes Spain on a second globe upon which America and Asia are visible. For Aldrete, the Spanish conquests of the time were thought to be a fundamental episode in the spread of Christianity. In fact, the Spanish Empire and the imperial nature of its language existed because of this religious phenomenon. In Aldrete's imagination, the advancement of the victorious Spanish banners and of the Castilian language were not just functioning as elements of a national history but fulfilling a role in the history of the salvation of the human race. He saw America as a protagonist in a history much greater than Spain's, a history whose setting in the modern era would eventually include the whole world.

Bernardo de Aldrete was not the only one who thought the propagation of Catholicism was concomitant with the spread of Spanish. The opinions of earlier writers, such as Pedro Moya de Contreras and Ortiz de Hinojosa, were somewhat well received by the Mexican council of 1585. Despite their ideas, Aldrete repeatedly asserted in his book that the spread of Spanish in America was not going well and that the diligence with which the Spaniards worked on its dissemination was lacking. That was all actually truer than his imperial imaginings. Furthermore, it was a paradoxical coincidence that his book was dedicated to Philip III, during whose reign the guidelines for the preservation of the American indigenous languages were more numerous than those promulgated for the expansion of Spanish. In fact, the ideas Moya, Ortiz and Aldrete expressed were still contradictory for their time because Catholicism was in fact spreading successfully in America, undoubtedly precisely because of the opposite process—preaching in Indigenous languages, which from a Christian ideological perspective was the most orthodox of practices. It is equally incongruous that it was an Islamist-turned-Christian monk named Enbaqom, in faraway Ethiopia, who predicted with much more precision than Nebrija, Valtanas, Medina, Aldrete, Moya, and Ortiz, the linguistic labor of the Empire in its vast colonial dominions.

In 1540, Enbaqom wrote *Anqasa Amin* o *Puerta de la Fe* (Anqasa Amin or The Gate of the Faith) to show the superiority of Christianity over Islam. It is a strange work that uses the following thesis: the Koran is a monolingual Arabic book, while the Gospels appear in many languages; therefore, Christianity may be experienced in many places. The Islamic attitude regarding the Koran makes translations of it nearly impossible. The faithful have to read or recite it several times a day in Arabic which may not be their own language. Naturally, the Koran's cultural impact was to Islamify and draw those who come into contact with it into one, single world-wide linguistic and governmental community (form an *uma* or monolingual Islamic nation which is still espoused by Koranic culture), while Christianity spread with more fluidity by addressing each people group in its own language and creating one unified yet multilingual community of faith. In other words, the spread of Christianity is antithetical to linguistic unification. Enbaqom welcomed the linguistic work of the great defender and disseminator of Catholicism—the Spanish Empire—in the coming years. Preaching in vernacular languages, and not following Nebrija or Aldrete's doctrines, was the appropriate linguistic strategy for an empire whose political strength would rest upon the expansion and preservation of the Catholic faith. There was no attempt to spread *one* language but *one* religion throughout the entire empire, through a pastoral strategy that called for a multitude of languages. That was the ancient Christian tradition from early times and the canonical one among its great thinkers.

How to Preach the Word of God

In his work *In libros Peri Hermeneias expositio* (On Interpretation), II, 2, Saint Thomas Aquinas makes this interesting assertion: "unde ille qui sunt diuersarum linguarum non possunt bene conuiuere ad inuicem" (one cannot live peacefully where there is a great diversity of languages). Apparently, Thomist thought supports those, who like Nebrija, believed that the Spanish language was a tool for peace. If it is true that where there are many languages it is not possible to get along, then spreading a common language amongst everyone should be enough to appease their spirits. The reality is, however, that Thomism turned out to be antagonistic to the concept of a Christian empire with only one language or the idea that the *pax hispanica* depended upon linguistic unification. Peaceful coexistence can also be achieved another way, more in keeping with that to which Saint Thomas was referring, more in accordance with the idea of the Christian city, i.e., with the creation of a community of nations of sorts in which each nation speaks its own language. The Empire's linguistic strategy, which sought religious unity over linguistic unanimity, was guided more by Thomism than by the ideas of Nebrija, as we have already seen.

None of these considerations would have had any effect at all in sixteenth-century Europe without the religious reformist movements that brought these debates to the forefront: the need to explain the Holy Scriptures in the everyday language of the people—and not in Latin. With the statutes of the Common (Catholic) Observance, meeting this need involved initiating a movement to revise and censor Holy texts that might appear in the vernacular language and a project for the pastoral conquest of the inhabitants of rural areas by religious orders that could speak to them in their own languages in order to combat the spread of reformational ideas with the same weapon that Protestantism used: vernacular languages. In this way, an empire such as the Spanish—based on Catholicism—did not repress but rather fostered a movement within it promoting the relevance of the vernacular languages within it. Between 1500 and 1670, there were 11,282 books published in Spain of which 5,835 were Catholic literature not written in Spanish. There are several strange stories that have been associated with this fact, such as one about the participation of Spanish clerics from religious orders in the promotion of the Irish language Gaelic.

Hugh O'Neill, a Catholic headmaster heavily supported by Philip II, led anti-Protestant uprisings in Northern Ireland that failed in 1590. This rebellion brought about a massive exile of Irish Catholics who sought protection in the Hapsburg domains. More than five thousand civilians went into the service of the Spanish army. Clergymen entered seminaries to educate themselves, some in Flanders, but many others in Salamanca and Santiago de Compostela, the latter under the King's sponsorship, according to the principles of the Council of Trent. In theory, they were preparing themselves to return to Ireland as transmitters of the Counter-Reformation, with preaching done in Gaelic. With works such as those by the Franciscan Flaithrí O'Maoil, which were translations of catechisms and breviaries sent from Spain, the city of Louvain became the literary capital of the Gaelic language. Gaelic discipline in the seminaries must have been formidable since in the 1624 *Memorial* a constant complaint raised by students from Irish schools in Spain to Philip IV was about the school's (clerical) directors: "[they] deny them communication with the Spaniards and keep them from learning their language so they cannot complain and, in that way, be more subject to said priests."

Languages and Catholic Orthodoxy in Spain

The Council of Trent (1545–1563), designed to reaffirm Catholic orthodoxy, did not pronounce any express linguistic precepts. Nevertheless, it did recommend that each bishopric follow local customs with regard to homiletics. Provincial councils in Spain often agreed on the need to sermonize in the local language. As the council in Urgell (1580 and 1630) and at the Provincial Council of Tarragona (1591) stipulated: "In hac Provincia omnes predicadores in Principatu Cathaloniae lingua catalana, in Regno Aragonum lingua maternal et naturals illius Regni, in Regno Valentia lingua valentine et non alia" (In this Province clergymen will preach in the Catalonian Principality's Catalan language, in the Kingdom of Aragon in the maternal and natural language of its Monarchs, in the Venician Kingdom in the Venician language, and no other). The Calahorra Bishop, Pedro Manso, considered it "useful that each province have the doctrine preached in its [own] mother tongue" and, in 1602, referring concretely to the domain of Vizcaya, he specified: "we order that in such places, sermons be given in the Basque language and that the priests allow nothing else, under penalty of law." In Catalonia, Valencia and the Basque province, at least, where for a long time councils often tended to be scrupulous on this point, Charles III's resolve concerning the teaching of Spanish grammar faltered, and even dictator Primo de Rivera would have confrontations with the most regionalist members of the clergy and the Catalan faithful. The case of Galicia, however, is special.

Galicia truly became a land of missions for many religious orders which considered that neither the priests nor the farmers of Galicia were true

Christians. Among many clergymen, their image of Galicia did not differ much from the one they might have had of an obscure American or Philippine mission. The great majority of clergymen came from Castilian areas, so the militant Church quickly identified itself with the local elites who had spoken the Castilian language for a long time. In 1595, Father Diego García stated: "We need to have Castilian men in these Galician schools—men who the Galicians appreciate and hold in high regard, so they can, with authority and religion, inform and establish ties with all possible returning priests." In fact, the most successful missionaries were priests from Castilian-speaking areas: Diego del Castillo came from Valladolid, Bartolomé Torres hailed from Seville, José Butrón was from Calatayud. Even Galician preachers like Manuel de Teixeira performed services in Spanish. Contrary to what went on in the Synods of Urgell, Tarragona or Calahorra, which would strongly recommend the use of Catalan or Basque, councils from Orestes (1543–1544) issued their decrees in Spanish, even translating them from Latin. A 1735 decree from Compostela recommends that the faithful "be made to memorize the catechism of Father Astete."

It cannot be said, however, that the Church, itself, was a force in the practical Castilianization in Galicia. It did elevate the regard for the Spanish language among those who already acknowledged it as the language of social ascension (e.g., all those who pursued an ecclesiastical profession) and contributed to the growth of the diglossic divide between the language of social prestige, Spanish, and the rural Galician. Even so, Galician continued being spoken in the fields, as would be expected, and no one—not parishes nor a still non-existent school system, thought of the possibility of eradicating it. Even when it only rudimentarily existed, in the second half of the nineteenth century, many Galician teachers were not proficient in Spanish, which was not the case of Hispano-Arabic in Granada. Furthermore, nobody seriously considered teaching Spanish in the countryside, and the Castilianization of the population was much more spontaneous in nature: the few countryfolk who owned a book kept it as though it were a treasure and reread it to the point of memorizing it, as was the case with the adventures of *Doce Pares* (noble warriors from France who perished at the Battle of Roncesvalles, mentioned in the "Chanson de Roland"). There is no dearth of instances where religious services were performed in Galician, since we must consider that at least one third of priests were Galician and lived in close proximity with the faithful in small hamlets. Nevertheless, there was one major obstacle to the success of this practice: the suspicion that rural priests officiated as such or as practitioners of witchcraft, depending on the need. Thus, short prayers written in Galician belonging to the common folk were translated into Spanish or Latin in order to protect them from any accusation of heresy. For example, in 1697 when Reverend Bolaño tried to find out if the emergency baptism of a young girl in the Castroverde parish was valid, the peasant who sprinkled the saving water on the child repeated the dictum prayer in front of the priest not in Galician or Castilian but in perfect Latin "learned the way the priests said it."

The Inquisition played a similar role. Given its propensity for promoting aristocratic and feudal ideas in Galicia, its documents were written in Spanish even though prisoners expressed themselves in Galician since the majority of them were of rural origin. Yet, because its effects were brief and sporadic, the Inquisition's linguistic practices did not make great inroads into the Galician countryside.

In order to understand what occurs with languages and the complex relationships that are established between them, it is important to understand one aspect about the ecclesiastical statutes of Imperial Spain: a career in the clergy was a means of social promotion, most likely the only one that assured a respectable position for the sons of peasants or younger sons. This explains the priestly obsession for the curate or parishes. There were areas like Galicia, where training occurred in Spanish, which rendered Galician less useful and undermined its success. However it did not cause its demise in areas where it was a geographical and sociological tradition. In other places, such as Catalonia, the Basque country and, to a lesser degree, Valencia (the case of America will be discussed later), the increasing penetration of Spanish was a real threat for the ecclesiastical functions that locals who were taught in Catalan, Basque or Valencian, performed. Thus, any defense of the language included two points: Christian ideological and strategic principles, i.e., to preach to everybody in their own language and, more importantly, the material interests of ecclesiastics and their families so that they could keep benefiting from their positions.

An important part of the ecclesiastical statutes in areas of linguistic contact tried to stop the growing ascendancy of Spanish in civil life, with an admonition that was frequently repeated from the beginning of the seventeenth century: "may bread be not taken away from our children and be given to those who are not," a reference to clergymen who came from Spanish-speaking areas. The Diocesan Synod of Urgell of 1610 stipulated a prohibition on hiring "either preachers or confessors who worked in the Castilian language." Notwithstanding, common people, especially in the cities, wanted to hear their sermons in Spanish, and many religious orders were willing to satisfy that demand of a sample of 67 sermons printed in Catalonia from throughout the seventeenth century, 45 were written in Spanish and included the name of the speaker as well as the location and the language they were given. In 1664, there were 26 sermons given at the parochial church of Blanes, with 25 preached in Spanish. In 1667, native Barcelona priest Magino Massò published his *Arbol fructuoso* (Fruitful Tree), a collection of twenty-two sermons that had been presented in Barcelona, all in Spanish. Additionally, the very same members of parliament who in 1637 demanded that there be requirement to preach in Catalan at the Tarraconense Council had no reservation about hiring Father Plácido de Aguilar to deliver a sermon in Spanish in honor of parliamentarians, judges and members of confraternities of Saint Jordi. All of this occurred at a time that could be considered the golden age of devotional literature written in Catalan.

Nevertheless the Church could not close its eyes to the increasing demand for Spanish with regard to civic activity because the preachers who delivered sermons in Spanish ensured public church attendance on important celebratory dates which was a threat to local ecclesiastical services. In addition, presented a danger that the councils tried to avert through their demand for sermons to be delivered in the language of the country, a tension which was sometimes resolved through strange compromises that allowed sermonizing in Spanish. Preaching in Catalan was not discussed as long as the preachers were of Catalan origin. Ultimately, a "defense of the language" was closely linked to the exclusion of foreigners from the benefits of ecclesiastical membership as well as to the need to guarantee the *modus vivendi* of the younger sons and, in that way, avoid the fragmentation of family patrimonies. In reality, this motive linked to the clergy's concrete interests restrained the penetration of Spanish particularly in rural areas: religious orders such as the Carmelites tended to preach in Catalan and Father Gregorio de Castilla learned Catalan when he realized that preaching in Spanish was not beneficial for him.

During the same era, the preservation of Eusquera (the language of the Basque region of Spain) was also tied to religious motives. Nine of every ten pages that were written between the sixteenth and seventeenth centuries contained devotional literature written to combat Protestantism. On the one hand, if Bishop Pedro Manso's demand that sermons be delivered in Basque reflected his concern for ensuring the orthodoxy of the pastoral message and protecting the *modus vivendi* of local priests—as was practiced in Catalonia—on the other, there was also no dearth of ideas issued by civilian policies that facilitated the successful incorporation of some Basques into society, with the antiquity of Eusquera providing justification. Such was the case with Andrés de Poza, a lawyer, who published a book in 1587 entitled *De la antigua lengua, poblaciones y comarcas de las Españas* (On the Ancient Language, Peoples and Regions of Spain), in Bilbao. Poza's work was a defense of the Basque language that argued that Eusquera was the first language spoken in Spain and the oldest of all the peninsular languages because it directly descended from the Babelian diaspora. Poza's ideas were not new; other period writers, although not necessarily Basque ones, used to debate the same question (the issue is still being debated, although now there is a greater critical apparatus and more information with which to do so, as Julio Caro Baroja has stated). However, Poza's intentions were not mainly philological in nature. What he wanted to communicate was that the roots of the Basque people and their language went back to the time of the Judeo-Christian Bible's book of *Genesis*. Thus, the Basque were Spain's most ancient people and, properly speaking, their right to fill the state's administrative positions was far greater than the right of many of the *conversos* who already had. In reality, Andrés de Poza's arguments about Eusquera's antiquity are actually concomitant with the attempt of many Basques to secure bureaucratic posts as secretaries, registrars, and administrators, careers in which some achieved well-deserved acclaim and from which they drove away many *conversos*. It is likely that the famous claim that Emperor Charles I spoke Eusquera well was a product of that context, but the reality of the Basque language at that moment was quite different. Due to the gradual assault of Spanish, Basque was in such decline that it stopped being used at the councils of Vizcaya during the time of Philip III. Many residents from neighboring Basque-speaking areas might not have aptly understood Calderón's religious plays or Lope's *comedias*, but it is a verifiable fact that theater companies did stage their works there with remarkable success.

Yet the ardor of the evangelization process caused peninsular conflicts in the colonial context to multiply. During the years of viceregal administration, the issue of languages in America and the Philippines was a veritable jumble of economic, political and ideological interests that was not easily addressed with the principle "Spanish for all" but with other, more situation-specific, complicated approaches. In general, though, there was not much interest in Spanish: in 1764, the fiscal (crown prosecutor) of the Council of the Indies informed Charles III that it would be easier to get all Spaniards to learn French than to make the natives of America learn Spanish. In fact, one should review the colonial world by beginning with one deservedly memorable case, because it, alone, exemplifies the American situation.

The American Case

In 1578, Philip II received a visit from a strange person, someone who was full of ideas on how to improve the governance of America. It was Fray Rodrigo de Loaysa, a veteran missionary from Peru. One of the matters that Fray Rodrigo discussed with the King was language. In the missionary's opinion, Church teaching could not be successful because many of the priests who were ordained had no knowledge of any Indigenous languages, which he thought should be avoided; in fact, this was an old complaint among the most experienced missionaries. In 1567, the Council of Lima had recommended to the bishops that they punish priests who did not learn Quechua (one should recall that in 1602 Bishop Pedro Manso demanded the same for those in Spain who did not preach in Basque, and that all the councils from that period uphold the need to preach in vernacular languages). Fray Rodrigo's opinion convinced the King, who in December of that same year only a few months after the missionary's visit, promulgated a law that forbade priests who did not know an indigenous language—in this case, Quechua—to be given the responsibility to teach Church doctrine to natives and ordered that *mestizos* not be ordained under any circumstances. This quasi-malicious and strategic addendum also reflected Fray Rodrigo's concomitant petition to Philip II: if vernacular languages were deemed to have value, the *mestizos*, who knew the indigenous languages better than the missionaries, would not have competition and were able to monopolize all parish positions. The King was told that *mestizos* were not reliable Christians, citing the authority of Father José de Acosta and his work *De Procuranda Indorum Salute* (On Ensuring the Indians' Well-Being) written in 1570, which stated that *mestizos* were "good at languages but had immoderate customs as a result of the ill effects of having suckled the milk of indigenous mothers."

Philip II's measure was popular with the most conservative groups in the viceroyalty's domains but came as a complete shock to the *mestizos* as well as some bishops. One from Cuzco, for example, was in favor of *mestizos* being ordained precisely "because they [were] very skilled in matters of language." Some *mestizos* appealed the law by using reports about their impeccable Catholic orthodoxy while more of them lobbied against it because of their language skills (half of the questions on the questionnaire about the *mestizos*' religious activities were directly concerned with linguistic issues). In 1583, the reports were sent to the Council of Lima which recommended that "the ordination of *mestizos* [would] be very useful because they are good with languages, can communicate with the Indians with whom they share a language, and know it very well."

Due to the intervention of both the bishop and the Vatican, Philip II repealed the prohibition of *mestizo* ordinations ten years later. Veteran missionaries and the most conservative groups of society, who did not look favorably upon the new classes' attaining ecclesiastical dignity through the mastery of Amerindian languages, then began to spread the idea that these languages could not properly reflect all of the subtleties of Catholic doctrine, as if Latin or Spanish could. Further, they also propagated the belief that allowing the teaching of the doctrine in Native languages was bound to bring about the creation of a possibly heretical "national" American clergy that would ruin efforts to spread the one and only faith.

All of these arguments were successful; for instance, a 1590 Royal Decree ordered that the *Audiencia* (Court of Hearing) of New Granada provide means by which the natives could learn Spanish. Since the *mestizos* also knew Spanish this law did not harm them. In the mid- to long-term, mission veterans were probably able to placate *mestizo* competition regarding Amerindian languages. In any case, since the question of using Amerindian languages to spread the doctrine corresponded to numerous interest, and the conflict surrounding it among religious groups continued, a compromise solution was agreed upon in 1596: to provide teachers so that the Natives would, voluntarily, make the transition to Spanish, while that the assignment of parish positions would be given preferentially to those who knew indigenous languages.

Fray Rodrigo's visit to Philip II—and everything that resulted from it for years—was in itself summed up by the linguistic circumstances in which the American viceroyalty was developing. This brings to the forefront illustrative issues that warrant further discussion, the first being the power of the state.

The Limited Power of the State

The political authority of states has been exaggerated in modern times as we now know that their transformational power is limited. In a contemporary sense of the term, the governing crux of the Spanish Empire had a linguistic policy, i.e., a plan with a specific goal—the spread of Spanish—through tenaciously employed administrative, educational, and juridical means created for that express purpose. Indeed, there were linguistic strategies: what American legislation revealed is the malleability of monarchic power when confronted by substantial American interest groups. Legislation from the Indies on language matters is extensive not because in a few generations the state had established a reachable goal for itself and persisted in trying to achieve it. Rather, it was due to the fact that the Court, the viceroys or the bishoprics saw the need to respond to the concrete demands—sometimes accepting, other times rejecting—establishments related to the Church, most often those for whom the protection of Amerindian languages, or the spread of Spanish, or some compromise between both, would serve their political, economic or job interests.

More than a linguistic policy, what we find in America, in the strictest sense, are strategies from different sectors, for the most part religious, on how to best become established in the New World where languages gained an essential value. These are strategies that the power structure pretended to either satisfy or frustrate via laws because the state's actual authority in matters of linguistic legislation was extremely limited during the colonial period. Speaking to everyone in his or her own language at the beginning of Pentecost might have been a positive ideological factor in the spiritual conquest of America and the Pacific, but the manner in which it was occurring in Spain often hid other issues.

One final factor must be considered when appreciating the state's weakness: Spain considered itself the most complete and advanced form of Catholic society, so much so that up until the time of Charles III, the vicarage with its direct papal authority over spiritual matters was responsible for the Antillean enterprise. In this sense, the Church enjoyed considerable autonomy. If regulations produced by civil courts favorable to the spread of Spanish contradicted priestly interests, they were either ignored or a document explaining the impossibility of implementing them was published. This happened with some frequency until 1769, when a reform aimed at reinforcing the king's authority over the Pope was attempted in the American Church. This initiative was not entirely successful, but, as far as the language issue was concerned, it did manage to get high-level American Church dignitaries to concur with Charles III's ministers about the need to observe the laws favoring Spanish with more enthusiasm than before.

There is one simple example that illustrates this point: Charles I initially gave his consent to the evangelical work of the first Franciscans, which was carried out with noticeable success in Amerindian languages. Notwithstanding, that same year, from June to July of 1550, when the general judge of Guatemala, Tomás López Medel, warned the emperor that the clergy were garnering a great deal of power amongst the Indigenous population and they were controlling too many of the Crown's economic resources, thus reducing the income that was available for the Crown because "only a few, who understand the language of these [Indians . . .], controlled the business, and they were never told exactly what was expected from them." The emperor issued three imperial decrees in an attempt to spread Spanish among the indigenous population, including two of them in Valladolid. Yet, the net results of those imperial orders could not have been widespread when one considers that the Council of Mexico recommended the extensive use of Indigenous languages during the same time period.

Obedience to the Mandate of Pentecost

Upon considering the limited power of the State and its malleability with regard to different peoples or groups opposing interests, one must also take into account the zeal for learning indigenous languages that spread among the first generations of missionaries. The strategy for spreading Catholicism as established earlier entailed multilingualism for even the most orthodox Catholic ideologues. In the prologue to *Arte y vocabulario de la lengua de los indios chaymas* (1680) (Rules and Vocabulary of the Chayma Indian Language), Fray Antonio de Fuentelapeña clearly stated: "Extendiéndose la Iglesia cada día por naciones diferentes, es necesario se multipliquen las versiones al paso que las lenguas se multiplican ("If the Church is going to spread through different nations every day, then its manifestations must multiply even as the languages do"). Despite this passion, it is reasonable to assume that from the very beginning legislators wanted the American population to be taught Spanish. Likewise, this is obvious from edicts that recommended the teaching of "how to read and write" [in Spanish] and from children's primers in Castilian and Latin that were exported to America in the New World. However, the recommendations did not specify in concrete terms the language or languages of instruction. Meanwhile, the need to preach in American languages can indeed be deduced with clarity from the Papal bull *Sublimis Deus*, written in June of 1537. Furthermore, given the prevailing situation of the vicariate, papal dispositions could actually carry more weight than any other laws. Papal doctrine concurred with the wishes of Spanish evangelizers, beginning with the very first one: Catalan native Ramón Pané who spent many of his missionary years learning Antillean languages. Papal doctrine was also in keeping with the ideas of Fray Bartolomé de las Casas, who considered the efforts to teach the Spanish language ridiculous and with those of Jerónimo de Mendieta who reported about missionaries who taught through hand gestures or in Latin but never in Spanish, with the hope of mastering the languages of the Natives. Finally, Papal doctrine also concurred with the ideas of Father Zumárraga, an indigenist held in high regard by Charles I.

Fray Juan de Zumárraga was a Franciscan whose native tongue was Basque. In 1539, he introduced a successful way to write bilingual catechisms for the American missions, stating: "I do not approve of those whose opinion is that idiots may not read divine scripture translated into the vernacular language because what Jesus Christ wants is for his secrets to be divulged over a long period of time." Zumárraga's power was extensive, and his ideas—acquired from Erasmus—were very influential. The Franciscans, Dominicans, Augustinians, and Jesuits were the orders most belligerently in favor of multilingual Indianism, but they were not the only ones. Without exception, all religious orders contributed in some measure to the colossal work of writing grammars of Amerindian languages and bilingual catechisms, an endeavor that contrasted with the modest attitude of the Portuguese Church.

If the first generations of missionaries who were in control until 1670, the time of Father Alonso de la Peña, did not ignore Spanish in their work, it is also true that there was frequent news about Indigenists who were convinced that they had singularly interpreted the ambiguity of the concept "to teach how to read and write." These were people who from very early on were capable of creating labor and pastoral networks utilizing Amerindian languages. Such was the case in 1537, when with the approval of Judges Davila Padilla and Cruz Moya, Sebastián Ramírez de Fuenleal, Bishop of the Audiencia of New Spain, tried a case in his court against Fray Domingo de Betanzos's missionary practices four years earlier. He accused him of being an "enemy of the Natives, a hater of doctrine and ignorant of the language and capabilities of the Natives." Through Fray Tomás de Torres, in the bishopric of Guatemala, the Natives had been taught only in their own language, at least until 1552. The conversion of great masses that were observed in the middle of the sixteenth century were made possible due to the preaching of simple messages in Amerindian languages. As Father José de Acosta noted: "We see that when the Natives hear a priest speak to them in their own language they pay a great deal of attention, and they greatly enjoy his eloquence." So, why was there this interest among the Spanish clergy to preserve Amerindian languages? There are two factors not very distinct from those affecting Spain or other areas of the Empire at play: one is ideological, the other material. The latter would prove to be more important than the former.

The concepts of "Thomism" and the spread of Christian ideas based on the principle of Pentecost that have already been discussed contributed mightily to an ideologically acceptable argument about the language issue. However, in looking at the Empire's theory of how to spread the faith, "the natives were considered individuals, persons sufficiently dignified and deserving of an educational policy that required an enormous quantity of patience, effort and hope." The fact that a Catholic Empire should act as such in the expansion of its doctrine, i.e., teaching each group in its own language, is an idea that many clergymen considered natural and, thus, acted in accordance with it.

Nevertheless, imperial theory was one issue while its practice was quite another. There was the expectation that the Natives, who were barely treated better than slaves, were to work and keep the system productive. Therefore, in practical terms, one cannot really refute the well-known arguments of José Vasconcelos or Paul Ricard about the Empire's interest in keeping Church doctrine remote through linguistic barriers. Hence, it became important to preserve indigenous languages.

Parishes and their teachings did not simply exist for the purpose of converting people but also to preserve a way of life for many clergymen who received income in direct proportion to the number of natives they managed and the religious services they offered. Thus, isolating the Indians by using a language that was unique to them was the equivalent of ensuring the survival of the *modus vivendi* of many clergymen: "We are proceeding in such a manner [speaking in the Guaraní language] to avoid any intermingling between our natives and the Spaniards, and so that our charges remain humble and simple." This was the strategy employed by Father Sepp, Jesuit of the Guaraní missions, a strategy that years later was considered "prejudicial to the state" by writers like Concolorcorvo.

The attempt here was not just to control all indigenous matters. The aforementioned case of Father Rodrigo de Loaysa clearly reveals another important function of the linguistic indigenism: the ability to reclaim the right to the land, the *ius soli*, by veteran missionaries, members of the *mestizo* class or even *criollos* in preference to the personnel that came from Spain or American areas where other indigenous languages were spoken. Father Loaysa's petitions to Philip II regarding this matter are just one of many examples that could be cited. Like Peninsular priests, American *criollos* who controlled the Franciscan order in Florida followed the custom of "constantly moving them around and sending them to miserable places so they could not learn any indigenous language," languages that the priests who lived in Florida did know. This allowed them to corner part of the potential competition for positions leading to an ecclesiastical career. Clearly, the result of this kind of linguistic particularism was not unlike the kind that developed in Spanish councils, which during the sixteenth and seventeenth centuries demanded that Church teachings be imparted in "national languages" sooner than in Spanish, in order to contain the penetration of and ascension into the ecclesiastical hierarchy of priests from purely Castilian-speaking areas (which was never successful). It should come as no surprise that the same practices occurred in America: in a letter to Philip III, Luis López Solís, the Bishop of Quito, recommended that the ordination of *mestizos* could produce many benefits because: "this could produce subjects who would be more successful with the Indians than anyone else who came from Spain because of the fondness with which Natives listen to their own language." Twenty years earlier, the petition of the council of Santiago de Guatemala to establish a university stated: "There are learned men in these parts, friars as well as priests, who understand how to manage the teaching of Church doctrine to the Natives. It is not necessary to bring such personnel to our kingdoms from Spain [. . .] because we have our own here, from our kingdoms, who aside from their education have skill in their mother tongues, which are of such importance." In fact, the university was established with professors who spoke Indigenous languages.

Yet the creation of a totally "national" American priesthood was viewed with resentment on the part of those with peninsular power. Some religious groups, *criollos*, *mestizos* and part of the American elite—as with the Valleumbroso case from which the subheading for this section takes its title—found a fabulous way to ensure privileges through the indigenous languages without having Spanish become the almost exclusive domain of the society's newest power elites. This explains a 1728 petition made to the Church by descendants of Indigenous aristocracies for unhindered and unfettered instruction in Spanish.

We have already discussed the role of ideological factors in the spread of the Catholic faith. Economic factors, too, can help explain both the rise and fall of the linguistic Indigenism that is appreciable by the end of the seventeenth century. With few exceptions, a careful examination of linguistic legislation and practices reveals that there was a cycle of decisions between the first third of the sixteenth century until the last third of the seventeenth century that favored the preservation of Indigenous languages. Bishop Alonso de la Peña Montenegro's ruling on this could be considered the highpoint of this trend. Montenegro went further than anyone else when he stipulated that those who did not know the languages would not just be removed from their posts but were also committing a serious sin. The Bishop's harshness was quite justifiable: the

Indigenous languages inspired little interest among new promotional missions, which was a threat to the groups that Montenegro represented. In fact, since the Viceroy of Peru's ruling in 1685, pro-Spanish language legislation continually increased until the years of Francisco de Lorenzana and the 1770 publication of *Tomo Regio* (Regional Book), which expressly recommended that Spanish be "spread and made the sole and universal" language [of the Empire]. During the second period, militant Indigenists like the infamous Bishop Juan Bautista Álvarez de Toledo seemed a bit of an anachronism.

Change of Direction

What caused this change in attitude toward Indianism? The factors are many, of course, but none of them seems completely separable from the way in which Indigenous labor, production and vassalage relationships were established through Church teachings and the missions. Until the end of the seventeenth century, protecting Natives was fiscally profitable for parish priests. The more natives they had, the more funding they received for their missions, and the easier the support of rural priests became. It was expected that each Native would bring in a total of 125 *maravedis*, a respectable sum for that time and place. Thus, leaving aside Pentecostal ideology, one can understand the interest there was in preserving the isolating and particularizing effects of Church teaching through the use of Indigenous languages. From this context emerged the popular expression: *"indio leído, indio ido,"* which loosely translated and defined in English means that once a subaltern [like an Indigenous person] has been educated [or empowered through education], he or she cannot be kept down.

Yet by the end of the seventeenth century, the organization of Indigenous labor changed drastically and Natives went from working in collective groups to being wage-earning peons, subject to contract by landowners, which brought about a very conflictive process—the transfer and migration of Indians from place to place. This, in turn, caused parish priests and *encomenderos* (Spanish holders of Indian territories) to lose interest in preserving a way to protect the Indians through their evangelization and communication in Amerindian languages, i.e., everything that was typical of the old collective system.

Nevertheless, teaching in vernacular languages did not cease completely. In 1771, the Synod of Charcas still recommended the use of Indigenous languages, but the new way in which production was organized left little reason for continuing the prior linguistic practices. This created a division between cities, where priests preferred speaking in Spanish, and the country, where vestiges of the old linguistic Indigenism still remained. More and more priests were ordained and given a "certificate of competence," that is, more sons of the wealthy, rent-collecting city families won out over poorer ones who were given a "language certificate." With time, there were more priests than available positions, so those with "competence" either occupied the positions in the cities or were destined to rural parishes without the requirement of knowing languages. This secular clergy, which generally spoke only Spanish, carried more weight in American religious administration and was decisive when it came to supporting the introduction of *regalismo* (regalism), that is, a policy directed at the recovery of the Crown's power in ecclesiastical matters vis-à-vis the *vicariate* (Papacy). This reform was carried out by Charles III and dealt a serious blow to the linguistic strategy of the Indigenists who lost privileges and saw their influence reduced even more. However, the dwindling number of Amerindian languages was not due only to religious reform but also for economic and market reasons as well. It is revealing that during the time of the *Tratado de Libre Comercio* (Free Trade Agreement) of 1778, the great innovator of American trade, the Viceroy of Corix, whose arguments turned out to be convincing to the Bourbon Court, was a staunch defender of the spread of Spanish.

With appropriate differences, the fate of vernacular languages in the colonial Philippines was similar to what took place in Spain and viceregal America. However, what the missionary colony did in the Philippines was to zealously guard Spanish for itself rather than protect Indigenous languages. In the end, however, the result was the same, and Spanish remained a true minority language in the midst of flourishing Indigenous ones and others, like Chinese which was also of greater commercial importance. This was easily accomplished: the Spanish population during colonial times in the Philippines never numbered more than twenty-five thousand with three thousand of them in Manila. It was only at the middle of the nineteenth century, under Isabel II's rule, that the scholastic spread of Spanish was secured. Given the circumstances of the time, it was considered a true success.

Priests from the colony were reticent to take native clergymen into their ranks and continued to be so until late in the eighteenth century; thus, they tried to make access to Spanish difficult for them. As one might expect, reports on the Philippine situation, like the two by Pedro Vértiz and Santiago de Salaberría dated 1788 and 1790 respectively, were not very charitable about the role of the religious orders regarding this matter.

Even though Saberría was more moderate than Vértiz in his judgments, it had become clear to both of them that the missionaries had accumulated absolute power by acting as intermediaries between the Natives and Spanish functionaries. Since that task kept them in a privileged position, they never bothered to evangelize or, much less, spread the use of Spanish. In fact, forty years earlier, Governor Pedro Manuel de Arandía encountered rigid opposition from the Philippine clergy when he wanted to spread the teaching of Spanish, an attempt that cost him his position. Nevertheless, there were those among the Natives who were favorable towards Spanish: the Tagalog printer Tomás Pinpin, who in 1610 published a Spanish grammar book for use in the Philippines, encouraged the learning of it: "The Spanish language is the source of many things. It is at the center of them. All the rest is like its covering." Tomás Pinpin soon learned that learning Spanish was important for achieving a satisfactory social position. The clergy knew this too: that is why they guarded it so zealously. In the Spanish Empire there was a place where Spanish was not only an invading language but was also guarded as a secret until the second half of the nineteenth century: that place was the Philippines.

The parallel between Spanish and Portuguese in the evangelization of America is interesting. In truth, the enormous amount of imperial rhetoric about Portuguese was even more fatuous than the rhetoric about Spanish. Like Spanish, Portuguese does not begin to spread massively in America until the beginning of the nineteenth century. For instance, Portuguese Jesuits refused to teach their language. However, Spanish missionaries handily beat their peninsular counterparts and excelled extraordinarily at publishing grammar books and catechisms in Indigenous languages, creating positions for their teaching, and, in short, seeing the issue of linguistic Indigenism as something relevant. If the limited introduction of colonial Portuguese had some effect on evangelization in vernacular languages, the fact that the Portuguese Church had a primary role to play in adapting slaves to their work in the new colonies was much more important. Proportionally, this was as much a source of the Portuguese clergy's *modus vivendi* as it was for the Spanish missionaries with their protective isolation of the Natives, except that Portuguese priests did not need expertise in Brazil's native languages, unlike the Spanish missionaries who did. There were a variety of reasons why the "black languages" were of no interest to Spanish or Portuguese clerics. Thus, the Portuguese Church remained uninterested in the aboriginal languages and did not help spread Portuguese through missionaries—as was the case with the Spanish religious clerics in the Philippines—because a more lucrative task had been superimposed onto the purely evangelical one.

Conclusion

The fact that linguistic Indigenism suffered a prolonged decline does not mean that Spanish spread with popularity. It is true that in a short time many Amerindian languages—almost all the Antillean ones—disappeared, sometimes because of the physical extermination of their speakers, although the decrease of the Indigenous population due to wars, epidemics or emigration was considerable. Moreover, many other languages were preserved, and some, like Quechua, spread beyond its pre-Colombian boundaries due to the work of missionaries. Even though between the end of the seventeenth and eighteenth centuries all of these languages ceased being ideological or economic instruments for colonizers and the Church, the use of Spanish in America after three centuries was still not pervasive, as José María Blanco described Cuzco: "two thirds of the population does not speak Spanish." Numerous writers of the time, including von Humboldt, Lázaro de Rivera, Juan Bautista Ladrón, Concolorcorvo, and the navigator Alejandro Malespina felt compelled to acknowledge the limited extension of this supposedly imperial language beyond the city-dwelling Spaniards, *criollos* or *mestizos* of the Empire's domains. It is notable that all of them agreed on this point. There were also ordinary reports, such as the one written by Monsignor Venura, the Bishop of Antequera (Mexico), submitted to the King in 1763. In it he pointed out that town judges did not know Spanish and that "the most important mayors stated that there was no one in the whole town who knew it." It would seem that Nebrija's prediction for his time did not come true after all.

The Construction of Nationhood (1997), by historian Adrian Hastings, contains interesting debates about the role of languages in the forging of national consciousness. About the Spanish case, he suggests "the Spanish linguistic community was subordinated for too long to imperial interterritorial politics to be a place in which a linguistically based concept of nationality could flourish." The supraregional character of the Spanish Empire and, above all, its "Catholic matrix" has linguistically affected the modern and contemporary era in two ways: together, they hindered the spread of Spanish in viceregal America and the formation of a national consciousness based on language, most notably in contemporary Spain, but also in other American countries where linguistic Indigenism has increased in great measure since 1960.

In its time, the Empire and the ancient regime did not meet with great success in the popular spread of Spanish but it must also be said that they did not seriously attempt it. Spreading a common language was not of great concern during those times. A major consideration, as Saint Paul recommended, was the forging of a Catholic Empire that would transmit the word of God to all peoples in their own languages. The Spanish Empire's claim to be the incarnation of Heaven on Earth was not entirely in vain.

Works Cited

[Due to the untimely and tragic death of Juan R. Lodares in 2005, the following incomplete and unorthodox list of Works Cited had to be reconstructed from the initial draft of the article he submitted].

Acosta, José de. *De Procuranda Indorum Salute,* 1570.
Aldete, Bernardo de. *De origen y principio de la lengua castellana o romance que oi se usa en España.* Roma, 1606.
Aquinas, Saint Thomas. *In libros Peri Hermeneias expositio,* II, 2, 1269–12.
Cervantes Saavedra, Miguel de. *El ingenioso hidalgo Don Quijote de la Mancha.* 2 Vols. Ed. Luis Andrés Murillo. Madrid: Castalia, 1978.
Despuig, Cristobal. *Colloquis de la insigne ciutat de Tortosa,* 1557.
Enbaqom. *Anqasa Amin o Puerta de la Fe,* 1532.
Fuentelapeña, Fray Antonio de. *Arte y vocabulario de la lengua de los indios chaymas,* 1680.
Gracian, Baltasar. *El politico.* Zaragoza, 1640.
Hastings, Adrian. *The Construction of Nationhood.* Cambridge: University of Cambridge, 1997.
Lorenzana, Francisco de. *Tomo Regio,* 1770.
Massò, Magino. *Arbol fructuoso,* 1667.
Menéndez Pidal, Ramón. *La idea imperial de Carlos V.* Madrid: Espasa-Calpe, 1963.
Nebrija, Antonio de. *Gramática de la Lengua Castellana.* Ed. Antonio Quilis. Madrid: Editora Nacional, 1980.
Pinpin, Tomás. *Librong Pag-aaralan nang mga Tagalog nang Uicang Castila,* 1610.
Poza, Andrés de. *De la Antigua lengua, poblaciones y comarcas de las Españas,* 1587.

◆ 2

Echoes of the Voiceless:
Language in Jesuit Missions in Paraguay

Fernando Ordóñez

In Latin America, there is a general consensus within Colonial studies that language was a powerful tool used by European *conquistadors* and missionaries in their political and spiritual conquest of the New World. In this essay I argue that linguistic policies in the Spanish empire were oriented pragmatically towards the fulfillment of its main goal: the creation of a '*Universitas Christiana*,' a Europe and a world ruled by the Emperor of the Holy Roman Empire (Charles V), and united under the spiritual leadership of the Catholic Church. I will discuss this perspective through an exploration of linguistic policies of the Jesuit missions in Paraguay as a model of a (different sort of) strategy that was employed at the empire's borders.

It is important to note that in the Spanish colonies, linguistic policies were not always intended to expand the use of Spanish over a greater geographic area. In some situations, Spanish was used as a medium for control, while in others, Spaniards employed Native American languages to establish and maintain their power. The Spanish administration was always guided by the need for a universal and Catholic empire. Consequently, they acted in response to challenges encountered in the Indies as they attempted to secure political, military, and economic power while disseminating Catholicism among the empire's nations.

There was an unquestionable imperial policy behind the Spanish linguistic policies: those principles were intricately connected to the Castilian experience of the *Reconquista*. It is important to note that this centuries-long process whereby the Peninsular Christian kingdoms reconquered Iberian territories under Muslim control is a marker in the process of construction of the Spanish national identity.

As was stated by Fernández Armesto, the conquest of Andalusia "was actually seen in Castile as an 'imperial' venture" (47). Under the rules of war, the Castilian crown expelled the confessional minorities from reconquered land in order to secure the border: "The scale of this displacement of population imposed on the conquerors a labor of resettlement which stretched manpower to the limit" (60) and demanded a policy of colonization. Two legal instruments, known as *repartimentos*, were implemented in order to stimulate the repopulation of the fertile south of Spain: the *donadíos,* "landholdings given to royal personages, aristocrats and military and religious orders for purposes of patronage or defense" and the *heredamientos,* "small units intended for direct exploitation by their owners and for to encourage settlement" (61).

The struggle to colonize these lands was ultimately resolved by the allocation of most of the *repartimentos* to soldiers and *caballeros* (knights). Despite the fact that people from different Iberian and European nationalities participated in the repopulation of Andalusia, most of the new settlers and those in administration were of Castilian heritage, which was expressed through language and other cultural elements. In other words, Castilian imperial enterprises and military actions during the *Reconquista* involved pragmatic population policies that brought about substantial cultural change. This model shaped subsequent imperial endeavors abroad, first in the Canary Islands and later in the Americas. In the fifteenth century, an empire was an accepted form of political organization amongst different nations. Moreover, the nation was understood within the framework of empire (García Alvarez 107). Given these circumstances, the perception of the local sphere was linked to an external "distant," and to a spatial notion of empire, a tension that always demanded diverse degrees of totality. This totality was represented by the utopian project of a '*Universitas Christiana,*' in which secular matters were under the absolute control of the emperor of the Holy Roman Empire.

While the Papacy had supreme control in the spiritual realm, with Charles V, Spain witnessed a unique opportunity to create this utopian kingdom because the emperor held title to the Holy Roman Empire and the right to claim the crown of Byzantium.[1] During the Diet of Worms, in 1521, Charles V vigorously embraced this imperial project with three main goals: a total war against the Protestant Reformation in Europe; the containment of the Ottomans in the Mediterranean; and the conquest and control of the New World. In the words of José Antonio Maravall, the main purpose of the Spanish empire was to honor God and promote the universal good of a Christian Republic (44).

It is interesting to note the incident that Charles V started in the papal court in 1536. While Charles V was defying Phillip I of France in the presence of Bishop Macon, the French ambassador argued that he did not understand Spanish, to which Charles V replied: "My Lord Bishop, understand me if you wish, and do not expect from me words other than [those I have expressed] in my Spanish tongue, which is so noble that it deserves to be known and understood by all Christian people" (quoted by Carrera de la Red 120) [my translation]. With this act, the emperor was defining Spanish as the language of the universal Christian empire. In essence, the rationale behind the Spanish geopolitical actions in Europe, the Americas, and everywhere else was both the Castilian model of conquest forged during the *Reconquista* and the creation of a universal Catholic empire. Thus, the Empire's linguistic policies should be seen in this context.

The interconnectedness of language and empire had already been acknowledged before Nebrija addressed it in his *Gramática de la Lengua Castellana* (*Castilian Grammar*). The use of language policies to strengthen imperial power had been the norm in prior imperial enterprises. The originality of Nebrija's argument was his recognition of the relevance of a standard language in an attempt to achieve national cohesion. Linguistic diversity had already functioned within the idea of an empire that ruled over different nations in the aftermath of the *Reconquista*, Castilian authorities perceived linguistic and religious diversity as a threat to political stability because they imagined a national identity that would unify race, language, and religion. Ultimately by connecting language and empire, Nebrija was not offering a prophecy about the imperial future but a lesson from the experiences of preceding empires and an analysis of Castilian expansionist efforts:

> Lo que diximos de la lengua ebraica, griega y latina, podemos mui más clara mente mostrar en la castellana; . . . La cual se estendió después hasta Aragón y Navarra y de allí a Italia, siguiendo la compañía de los infantes que embiamos a imperar en aquellos Reinos. I assí creció hasta la monarchía y paz de que gozamos, primeramente por la bondad y providencia divina; después por la industria, trabajo y diligencia de vuestra real majestad. En la fortuna y buena dicha de la cual, los miembros y pedaços de España, que estavan por muchas partes derramados, se reduxeron y aiuntaron en un cuerpo y unidad de Reino. (Nebrija 100)

(What we said of Hebrew, Greek and Latin, clearly can be shown for Spanish; ... [Spanish] later extended to Aragon and Navarre and from there to Italy, following the *infantes* that we sent to reign in those Kingdoms. And thus it grew into the monarchy and peace that we now enjoy, first of all thanks to goodness and divine providence; and later by the industry, work and diligence of your royal majesty. To such luck and good fortune were the members and parts of Spain spread, and reduced and joined in one royal and united Kingdom.) [my translation]

Nebrija's allegations were in perfect accordance with the program of religious nationalization initiated by Queen Isabella and which "later monarchs carried on towards the identification of Catholicism with Castilianization" (Heath 6). Thus, if the empire had the essential mandate to promote the Catholic faith by unifying different people, Castilian was the language to express that unity.

In America, there was an analogous linguistic desire for domination specifically with regard to the Aztec and Incan empires, where there were a variety of native languages. The imperial administration—including its pastoral efforts—and trade required a lingua franca in places where there were many different languages spoken. In Mexico and Peru, the Spanish established similar linguistic practices, with Nahuatl and Quechua being the official languages of the Aztec and Incan empire respectively. La Rosa indicates: "when the two empires collided, however, the traditional language policies of both empires, which were to impose the language of the politically dominant group on all others, initially collapsed" (2) [my translation]. Given the vast dimensions of the new territories, Spanish could not prosper concomitantly with military expansion. The use of language, itself, whether Spanish or a Native American language, played a crucial role in establishing European domination in the Americas since the very beginning of the Conquest.

The Pope granted the Spanish Crown the right and responsibility for the conversion of the natives. 'Conversion' basically meant the right to crush nations and dominate their lands if they declined to accept the empire, i.e., if they rejected European control and the Christian faith. That prerogative implied that the Spanish administration had to invest in the natives' evangelization which was unavoidably linked to language.

Columbus understood the correlation between language and evangelization on his very first voyage. On November 27, he reports in his journal: "... Faré enseñar esta lengua a persona de mi casa, porque veo que es toda lengua una fasta aquí; y después se sabrá los beneficios y se trabajará de hacer todos estos pueblos cristianos ..." (Colón 72) (I will have the language taught to one of my people, since I perceive that it is a tongue spoken everywhere. Thereafter it will be possible to assess the benefits and work toward the conversion of all of these people to Christianity) [my translation].

Columbus acknowledged the need to learn the language of the natives and, for that reason, he took a group of them to Spain. The Spanish administration also recognized the importance of language in the enterprise of Conquest, but opted to force the natives to learn Spanish. In a royal decree, Emperor Charles V ordered the Dominicans to teach language in conjunction with their pastoral duties:

> Os encargo a vuestra merced y a todos los religiosos de su Orden, en las provincias donde residen, que traten por todos los medios posibles de enseñar nuestra lengua castellana a los indios, y poned en ello todo el cuidado y diligencia, pues es una tarea de primerísima importancia, porque . . . parece que ésta es la forma más rápida para que estos pueblos sean capaces de tener una acabada comprensión del Dios verdadero y de ser instruidos en nuestra santa fe católica. (de Solano 49)

> (I supplicate and charge you and other clergymen of your Order in the province where you reside, to attempt in all possible ways to teach our Castilian language to the Indians, and to put all care and diligence in this task, as it is of primary importance, because . . . it seems that it is the quickest way for these people to be able to have an understanding of the true God and to be instructed in the our holy Catholic faith.) [my translation]

Evangelization was a colossal venture without precedent in the history of Christianity. The Spanish had some immediate earlier references for this enterprise: the literacy campaign of Castile; the catechism of the Moriscos in Andalusia in the fifteenth and sixteenth centuries, and the experience of the Spanish religious orders in their missions overseas (Hernández Aparicio 573). The missionaries first preached with signs and gestures but soon recognized the needs for language: ". . . Los religiosos utilizan los métodos de enseñanza europeos: cartillas, carteles con el alfabeto y la formación de silabas, dibujos que representan hechos y personajes de la Sagrada Escritura" (578) (They tried to teach the Spanish tongue to the Indians; so the priests used European methods of teaching: handbooks, posters with the alphabet and the formation of the syllables, drawings that represent event and people from sacred scripture) [my translation] and so on.

Relocated in towns, or in *encomienda*[2] the natives were gathered to receive the faith jointly with the new language. In the Laws of Burgos (1513), the Crown delineated its policies regarding religious education in America. In this plan, the sons of the *caciques* (chieftains), particularly those under thirteen years of age, had to be taught by priests—*doctrineros* (doctrinaires) who imparted them with reading and writing skills as well as an indoctrination in Catholicism (de Solano 8). After four years of education, they were supposed to return to their communities in order to teach language and religion.

This program of religious and language teaching proved to be unfeasible due to the vast demographic and geographic dimensions of America. Since evangelization was one of the empire's main goals, a new linguistic and pastoral system was put into place, one which switched from Castilian to native languages for the preaching and teaching of catechism. In December 1578, Phillip II established that to be a doctrinaire priest in America, one had to know the particular language of the local natives. Moreover, those provisions were ratified by the Crown in ordinances written in 1580 and 1582. In order for these policies to be put into effect, Phillip II decreed the implementation of courses on native languages at the Universities of Lima and Mexico as well as in major jurisdictions (Castro 487).

Moreover, under this model the clergy would be able to control the reception of the faith and, therefore, could ultimately prevent heresy. Priests, as a social group, retained the role of mediators between the Indians and colonial society, as they were the principal link between the colonial administration and the native communities.

Another reason the missionaries preferred learning indigenous languages was that they wanted to keep track of the religious education of the natives. If they could not understand their native languages, there was no way of knowing whether the Indians had correctly understood their teachings, or if they were spreading heresy in the indigenous languages. Effective communication was necessary for conversion, and it was believed to be necessary to learn the language and culture of the people in order to convert them (Gómez Mango 119). Consequently, priests were among the first Europeans to learn indigenous languages.

Religious orders and the clergy undertook an enormous effort to learn and codify native languages. Yet, despite the fact that the easiest course of action for the Spanish colonial administration would have been to use the common languages of the preceding empires, there was resistance to such language diversity. Because native languages were perceived as inferior, many missionaries questioned their ability to convey abstract notions of Catholic doctrine. Sánchez Herrero has stated that it "Se trata de hacer pasar a los idiomas indígenas conceptos que jamás se habían expresado en ellos ... tales como Trinidad, Espíritu Santo, redención, etc." (643) (Was a matter of translating into native languages concepts that had never been expressed in them . . . such as Trinity, Holy Spirit, redemption, etc.) [my translation]. The missionaries faced two options: they could incorporate Spanish words whose concepts were very difficult to translate into native languages or they could translate everything, even using some paraphrasing (642). Generally, they preferred the first option. In fact, missionaries in Mexico did not refer to God using the Nahualt word *'teolt'*: they favored using the Spanish *'Dios.'* Another interesting example is the word *'papa'* in reference to the Pope, "In order to avoid any confusion between the word for the Pope or a native priest, who were called *'papas,'* Bishop Zumárraga[3] ordered that *'pontifex'* or 'pontiff' be used instead of the Latin and Spanish word *'papas'* (Sánchez Herrero 642) [my translation].

These prejudices in addition to many concrete problems ultimately determined a new linguistic policy that basically enforced the use of Spanish for pastoral purposes, specifically catechism, while Latin, Greek and Hebrew were reserved for the liturgy and theological and biblical studies.

The Society of Jesus (the Jesuit order) was the last religious order to arrive in America around 1540, only a decade after its founding. While it established missions in all of the major colonies, in Spanish America it had a special interest in the empire's borders, specifically California and the northern regions of New Spain, and in the area around the River Plate in the South.

In those areas, the Jesuits set into motion many evangelization programs, but their most significant experience was with the *Reducciones* that they founded in Paraguay. This Resettlement plan must be understood within the context of the political conditions that prevailed upon the Jesuits' arrival to the Plate River area. Juan Díaz de Solís explored this area around 1516, but its conquest was gradual due to the resistance of local tribes. Consequently, by 1590, a small number of cities and forts were established in the region. At the same time, the Portuguese represented a hostile front, constantly threatening the border, since they visualized the River Plate itself as the natural limit of their own empire in the South.

As in the rest of the Spanish colonies, the natives who were 'reduced' by force or who were voluntarily submitted to the Spanish administration were brought primarily into the *encomienda* system. Due to the cruelty of this system, there were frequent uprisings in the area, and many villages, including Buenos Aires, were destroyed multiple times by Indians.

Franciscans established the first missions, but other orders such as the Dominicans, Mercedarians, and Augustinians also played an important role in instituting the Catholic hierarchy in the region. Since it was a vast territory, three dioceses were created: Asunción (1547); Tucumán (1570); and Buenos Aires (1582) (Dussel 1981).

In 1581, Bishop Francisco de Victoria of Tucumán requested the assistance of the Jesuits who arrived in Tucumán in 1586, and they went to Asuncion in 1587. In just a few decades, the Jesuit founded homes, seminaries and missions in Asunción, Buenos Aires, Córdoba (a university since 1621), Corrientes, Tarija, Salta, Santiago del Estero, San Miguel de Tucumán, Santa Fé, and La Rioja, where they worked mainly as teachers in the cities and ministered among the Indians in the *encomiendas*. Moreover, from the very first moment, the Jesuit started their countless travels in every direction of the vast territory looking for tribes that had not yet been 'resettled.'

The Jesuit came up with a plan for a more efficient administration of those borders of the Empire, proposing a different approach to the evangelization and colonization of the people in the region of La Plata. The Resettlement program was connected to a utopian representation of the Christian empire, seeking to avoid the main difficulties that the *encomienda* system presented in the conversion of the natives: the oppression of natives by force, the resulting rejection of the religion of the oppressors, and the poor example of the colonists. In *Conquista Espiritual del Paraguay* (Spritual Conquest of Paraguay), Antonio Ruiz de Montoya perfectly summarized his analysis of the colonial situation:

> Hay otra provincia que llaman Calchaquí cristianos bautizados, en que Su Majestad tenía un pueblo suyo que le daba no pequeño tributo. Había en las doctrinas clérigos y en la ciudad religiosos. Viéronse estos indios tan apurados del continuo trabajo del beneficio del algodón y tejumbre de lienzos, y sus mujeres tan afanadas con el perpetuo hilado y rigor con que se les pedía tarea, aún a la mas ocupada en criar sus hijos, que les obliigo la necesidad a buscar desahogo, Alzáronse, mataron buen numero de españoles, y fue fuerza a los vivos desamparar la ciudad y sus bienes, que no eran pocos; y guarecerse a la ciudad de Corrientes; y aunque se ha hecho esfuerzo para volver a recuperar aquella tierra, no ha sido posible . . . . (69)

(There is another province that the baptized Christians call Calchaquí, in which your Majesty had a people that paid him no small tribute. There were clergymen there for the teaching of the Doctrine and priests in the cities. These Indians found themselves in such a bad state because of their continuous labor in cotton and weaving, and its women so overworked with the constant spinning and rigor with which they are expected to work, even the busiest of them, who is raising children, that they saw a need to seek some form of relief. They carried out an uprising and killed a good number of Spaniards, and those who survived felt forced to abandon the city and their goods, which were not few; they sought shelter in the city of

Corrientes; and although there has been some effort to return to recover that land, it has not been possible.)

Under the Jesuit plan, the Indians would gain their liberty and be released from the compulsory personal service that was forced upon them by the colonial system. This plan evoked a strong reaction against the Jesuits among the colonists, including members of the clergy, resulting in the Jesuits' expulsion from their colonies. Yet King Philip III, an open supporter of the Jesuits, backed their plans with many royal decrees and endowments from the public treasury. In a *Cédula Real* dated December 18, 1606, he ordered Hernán Díaz de Saavedra—governor of Asunción—that, "even if he could conquer the Indians by force of arms he must not do so, but must win them over solely through the sermons and instructions of the clergy who had been sent for that purpose" (Sánchez Herrero 643). Furthermore, a *Cedula Real* dated January 30, 1607, guaranteed that the Indians who converted to Christianity would be excluded from servitude and would be exempted from taxation for a period of ten years. On the contrary, in 1609, a new royal pronouncement decreed "the Indian should be as free as the Spaniard" (Sánchez Herrero 644).

The problem of language and evangelization arose here, too. Despite the fact that in the empire's other regions Spanish was the language of catechism, the Jesuits thought that Guaraní should be the language of their pastoral enterprise, since they recognized the relevance of language in the evangelization process and because they understood the semiotics of colonial interaction. According to Walter Mignolo, "colonial semiosis refers to a conflictive domain of semiotic interactions among members of radically different cultures engaged in a struggle of imposition and appropriation, on the one hand, and of resistance, opposition and adaptation on other" (7). Aware of that cultural clash, the Jesuits identified a need to address the plurality of traditions. This would eventually imply a plurality of loci of enunciation and of understanding (95). Recognizing that a new language was needed, they recreated one by transforming a common one belonging to the Tupi-Guaraní linguistic family, a language utilized in South America, from the Atlantic to Amazonia, in the North to the Plate River region.[4] The result was the *Guaraní Jesuítico* (Jesuit Gurani) that the Fathers used in the missions, which was accepted by the Indians despite the fact it was an artificial creation. This process was not exempt of violence, however, as Zajícová states:

> Es difícil darnos cuenta de la violencia lingüística de este proceso. Por ejemplo, el simple hecho de intentar aplicar las categorías gramaticales que más o menos

funcionan en las lenguas indoeuropeas al guaraní es muy violento. En el guaraní no existe, p. ej., la distinción entre verbo y sustantivo: 'soy loco', 'hago tonterías' y 'mi tontería', los tres conceptos se expresan igual con la ayuda de *che,* 'yo' y 'mío' a la vez; no existe el verbo "ser," ni su concepto. Con la lengua reducida quedó también reducido el imaginario religioso, político y social de los guaraníes. (2)

(It is difficult to comprehend the linguistic violence of this process. For example, just the attempt to apply the grammatical categories more or less prevalent in Indo-European language to Guaraní was very violent. In Guaraní, there is no distinction between a verb and a noun, for example: the following phrases, 'I am crazy,' 'I am engaged in nonsense' and 'my nonsense,' are all expressed the same way with the help of *che,* both 'I' and 'mine': there is no verb 'to be' nor does its concept exist. As the language became 'reduced,' so did the religious, political and social imaginary of the Guaranís.)

Although violence is implicit in such actions, those modifications affected the lexicon but not the grammar of Guaraní, as Dietrich astutely observes:

Esta lengua moderadamente planificada se refleja también en las obras de Ruiz de Montoya, tanto en la terminología cristiana que contienen como en algunos términos de la vida social. Pero esto afecta sólo una parte del léxico, apenas la gramática. El guaraní "jesuítico" conservó las estructuras básicas de la semántica léxica y de la gramática del guaraní original, tanto que se pueden ver fácilmente las correspondencias semánticas y morfológicas con las demás lenguas de la misma familia. (289)

(This moderately planned language can be seen in the works of Ruiz of Montoya, both in their Christian terminology and in some terms referring to social life. Yet, although this affects only part of the lexicon it barely affects the grammar. Jesuit Guaraní kept the basic structure of the lexical semantics grammar of the and original Guarani, so much so that it is easy to trace its semantics and morphological correspondence with other languages from the same linguistic family, today.)

This new language was a synthesis of previous linguistic practices, since in using a native language, it was modified in order to ensure an unambiguous transmission of Catholic dogma. Ruiz de Montoya offers an excellent example of this:

Este nombre *Tupá* aplicaron los indios a Dios, que concibiendo por la predicación de Santo Tomé Apóstol (como se presume con buenos fundamentos) su incomprehensibilidad, y inexplicabilidad, se acogieron a admirarle con rendida admiración con solas dos dicciones en que dicen mas de Dios que si con multiplicidad de palabras y conceptos quisieran definirle, porque en esta admiración encierran su ser increado, su simplicidad, su inmortalidad y hacen aprecio y estimación de sus divinos atributos y así en una admiración adoran lo que no pueden entender ni explicar como nosotros con el nombre de Dios. (Quoted by Meliá 25)

(The Indians used the name *Tupá* to refer to God, who according [with good reason] to the Apostle Saint Thomas, was an incomprehensible and inexplicable concept. Yet, they took to worshipping Him with true devotion using only two words which, according to them, say more about God than any multiplicity of words and concepts that might try to define Him, because by them they invest in Him all of His uncreated nature, His simplicity, His immortality, and they manifest all their appreciation for Him and for His divine attributes, and in that way they manifest their adoration and devotion for something they can neither understand or explain what we do when we call His name, God.) [my translation]

In this example, Ruiz de Montoya is rethinking the colonial semiosis by acknowledging the possibility of a different locus of enunciation present in language: he is stating the possibility that the Indians had a different voice in which to address the way in which they experienced God. While, according to Montoya, they could not have 'explained' this without having first received the Christian revelation—which was the role that the Jesuits were claiming for themselves Guaraní, as a language, and the Guarani as a people, had the agency to express the reality of God.

Moreover, the *Guaraní Jesuítico* had incorporated some terms whose meaning was ideologically transformed. The case of 'money' is a very well-known example. Since currency was not allowed in the missions, Ruiz de Montoya used the word *kuarepotí ju* (golden money, or yellow money), and *kuarepotí* (silver money or white money). The term *kuarepotí* was created from *kua.r* (hole) and *t-epotí* (excrement), thus the meaning of "metal" is represented by the phrase "excrement of the mines" (Dietrich 289).

Missionary linguistic policies could be seen within a broader agenda, too, since the Jesuits were building a new utopian community that, in my opinion, was a new form of imperial administration. Education had an important role in this context. Each *Reducción* (Settlement) had a basic school system, although some lessons were given at home. The teachers were natives educated by the Jesuits, and they taught in Guaraní. In the beginning, the social organization of schools included boys and girls, but the system became progressively more selective, focusing specifically on the children of the *caciques* (chieftains). At school, students could learn reading, writing, and arithmetic, mainly in Guarani, but there are documents that show that some students could read Spanish and Latin (Meliá and Nagel 166). Students who were particularly gifted also received enough instruction in Latin to enable them to perform sexton's duties and, eventually, read in college.

Spanish was secondary in the curriculum and only the *notarios* were specifically trained in it. The supremacy of Guaraní over Spanish was so conclusive that after the expulsion of the Jesuits, in 1796, the governor of Buenos Aires, Lázaro de Ribera, in reporting to the king, commented:

> Al tiempo de la expatriación de los jesuitas se establecieron en estos pueblos con arreglo a las leyes, escuelas de primeras letras con el importante fin de que los naturales aprendiesen la doctrina cristiana en lengua castellana, a leer y escribir y contar. Pero, ¿qué es lo que hemos adelantado en 28 años de fatiga? Nada más que estar viviendo la pérdida efectiva de más de cien mil pesos que se han llevado las dotaciones de unos maestros inútiles por no decir perjudiciales. Los indios se mantienen en una ignorancia absoluta de nuestra lengua y como en la de ellos conocida con el nombre de guaraní, es imposible explicar bien las verdades eternas de nuestra religión, resulta de que el bien espiritual de estos infelices está cercado y envuelto en las tinieblas de la ignorancia y a veces del error [. . .] Por una fatal desgracia y por varias causas que no precisa referir aquí, hemos llegado al extremo de que la lengua del pueblo conquistado sea la que domine y dé la ley al conquistador, que los indios se mantengan intratables y separados de nosotros [. . .]. (Massare 384)

> (Upon the expulsion of the Jesuits, primary schools were established in these towns, according to law, so that the natives could learn Christian doctrine in Spanish, and to read, write and count. But, what progress have we made in twenty-eight years of hard work? Nothing more than to be living with the loss of more than a hundred thousand pesos that staff members of some useless (if not dangerous) teachers have taken. The Indians continue in absolute ignorance of our language and because it is impossible for us to effectively explain the eternal truths of our religion in their language, called Guaraní, the spiritual wellbeing of these poor creatures is enveloped and trapped in the darkness of ignorance and, sometimes, even error [. . .] Due to a terrible misfortune and several other reasons we need not here explain, we have come to a situation whereby the language of a conquered people is the dominant one and rule over the *conquistador,* that the Indians remain unapproachable and separate from us [. . .].)

In fact, it might be argued that "Las reducciones aislaron al guaraní del español y facilitaron su supervivencia, lo mismo que facilitaron la supervivencia de los hablantes indígenas" (Zajícová 2) (*reducciones* isolated the Guaraní from the Spanish and facilitated their survival, and also facilitated the survival of the native speakers) [my translation].

Formal and artistic education had a practical sense and purpose in the missions since they were conceived to prepare children to live in a traditional community that was sacred and close by definition. Moreover, the core of education in the *reducciones* was the socialization of children through a set of instrumental community skills and religious practices that were organized around a strict schedule (Meliá and Nagel 166).

The implementation of this program required many cultural strategies: music and theatre were perceived as excellent resources according to the experiences of different missionary group (Caraman 213). In the Paraguay mission, schools for singing and music were very successfully managed, so that each *reducción* had a capable church choir and orchestra. Those spheres were in fact very important in the process of cultural assimilation of the natives. The catechism, itself, was interconnected to music and dances. Furthermore, "before 1619, a whole Christian catechism through sensible symbols and pictorial dances had been developed" (Caraman 214). All these cultural tools, but specifically the use of their own language, gave the *Guaranís* an agency that other indigenous group would never have anywhere else in the Spanish colonies.

In the early stages of the missions the Jesuit brought with them a printer and published many books in Guaraní including *Guaraní Sermons,* by José Serrano S.J. (1705), and *Catecismo y Sermones,* written by Nicolás Yapuguái (1724), a local cacique. This last example shows that the missions gave the Guaranís—at least some of them—the possibility of expression, something improbable in the rest of the Spanish colonies, particularly in rural areas. Each *colegio* (school) had a library, and the Jesuits had an enormous interest in printing their own books, most of them in Guaraní.

In conclusion, linguistic policies in colonial Spanish America were always guided by the requirements and designs of the Catholic empire. Despite the fact that language and empire were inextricably linked, and many groups in Spain—especially in Castile—understood Spanish as the language of Catholicism, there was always tension between religion and empire. A colony with a different language was conceivable—as was the case of the Philippines—but it was unacceptable for a colony not to have Catholicism as its only and official religion.

In the *Reducciones* of Paraguay, Jesuits implemented a new model. Yet, ultimately, a more traditional imperial model was put into place. Even if religion and empire were interconnected in the Jesuit missionary experience, they attempted to build millennium[5] at the borders of the empire, where the natives could have much better and humane conditions and their freedom was restricted but still effective. Through this missionary program, the Guaranís were 'resettled' (assimilated) to one place, as was their culture and language. From the perspective of the Jesuits, the new language—*Guaraní Jesuítico*—was an excellent strategy since it made possible the creation of a community distinct from the Europeans, and from other native groups. But from the *Guaraní* point of view, one might argue that the *indios misionales* (missionary Indians) lost their original identity and that their language "sufrió un profundo proceso de reducción: reducción a escritura, reducción a gramática, reducción a diccionario y reducción en las formas de discurso" (Meliá and Nagel 160) (suffered a deep process of assimilation: assimilation in their writing, grammar, dictionary and discursive forms) [my translation]. Those transformations meant, for example, the loss of their mythology, their religious poetry, etc.

From a geopolitical perspective, the Guaranís did not have better options, living as they did at the borders of two empires. The *Reducciones* were a possibility for them, but they had to pay the price of a transformed identity. As Fernando Gómez has stated: "Early Modern utopianism fundamentally means the implementation of a regulated society" (*Jesuit Proposal for Regulated Societies* 93) and such was certainly the case in the missions of Paraguay. Since the natives had no agency in these regions, slavery was their only destiny. They were voiceless, and, like echoes, they only had the right to a voice, but a voice that was modulated—even with good intentions—by others.

Notes

1. According to García (113), Andrea Paleólogo, the heir of the Byzantine Empire signed in his will, in April, 1502, to confer to Charles V rights over the *Eastern Roman Empire*.
2. The *encomienda* system was a colonial trusteeship system implemented by the Spaniards in the New World and later in the Philippines. Under this economic system the conquistadors were granted the towns of the indigenous people they conquered. These communities had to work for the *encomenderos* and in return they received protection and indoctrination in Catholicism.
3. Juan de Zumárraga was born in Durango, in the Basque Country, in 1468; and died in Mexico, June 3, 1548. In 1527, Zumárraga was appointed first bishop of Mexico.
4. Today that region is located in Northern Argentina, Southeastern Bolivia, Brazil, Paraguay and Uruguay.

5. Based on the book of Revelation Chapter 20 (New Testament), many Christian groups have literally understood that Jesus and his faithful followers are to rule on earth for a thousand-year period of holiness. In these visions, the heavenly kingdom will appear after an eschatological battle between good and evil. In preparation for these final times, a community of chosen is usually required.

Works Cited

Caraman, Philip. *The Lost Paradise: An Account of the Jesuits in Paraguay, 1607–1768*. London: Sidgwick and Jackson, 1975.

Carrera de la Red, Avelina. *El problema de la lengua en el humanismo renacentista español*. Valladolid: Universidad de Valladolid, Secretariado de Publicaciones, 1988.

Castro y Castro, Manuel. "Las lenguas indígenas americanas transmitidas por los Franciscanos del Siglo XVI." *Actas del II Congreso Internacional sobre "Los Franciscanos en el Nuevo Mundo (Siglo XVI)."* Madrid: Ed. Deimos, 1988. 485–571.

Cristóbal Colón. *Los cuatro viajes del almirante y su testamento*. Ed. Ignacio B. Anzoátegui. Digital Edition based on 10th. ed. Madrid: Espasa-Calpe, 1991. <www.cervantesvirtual.com/servlet/SirveObras/79138363878579052532279/index.htm>.

de Solano, Francisco. *Documentos sobre política lingüística en Hispanoamérica (1492–1800)*. Madrid: Consejo Superior de Investigaciones Científicas, 1991.

Dietrich, Wolf. "La importancia de los diccionarios guaraníes de Montoya para el estudio comparativo de las lenguas Tupí-Guaraní de hoy." *Amerindia: Revue d'Ethnolinguistique Amérindienne* 19–20 (1994–95). Villejuif: Centre André-Georges Haudricourt C.N.R.S. <www.vjf.cnrs.fr/celia/FichExt/Am/A_19-20_26.htm#_ftnref4>.

Dussell, Enrique. *A History of the Church in Latin America: Coloniality to Liberation (1492–1979)*. Trans. and revised Alan Neely. Grand Rapids, MI: Eerdmans, 1981.

Fernández Armesto, Felipe. *Before Columbus: Exploration and Colonization from the Mediterranean to the Atlantic 1229–1492*. Philadelphia: University of Pennsylvania Press, 1987.

García Alvarez, César. "Ensayo para una teoría del imperio español: Europa-América-Bizancio." *Bizantino Nea Hellas* 13–15. Santiago de Chile: Editorial Universitaria, 1996.

Gómez, Fernando. "Jesuit Proposal for Regulated Societies: The Cases of Antonio Ruiz de Montoya y Antonio Vieira." *Mester.* Los Angeles: UCLA Department of Spanish and Portuguese Studies, 1998.

Gómez Margo, Lidice M. *Las lengua en la formación de los pueblos hispanoamericanos*. Lima: Vida y Espiritualidad, 1994.

Heath, Shirley Brice. *Telling Tongues: Language Policy in Mexico, Colony and Nation*. New York: Teachers College Press, 1972.

Hernández Aparicio, Pilar. "Grámaticas, vocabularios y doctrinas franciscanas en las bibliotecas de Madrid." *Actas del II Congreso Internacional sobre "Los Franciscanos en el Nuevo Mundo (Siglo XVI)."* Madrid: Deimos, 1988. 573–88.

La Rosa, Zhenja. "Language and Empire: The Vision of Nebrija." *The Loyola University Student Historical Journal* 27, 1995–96. <www.loyno.edu/history/journal/1995-6/rosa.htm>.

Maravall, José A. *Carlos V y el pensamiento político del Renacimiento.* Madrid: Instituto de Estudios Políticos, 1960.

Massare de Kostianovsky, Olinda. *La instrucción pública en la época colonial,* 2nd ed. Asunción: Archivo Nacional, 165, 1975.

Meliá, Bartomeu, and Liana Maria Nagel. *Guaraníes y Jesuitas en el tiempo de las Misiones: Una Bibliografía Didáctica.* Universidade regional Integrada do Alto Uruguay e das Missioes—Centro de Cultura Missioneira. Santo Angelo, 1995.

Meliá, Bartomeu. *La lengua guaraní del Paraguay: Historia, sociedad y literatura.* Madrid: Mapfre, 1992.

Meliá, Bartolomeu, and Mane Ángel. *Guaraníes y Jesuitas en tiempos de las Misiones: Una bibliografía didáctica.* Asunción: Centro de Estudios Paraguayos Antonio Guasch, 1995.

Mignolo, Walter. *The Darker Side of the Renaissance: Literacy, Territoriality, and Colonization.* Ann Arbor: University of Michigan Press, 2003.

Nebrija, Antonio de. *Gramática de la Lengua Castellana.* Ed. Antonio Quilis. Madrid: Editora Nacional, 1980.

Ruiz de Montoya, Antonio. *Conquista espiritual del Paraguay hecha por los religiosos de la Compañía de Jesús en la [sic] provincias de Paraguay, Paraná, Uruguay y Tape. Estudio preliminar y notas.* Ernesto J. A. Maeder. Asunción: El Lector, 1996.

Sánchez Herrero, José. "Alfabetización y catequesis franciscana en América Latina durante el siglo XVI." *Actas del II Congreso Internacional sobre "Los Franciscanos en el Nuevo Mundo (Siglo XVI)."* Madrid: Deimos, 1988. 589–647.

Zajícová, Lenka. "Interacción entre español y guaraní: Desarrollo histórico y situación actual." *El Hispanismo en la República Checa II.* Filozofická fakulta Univerzita Karlova, 2001. <http://oldwww.upol.cz/res/ssup/hispanismo2/zajicova.htm>.

◆ 3

Languages and Imperial Designs in the Andes

Juan C. Godenzzi

(Translated by Sara Smith)

Before the European invasion, the Inca annexed territories and peoples and organized an empire whose principal instrument of communication was Quechua. The Spanish colonial regime, in the sixteenth century, began to organize its economic and religious domination of the Andes. This was achieved not only through the use of Spanish, to the extent that it was the hegemonic language—albeit a minority language in those times—but also through regional languages (Puquina and Aymara) and, above all, through the "truly general" language (Quechua). At the conclusion of Spanish imperial sovereignty, the new republics did not alter the relationship between social classes, such that Spanish colonialism persisted under national forms of *coloniality of power* from the nineteenth century until present (Quijano 228–32). During this last period, the same language hierarchy has subsisted and an expansion of Spanish has occurred, first gradually and later, from the second half of the twentieth century, in an accelerated and massive way.

In this essay, through a social and historical revision of the Andean linguistic formation, we will attempt to show how considering the relationship between *language* and *empire* can be a fruitful way to discover not only how political power utilizes language for the purpose of imposing its dominance, but also the role of these same languages in the emergence of resistance forces and democratisation. In operative terms, and for the purposes of this essay, *language* is understood as a system of socially and historically constituted signs, while *empire* is understood to be the political unit that has imposed its sovereignty onto foreign peoples and territories.

Early Andean Linguistic Formation

Little is known about the linguistic situation during the long *pre-Hispanic period* in the Andes. Not having access to direct knowledge of such a situation has led specialists to a reconstruction based on the internal and external history of languages, on the present language distribution, on toponymy and on the information obtained from colonial chronicles. It is believed that the peopling of the Andean region began some ten thousand years ago. The peculiar evolution of languages in the Andes can be explained by peoples' movements, sedentarization and the appearance of regional states. It is believed that some thousand years before our age, there was a period of regional exchanges that accrued in size, even though it is not known with certainty which languages would have been involved. There is some evidence indicating they may have been languages from two linguistic groups, probably expanding at that time: Arahuaco and Tupi (Torero 2002: 37–38).

Towards the year 500 of the Common Era, the geographical distribution of languages would have been as follows: *Cunza* (Atacama oasis, Chile); *Uruquilla* (near Lake Poopó and saltpeter deposits of Coipasa and Uyuni, Bolivia); *Puquina* (around Lake Titicaca, extending towards the mountain top, the Pacific coast and zones near Cuzco); Aru languages, i.e., *Aimara, Cauqui* and *Jaqaru* (southern mountains and coast in Peru); *Quechua* (central coast and mountains); *Quingnam* (central-north coast); *Mochica* (northern coast); *Tallán* (northernmost coast); *Culli, Den* and *Cat* (northern mountain); *Bagua* (Jaén-Bagua basin, in north-east Peru) (48–49). Some centuries later, Quechua became divided into mountain varieties (*Quechua I*) and coastal varieties (*Quechua II*). Aru languages are extended to the Ayacucho region. *Puquina* increases its preponderance in the Altiplano through Tiahuanaco society. Several languages disputed hegemony in the north, without covering vast territories along the coast, the mountain or the upper expanse of the jungle, as had happened in the center and south. It is probable that during the sixth and seventh centuries, which were periods of intense regional exchange, the Aru and Quechua languages intensified their mutual influence and contact (47–52).

Likewise, the coastal peoples built cities (Pachacamac, Chanchan, and

Chincha) and extended their exchanges through commerce and navigation as far as Ecuador and probably Colombia, Central America and Mexico. Beginning with the eighth century, the economic and political power of Pachacamac and the central coast favored the spread of Quechua II to the northern mountains (*Yungay variety*) and the southern coast (*Chinchay variety*), displacing *Aru* from its former territories (Torero 1974: 79–80, 141).

The Language of the Inca

Peoples from the southern coast, speaking Quechua Chinchay, established commercial links and demographic exchanges with northern Peru and Ecuador, Ayacucho, Cuzco, the Peruvian-Bolivian Altiplano, and perhaps northern Chile and Argentina. The pre-eminence of Chincha explains the wide spread of their language.

After consolidating its power, towards the fourteenth or fifteenth century, the Inca Empire adopted *Quechua chinchay*, due to its great expansion, and turned it into the administrative language of its territory, Tahuantinsuyo (132). In 1470, the Inca Tupac Yupanqui, conquered the new Kingdom of Chimor, which had under its control the coastal territory going from Tumbes to Paramonga. *Quingnam*, the kingdom's language, according to Calancha, did not have enough time to displace the other languages from the northern coast. Rather it was displaced by *Quechua Chinchay* in its function as a general language, while the Amazon region was only partially integrated to the Inca territories.

Despite its expansion and its prestige, *Quechua Chinchay* did not exclude other languages and instead co-existed with them (Cerrón-Palomino 137–38). In general terms, the linguistic group of Ancient Peru consisted of a polyphonic choir with multiple and varied voices, as testified by some Spaniards shortly after the European invasion in the Andes. In 1577, Joseph de Acosta wrote:

> Dicen que en otros tiempos con setenta y dos lenguas entró la confusión en el género humano; mas estos bárbaros tienen más de setecientas . . . ("De procuranda ‚indorum salute"; quoted in Mateos 399)

(It is said that in ancient times seventy-two languages were enough to create confusion among human kind; but these barbarians have more than seven hundred.)

And in 1590, Miguel Cabello Valboa wrote:

... son tantas y tan diferentes las lenguas que ablan ... que creo faltaran letras en la Arichmetica para numerarlas según son muchas, y en esto en tan notable manera que en muchas Prouincias no se andara legua que no se alle lengua diferente ... (Cabello Valboa 104)

(they speak so many languages, so different from each other ... that I believe there aren't numbers high enough to count them, there are so many. This is so notable that in many provinces one doesn't go a league without coming across another language.)[1]

The Irruption of Spanish

In the Iberian Peninsula, the linguistic formation of Spanish developed alongside the process of the *Reconquista* of the territories occupied by the Arabs, such that it developed in tandem with the unification of Spain. Beginning as a local tongue, Castilian began to expand not only at the expense of Mozarabic, but also to the detriment of other dialectal varieties: Galician, Leonese, Aragonese and Catalan (Darbord and Pottier 23). The thirteenth century saw great developments in Castilian, including the amplification of functions, the first linguistic normalization, and an abundant production of prose. By the fifteenth century, Castilian had become a national and literary language (Rivarola 17–20). Two singular events which occurred in 1492 promoted the expansion of the Spanish Empire overseas: the expulsion of the Jews, who transferred Spanish to the territories of the Ottoman Empire and the occupation of the New World territories.

In the Andean context, the irruption of Spanish altered the entire linguistic outlook of the sixteenth century. The language and its alphabetical writing confined other languages and their discursive manifestations to a subordinate place. Nevertheless, noting that Quechua (in its *Chinchay* varieties and in some of its *Yungay* varieties) constituted a "truly general language," the Spaniards promoted it as a lingua franca. They made efforts to find natives who spoke the language in order to make *ladinos* of them (Indians who adopt Spanish ways). During the first decades of the sixteenth century, *Chinchay* varieties were spread from central Chile and northern Argentina to Ecuador (and perhaps part of Colombia), as well as to the Amazon River.

In 1560, Domingo de Santo Tomás printed his *Vocabulario* and his *Gramática* of the General Language in Peru, whose main references were the dialectal varieties of the language spoken by societies living along the coast on the brink of disappearance. At the end of the sixteenth century, Quechua was eliminated from coastal zones, while varieties from Cuzco acquired greater importance. Several languages were spoken on the northern coast between the seventeenth and eighteenth centuries: *Tallan (or Colan or Catacaos), Sechura, Olmos, Mochica (or Yunga), Quingnam (or Pescadora)* (Torero 1986: 529). During the Inca period, general Quechua did not prevail on the coast where it was no more than a mere tool for the public administration. With the imposition of colonization, Spanish became the general language, thus subordinating Quechua. The strong presence of Spaniards in the region, attracted by the richness of the valleys, produced the phenomena of land expropriation, expulsions and illnesses; hence, this explains the rapid imposition of Spanish along the coastal region.

On the contrary, in the northern mountains, ancestral languages and customs had a greater persistence. Some native geographical names still remain. Based on the toponymy, Torero succeeded in delimiting linguistic areas that might have existed for more than a millennium, until Quechua or Spanish were imposed (523–45). These area include *Den, Chacha, Culle* and *Cat*. In the southern Andean Altiplano, four languages were spoken in the sixteenth century: *Puquina* (around Lake Titicaca and nearby mountains), *Uruquilla* (south from Lake Titicaca and around Lake Poopó), *Aimara* (vast zones of the Altiplano) and *Quechua*. Later on, Puquina and Uruquilla would start to lose their importance and relevance.

At the end of the eighteenth century, the situation of many ethnic groups had radically changed. For many people, contact with colonizers meant cultural, linguistic and physical death. The overall linguistic panorama during the colonial period consisted of Spanish hegemony, the use and expansion of Quechua, aimed at politico-administrative control and evangelization, and the precarious subsistence of numerous other languages—subordinated, despised, and excluded—many of which ultimately disappeared.

Presently, in spite of the strong pressure exerted by Spanish, several ancestral languages still subsist. Ecuador, Peru, and Bolivia host the largest percentage of indigenous language speakers in the Andean region. It is believed that 34 percent of Ecuadorians, 37 percent of Peruvians and 62 percent of Bolivians belong to indigenous communities speaking different languages. Besides Spanish, the languages spoken by most people are Quechua (more than ten million speakers) and Aymara (2.5 million speakers). Furthermore, there are other vulnerable languages spoken by minorities, particularly in the Amazon area with ten languages in the jungle region in Ecuador, forty in Peru, and thirty four in Bolivia (Zimmermann 67–69; López and Küper).

Politics of Language

The expansion of the Inca Empire resulted in the servitude of several peoples. Violence as well as death were part of the process. Quechua or *runa simi* (language of the human being) started to work as an instrument of that expansion even though it never became a completely hegemonic language. Perhaps this is because the Inca were interested in a certain degree of coexistence and reciprocity with other languages, or simply because the process was interrupted by the arrival of the Spanish *conquistadores* (Mannheim 1991: 80).

Shortly after the fall of Granada in 1492 and while Columbus was sailing to America, Antonio de Nebrija's *Gramática Castellana* was published. In the foreword of his book dedicated to the Queen, the author states that his work will contribute to the imperial project of the Crown: by helping "the barbarian peoples and nations who speak lesser languages" learn the conqueror's language. He then adds that the Castilian language, "the empire's companion," must play a central role in dominating all conquered territories (Rivarola 93–94).[2] Inspired by this ideology, the official colonial linguistic policy sought to impose Castilian as the language of the Spanish empire. Nevertheless, this project was not made possible due to the fact that a good part of the indigenous population, having been obliged to live in *reducciones* (settlements of Indians converted to Christianity), had little exposure to Spanish. Instead, the missionaries were the ones who made an effort to acquire indigenous languages (Heath and Laprade 119).

Another linguistic policy existed that was more open to everyday communicative praxis and supported by colonial authorities as well by vast Church sectors (Carrión Ordóñez 57). In 1563, the Council of Trent allowed the Crown to impart sacramental catechesis in vernacular languages (Schroeder 197–98; Heath and Laprade 122). Likewise, all five Lima Councils between 1552 and 1601 insisted that priests, both regular and secular, learn native languages. This church practise found a privileged support in the university. Porras Barrenechea points out the great concern of the colonial universities in discovering and studying indigenous languages ([1951] 1973: 7–8). The Universidad de San Marcos, among them, in the seventeenth century, became "the main center for the study of South American languages." Here it was possible to criticize those who attacked Quechua for considering it a barbarian language with the sole intention of justifying their abuses against the Andean population, which they viewed as inferior in nature. Domingo de Santo Tomás reveals that Quechua is a subtle and rich language, "just like those who speak it." He addresses the King, saying: "Your majesty must know that people from the kingdom of Peru are wise and orderly, and that those who say otherwise want to deceive you, in order to obtain personal gain" ([1560b] 1951: 10–11).

Quechua was the language used by missionaries to catechize and evangelize. Some of them wrote grammars, arts and vocabularies. They had to face the difficulty of translating in a multicultural context by resignifying words or creating Quechua neologisms in order to express European moral and religious concepts. Linguistic representations were, in general, religiously biased. In the foreword of his *Gramática,* Diego González Holguín states that the most important deed is to "help souls repent for their mistakes and evil lives" and that the best way to do so is by "learning languages, necessary to the conversion of souls" (folio 4). Not all missionaries were interested in the revaluation of Quechua and its speakers from the realm of religion. Beyond the goals specific to evangelization, there was persecution and destruction of native cultures as well as abuses and arbitrary acts in the name of religion. The origins of the Huarochiri manuscript were related to Francisco de Avila's work that started in 1608 by eradicating superstition and idolatry. He sought to know all about cults and the emplacement of *huacas* (ancient sepulchres) not only in order to destroy the "idols" but to gain possession of their treasures (Taylor 16–17).

Under the rule of Carlos III, there was a reaction against the predominant linguistic ecclesiastical policy. In the Real Cedula of March 10, 1770, it became mandatory to help "extinguish all different spoken languages." Obedient to that legislation, Cuzco's Bishop, Juan Manuel Moscoso, writes a letter to the Visitador Areche, during the rebellion of Tupac Amaru:

> Más de doscientos años he dicho tenemos de conquista, y cuando el sistema de todo conquistador es traer a su idioma la nación conquistada, nuestros españoles en nada más parece que han pensado que en mantenerles en el suyo, y aun es acomodarse con él, pues vemos le usan con más frecuencia que el propio. Los inconbenientes que de ellos se siguen son obvios al más ciego y mucho es lo que padecen, Dios, el Rey y la causa pública por esta reprobable práctica. (Quoted in Rivarola 1990: 108–109)

> (We have had more than 200 years of conquest and even though conquerors bring their language to the conquered, our Spaniards have not thought about anything else than letting them hang on to their language, and have even accommodated to it, since we see that they (the Spaniards) use it more often than their own language [Spanish]. The inconveniences that this causes are obvious to the most blind person, and God, the King, and public interest suffer greatly from this reprehensible practice.)[3]

From a different perspective, we see another tendency: by the end of the seventeenth century, members of Cuzco's local elite had adopted Quechua as a literary tool and also as a symbol. They claimed legitimacy invoking the Inca past while at the same time exploiting indigenous people. The marquises of Valle Umbroso are a good example of this: they claimed to be of Inca descent, dressed as Incas, had people address them with the name of *Apu* and spoke in Quechua. But the ideological use they made of Quechua and other Andean symbols was clear. Those landowners sought to legitimize their properties, wealth, and political autonomy before the colonial authorities, while at the same time exploiting the impoverished "Indians" (Mannheim 1991: 71; 1992: 15–22).

During the republic, the official Peruvian policy was still to impose Spanish as a means of building a national identity. Nevertheless, the historic conditions of daily life prevented the imposition of the law. In the period where landowners or *gamonales* (caciques) had control over the indigenous peasantry, the former, fearing the latter's participation in politics, preferred them to remain illiterate and monolingual in Quechua. The struggle to attend school was an important peasant demand during the 1920s. Beginning in 1950, social changes in the Andes became more evident. Some of the triggering factors of this process include the following: the modification of landownership, causing the weakening or disappearance of the *gamonales*, the expansion of public education, and the massive migration of the peasant population to the cities. All these factors favored a substantial Hispanicization in vast zones of the southern Andes. General Velasco's military government (1968–1975) became characterized by an Indigenist revival, with the promulgation of certain legal provisions favoring vernacular languages. The General Law of Education (law decree 19326 of April 21, 1972) states: "the educational approach will consider the existence in the country of diverse languages, which are a means of communication and an expression of culture; thus, it will contribute to their conservation and development." In the law decree 21156 of May 27, 1975 we read: "Quechua, as well as Spanish, is considered an official language of the Republic." The results obtained from these measures were meagre. It is legitimate, then, to ask oneself whether or not these measures were simply ideological strategies lacking technical foundations and only in the service of political interests. At present, there exist new official measures.[4] However, one must also ask oneself if, behind these new pronouncements, there truly exists a political will capable of achieving real change.

A contemporary example of local linguistic ideology is that of the Academia Mayor de la Lengua Quechua (Regional Academy of Quechua), based in Cuzco. In one of the items of its Resolution 01–90–P–AMLQ, we read that "Imperial Quechua from Cuzco keeps the most genuine *runasimi*," that "imperial Quechua has a considerable number of lexical, morphological and syntactical elements showing that it is a more evolved language," and therefore academics must "look after the purity of Quechua and its linguistic expansion." As a matter of fact, imperial Quechua is a sociolect, that is, a variant used by the social group of *mestizos*, who claim to be the descendants of the great and powerful Inca (not the "Indians"). That is the reason why this sociolectal variety is called *Inka simi* (the language of the Inca) or *Qhapaq simi* (the language of the powerful), in contrast with *runa simi* (the language of the common people). Sociolectal variants of peasant communities would then be considered as impure, bastard or ignorant forms. According to this ideology, all varieties of Quechua diverging from Imperial Quechua would be ruled out.

In sum, as Mannheim points out:

> From the European invasion until today, the politics of language has been a politics of social subordination. Overtly, colonial language policy was schizophrenic in its shifts between maintaining the Native Andean languages as a step toward assimilation and suppressing them altogether. Covertly, the entire political spectrum was suffused with social domination; [...] before the European invasion, the Andes were a linguistic mosaic of interspersed languages and peoples. The heterogeneity encountered by the first European soldiers, travelers, and settlers has been replaced by a situation in which language difference maps directly onto political domination. (77–79)

Spanish-Quechua Struggles

Spanish became legitimate as a result of the many interventions in the process of regulating languages in the Andean region. We can see this in attitudes of open or subtle glossocentrism detrimental to other languages. Thus, the exaltation of Spanish and the claimed inferiority of native tongues have become traits characterizing the linguistic imaginary of the Andean region. Colonial glossocentrism, documented by works such as that of Rivarola (98–109), is still present nowadays at every socio-cultural level and is viewed as one of the main components of "common sense." Sometimes this view manifests itself in an openly violent form, as Kapsoli (13) relates, based on his own experience:

> Cuando estudiábamos en la escuela Pre-vocacional de Pomabamba (Ancash) fuimos testigos de una 'ingeniosa' represión del quechua. El profesor impuso un

castigo psicológico, con efectos violentos de apocamiento. Los alumnos sorprendidos hablando quechua eran conducidos al centro de la Plaza con una corona de papel rotulado *El Rey de los Quechueros*. Las víctimas, generalmente alumnos de las estancias y caseríos, eran pasto de burla y hazmerreír de los citadinos.

(When we were students at the pre-vocational school of Pomabamba (Ancash), we witnessed an 'ingenious' repression of Quechua. The teacher imposed a psychological punishment causing students to feel violently embarrassed. Students who were caught speaking Quechua were led to the main square, bearing a paper crown that read *The king of Quechua*. The victims, who came generally from farms and small towns, were scornfully laughed at by students coming from the city.)

A language imposes its hegemony not only by force but also, and perhaps more decisively, on the basis of a more or less generalized consensus. No wonder wide sectors of Quechua speakers have internalized, at least partially, their subordination and have an attitude of rejection towards their own language. There are Andean indigenous discourses that tackle this linguistic problem and its consequences. However, some of them are ambivalent: while they want to reaffirm the vernacular language, they continue to accept Spanish preeminence.

Edgar Vera, born in Urcos-Cuzco, has written a story in Quechua that he heard in the community of Pampachulla.[5] The story is about a verbal clash between "the man from Spain" and "the man from Cuzco":

Unay pachas, kay Qusqu llaqtanchikman Ispaña runakuna chayamusqaku; tukuy manchay runas. Hinaspas huk kutinsi, kay Qusqu k'iklluta purikaspa kay Ispaña runaqa, Qusqu runawan tupasqa, hinaspa parlata tupachisqaku. Ispaña runa Qusqu runata ñisqa: "ñuqaykuqa allin, chanin, sut'i misti siminta rimayku, chaypa sutin kastillanu, qankunaqa mana sutiyuq simita, ima simitachá rimakunkichikpas." Hinaspas Qusqu runaqa suyakusqa Ispaña runap rimasqanta tukunankama, chaysi Qusqu runaqa allinta yuyaymanaspa ahinata kutichisqa: "'Ñuqaykup simiykuqa Inkariypa, runakunap simin, llaqtap siminmi" ñispa, "ichaqa qankunap kastillanu ñisqa simiykichisqa sutinqa *allqu simi*; manam pipas chay simitaqa yachanchu."

(A long time ago, people from Spain arrived in our town of Cuzco. Everybody said they were scary. Once, when the man from Spain was walking in the street, he came across the man from Cuzco, and they started to talk. The man from Spain said to the man from Cuzco [in a badly pronounced Quechua]: "We speak a good language, a just language, a true one, the language of the people from the city. Its name is *Castilian*. But you speak a tongue without a name! What is that language?" The man from Cuzco waited until the man from Spain had finished and, after thinking about it he said: "Ours is the language of the Inca King, the language of the people. Instead, that language of yours, the one you call Castilian, has the name of *language of the dog*. Nobody speaks that language.")[6]

In this linguistic confrontation, the man from Spain values his language by saying that it has a name and despises Quechua by arguing that it does not have a name. The judgment is made from the perspective of social recognition and political power of *conquistadores*, "scary people." The man from Cuzco is shrewd enough to change the focus of the polemic to the axis of meaning: Quechua is the language that everybody speaks and understands, including the man from Spain, because the discussion is taking place in Quechua. On the other hand, while Spanish is the language of power, it has a reduced usage and people do not understand it. On that basis, he revaluates his language giving it its name: *runa simi* (the language of the human being) as opposed to Spanish, which is presented as *allqu simi* (the language of the dog). From a subordinate linguistic position, the man from Cuzco produces a symbolic revenge in order to affirm his own dignity before Spanish domination.

Other stories refer to the inseparable ally of the Spanish language: alphabetic writing. Gregorio Condori Mamani said: "Inkakunaqa manan papilta riqsirqankuchu, qillqata, taytacha papilta quyta munaptinpis paykuna richasasqaku; purki paykunaqa mana nutisyasta papilpichu apachinakurqanku, sinu wik'uña q'aytukunallapi" (Valderrama and Escalante 1977: 50) (the Inca did not know paper nor writing; when the *taytacha* tried to give them paper, they refused because they would use vicuna threads to send the news). This is another manifestation of a linguistic clash: two different systems of writing or registering data. In this case, the Andean system also ended up losing the game. Apparently, the Inca voluntarily rejected the "superior" writing system and were, therefore, surpassed by the Spaniards. Another story, also gathered by Valderrama and Escalante (1992), makes a comparison between "being able to read" and "having eyes." The Inca defeat, thus, is due to their disadvantaged point of view, having to blindly face the Spaniards, who could see:[7]

> Paykunaqa mana liyiyta yachasqakuchu. Mana ñawiyuq kasqaku chay inkakuna. Chay ispañulkunaqa liyiyta yachasqaku. Hinaspanñataq chay Inkakunata abansapuyta munasqa. Hinaspa mana pasamusqakuchu chay Inkakuna, sumaq llaqta phurmaqkuna. Paykunalla Qusquta rurasqa. Chayqa, Inkakuna mana ñawiyuq kasqakupas piru kartata apachinakusqaku, khipuspalla q'aytullapi: "kaymanta haqaykama apanki." Chay khipullapi yachanakusqaku. Imaynatachá khipurqanku q'aytuta.

(The Inca did not have eyes; they didn't know how to read. The Spaniards did know how to read. That is how they intended to surpass the Inca. So, the Inca that made beautiful towns did not come this way. They only made Cuzco. Nevertheless, in spite of not having eyes, they sent letters with knotted threads: "bring this from here to there" they would say. They got in touch by means of those knotted threads. How were they knotted?)

The linguistic imaginary makes the power of Castilian and its writing appear to be invincible. To only speak Quechua in the Andean countries is to be deprived of citizenship rights and to be doomed to social exclusion. This explains why Quechua speakers feel the need to master Spanish even if it is painful. In the story *Kastillanu rimayqa ancha karun kasqa* (You have to pay dearly to speak Spanish), gathered by Ortiz Rescaniere (176–83), we see, beyond the bitterness present all along, a painful reality: the national diglossic situation excludes and despoils those who, because they don't speak Spanish, ignore their rights and are incapable of making themselves respected.[8]

Apart from a few exceptions, Quechua does not have public, formal, or official functions. It is circumscribed to the realm of the informal and domestic and is, therefore, dysfunctional for the state and institutional apparatus. Testimonies gathered in Puno by Hornberger (128) are eloquent:

Munani kastillanuta kunwirsanaypaq may trawahukunapipis, may uphisina waykunapaqpis.
(I prefer to speak Spanish at work, and I use it when I go to offices.)

Kastillanu impurtanti, allin parlananchikpaq wardiyakunawan.
(Spanish is important to speak well with policemen.)

Kastillanu liyinapaq, qhichwa parlanaypaq.
(Spanish is so that I may read, Quechua is so that I may speak.)

At the same time, we see affection and loyalty to the language and openness to multilingualism in the Quechua speaking population. Acquiring a relative competence in Spanish does not amount to despising Quechua. We see this in the following testimonies (Hornberger 131–32):

Mana munarqanichu [qhichwata qunqayta], mas wiyin kastillanuta parlayta munarqani, aswanta duminayta munarqani.
(I did not mean to forget Quechua, I just wanted to improve my Spanish.)

Iskaynintan yachanan rimayta.
(It is necessary to speak both languages.)

Qhichwa rasallay, qhichwa parlaqkuna chayta qhichwamanta rimapayani, kastillanu parlaqkunataq kastillanumanta parlapayanitaq.
(I speak Quechua with my own kind, with Quechua speakers; with those who speak Spanish, I speak Spanish.)

Lliwnintin allin, kastillanu, quechwa, inlis, latin, aymara.
(They are all good, Castilian, Quechua, English, Latin, Aymara.)

Imperial Languages as Resources of Decolonization

Quechua, which once superimposed itself on other Andean languages due to its diffusion during the Inca and Colonial periods, has been converted into a Pan-Andean symbol of "indigenous authenticity" opposite the dominant culture, whether colonial or post-colonial. In this way, for example, as Calvet (129) signals, today Indigenous communities in Ecuador maintain close sentimental and ideological ties to Quechua, a language that, nevertheless, came to them from abroad. The imperial expansion of Quechua has also meant that it can serve as an instrument that links together colonized and discriminated peoples.

In the same way, by the beginnings of the Colony, the Spanish acquired by some indigenous people served them as a way to denounce and resist the abuse and tyranny of the colonial authorities. For example, in the sixteenth century, Guaman Poma de Ayala wrote his famous chronicle, addressed to the King of Spain, in an Andean modality of Spanish (Guaman Poma de Ayala [1615] 1980). In the eighteenth century, Gabriel Tupac Amaru wrote memorials, letters, edicts and proclamations in Spanish, which preceded or accompanied uprisings and rebellions against fiscal pressures, and the exploitation of indigenous people in textile factories (*obrajes*), ranches (*haciendas*) and mines (Lewin 1967). By the second half of the twentieth century, a massive migration of the indigenous population began to direct itself towards the cities, expelled from a deteriorating rural economy and in search of better living conditions. A physical displacement is also a social, cultural and linguistic one. Spanish has become essential such that its acquisition as a second language occurs in urgent conditions without the help of the education system. New varieties of Spanish have been configured that include transferences from Quechua or other indigenous languages. These serve to express the new desires and needs of migrants, to reconstruct their identities, and to gain physical and social spaces in the city.

One of the demands of indigenous organizations in Andean countries is the right to participate in the design and management of education. From this perspective, better quality and more pertinent education innovations have emerged. Such is the case with Bilingual Intercultural Education (BIE), which, in synthesis, proposes to develop both the maternal language and Spanish in a manner that accommodates culturally diverse ways of interacting and constructing knowledge. These approaches underline a new linguistic imaginary that considers language diversity to be an asset and an opportunity to make living together possible. In the case of BIE in Ecuador, Cotacachi has expressed the following:

> In Ecuador, Bilingual Intercultural Education (BIE) is not imposed by anybody. It is an aspiration of the indigenous organizations and is directed by them. . . . Actually, we, the indigenous, are convinced that neither our language nor our culture will disappear. BIE has become the crucial pillar of an awakening national and international consciousness that indigenous peoples contribute to national and international cultural life with their own resources and in their own terms. (285)

During the past few decades, indigenous communities have assumed an increasingly greater leading role in the political and economic life of the region and the continent. The indigenous social movement questions economic development, citizenship, and the way in which the nation is constructed. During the 1990s, this movement confronted authoritarianism and neoliberal market reforms. Its demand for a transformation in the relationship between State and Society and in the form of exchange between North and South has been felt (Lucero 1–2). Indigenous communities and their leaders have strengthened their organizations, rearticulated their memory, and are formulating their proposals in the current context of globalization. All of this process requires, in addition to particular indigenous languages, a common language of diffusion that will guarantee an ample communication. Spanish is the language that fulfills the function of *lingua franca*.

Thus, the language of the Inca Empire has become an oppressed language and a symbol of resistance against discrimination. For its part, Spanish, the "Empire's companion," is no longer solely the language of the dominant power; it is also the language of the peoples and multitudes that use it in order to resist oppression and formulate new projects.

Conclusion

Throughout this essay, Quechua and Spanish have appeared as means of communication and instruments of power that serve not only the dominant power but also colonized peoples, permitting the latter to question the inequalities produced by the imperial order. The inter-subjective nature of language makes languages that are limited to a unidirectional and oppressive communicative framework seem like deviations. Languages carry the seeds of a renewed utopia: the elimination of fragmentations and divisions. In this sense, the power of languages surpasses the time and space of empires as its strength lies in the permanent human need to establish reciprocal ties and exchanges.

In an analytical perspective, the fact of having established a correlation between *language* and *empire* has contributed to enriching the explicative power of these concepts. In effect, the concept of *language* recaptures the function that language serves within the geopolitical designs that generate economic, social, ethnic, and cultural polarities. For its part, the concept of *empire* becomes complete by being expressed in relational and exchange modality terms. In this way it serves to explore the competition and interdependence between centre and periphery, between colonizers and colonized, between the accumulation of wealth and poverty, and between the reduced concentration of consumption and ever growing exclusions. In sum, by challenging the notions of language and empire, one discovers the connections that are established between the obverse and the reverse sides of political and communicative practices.

Notes

1. The translation of this fragment is by Mannheim and taken from Mannheim (1991: 36).
2. We must also point out that Nebrija's work, particularly the ones pertaining to Latin (*Introductiones latinae*, 1481; *Dictionarium latino-hispanicum*, 1492; *Introductiones in latinam grammaticem*, 1540), served as a model to document indigenous languages found in the New World. Metalinguistic description contributes to the "colonization of vernacular languages" (Mignolo 1990: 171–99).
3. The translation of this fragment is by Mannheim and taken from Mannheim (1991: 74–75).
4. In Peru, the 1993 Constitution establishes that every person has the right to an ethnic and cultural identity and that the state recognizes and protects the nation's ethnic and cultural plurality. It also establishes that the state "promotes Bilingual Intercultural

Education in accordance with the characteristics of each area, preserving the diverse cultural and linguistic expressions in the country" (art. 17). The 1993 Constitution also declares Spanish as the official language, as well as Quechua, Aymara, and other aboriginal languages in the areas in which they are predominant (art. 48). The 2003 *Ley General de Educacion* (General Law of Education), the 2003 *Ley de Preservación y Difusión de las Lenguas Aborígenes* (Aboriginal Languages Protection and Dissemination Law), and the 2002 *Ley para la Educación Bilingüe Intercultural* (Bilingual Education Law) attempt to put into practical terms that which is formulated in the Constitution.

5. The story was told by Don Luis Haqqiwa Qarwarupay, an 85-year Quechua speaker, coming from the community of Pampachulla, District of Urcos, Province of Quispicanchi, Departament of Cuzco; Quechua writing was normalized. Quoted in Godenzzi, ed., (1992: 67).
6. The translation into English is based on the Spanish version by Edgar Vera.
7. This story was told by Wikturyanu Tarapaki Astu. Quoted in Valderrama and Escalante (1992: 3). For other Andean discourses or testimonies concerning writing, see Ortiz Rescaniere (1973: 143–49), Montoya (1987: 311–12; 1990: 91–94), Rivarola (1990: 102–105), Salomon (2001a, 2002b).
8. We do not present the text here because there is an available English translation of the story in Mannheim (1991: 82–84). Similarly, Harrison (1989: 85–86) and Montoya (1990: 95–96) quote and comment on this story.

Works Cited

Calvet, Louis–Jean. *La guerre des langues et les politiques linguistiques*. Paris: Hachette Littératures, 1999.

Cabello Valboa, Miguel. *Miscelánea antártica, una historia del Perú antiguo*. Lima: Universidad Mayor de San Marcos, [1590] 1951.

Calancha, Antonio de la. *Crónica moralizada*. 6 vols. Ed. Ignacio Prado Pastor. Lima: Universidad Nacional de San Marcos, [1638] 1977.

Carrión Ordóñez, Enrique. "La política lingüística en el Perú durante la colonia." *Temas de Lingüística Aplicada*. Ed. Luis E. López, Ines Pozzi–Escot, and Madeleine Zúñiga. Lima: CONCYTEC and GTZ, 1989. 55–76.

Cerrón-Palomino, Rodolfo. *Castellano Andino. Aspectos sociolingüísticos, pedagógicos y gramaticales*. Lima: Pontificia Universidad Católica del Perú and Cooperación Técnica Alemana GTZ, 2003.

Cotacachi, Mercedes. "Attitudes of Teachers, Children and Parents towards Bilingual Intercultural Education." *Indigenous Literacies in the Americas*. Ed. Nancy Hornberger. Berlin & New York: Mouton de Gruyter, 1996. 285–98.

Darbord, Bernard, and Bernard Pottier. *La Langue Espagnole. Éléments de grammaire historique*. Paris: Éditions Nathan, 1994.

Godenzzi, Juan C., ed. *El quechua en debate: ideología, normalización y enseñanza.* Cuzco: Centro de Estudios Regionales Andinos Bartolomé de Las Casas, 1992.

Gonzalez Holguín, Diego. *Gramática y arte nueva de la lengua quechua general de todo el Perú llamada lengua Quechua o del Inca.* Ciudad de los Reyes del Perú, Francisco del Canto, impresor, 1607.

Guamán Poma de Ayala, Felipe. *El Primer Nueva Coronica y Buen Gobierno.* 3 vols. Eds. John V. Murra and Rolena Adorno; translation from Quechua by Jorge L. Urioste. México: Siglo XXI; Lima: Instituto de Estudios Peruanos, [1615] 1980.

Harrison, Regina. *Signs, Songs, and Memory in the Andes: Translating Quechua Language and Culture.* Austin: University of Texas Press, 1989.

Heath, Shirley Brice, and Richard Laprade. "Castilian Colonization and Indigenous Languages: The Cases of Quechua and Aymara." *Language Spread, Studies in Diffusion and Social Change.* Ed. Robert L. Cooper. Bloomington: Indiana University Press, 1982. 118–47.

Hornberger, Nancy. *Haku yachaywasiman. La educación bilingüe y el futuro del quechua en Puno.* Lima-Puno: Proyecto de Educación Bilingüe de Puno, 1989.

Kapsoli, Wilfredo. "Estudio preliminar." *Nosotros los maestros.* Ed. José María Arguedas. Lima: Editorial Horizonte, 1986. 9–28.

Lewin, Boleslao. *La rebelión de Túpac Amaru y los orígenes de la independencia de Hispanoamérica.* Buenos Aires: Sociedad Editora Latino Americana, 1967.

López, Luis E. and Wolfgang Küper. *La educación intercultural bilingüe en América Latina: balance y perspectivas.* Cochabamba: PROEIB Andes; Lima: PROFORMA, Ministerio de Educación del Perú, 2001.

Lucero, José Antonio, ed. *Beyond the Lost Decade: Indigenous Movements, Development, and Democracy in Latin America.* Program in Latin American Studies, Cuadernos 6. Princeton, NJ: Princeton University Press, 2003.

Mannheim, Bruce. "El renacimiento quechua del siglo XVIII." *El quechua en debate: ideología, normalización y enseñanza.* Ed. Juan C. Godenzzi. Cuzco: Centro de Estudios Regionales Andinos Bartolomé de Las Casas, 1992. 15–22.

———. *The Language of the Inka since the European Invasion.* Austin: University of Texas Press, 1991.

Mateos, Francisco, ed. *Obras del P. José de Acosta.* Madrid: Biblioteca de Autores Españoles 73, [1577] 1954.

Mignolo, Walter. "Teorías renacentistas de la escritura y la colonización de las lenguas nativas." *Primer Simposio de Filología Iberoamericana.* Sevilla, 1990. 171–99.

Montoya, Rodrigo. *Por una educación bilingüe en el Perú. Reflexiones sobre cultura y socialismo.* Lima: CEPES and Mosca Azul, 1990.

Montoya, Rodrigo, Edwin Montoya, and Luis Montoya. *La sangre de los cerros/Urqukunapa yawarnin.* Lima: CEPES, Mosca Azul Editores and UNMSM, 1987.

Nebrija, Antonio. *Gramática Castellana.* Facsimile edition with an introduction by E. Walberg. Halle: Niemeyer, [1492] 1909.

Ortiz Rescaniere, Alejandro. *De Adaneva a Inkarri (Una visión indígena del Perú)*. Lima: Ediciones Retablo de Papel, 1973.

Porras Barrenechea, Raúl. *Mito, tradición e historia del Perú*. Lima: Ediciones Retablo de Papel, [1951] 1973.

Quijano, Aníbal. "Colonialidad del poder, eurocentrismo y América Latina." *Globalización y diversidad cultural. Una mirada desde América Latina*. Ed. R. Pajuelo and P. Sandoval. Lima: Instituto de Estudios Peruanos, 2004. 228–81.

Rivarola, José Luis. *La formación lingüística de Hispanoamérica. Diez estudios*. Lima: Pontificia Universidad Católica del Perú, Fondo Editorial, 1990.

Salomon, Frank. "Para repensar el grafismo andino." *Perú: el legado de la historia*. Ed. Luis Millones. Sevilla: Fundación El Monte and Promperú, 2001a. 107–27.

———. "How an Andean *Writing Without Words* Works." *Current Anthropology*. Vol. 42, 1, (2001b): 1–27.

Santo Tomás, fr. Domingo de. *Lexicon, o Vocabulario de la lengua general del Perú*, Edición facsimilar. Lima: Universidad Nacional Mayor de San Marcos, [1560a] 1951a.

———. *Gramática o arte de la lengua general de los Indios de los Reynos del Perú*. Lima: Universidad Nacional Mayor de San Marcos, [1560b] 1951b.

Schroeder, J. J. *Canons and Decrees of the Council of Trent*. Saint Louis: B. Herder, 1950.

Taylor, Gerald, ed. *Ritos y tradiciones de Huarochirí del siglo XVII*. Lima: Instituto de Estudios Peruanos e Instituto Francés de Estudios Andinos, 1987.

Torero, Alfredo. *Idiomas de los Andes. Lingüística e historia*. Lima: Instituto Francés de Estudios Andinos y Editorial Horizonte, 2002.

———. "Deslindes lingüísticos en la costa norte peruana." *Revista Andina* 8, Año 4, 2 (1986): 523–48.

———. *El quechua y la historia social andina*. Lima: Universidad Ricardo Palma, 1974.

Valderrama, Ricardo and Carmen Escalante, eds. *Gregorio Condori Mamani. Autobiografía*. Cuzco: Centro de Estudios Regionales Andinos Bartolomé de Las Casas, 1977.

———. *Nosotros los humanos/Ñuqanchis runakuna. Testimonios de los quechuas del siglo XX*. Cuzco: Centro de Estudios Regionales Andinos Bartolomé de Las Casas, 1992.

Zimmermann, Klaus. "Formas de agresión y defensa en el conflicto de las lenguas española y portuguesa con las lenguas amerindias." *Threatened People and Enviroments in the Americas*. Ed. M. Mörner and M. Rosendhal. Proceedings, 48th International Conference of Americanists. Stockholm: Institute of Latin American Studies, Stockholm University. Vol 1, 1995.

**Part II
Language and Resistance—
The Fight for National and Individual Identities**

4

Exploring the Problematics of Non-Castilian Emigration to the Americas through *la vida cuartizada* of Joan/Juan Torrendell

Thomas Harrington

The contemporary study of literature and cultural history is inextricably linked to the rise and consolidation of the nation-state during the nineteenth century. The drive to institutionalize the concept of national memory (first evoked by early nineteenth century Romantics) through the scientific study of historical texts (philology), was pioneered in the emergent Germany of the mid- and late-1800s. However, this technique was soon adopted by the leadership classes of other continental nations, including Spain, who saw its potential for soothing the social fractiousness induced by the dislocations of industrial modernity. This social dislocation in the face of epochal change was not, in and of itself, anything new for humankind. What was new, however, was that it was taking place in an environment where religious certainties (and with them previous notions of social hierarchy) were under active assault. In this context, the narratives of transtemporal continuity of the national spirit generated by philologists evolved into new receptacles for the heretofore religiously-channeled transcendental yearnings of the populace. Given that the growth of Europe on the world stage had occurred under the sign of Christianity, it is not surprising that these new philologically-generated creeds of national identity would possess a decidedly *monistic* discursive logic, that is, they would place a great premium on the indivisible oneness of the national "body."[1]

In the Iberian context, this meant exalting the Castilian language and culture to the point where institutional manifestations of the "other" culture-nations of the peninsula (Catalonia, Galicia, Portugal and the Basque Country) became virtually nonexistent. However, in the period between 1890 and 1920, politicians and intellectuals from these so-called "peripheral" cultural systems (especially those in Catalonia) began to mount a counterattack against the state-sponsored Castilianist national pedagogy by creating institutions designed to greatly expand the extant repertoire of autochthonous cultural material. While some nationalist pedagogues working within these movements in Catalonia, Portugal and Galicia sought to create a new discursive architecture which would allow for the expression of multiple and/or overlapping schemas of national identity,[2] the dominant tendency on the periphery was to imitate, and install as normative, the monistic logic of Castilianism. The result after 1906, and more particularly after 1911, was a situation in which the most influential nationalists of each of the five culture-nations of the peninsula were actively touting the stand-alone nature of their particular national tradition at the expense of the long-standing history of co-existence and co-operation between them.[3]

Though it is not always readily acknowledged, the institutionalization of literature in the "new" nations of the Plata region was deeply influenced by the models of national pedagogy generated in Europe in general and Spain in particular. There, as on the Peninsula, what started as romantic reactions against the status quo in the 1830s and 1840s were gradually transformed into integrated and forward-looking plans of social action during the second half of the nineteenth century. There were of course also key differences. One of these was the positionality of the early nationalist writers of Argentina and Uruguay. In Europe, the Romantic rebellion for the most part was a reaction against the imposition of modernity by a seemingly heartless class of city-dwellers. In the Plata, as Jean Franco reminds us, the Romantic wrote *from the city* against the chaos of a vast and seemingly heartless natural environment (68–82). Another important difference (arguably intertwined with the first) was the relative weight of *self-conscious* social conservatism within the late nineteenth century pedagogies of nationhood. In the Iberian nations, the nationalist discourses of the period oscillated between a dominant historicism (with its implied religiosity and exaltation of ethnic difference vis-à-vis the other) and a minority strain of French-style social contractualism. In the republics of the Plata, this relationship was reversed. There, as is fitting in societies that had identified immigration as their main engine of economic and social growth, Renan's notion of the nation as "a daily plebiscite" (as opposed to the Herderian idea of the nation as an enlarged ethnic clan) was the prime concept of social cohesion.[4]

While these changes of emphasis would have important effects on the future development of the cultural systems of both Argentina and Uruguay, they did not substantially challenge the underlying *unitary logic* of inherited models of nationalist pedagogy. Put another way, a dialogic approach to otherness, symbolized by an openness to linguistic and cultural hybridity, was no more a part of the nationalist discourses of the Southern Cone than those on the Peninsula. Emblematic of the extreme desire of the intellectual classes in the region to solidify (and homogenize) the internal cultural landscape in unitary terms against the "threat" of a potentially avenging "other" was the campaign led by important writers during the 1870s and 1880s to reject any Argentine cooperation with Spain in the effort to establish the institutional bases of the "national" language.

These historical realities continue to exert enormous influence on our present day study of Hispanic culture. As I have argued in other places, the institutionalized fixation on unitary and fundamentally non-interactive concepts of identity on the Peninsula, has seriously crippled our understanding of the Iberian past, and with it, our ability to imagine new schemas of democratic co-existence within the Spanish state.[5] Much the same can be said of the burgeoning area of transatlantic studies, especially as it relates to the contemporary Iberian emigrations to the Southern Cone.[6] Owing to the predominance on both the Peninsula and in the Plata region of the unitary and/or *statist* framings of national culture briefly described above, these migrations have been analyzed, more often than not, as a cultural negotiation between the immigrant's sense of Spanishness on one hand, and the national identity of his or her country of adoption on the other.[7] While this model can no doubt be applied to the experience of many Iberian emigrants to the Americas in general, and the Plata region in particular, it ignores an important fact: that a probable majority of "Spanish" immigrants to the Americas (and the region of the Plata) in the nineteenth and twentieth centuries came from areas of the Peninsula (Galicia, Catalonia, The Balearics, Valencia, the Basque Country and Navarra) where state-sponsored, Castile-centered pedagogies of national identity were either poorly established or under active assault.[8] Moreover, these so-called peripheral identities were themselves often driven by intensely-felt local divisions. This meant that for large numbers of Iberian immigrants to Argentina and Uruguay, the process of assimilation was far more complicated than at first it might appear as they were often bringing a doubly or even triply contested idea of national identity to their new country. In fact, for many of them,

Castilian was a second language only spoken outside the home and life tended to revolve around friendships and institutions where the so-called "peripheral" languages of Spain were the preferred codes of communication. Summing up, issues of identity faced by *gallegos*[9] in the Plata region were often much more complex than extant models of analysis have permitted or encouraged us to acknowledge.

It is in the hope of illustrating the extent to which overlapping identities were, and are, part of the experience of Iberian immigrants to the Plata region that we turn now to the life and work of the novelist, playwright, critic, editor and publisher Joan and/or Juan Torrendell. The treatment of his extraordinary professional trajectory, which took place across four distinct socio-cultural environments (Palma, Barcelona, Montevideo and Buenos Aires) and involved the use of at least five national or proto-national identities (Mallorcan, Catalan, Spanish, Uruguayan, and Argentine) over nearly half a century, lays bare the symbolic violence that has so often been applied to individuals by meditating institutions of national culture. Torrendell's body of work has, in effect, been neatly *cuartizado*, with scholars from each of the national cultural fields in which he worked occupying themselves almost exclusively with what he did in their particular realm of identity.[10] Lost in this approach is the fact Torrendell himself apparently never felt the need to obscure or jettison any of the five identities he carried within him. In fact, when we view his overall production closely, we can see that it was marked by a constant and passionate drive to place readers and associates from each of his worlds in contact with one another other. In the pages that follow, I will seek to reassemble from extant scholarly fragments his long-running experiment in what I like to call the "alchemy of identity."

Joan Torrendell i Escalas was born in Palma, Mallorca on August 31, 1867. Like many intellectually gifted and economically disadvantaged young men of his time, he enrolled in the seminary as a teenager. To enter the seminary in Mallorca in this era was, as Antoni Marimon makes clear,[11] to enter an environment dominated by an extremely strong, almost overpowering, identification with the centralized Spanish state and the cultural hegemony of the Castilian language. While there, he published twelve poems and eleven articles in Castilian in a bilingual journal, the *Semanario Católico*. In them, he sings the praises of Pope Leo XIII, motherly love and the beauty of the island while defending the church's postures on issues such as papal prerogative, the threat of socialism and the dangers of rational modernity.[12] What is not clear, and probably cannot ever be known for sure, is the degree of sincerity with which he wrote them. The ideological contents of the writings produced during the subsequent decade of his life, with their strong attacks on the existing social order, would seem to suggest that he was a young man writing under the duress of institutionally-imposed norms.[13] However, this conclusion is thrown into some degree of doubt when we realize that for all his apparent suspicions of the church, he would, according to his granddaughter, remain a practicing Catholic for the rest of his life.[14]

What we do know for sure is that in late 1888, a very short time before he was scheduled to take his vows as a priest, he decided to emigrate to Montevideo, Uruguay. In so doing, he was not alone among his countrymen. During the last two decades of the eighteenth century, the Balearics, like other impoverished non-Castilian areas of the peninsula such as Galicia, Asturias, and the Basque Country, were affected by large-scale emigrations to the Americas (mostly Cuba and the Plata region) as well as France and Algeria. Among the "push factors" in the Mallorcan context were rural overpopulation, the arrival of the phylloxera plague (1891) and the loss of the Caribbean market owing to the outbreak of the Cuban War of Independence (1895). The major "pull factor" was the desire of American officials, especially those in the countries of the Southern Cone, to populate their territories with European workers. According to Buades Crespí, the year of Torrendell's departure was a watershed in this process in that it was the first time that emigration (heavily encouraged by on-site agents in the pay of the Argentine government) grew so large as to engender a net decline in the population of the island.[15]

If, as his friend and fellow critic Eduardo Ferreira later suggested, Torrendell left Mallorca in the hope of exploring ideas that had been previously forbidden to him (Ferreira xii), there was arguably no better place for him in the Spanish-speaking world than the small South American Republic, a place where the modern ideals of Batlle y Ordóñez were about to usher in a Golden Age of material and intellectual progress, a leap forward made possible, in no small part, by the egalitarian and decidedly non-theocratic attitudes (even among the clergy and the so-called Spiritualists) of previous Catalan immigrants to the country.[16]

Torrendell was quick to lend his energies and talents to what one important member of Uruguay's contemporary Catalan community has called this unique "emigration of ideas" "emigració de idees" (Coll) from the peninsula's northeast corner. He gained employment by day as a teacher of Latin at the *Escuela Barceló*, an institution founded by his fellow Mallorcan and future vice-president of the Uruguayan *Dirección General de Instrucción Pública*, Jaume Ferrer Barceló. At night, he dedicated himself to writing theatre criticism under the pseudonym of *Blandengue*[17] for *El Día*, the newspaper controlled by Batlle y Ordóñez. In this latter role, he soon gained a reputation for great rigor and fierce independence. His notoriety as a principled but sometimes harsh *francotirador* was so great that the aforementioned Ferreira writes of needing to suppress his feelings of antipathy for the brash newcomer in advance of their first meeting (ix). But behind the firebrand image was a supple and perceptive mind that whose implied directives brought a great deal of change to Montevideo's artistic life. Writing in 1926, the Uruguayan poet and essayist Victor Pérez Petit speaks of the contrast between false and stultifying mediocrity of turn-of-the-century Uruguayan literary society and the fearless honesty and erudition of "Blandengue." The result of this clash, he suggests, was nothing short of a renovation of the national literary system.

> [Torrendell] Puso cátedra de buen gusto sin buscarlo de propósito—porque la más sólida y fecunda de las enseñanzas fluía naturalmente de sus escritos—y enseñó a pensar y a sentir, a pensar bien y hondo, a sentir artísticamente. Su influjo, pues, en las letras uruguayas . . . es indiscutible. Dio un certero golpe de muerte a los simuladores, a los arrivistas, a las nulidades engreídas, a los gansos consagrados—barriendo para el estercolero toda aquella producción fatua, vacía, rimbombante y cursilona—y al mismo tiempo, señaló los verdaderos derroteros del arte, fijó normas de elegancia y de buen gusto, enseño muchas cosas que se ignoraban por completo, ensanchó los horizontes sugiriendo ideas creadoras y sensaciones artísticas. Al lado del demoledor estuvo constantemente el constructor, y eso es lo que avalora aún más su crítica. (Pérez Petit 173–74)

> ([Torrendell] established himself as the arbiter of good taste without explicitly setting out to do so—solid and suggestive teachings flowed naturally from his writings—and taught his readers to think and to feel, that is, to think deeply and well and to feel artistically. His important influence upon Uruguayan letters is . . . beyond dispute. He administered a well-aimed final blow to the fakers, the social climbers, the bitter ones without talent and the sacred cows and banished their fatuous, empty, high sounding and kitschy literary production to the manure pile. At the same time he signaled the true path of art and established norms of elegance and good taste, re-teaching things that many had forgotten. He broadened horizons by encouraging creative ideas and artistic sensibilities. In Torrendell, the builder always worked beside destroyer and this is what makes critical work so valuable.)

This exalted view of Torrendell's critical labor in Uruguay is echoed by the famed Chilean writer Eduardo Barrios who described it as a necessary precursor to Rodó's celebrated *Revista Nacional*. "Llegó directamente a Montevideo; y allí, con Victor Pérez Petit y Eduardo Ferreira, fundó la primera crítica seria en los diarios uruguayos. Aquella actuación iniciada en el año 90, fue la precursora de la famosa Revista Nacional, que dió a conocer a José Enrique Rodó" (269) (He emigrated straight to Montevideo. There, along with Victor Pérez Petit Eduardo Ferreira, he began producing the first serious criticism ever seen in Uruguayan newspapers. This enterprise begun in 1890 was the precursor of José Enrique Rodó's famous *Revista Nacional*).

While modeling declensions for the young by day and trying to cleanse Uruguayan literature of insincere cant by night, Torrendell was also writing theater and narrative fiction. At the time, the Uruguayan intellectual world was engaged, as Arturo Ardao has explained in great detail, in an intense debate between partisans of spiritualism on one hand, and positivism (and its literary correlate Naturalism) on the other. Torrendell wasted little time in making his own preference for the latter posture clear, first with *La ley y el amor*, a drama which debuted at the Teatro Solís in April 1893 then with *El picaflor*, his 1894 novel about corruption and social climbing among Montevideo's cultural elites. In writing these works under the unambiguous influence of Zola's Naturalism, with its emphasis on conveying the particularities of "real" social spaces, Torrendell was, in effect, assuming the identity of a person-in-the-culture, that is, of a Uruguayan who is fully cognizant of the social and linguistic registers of his adopted city. According to Pérez Petit, who strongly criticized other aspects of *El picaflor*, Torrendell succeeded quite admirably in this essential task of conveying to readers a sense of the "real life" of the nation "Es todo un 'documento humano,' tal como lo exigía Zola, y ese es, acaso, el más grande y superior mérito de la novela. Yo no recuerdo otra, que no sea la *Beba* de Carlos Reyles, que nos dé una sensación de 'realidad vivida,' entre todas las novelas uruguayas de la época" (176) (It is very much a 'human document' of the type that Zola encouraged us to create. This is probably the novel's greatest accomplishment. With the possible exception of Carlos Reyles's *Beba,* I cannot remember any other Uruguayan novel from the time that provides us with such a strong sense of lived reality).

However, Torrendell's sense of allegiance to the Uruguayan imagined community was not as clear-cut as it might have appeared to the outside observer. At the same time he was apparently establishing himself as a fully assimilated and widely recognized member of the Uruguayan creative class, he was writing articles under the pseudonym of Fernán-González for *La Almudaina* in Palma that make evident his disappointment with the cultural life of Uruguay and his desire to return to the Balearics. This was confirmed in 1893 by his colleague Ferreira: "Una idea dulce acaricia incesantemente: la de regresar a su patria y dedicarse a la escabrosa carrera de las letras, que aquí, entre nosotros no ofrece en recompensa más que amargas decepciones" (xvii) (A sweet dream constantly caressed his consciousness: the idea of returning to his homeland and dedicating himself to the unpredictable life of the full-time writer, a career that here among us promises little more than bitter diappointment). Torrendell, who in the seminary had published doctrinal tracts while probably wanting to write progressive social criticism, once found himself between worlds balancing two distinct identities.

Fate soon intervened in the form of a lottery ticket; Torrendell won the "premio gordo de la Lotería de Montevideo" (Pérez Petit 181) (the jackpot in the Montevideo City Lottery). He immediately married his betrothed, Sara Fariña, a niece of the famed Uruguayan writer Zorilla de San Martín, and left for Palma, arriving in the island capital on December 2, 1894. After a brief residence in Barcelona in 1895, apparently dedicated to the task of finding a publisher for two books finished during his last months in Montevideo (*Clarín y su ensayo* and *Pimpollos relatos*) as well as securing a Spanish debut for his play *Currita Albornoz*, he settled down in Palma at the beginning of 1896.

Torrendell arrived in Mallorca at a very special moment in the cultural history of the island.[18] Most students of Peninsular culture are, by now, more or less familiar with broad outlines of the heterodox social and artistic movement known as Catalan *modernisme*. The bulk of the analysis of this phenomenon has centered on creative projects that took place in Barcelona and its immediate environs: the architecture of Gaudí and Domènech as well as the varied activities of creators such as Santiago Rusiñol, Ramón Casas and Joan Maragall among numerous others. Much less widely understood and discussed is the Mallorcan branch of the movement whose leading voices were Miquel dels Sants Oliver, Gabriel Alomar, Fèlix Escalas, Bartomeu Amengual and eventually, Joan Torrendell.

For the most part, Catalan historiography has never known quite what to do with this Mallorcan *modernisme*. The general tendency has been to treat it as a very peripheral sideshow, clearly part of the "national cultural space" for bragging purposes, but only worthy of detailed analysis in terms of its direct effect (e.g., the famous series of lectures at the *Ateneu* in 1904) on the cultural life of Barcelona. What goes missing in this approach is an analysis of the unique and complex dynamics of the island's cultural life. Perhaps the best way to describe it would be as a literary and cultural "intersystem,"[19] an environment subject to a constant and unbreakable dialogue with Barcelona, but conditioned by very real and often very different local imperatives which render it somewhat "foreign" to the metropolitan gaze. The result was a group of thinkers who demonstrated an extraordinary ability to juggle multiple schemas of identity, to be and live *in* a place (often Barcelona) but never be fully beholden to its claims on the soul.

If the prime emphases of mainland literary *modernisme* were the bohemian artist and the cafe (*Cau Ferrat* and *Els Quatre Gats*), then the focal points of the Mallorcan branch of the movement were the journalist and the press room, especially that of the previously mentioned *La Almudaina*, which M.S. Oliver ran with considerable vision and charisma from 1887 to 1904.[20] The early and forthright embrace of social pedagogy (as opposed to individual artistic expression) by the Mallorcans led them to generate a number of important innovations within the Catalanist discourse, changes that, in many cases would only become fully ensconced on the mainland later on. One was to largely decouple the question of increased local autonomy from issues, both pro and con, concerning clerical prerogative. Another was the practice of locating (rhetorically, at least) the regionalist cause, as it was then called, within the broader ideological framework of Spanish Regenerationism. A third was to create an intimate association in the minds of citizens between the revival of local culture and the creation and maintenance of civic institutions. There were, however, two distinguishing features of Mallorcan *modernisme* that would never reach the "center zone" of the mainland system of nationalist expression. These were a relative openness to the idea employing Castilian for Catalanist ends and the earnest pursuit of an all-encompassing Iberianist solution (as opposed to a bilateral Barcelona/Madrid solution) to the Catalan problem.

As he had done in Montevideo, Torrendell threw himself into the new, if still largely familiar, situation with abandon. He quickly became a very important presence at *La Almudaina* and the other publications on the island (such as *La Roqueta*) with which it tended to share writers. Another such publication was *La Última Hora*, which named him interim editor-in-chief in June of 1897. During his first year on the job, he published very little under his own name. However, after the Spanish debacle of 1898, Torrendell began contributing much more frequently, with articles that were far more politically radical than anything he had written previously in either Uruguay or Mallorca. Among the topics in these pieces were the need for real democratization of local government, the evils of *caciquismo*, the miscarriages of justice in both the Dreyfus Affair and *El Procés de Montjuic*. He also imbued the paper with a markedly more strident tone on the issues of regional autonomy and the institutional use of the Catalan language. Irritated with his new and pointed aggressiveness, the owners of the paper fired Torrendell in September of 1899. He was quickly hired as editor of *La Unión Republicana*. In this capacity, he sought to reconcile the historically antagonistic relationship between the regionalists and republicans, implicitly challenging the former to lighten their devotion to social conservatism and the latter to dispense with their traditional adherence to centralism. In this sense, *La Union Republicana*, under his brief two month stewardship can be seen as an important precursor to *El Poble Català*, the seminal journal of Catalanist republicanism founded in Barcelona in 1904.

In January of 1900, Torrendell left *La Union Republicana* to launch his own Catalan-language weekly, *La Veu de Mallorca*, dedicated almost exclusively to politics. This was not the first—and it would certainly not be the last—time that Torrendell engaged in intellectual entrepreneurship. In late 1898, a time when he was editing *La Ultima Hora* and contributing articles to a number of publications on the island and the mainland, he had founded *Nova Palma*, a bilingual fortnightly which aimed to bring the creative spirit of mainland literary *modernisme*—though not its sometime embrace of decadentism—to Mallorca. In its four issues we find texts by non-Catalan icons such as D'Annunzio, Nietzche and Unamuno beside those of the Barcelonans, Maragall, Pérez Jorba, and Rusiñol and of course the *Mallorquins*, Oliver, Escalas and Alomar. In July of 1899, Torrendell founded *Fígaro*, a general interest journal whose *raison d'etre* appears to have been much more economic than ideological. It failed after only one issue.

In starting *La Veu de Mallorca* in early 1900, Torrendell was tipping the Nationalist/Republican balance on the island ever so slightly toward the former in the belief that language and culture will always have a broader and more constant appeal than rationally constituted ideologies. In so doing, he was following the previous example of the Federalist cum Particularist Valentí Almirall. It was also a savvy choice considering the ever-increasing power of historicist Catalanism on the mainland following the events of 1898. As the power of these forces under the leadership of Prat de la Riba continued to grow, Torrendell would, as we shall see, be drawn increasingly into their orbit. As this occurred, he would face pressure to restrict his openness to Republicans and others who, for one reason or another, were viewed with suspicion by the *Lliga*. He very seldom, if ever, ceded to these coercions, preferring instead to constantly reaffirm his belief in an "ecumenical" approach to questions of politics and identity.

Despite breaking much new ideological and stylistic ground in the Mallorcan context—some have described it as *the* foundational journal of modern Mallorcan nationalism[21]—*La Veu* closed after only three months of operation. After its failure, Torrendell returned with renewed vigor to what was his most intense passion: the theater. In May, 1901 his drama *Els Encarrilats*, which starred the most popular and skilled Catalan actor of the day, Enric Borrás, debuted to very favorable reviews in Barcelona. A Castilian version of the Ibsen-influenced work met with similar praise when it opened in Palma and Valencia later in the same year. It is still viewed by many critics today as a key work of contemporary Mallorcan theater as well as the regenerationist strain of Catalan *modernisme*. At its core, it is a tribute to the social power of individual passion. The young protagonist, Guillem, an intellectual disgusted by the injustices of *el caciquismo*, seeks to wake his fellow citizens (*els encarrilats*) from their conformist apathy. When he cannot, he takes the drastic step of killing the local boss in the belief that the egregious act will break the reigning system of oppression. No doubt some of the play's success was derived from its relevance to current events. Just a month before its debut, the *Lliga* had been founded (through the fusion of the *Centre Nacional Català* and the *Unió Catalanista*) with the expressed goal of breaking the cacique-dependent duopoly of political power in Restoration Spain.

In his next play, *Els dos esperits*, which was first performed in Barcelona in September of 1902, Torrendell creates a similar modernist hero. However, this time his dilemmas are played out upon a backdrop of explicitly-drawn class conflicts. Its popular and critical reception was nowhere near as positive as that received by *Els encarrilats*, perhaps indicating a reticence among many bourgeois nationalists—which is to say the majority of them at this point—to conflate the cause of national autonomy with that of sweeping social reform.

The tepid response to the play was the beginning of the end of Torrendell's social radicalism. While he would continue to call for social reform on the basis of class precepts in articles and lectures written during 1903, he had by 1904 adopted an approach much more in keeping with the core currents of mainland Catalanism. A major factor in this realignment was the decision of the *Ateneu* of Barcelona, then under the leadership of Maragall, to sponsor a series of lectures by the those he regarded as the brightest lights of Mallorcan intellectual life: Miquel Costa i Llobera, Gabriel Alomar, Joan Alcover, Miquel dels Sants Oliver and Joan Torrendell. Not only did these lectures provide the iconoclastic outsider Torrendell with a long-desired dose of big-city legitimacy, but also a new responsibility. Shortly after showcasing his talents in his talk to the *Ateneu* in May of that year, Oliver was offered—again thanks to the mediation of Maragall—the job of director of the *Diario de Barcelona*,[22] a change which, in turn, catapulted Torrendell to the directorship of the *La Almudaina*. Acutely aware of the paper's historic role in binding together the disparate coalition of islanders interested in the struggle for greater self-determination, he decided to dispense the more potentially divisive elements of his discourse.

This tolerant pragmatism—which would accompany him for the rest of his life—came into particularly clear focus in the last of Torrendell's Mallorcan enterprises, the weekly *La ciudad*, founded in October 1905. After working so hard to promote Catalan as the prime language of cultured social discourse,[23] he once again reverts to using Castilian as the journal's sole language of communication, presumably for its ability to reach a wider readership. But perhaps more surprising still was the great attention he paid to economic issues framed not from the point of view of the poor or the disaffected intellectual as in his recent works of theater, but from that of businessmen and economists. In doing this, he was really just returning to the roots of the Mallorcan regionalist discourse as conceived by Oliver in the late 1880s and 1890s. Nonetheless, it is still somewhat shocking, given the social stridency he had exhibited only two years before.

While working on the island, Torrendell continued to cultivate the contacts made in his triumphant 1904 visit to Barcelona. In May 1905, he attends the *Jocs Florals* in that city. In October of 1906, he returns to give a talk on "Trascendència del periodisme pera la propaganda i consolidació del Renaixament y restauració de la nostra llengua at the Primer congrès internacional de la llengua catalana" (The Transcendant Role of Journalism in the Creation of Propaganda, the Consolidation of our Literary Revival and the Restoration of our Language), perhaps the most important institutional manifestation to date of the rising strength of the Catalanist cause. In fact, by the time he made this last trip to the mainland, it would seem that Torrendell had already decided that he had to live in a capital city that was rapidly reinventing itself along new cultural, linguistic, and governmental lines. Helped no doubt by Oliver, he lined up a job at *La Veu de Catalunya*, the official organ of Prat de la Riba's *Lliga*, where Eugeni D'Ors was then writing the first of the daily *Gloses* that would, over the next 14 years, do so much to define the linguistic and esthetic bases of *noucentisme*. With this offer of steady employment in hand, he set out to Barcelona from Palma on December 11, 1906.

But, as we have seen, Torrendell was seldom content with merely writing for others. So it should probably come not as a surprise that just months after his arrival in the capital, while adjusting to a high-profile job at *La Veu de Catalunya* and still writing frequent articles as Barcelona correspondent for *La Almudaina*, he launched another journal, *La Cataluña* with his fellow Mallorcan (and long-time Barcelona-based contributor to *La Almudaina*) Bartomeu Amengual and the moral, if not financial support of the *Lliga*. It would prove to be the most successful of Torrendell's peninsular enterprises (lasting nearly three years under his control and several more under different leadership) and one of the more fascinatingly heterodox journals of its time. It is also perhaps for this last trait that it remains one of the least examined publications of early twentieth century Catalonia.[24]

The philosophy behind *La Cataluña*, which debuted on October 5, 1907, was much the same as that which had animated the founding of *La ciudad* in the Mallorcan context two years earlier: create a Catalanist journal in Castilian which would appeal to the broadest possible band of collaborators and readers. As occurred with *La ciudad*, it quickly became a magnet for those, as such as Guillem Graell and Federico Rahola, who were interested in the economic and foreign trade dimensions of Catalanism and had felt somewhat marginalized by the dominant literary and artistic focus of the extant Catalanist discourse. But it also gained some entirely new constituencies; perhaps the most important of these were the Iberianists.

When we speak of Iberianism today, we speak almost exclusively of Joan Maragall who, in his now famous correspondence with Unamuno spoke of the need to engender ideals and institutions that would reflect the reality of a Peninsula made up of three essential culture-nations: Catalonia, Castile (which included the Basque Country) and Portugal (which included Galicia). But in fact, the movement was far deeper and broader than this. Viewed in historical terms, this Tripartite Iberianism, which owes as much to Casas-Carbó and Ignasi Ribera-Rovira as it does to the famous poet, was a bold attempt to bridge the gap between historicists and federalists within the Catalanist movement.[25] The more conservative historicists, whose outlook was exemplified by Prat de la Riba and the *Lliga,* believed that the key to Catalonia's future lay, above all, in leveraging its relationship with Madrid. However they also knew that speaking openly about such plans would provoke strong negative reactions in the rest of the Peninsula. Their solution was to develop a rhetorical defense of integral peninsular reform. That it was so vague as to be forever inoperative did not matter. The important thing was to inoculate the *Lliga* from the frequent charge of trying to blackmail the central government for its own narrow ends. Conversely, Catalan federalists had long dreamed about reshaping the entire peninsula. However, as exponents of rational modernity, they were uncomfortable with doing so solely on the basis of what they viewed as essentially "atavistic" considerations such as language and culture. Rather, they believed that such arrangements needed to be formulated largely on the basis of a voluntaristic consensus. The position of the Tripartite Iberianists was like that of the historicists in its insistence on the important role of language and culture in the creation of collective entities. However, it was similar to that of the federalists in its concern with generating a durable framework for intra-peninsular cooperation where identities are never impenetrable or exclusive but rather hybrid and fluid. It is easy to see why Torrendell, with his "catholic" sensibilities and roots in the Mallorcan branch of Catalanism, where creating broad alliances was common and where sincere talk of "Peninsular solutions" had long been present, would provide such a warm welcome to the Iberianists and other "in-betweeners" of the Catalanist movement.

What his natural iconoclasm and expansiveness did not allow him to see was the extent to which his journal's eclecticism would begin to irritate the higher-ups at the *Lliga*. Initially the party seems to have viewed publication as an escape valve for its internal tensions and a potentially valuable tool for winning over hearts and minds in the rest of the Peninsula. Especially supportive of this last goal was Prat's more charismatic and more sincerely Iberianist collaborator, Francesc Cambó. However, as *Solidaritat Catalana* began to fracture, so too did tolerance for Torrendell's brand of ideological ecumenism. A key moment in this process was the Tragic Week of July 1909, which brought previously submerged class and religious tensions to a boil. The *Lliga* reacted by embracing the central government's crackdown of the anti-bourgeois and anti-clerical rebels. No longer believing in the possibility of maintaining a broad heterodoxically-constituted Catalanist front, it further sharpened its ideological profile in the ensuing months and years. Emblematic moments of this process were the celebrated re-issuance of Prat's *La nacionalitat catalana* in December of 1910 and the publication of Eugeni d'Ors two most overtly catechetical works (*La Ben plantada* and the *Almanac dels noucentistes*) in the latter half of 1911.

Torrendell left, or was forced out, as the head of *La Cataluña* in July of 1910, at the very same time that he either left or was forced out of his other job as editor at *La Veu de Catalunya*. While the exact reasons for his departure from these posts have never been revealed, tributes written about him at the time of his departure suggest quite clearly that he had been betrayed by those that did not possess his equanimity or breadth of vision.[26] The best supposition, in my view, is that he, like his admired Maragall, had been unable to suppress his disgust at the growing authoritarianism of the *Lliga*. But whereas the poet had had enough family money to publish as much or as little as he pleased, Torrendell lived by his pen. Having bravely straddled the spaces between political factions, he now found his loyalty questioned by people on both sides of the political equation. So on July 30, 1910 at the age of 43 he set out with his wife and three children to "hacer la América" once again.

Back in Montevideo, he once again donned his Uruguayan identity and returned to work as a writer and critic at Batlle's *El Día* which, as we have noted, was located at the very epicenter of the country's intellectual and political life. But just as he had maintained his Mallorcan identity by writing for *La Almudaina* during his first residence in the country, he now exhibits his profound devotion to the broader idea of Catalonia by quickly founding *El Correo de Cataluña* in the Uruguayan capital. The publication ran for 33 weeks in Montevideo before Torrendell decided to move again, this time to Buenos Aires in early 1912. There he would publish *El Correo de Cataluña* for another year and then move on to work as an editor and book critic at the weekly magazine *El Hogar*.

As has been noted, Argentina enjoyed an enormous rate of population growth in the latter half of the nineteenth century, most of it coming through European immigration. By 1890, Buenos Aires was a massive multi-ethnic city known primarily for an economic dynamism rooted in *unskilled* labor. Over the next two decades, however, this would change, thanks in large measure, to the fact that free and obligatory state education had been instituted in 1884. By the first decade of the twentieth century, we can begin to speak of the existence of "literate masses" in Buenos Aires, a situation that contrasted markedly with that of Spain where illiteracy rates were still extremely high. Quick to realize the implications of this change for the publishing industry in the country was the Anglo-Argentine entrepreneur Alberto Haynes, who, encouraged by the example of *Caras y Caretas* (1898), founded *El Hogar* in 1904. Over the next several decades Haynes would, through this publication and others like *Mundo Argentino* and *El Mundo*, provide what we would now call a "middlebrow" vision of the national reality. In contrast to today, however, such a framing of the national ontology still provided ample room for literature. While one section of *El Hogar* was providing cooking tips and news of the latest engagements among Buenos Aires' prosperous families, another was providing articles and literary texts by writers such as Horacio Quiroga Roberto Arlt, Ezequiel Martínez Estrada, Enrique Amorim, Ramón Gómez de la Serna, and later on, Jorge Luis Borges. In effect, Torrendell as book critic became the one of the fulcrums of "high culture's" new engagement with the public.

Torrendell's time at *El Hogar* was notable for another reason. It was there that he established a strong relationship with Constancio Vigil, the man who would furnish him with the position for which he is perhaps best known in the Argentine context: that of book critic for the weekly, *Atlántida*. The Uruguayan-born Vigil worked for Haynes at *El Hogar* from its inception, learning the still new science of mass-market magazine journalism. In December 1917, he left the Haynes group and founded *Atlántida*. Three months later, its first issue appeared in kiosks. Where the social pedagogy of *El Hogar* had been largely conservative, concerned with the family and a sort of simplistic patriotism, that of *Atlántida* was a clear reflection of Vigil's optimistic progressivism. He was a convinced humanist, democrat and pan-Americanist who saw the publication as a key instrument of democratic education. Consequently, he did not shrink from chiding the political class when they fell short of these noble goals. And needless to say, he saw the reading and discussion of good literature as an integral element of his pedagogical project.

Torrendell wrote a book review essay for *Atlántida* every week from 1918 to 1923, the first five years of the magazine's meteoric rise in the world of Argentine publishing. The focus of "El libro de la Semana"[27] was almost entirely on national literature, a situation which meant that Torrendell, formerly a leading taste-maker in Uruguay, Mallorca and mainland Catalonia, was now a leading arbiter of artistic quality in yet another national literary system. He took his responsibilities in this role quite seriously, dispensing opinions with the same freedom and severity, but also intuitive sympathy, as he had three decades earlier as *Blandengue*. As a result, encomiums to his probity and incorruptibility are ubiquitous in the accounts of the Argentine phase of his life.[28]

However, while clearly working as an "Argentine" and/or rioplatense literary critic in these years, Torrendell never abandoned his Catalan identity. Indeed, he often sought to share his native culture with his American readers. For example, in critical essays about Jorge Rohde and Fausto Burgos we find extensive disquisitions on Eugeni d'Ors and *noucentisme*. In a review of Pérez Petit's famous biography of Rodó, he compares the work of the author *Ariel* to his friend and fellow Mallorcan, Gabriel Alomar. He then goes on to argue that Rodó, whose father was Catalan, "imprime en todos sus ensayos una marca esencialmente catalana, el distintivo de todo el pensamiento nacional de aquel pueblo... la tolerancia... el criterio justo, el termino medio, la prudencia, la cordura, *el seny*, en fin, catlanísimo, ... aparece rezumando de toda su obra" (II, 88) (imbues all of his essays with an essentially Catalan sensibility. That markers of that people's national philosophy... tolerance, exacting criteria, moderation, prudence, sanity and, of course, *seny*, that most Catalan of qualities, are present throughout his body of work). Similarly in his review of Carlos Octavio Bunge's *Nuestra América*, Torrendell fiercely attacks the author's reliance of a Castilian-generated concept of Iberian culture that presumes the ethnic unity of the Peninsula.

Seeing the financial success obtained by Haynes and Vigil in selling "culture" to the country's newly literate middle classes led Torrendell to found the *Editorial Tor* in 1916. Over the next several decades, it would serve as the publisher of economical editions of an extremely broad range of writers. Among the Hispanic writers were contemporary Argentines (Manuel Galvez,

Baldomero Fernández Moreno Alfonsina Storni and Adolfo Bioy Casares), contemporary non-Argentines (Amado Nervo, Darío, Martínez Sierra and Ganivet) as well as "classic" Spanish writers from previous eras (Luis de Leon, Lope de Vega and Moratin). The offering from the non-Hispanic world ranged from Shakespeare to Kipling by way of Rousseau, Voltaire, Spencer, and Torrendell's much-admired Ibsen. His devotion to the new idea of book as market commodity later led Torrendell (and/or his son Juan Carlos) to the extreme of selling books priced by the kilo on the sidewalk in front of his bookstore on la *Calle Florida*, an act which drew a formal rebuke from the *Academia Argentina de Letras*.[29]

This devotion to what we would today call the "mass-marketing" of literature might give the impression that Torrendell had abandoned his desire to wield influence among the nation's cultural elites. Nothing could be further from the truth. This is made clear by his constant collaboration in what was arguably the most important "high culture" publication of the era, *Nosotros*, founded by Roberto Giusti and Alfredo Bianchi in 1907. But while Torrendell acted primarily in the context of an "Argentine" identity before the broad public, he retreated to his Iberian roots in this more erudite company. Beginning in 1918, he wrote articles in *Nosotros* on *Letras catalanas*, taking over a section of the journal instituted years earlier by another prestigious Catalan writer in Buenos Aires, Juan Más i Pi. During the late 1920s, Torrendell's attempts to explain the Catalan struggle to the readers of *Nosotros* grew still more explicit. One probable motivation for the change was the great international furor caused by Macià's failed uprising at Prats de Molló in 1926 and his subsequent trial in Paris. In July of 1927, the Republican leader notified all the Catalan organizations of America that he would be arriving in Buenos Aires from Belgium (where he had gone after being expelled from France) at the very beginning of 1928. A very short time later, the editors of *Nosotros*, Bianchi and Giusti, ever attentive to the course of world events, asked Torrendell to write an extensive article for their twentieth anniversary issue of the journal (October 1927) on "Catalan Literature in its Present-Day Revival" "La literatura Catalana en su actual renacimiento."[30] In 1933, he uses an invitation from the *Instituto Popular de Conferencias* of the newspapaer *La Prensa* to speak on the topic of the subject of "Las lenguas de España" (The Languages of Spain). The speech, the text of which was subsequently published by *Nosotros*, is an impassioned defense of Iberianism.[31]

Where did all this work as an "Argentine" and a "Catalan" leave Torrendell's identity as a Mallorcan? Firmly intact it would seem. In 1916, two immigrants to Buenos Aires from the Mallorcan locality of Pollença, founded the Catalan language journal *L'Oranella* as *L'organ de la collectivitat de Pollença a l'Argentina* (The Organ of the Pollensan Community in Argentina). When the publication foundered, Torrendell took over as its director and greatly expanded its cultural reach, describing it as "Periodic quinzenal. Informació de Balears i Cataluña" (A Fortnightly with Information on the Balearic Islands and Catalonia). Though his *l'Orenella* (he changed the spelling from the more archaic usage to the modern and presumably more pan-Catalanist form) failed after only a few issues, Torrendell continued to write about Mallorcan culture for *El balear* the monthly organ of the *Centro Balear* of Buenos Aires as well as *L'Almoina*.[32] During the 1920s, Torrendell was also a regular contributor to *El Día* in Palma, writing regularly about Mallorcan and Argentine culture for a Mallorcan readership. In early 1928, two writers from that island paper, M.A. Colomer and Joan Alomar (the son of Torrendell's great friend from his Palma days, Gabriel Alomar) came up with the idea for *Missió d'Art a L'Argentina* (Art Mission to Argentina). The idea was to promote the island's landscapes and artistic culture among Latin Americans. As a regular contributor to *El Día* and an active member of the *Centro Balear* of Buenos Aires Torrendell was absolutely key to its successful execution, a fact made clear by his presence beside the President of Argentina, Manuel Alvear, at the ceremony marking the inauguration of the exhibition.[33]

In the last six years of his life, Torrendell's production remains prodigious. There is, however, a marked changed in focus; he largely dispenses with his Mallorcan and *rioplatense* identities and begins to write alternately as both a "Spaniard" and a "Catalan."[34] This two-headed approach to things Iberian can be seen in Torrendell's work at *Nosotros*. In the second cycle of the journal's life,[35] Torrendell continues with his articles on *Letras catalanas*. However, he also adds a section on *Letras castellanas*, thus carefully balancing the two identities in the eyes of his Argentine readership. In adopting this bifurcated yet simultaneously integrated approach to Iberian affairs at *Nosotros* in early 1936, Torrendell was effectively mirroring what he had already done in two sizable works written in the preceding five years.

When the Spanish Republic was declared in April of 1931, Torrendell began a series of articles that he will later publish under the title of *La república española en su primer hervor: Diario de un periodista residente en Buenos Aires* (1935) (The Spanish Republic in its initial ardor: The Diary of a journalist living in Buenos Aires). As the title indicates, he writes not as an Argentine, but rather as a Spaniard who *happens to be residing* in Buenos Aires. The focus is on the political actions of the central government. The book is similar in tone to the Civil War writings of another great Catalan journalist of the time, *Gaziel*; both men saw themselves as reasoned moderates who were above the partisan fray and thus able to verbalize many things that others were afraid to say, especially about Republican policies. Its most notable elements have to do with the problem of Church-State relations. As a longtime Republican, Torrendell makes clear that he was glad to see the end of the monarchy. However, as a Catholic he was deeply disturbed by what he saw as Azaña's needlessly aggressive anti-clericalism. In trying to strike a balance between Republicanism and the preservation of a meaningful role for Church within Spanish life, Torrendell can be seen as an important precursor to the distinctive body of thought that would be enunciated with great force and eloquence by Basque *lehendakari* José Antonio Aguirre in the ensuing years.

Torrendell's valedictory as writer was entitled *Cataluña y la República española: Diario de un periodista residente en Buenos Aires* (Catalonia and the Spanish Republic: The Diary of a journalist living in Buenos Aires) published in late 1936, just months before his death. As the title suggests, the book contains considerable analysis of the ongoing evolution of Spanish decentralization. But even more than this, it is a ringing defense of the ideals that had led him to found of *La Cataluña* thirty years before. As he looks back, Torrendell stridently reaffirms the need to both reject Castilian centralism and to locate the search for greater Catalan autonomy within a broader effort to create a truly multi-polar (Iberianist) understanding of the peninsular reality. The text also includes frequent mentions of his admired colleagues and mentors from that earlier time. Among them are Oliver, Salmerón, Maragall, Prat de la Riba, Alomar, and Cambó. When we look at this personal pantheon, we can see that it is, in ideological terms, a very mixed bag with no apparent ideological coherence. Yet Torrendell, presents them as perfectly complementary pieces of a larger puzzle.

How can this be explained? One way to view it is as an act of romantic self-delusion by an old man at the end of his life. Perhaps a better way, however, is to place this act of "ideological alchemy" in the broader context of Torrendell's astonishingly varied and productive life. Along with his facile pen and incisive mind Torrendell possessed a deep almost religious belief in the possibility of establishing respectful dialogue between disparate cultural options, *including the many he carried within himself.*

At the outset, I spoke of how institutions of national culture, forged for the most part in the monistic or unitary ethos of the nineteenth century, have encouraged us to frame the contemporary Iberian emigrations to the Southern Cone in largely bilateral and bicultural terms. I believe Torrendell's vital and professional trajectory should make us pause to consider the true effectiveness of these paradigms. While his "literariness" clearly sets him apart from the broader currents of late nineteenth and early twentieth century Iberian emigration to the Southern Cone, his multiculturality does not. How many others living beyond the pale of the printed record, were able, like him, to quietly juggle a number of passionately-lived "national" lives? My sense is that there were many. However, we will not know for sure until we develop frames of analysis that will put us in a place where we can actively seek out and hear their stories.

Notes

1. For a more detailed view of this historical progression see Harrington, "Rapping," 107–24.
2. For more on the long-overlooked pluralist strain of Catalanism, see Harrington, "El Cercle Maristany," 107–27.
3. For more on this multi-polar standoff, see Harrington, "Las cinco cabezas," 64–73.
4. I am well aware of the dangers inherent in highlighting the predominance of contractualism over ethnically based concepts of nationalism in the Argentine and Uruguayan contexts. For while it was certainly true that there was much less *formal* recognition of ethnic peculiarities here than in the nationalist discourses of Europe, it is also true that this more universalizing approach to generating social cohesion only existed within the carefully delimited space of social "whiteness." Given that whiteness can only exist in opposition to non-whiteness, we can see that Sarmiento and others like him were quite far from having freed themselves from European-style fixations on difference. Indeed, it could be argued that they simply transferred the locus of exclusion from the realm of the ethnic group to the realm of race.
5. See "Catalanism in the Portuguese Mirror," 257–80.
6. During the last decade or so, the history of transatlantic migrations has achieved a much-enhanced currency within contemporary Peninsular Studies. Though it is always difficult to pinpoint the origin of scholarly trends, I believe it is possible to adduce a number of probable reasons for this change. On the most general level, there is the ever-increasing presence of immigrants and imported cultural materials in the daily lives of Europeans and North Americans (the core group disposed to reflecting upon such things in publications of this type), a reality that underscores the essential dynamism and permeability of what were long-presented as largely static and autonomous national cultural systems. More specifically, there was the decision made by the newly "Europeanized" (and hence newly wealthy) governments of Spain and Portugal to stage elaborate celebrations for their transoceanic legacies during the 1990s. While clearly distasteful to some, this symbolic re-conquest of America (and Africa) nonetheless provided institutional incentives for many scholars to reflect anew

upon the global aspects of Iberian culture. Another was the gradual splintering of the Spanish *pacto de olvido* during the same period. The understandable desire of Spanish citizens and scholars alike to insure the success of the Transition to Democracy had led in the seventies and eighties to a generalized tendency to downplay the narratives of those who had suffered as political and economic exiles during Francoism. The apparent consolidation of the democratic system in the early and mid 1990s gave scholars the confidence to finally begin exploring these difficult narratives of displacement. Adding to this impulse was the growing realization that the window for gathering testimonies of these experiences was quite limited owing to the advanced age of the participants in this transatlantic epic. Also playing a role in fomenting interest in contemporary Iberian interactions with America was, and is, the increasing precariousness of Peninsular Studies within the North American academy. As the balance of resources within North American Hispanism has shifted ever more sharply toward Latin American issues during the past two decades, scholars of Iberian culture began to believe (rightly or wrongly) that forging thematic links to Latin American might help to attenuate their growing sense of institutional impotence.

7. Emblematic of this tendency is Doris Schwarzstein's *Entre Franco y Perón: Memoria e identidad del exilio republicano español en Argentina*. While this finely written and richly documented study does an excellent job of relating both the bilateral negotiations surrounding the transatlantic movement of Republican exiles as well as the personal difficulties many of them suffered while adapting to Argentine life, it largely elides the issue of the unique "trilateral" cultural negotiation faced by Catalan, Basque and Galician emigrants in the country.

8. For a statistical breakdown of the turn-of-the-century Iberian emigration to the Américas, see Naranjo, 177–200.

9. This popular usage is itself quite revealing of the general tendency to overlook the specifics of non-Castilian identities in *La Plata* region. By constantly using a part (Galicia) to refer to the whole (Spain), rioplatenses are both announcing their general indifference to the question of Iberian diversity and effectively denying Galicians themselves the possibility of being understood in terms of their own unique cultural ontology.

10. Critical "vivisections" of this type have occurred in the case of a number of other prominent Catalan cultural producers. The one that comes most immediately to mind is Eugeni D'Ors. Until the mid-1980s, this absolutely essential figure of Catalan thought and letters was widely shunned in Catalonia as an object of serious study because of his post-1920 apostasy from the nationalist cause. This issue has now been "resolved" by essentially treating d'Ors not as a single writer with a single artistic trajectory but rather as two distinct and autonomous literary beings. One is the high priest of Catalanism from 1906–20 the other the Castilian language apologist for right wing centralism. Perhaps even more germane to this study is the critical fate the Catalano-Uruguayan painter Joaquin/m Torres-Garcia around whom there has been erected two separate and nearly mutually-exclusive critical discourses, one dealing

with his time as a "Catalan" figurative painter (1891–1920) and the other as an internationally-minded "Uruguayan" master of Constructivism (1920–1949). What makes the case of Torrendell so interesting is that both his Catalan and *rioplatense* trajectories were themselves divided by competing concepts of national culture.
11. See Marimon, 83–97.
12. See Pons, "Aproximació," 106–108.
13. Eduardo Ferreira's description of Torrendell as someone who had studied for the priesthood "more out of obligation than devotion" "más por obligación que por devoción" (xii) seems to confirm this vision of the incongruously "orthodox" articles.
14. See Torrendell, Larravide.
15. Joan Buades Crespí, "La emigración masiva . . ." s.n.
16. The question of the role previous emigrants from *els països catalans* played in creating the uniquely progressive and forward-looking culture which made Batllismo possible deserves much more critical attention than it has received to date. The roster of Uruguayans of Catalan descent (either immigrants or children of immigrants) who played important roles in the formation of the nation's cultural and social infrastructure in the nineteenth century is quite extensive, constituting a virtual who's who of the nation's leadership in fields such as government, religion, arts and ideas, international commerce and meat packing, architecture, medicine, viticulture, and especially, education. A very partial list includes such key figures as José Batlle i Carreó, Lorenzo Batlle i Grau, Francisco Giró, Franciso Llambí, Francisco Vidal, Mariano Soler, Pedro Blanes Viale, Miguel Jaume y Bosch, José Enrique Rodó, Carlos Roxlo, Orestes Araújo, Francisco Sunyer i Capdevila, Jaime Cibils, Aleix Rossell i Rius, Juan Carrau, Felix Buxareo, Francisco Juanicó, Antonio Fongivell, Cayetano Buigas, Teodoro Villardebó, Alejandro Fiol de Perera, Francisco Vidiella, Pedro Giralt, Tomás Claramunt, Adolfo Pedralbes, Joaquim Pedralbes, Enriqueta Compte i Riqué, Jaime Roldós y Pons and Benito Riqué. The enormous influence of Catalans and their direct descendents in Uruguayan life continued into the mid-twentieth century through the work of (among many others) figures such as Joaquín Torres-García, Margarida Xirgu, Carlos Sabat Ercasty, Julio Villamajó and Antonio Bonet Castellana. For an introduction to this long-neglected field of inquiry, consult Paris de Oddone and Puiggros.
17. Torrendell's choice of this pseudonym demonstrates his early sensitivity to the problem of juggling national identities. The Blandengues were the elite corps of soldiers formed by the Spanish viceroy (the Catalan Antonio Olaguer Feliu) in 1797 to protect the Banda Oriental of the Plata from the encroachments of the Charrúa, and eventually, the Portuguese and British. José Gervasio Artigas joined the militia in the year of its creation. In 1811, he would become its commander and transform the regiment into the principal "sword" of his new campaign for independence from Spain. It is safe to assume that Torrendell was well aware of Artigas's double condition as esteemed servant of the Spanish crown and Uruguayan patriot when he chose to adopt *Blandenque* as his *nom de plume*.

18. For more on the overall intellectual and cultural environment of the island capital at this time, see Pons, *Ideología i cultura*.
19. For more on the concept of intersystems see Harrington, "Agents of an intersystem" 95–99.
20. See Pons, *El diari La almudaina*.
21. See Carrió, "Les publicacions" and Serra, "La Veu."
22. Two years later Oliver would leave *El Diario de Barcelona* to begin his famous run as editor in chief of *La Vanguardia* a job he would occupy (among many others!) until his death in 1920.
23. See Torrendell, "Don Joan Palou."
24. This conspicuous gap in the scholarship of turn-of-the-century Catalanist thought has finally begun to be addressed in recent years by Guirao Motis and Costa Ruibal.
25. See Harrington, "Belief."
26. See Rucabado, 458–59.
27. The articles from Torrendell's first year at Atlántida were gathered in the volume *El año literario* (1918). This same volume was republished in 1933 as *Crítica menor I*. The following year, *Crítica Menor II*, a collection of articles from the subsequent years of his *magisterium* at *Atlántida*, appeared. In the prologue to this volume, it was suggested that other volumes of his collected criticism would soon follow. However, it does not appear to have occurred.
28. Typical of the praise that one finds when researching the Argentine phase of Torrendell's career are these words of Manuel Gálvez: "Era Torrendell un mallorquín muy culto e inteligente. Había sido seminarista, por lo cual entendía cosas de religión y de moral. Era un crítico excelente: a su conocimiento, fino espíritu, buen gusto y sano criterio se unía su honradez y sinceridad. Erguido, de grandes mostachos canosos. Nuestras letras, que empezó a juzgar en *Atlántida* desde fines de 1916 o principios de 1917, le deben mucho. Fue un mentor comprensivo y exacto, sin severidades excesivas ni benevolencias amistosas" (480–81) (Torrendell was an intelligent and highly cultured Mallorcan. He had been a seminarian, an experience which allowed him to understand issues of religion and morality. He was an excellent critic who combined knowledge, generosity of spirit, good taste and solid criteria with honesty and sincerity. He stood upright and wore a bushy grey mustache. Our (Argentine) literature, which he began to comment upon in the pages of *Atlántida* in late 1916 or early 1917, owes him a great deal. He was an understanding mentor, encumbered by neither excessive severity nor friendly benevolence).
29. Abós s.n. In recent conversations wih Torrendell's grandchildren, the consensus opinion was that it was probably Juan Torrendell's more flamboyand son Juan Carlos, his founding partner in Editorial Tor, who was probably the mastermind behind this marketing stunt.
30. The troubled arrival of Macià in Buenos Aires—he was arrested by the Alvear government while walking down the Avenida de Mayo and deported to Uruguay—only further enhanced Argentine interest in Catalan culture, and one can assume, Torrendell's

role as an in-house expert. As Hipolit Mallol, then one of the leading Argentine-based Catalan intellectuals put it at the time: "El cas Macià interessa tothom, i Catalunya i els seus ideals de llibertat, la seva cultura, l'art, la ciència, els costums, la seva personalitat nacional, en suma, són coneguts per tot el món. No passa dia que els diaris argentins no en parlin i que les agències no envïien telegrames que es refereixen als fets que es desenvolupen" (Fabregat I, 95) (The Macià case interests everyone. Catalonia and its ideal of liberty, its culture, its art, its science, its customs, in short, its national personality are known to all. Not a day goes by without the Argentine newspapers talking about it and the wire services sending telegrams that transmit the latest developments in the story).

31. Up until 1930, Torrendell apparently also wrote a column called "Llibres, llibres, llibres" for *Catalònia,* the sponsored publication of the *Centre Català,* an organization which would merge with the *Casal Català de Buenos Aires* in 1941. The joint organization adopted the name of the *Casal de Catalunya.* See Rocamora 215.

32. A bilingual journal published in Buenos Aires from 1921 to 1926 and again from 1934 to 1936. In the first period it was described as a publication centering on "Información pollensina, balear y catalana." In its second incarnation it was described as a "Quincenario balear, Arte, Literatura e Información." For more on this publication see Surroca 340–41.

33. Alcover 96.

34. Given what we have seen so far, the assumption of this first identity might at first seem incongruous. However, when we look more closely, we can see that it is very much in keeping with his overall intellectual outlook. Though Torrendell had always identified quite strongly with the Catalan nationalist project, he had never done so in a way that obviated (either politically or discursively) the existence of Spain or his condition as a Spaniard. As we have seen, he, like his mentor Miquel dels Sants Oliver, never saw any contradiction in using the Castilian language for Catalanist purposes. More telling still, was his openness to Iberianism while at *La cataluña,* a posture which gained him the enmity of the hierarchy of the *Lliga.* To embrace Iberianism is to accept *unambiguously* (rather than through an accidentalist focus) the enormous political and cultural weight of Castile in the Peninsula, and the need for its cooperation in any future solution to the Catalan national problem. Upon arriving in Argentina, Torrendell's "catholicity" on the issue of identity was made manifest yet again when he signed on as an occasional collaborator with *El diario español,* the most important "Spanish" publication in the Plata Region.

35. In 1934, the venerable journal of Bianchi and Giusti fell on difficult financial times and had to cease publication. It finally re-appeared at the beginning of 1936, thanks in large part to the support given to it by Torrendell and Rafael Vehils, a fellow Catalan and long-time manager of Francesc Cambó's South American utility company, CHADE (Compañía Hispanoamericana de Electricidad). See Zuleta, 23.

Works Cited

Abós, Álvaro. "Pasión por los libros." *La Nación Line* 4 enero 2004. <www.lanacion.com.ar>.
Actes del Primer Congrés Internacional de la Llengua Catalana. Barcelona: Estampa de Joaquim Horta, 1908.
Aguirre y Lecube, José Antonio. *De Guernica a Nueva York pasando por Berlín.* Bilbao: EKIN, 1992.
Alcover, Manuela. "La 'Missió d'art a l'Argentina.'" *Actes del congrés internacional d'estudis históricos de Les Balears i América.* Coord. Román Piña Homs. *Palma* III. Palma: Institut d'Estudis Baleàrics (gener 1992): 89–110.
Amengual, Bartolomeo. *El optimismo que debemos tener. Cosas de hoy en artículos de ayer.* Barcelona: Artes Gráficas, 1924.
———. *La industria de los forasteros.* Pròleg de Joan Alcover. Palma: Amengual i Muntaner, 1903.
Ardao, Arturo. *Etapas de la inteligencia uruguaya.* Montevideo: Departamento de Publicaciones, Universidad de la República, 1971.
———. *Espiritualismo y positivismo en el Uruguay: filosofías universitariás de la segunda mitad del siglo XIX.* México, D.F.: Fondo de Cultura Económica, 1950.
Barrios, Eduardo. "Figuras de América: Juan Torrendell." *Nosotros* 1–161 (octubre 1922): 268–71.
Bastons, Carles i Moisés Stankowich. "La correspondència de mallorquins a Unamuno. Cartes de Joan Torrendell." *Estudis de llengua i literatura en honor de Joan Veny* II. Barcelona: Publicacions de l'Abadia de Montserrat. 355–76.
Beretta Curi, Alcides. "La burgesía catalana, el comerç amb América i el port de Barcelona." *Quaderns d'America/Revista Americanista de Catalunya* 1 (maig 1987): 8–13.
Biagini, Hugo. *Intelectuales y políticos españoles a comienzos de la inmigración masiva.* Buenos Aires: Centro Editor de América Latina, 1995.
———. "Els intellectuals catalans a l'Atenes del Plata." *L'Avenc* 143 (1990): 62–65.
Bianchi, Alfredo. *Veinticinco años de vida intelectual argentina. Historia sintética de 'Nosotros.'* Buenos Aires, 1932.
Buades Crespí, Joan. "La emigración masiva de de mallorquines a Argentina y a Chile en el año 1889. Las causas y el debate que origina en la prensa local." <http://www.uib.es/catedra_iberoamericana/>.
———. "Panorama bibliográfico sobre la emigració balear a Ultramar." *Iberoamericana* I. 3 (2003): 229–40.
———. "L'emigració balear a l'Uruguai en els Segles XIX i XX. El movement associatiu." *Actas del congrés internacional d'estudis históricos de Les Balears i América.* Coord. Román Pina Homs. *Palma* III. Palma: Institut d'Estudis Baleàrics (gener 1992): 129–49.
Carrió Trujillano, Bartomeu. "Les publicacions nacionalistes a Mallorca al primer terç del segle XX." *La premsa, la ràdio i la televisió des d'una perspectiva histórica.* Palma: Institut d'Estudis Baleàrics, 1993. 69–83.

Coll, María Rosa. Personal Interview, March 24, 2004.
Costa Ruibal, Oscar. *L'imaginari imperial: el Noucentisme català i la política internacional.* Barcelona: Institut Cambó, 2002.
Diccionari dels catalans d'América; contribució a un inventari biogràfic, toponímic i temátic. 4 vols. Barcelona: Comissió Amèrica i Catalunya 1992, Generalitat de Catalunya, 1992–1993.
"En honor de Torrendell." *La cataluña* 146 (23 julio 1910): 465.
Escalas y Chamení, Fèlix. *Bartolomé Amengual y Andreu: Hijo Ilustre de Felanitx.* Barcelona: Gráfica Moderna, 1929.
Fabregat, Ramon, ed. *Macià, la seva actuació a l'estranger.* 2 vols. Mèxic: Edicions Catalanes de Mèxic, 1952.
Ferreira, Eduardo. "Semblanza literaria" prólogo de Juan Torrendell. *El picaflor. (cuadros montevideanos).* Montevideo: Cuspinera, Teix y Cia., 1894.
Franco, Jean. *Historia de la literatura hispanoamericana.* 5a edición. Barcelona: Ariel, 1983.
Gálvez, Manuel. *Recuerdos de la Vida literaria 1 (Amigos y maestros de mi juventud, En el mundo de los seres ficticios).* Prólogo Beatriz Sarlo. Buenos Aires: Taurus, 2002.
Giusti, Roberto. *Crítica y Polémica.* 4 vols. Buenos Aires: Nosotros, 1917–1930.
Guirao Motis, Antoni. "La Cataluña. Ideologia i poder a la Catalunya noucentista (1907–1914)." Ph.D. Diss. Universitat de Barcelona, 1998.
Harrington, Thomas S. "Belief, Institutional Practices and Intra-Iberian Relations." *España fuera de España.* Ed. Luis Fernández-Cifuentes. Lewisburg: Bucknell University Press, 2004.
———. "Rapping on the Cast(i)le Gates: Insurgent Culture-Planning in Twentieth Century Spain." *Ideologies of Hispanism.* Ed. Mabel Moraña. *Hispanic Issues* 30. Nashville: Vanderbilt University Press, 2004. 107–37.
———. "Las cinco cabezas del nacionalismo ibérico." *Claves de Razón Práctica* 130 (Marzo, 2003): 64–73.
———. "El Cercle Maristany y la interpenetració dels sistemes literaris de la Península Ibérica." *Revista de Catalunya* 175 (juliol/agost 2002): 107–27.
———. "Catalanism in the Portuguese Mirror: Skirmishes Between 'Unitarians' and 'Pluralists' for Control of the Movement (1900–1925)." *Revista de Estudios Hispánicos* 35 (2001): 257–80.
"Los catalanes en la República Oriental del Uruguay." *El progreso Catalán en América.* Vol. 3 Santiago: Blaya y Giralt, 1925. 433–82.
Manresa Montserrat, Maria Antonia i Margalida A. Mas Barceló. "El Balear: Publicació dels Emigrants illencs a L'Argentina." *Actas del congrés internacional d'estudis històrics de Les Balears I América.* Coord. Román Pina Homs. *Palma* III. Palma: Institut d'Estudis Baleàrics (gener 1992): 277–95.
Marimon Riutort, Antoni. *La crisi de 1898 a les Illes Balears: repercussions polítiques i ideològiques de les guerres de Cuba i de les Filipines.* Palma: El Tall, 1997.
Mas i Pí, Juan. *Letras españolas.* Buenos Aires: N. A., 1911.

———. *Ideaciones. Letras de América, Ideas de Europa*. Barcelona: F. Granada y Cia, 1908.
Morató Rodríguez, Octavio. "Víctor Pérez Petit." *Revista Nacional* (Montevideo) 189 (julio-septiembre 1956): 1–8.
Moya, José. *Cousins and Strangers: Spanish Immigrants in Buenos Aires, 1850–1930*. Berkeley: University of California Press, 1998.
Naranjo, Consuelo. "El Aluvión, 1880–1930—Análisis cuantitativo." *Historia general de la emigración española a Iberoamérica*. Vol I. Madrid: Historia 16 (1992): 177–200.
Oddone Falcón, Juan. "Federico Rahola i Trémols, promotor de l'americanisme català." *Jornades d'Estudis Catalano-Americans 3*. Ed. Carlos Martínez Shaw. Barcelona: Generalitat de Catalunya, Departament de la Presidència, Comissió Amèrica i Catlunya. 171–82.
Oliver, Miquel dels Sants. "Ratificación." *La cataluña* 146 (23 julio 1910): 458.
Paris de Oddone, M. Blanca. *Figuras e instituciones catalanas en el Uruguay*. Montevideo: Florensa y Lafón, 1960.
Pereyra, Washington. *La prensa literaria argentina*. 2 Vols. Buenos Aires: Colonial, 1993.
Pérez Petit, Víctor. "Juan Torrendell." *Nosotros* 53–204 (mayo de 1926): 163–206.
Pericay, Xavier, ed. *Julio Camba. Gaziel. Josep Pla. Manuel Chaves Nogales: cuatro historias de la República*. Barcelona: Destino, 2002
Pons i Pons, Damià. *El diari "La Almudaina" en l'epoca de Miquel S. Oliver*. Binissalem: Edicions Di7, 1998.
———. *Ideología i cultura a la Mallorca d'entre dos segles (1886–1905)*. Palma: Lleonard Muntaner, 1998.
———. "Joan Torrendell: Entre el modernisme vitalista i el regeneracionsime d'esquerres." Introducció de Juan Torrendell. *Els encarrilats*. Barcelona: Publicacions de l'Abadia de Montserrat, 1998. 6–78.
———. "Aproximació a Joan Torrendell (1869–1937)." *Affar* I (1981): 105–118.
Puiggros, Ernesto, María del Carmen Medina Pintado and Uruguay R. Vega Castillos. *La inmigración española en el Uruguay: catalanes, gallegos y vascos*. Mexico: Instituto Panamericano de Geografía e Historia/ Organización de Estados Americanos, 1991.
Rahola y Tremols, Federico. *Sangre nueva*. Buenos Aires: El Elefante Blanco, 2002.
———. *Comercio de Cataluña con América en el siglo XVIII*. Barcelona: Henrich y Cía., 1931.
Reyes Abadie, Washington. *Españoles en el Uruguay*. Montevideo: Banda Oriental, 2000.
Rocamora Cuatrecasas, Joan. *Catalanes en la Argentina*. Centenario del Casal de Cataluña. Buenos Aires: Arte Gráficas el Fénix, 1992.
———. *El casal de Catalunya a Buenos Aires. Catalans a Buenos Aires*. Barcelona: Curial, 1991.
Rucabado, Ramón. "Torrendell." *La cataluña* 146 (23 julio 1910): 458–59.
Sarramone, Alberto. *Cataluña y los catalanes en el Plata*. Azul Argentina: Editorial Biblos Azul, 2004.
"Saludo a D. Juan Torrendell." *La Cataluña* 148 (6 agosto 1910): 497.

Schwartzstein, Dora. *Entre Franco y Perón*. Barcelona: Crítica, 2001.
Serra, Antoni. *Gabriel Alomar (l'honestidat difícil)*. Palma: Ajuntament de Palma, 1984.
Serra Busquets, Sebastià. "Les publicacions periòdiques dels emigrants de les illes Balears a América." *La premsa, la ràdio i la televisió des d'una perspectiva histórica*. Palma: Institut d'Estudis Baleàrics, 1993. 551–60.
———. "La emigración de la Islas Baleares a Iberoamerica." *Historia general de la emigración española a Iberoamérica*. Madrid: Historia 16 (1992): 87–114.
———. "L'emigració de les Illes Balears a América." *Actas del congrés internacional d'estudis històrics de Les Balears I América*. Coord. Román Pina Homs. *Palma* III. Palma: Institut d'Estudis Baleàrics (gener 1992): 9–46.
———. "*La Veu de Mallorca*: una publicació nacionalista entre 1900 i 1931." *Mayurga* 20 (1981–84): 293–318.
Solé i Cavallé, Josep. *Casal català de Montevideo 1926–1996*. Montevideo: Editorial Blanes, 1997.
Surroca i Tallaferro, Robert. *Premsa Catalan del'exili i de l'emigració*. Barcelona: Generalitat de Catalunya, 2004.
Torrendell Larravide, Beatriz. Personal Interview. April 19, 2004.
Torrendell, Juan. *Cataluña y la República Española: Diario de un periodista residente en Buenos Aires*. Buenos Aires: Editorial Tor, 1936.
———. *La república española en su primer hervor: Diario de un periodista residente en Buenos Aires*. Buenos Aires: Editorial Tor, 1935.
———. *Crítica menor II*. Buenos Aires: Editorial Tor, 1934.
———. *Crítica menor I*. Buenos Aires: Editorial Tor, 1933.
———. *Las lenguas de España*. Buenos Aires: Centre Català, 1933. (Re-edición de un articulo aparecido en *Nosotros* en julio y agosto de 1933).
———. *La literatura catalana en su actual renacimiento*. Buenos Aires: Centre Català, 1928.
———. *Los concursos literarios y otros ensayos*. Buenos Aires: Editorial Tor, 1925.
———. *El año literario 1918*. Buenos Aires: Editorial Tor, 1918.
———. *Els dos Esperits*. Palma de Mallorca: Tipogràfic de Francisco Soler, 1902.
———. *Don Joan Palou i Coll. Estudi Crític*. Palma: Estampa d'Amengual i Muntaner, 1902.
———. *Els Encarrilats*. Barcelona: Tipografía L'Avenç, 1901.
———. *Los encarrilados*. Palma: Tipo-litografia de Bartomeu Rotger, 1901.
———. *Clarín y su ensayo*. Barcelona: López Editor, 1895.
———. *Pimpollos. Novelitas montevideanas*. Barcelona: A. López, 1895.
———. *El picaflor. (cuadros montevideanos)*. Montevideo: Cuspinera, Teix y Cia., 1894.
Ulla, Noemí. *La revista Nosotros*. Buenos Aires: Galerna, 1969.
Zuleta, Carmen de. *Relaciones literarias entre España y la Argentina*. Madrid: Ediciones Culutra Hispánica del Instituto de Cooperación Iberoamericana, 1983.

◆ 5

The Foxes by José María Arguedas: A Death Warrant for Peru's Modern National Project

José Antonio Giménez Micó

(Translated by Kate Alvo)

In 2001, after almost a decade of neo-populist and neo-liberal authoritarianism led by *El Chino* Alberto Fujimori, Alejandro Toledo, *El Cholo*, takes on the presidency of Peru. The word *cholo*, which has no direct translation into English, refers both to people of mixed race as well as to Indians who have adopted occidental habits and customs. It is important to point out that *cholo*, like *indio*, has been—and continues to be—a pejorative term, similar to *chicano* in the Southwestern United States or *mambí* in Cuba (Giménez Micó 2001: 320–21); and, just as these terms were vindicated under particularly rebellious historical circumstances, Toledo's electoral discourse submits *cholo* to a total axiological inversion: it is time, for the presidential candidate and for those who identify with him, to be proud to be *cholos*.

Toledo is not, however, a regular *cholo*: the new president can also pride himself on being a self-made man who, through hard work, has gone from being a shoe-shiner and door-to-door salesman as a boy to receiving a scholarship that allowed him to pursue his studies in the USA, where he obtained a Ph.D. in Economics from Stanford University. This, however, does not change the fact that one of the most important trump cards in his electoral campaign is precisely that of his native heritage. In his most impassioned discourses, the presidential candidate summons *el Perú profundo* (deepest Peru) presenting himself as the genuine descendant of the Incas: the new *Pachakutek Inca* who will restore, at least symbolically, the *Tawantinsuyo* or "Inca Empire." The "Andean Utopia" or "return of the Incas," that fundamental component of the Andean imaginary that emerged in colonial times (Burga 52–53), once again shows its cohesive strength.

Born in the Andes in the mid-1940s, Toledo immigrated with his large family to the coastal city of Chimbote when he was five years old. His family was one out of many who, since the 1940s and, in greater numbers since the 1950s, have been massively emigrating to the coastal cities of Peru that were, up until then, reserved mainly for *criollos* (descendants of the European colonizers). This erruption of large segments of the Andean population in the coastal cities, studied by Peruvian sociologist José Matos Mar in his book *The Popular Overflow* (1984, 2004), has radically modified all aspects of Peruvian life: urban, socio-political, linguistic, and cultural.

The Foxes: A Snapshot of the "Popular Overflow"

The literary work that best dramatizes this "popular overflow" is probably José María Arguedas' novel *El zorro de arriba y el zorro de abajo* (The Fox From Up Above and the Fox From Down Below), 1969; from now on, *The Foxes*.

The Foxes is indeed a post-indigenist and post-realist novel about migration: the majority of its characters are *serranos* (highlanders), most of whom have just arrived in the Peruvian coastal city of Chimbote. The young Alejandro Toledo, who lived in Chimbote between 1950 and the mid-1960s, could well have been one of the novel's characters.

The Foxes is a Babelian work in which the Spanish and Andean languages are in contact and constant conflict. The means of expression used by the two worlds ("from up above," i.e., the Andean communities, and "from down below," the coastal cities) are presented as radically different, if not opposites of each other.

History: Quechua in the Viceroyalty of Peru

In order to understand the novel's diglossic, dialogical and Babelian implications, it is essential to take into account the conflictive history of languages in Peru since the Conquest, a history which is inextricably related to the genesis and development of what Fernando Aínsa called the "dialectic of antimonies"

(Aínsa 2). Broadly speaking, this dialectic comes into play in the initial opposition between "White vs. Indian" that is established during the time of conquest and colonization and reappears in the other, more subtle opposition of "nationality (Mexican, Bolivian, Peruvian, and so on) vs. Indigenous Peoples" that we find in the nineteenth and twentieth centuries.

Unlike the Spanish Empire, the Tawantinsuyo never aimed to homogenize the great cultural diversity of its territory, which consisted of numerous macro ethnicities and their own habits, customs and languages (Rostworowski 3–28); the farthest it got was to impose Quechua as the language of communication, or rather to recognize it as such, since this language had been used for centuries between the different communities for commercial purposes (Torero 145–50).

In 1550, a royal order stipulated that, since "even in the most perfect Indian language the mysteries of our Holy Catholic Faith [cannot] be well and properly explained . . . , it would be worthwhile to introduce the Spanish language," for which it was ordered "that the Indians become teachers, that they teach whomever wishes to be taught, in the easiest way and without cost" (quoted in Torero 195).[1] The complex and stubborn reality would deal with thwarting the imperial plans of Charles I. Quechua not only did not diminish in importance during the sixteenth and seventeenth centuries, but it extended to regions that it had never before accessed (Potosi, Quito, Santiago del Estero, part of the Amazon), to the point that the clergy began calling it "Indian's Latin."

The Spanish, far outnumbered by the "Natives," quickly discovered that it would be impossible to impose Spanish, as well as the virtues of this "general language" that allowed them, more than any other language, to spread their colonial dominion, not only in purely military terms, but also from a commercial and, of course, religious perspective (Glave 455). "It was only from this utilitarian perspective that they showed interest in their learning, turning it into a refined instrument for domination, particularly in the ideological imposition of the dominant class" (Cerrón Palomino 42). Let us remember that, at the time of the conquest, the "Natives" did not make up one undifferentiated population, but rather an extremely complex social fabric in which, for example, Natives from Cusco were considered to be oppressors by most others.

The progression of Quechua, with the consequent (and very relative) dissolution of the different local identities into "one" Indigenous voice (to which those of the popular sectors of Hispanic and African origin would be added as a result of colonization), did not prevent, but rather facilitated the establishment of a diglossia of Spanish/Indigenous languages, which reflected, in general terms, the opposition between writing and orality.

The progression of the main languages of a dominated people at its most subjugated as well as the relative autonomy of its cultural practices, can only be adequately understood if we take into account the complexity of the relationships that are established in any colonial situation. The opposition between "oppressors" and "oppressed" surely exists and has devastating effects, but we should resist the temptation to reduce this to a simple deterministic dichotomy that clumsily imitates the dialectic between master and slave, according to which the oppressor forcibly imposes his language, culture, religion and world view on a population that can only submit or openly rebel. We know it is not that simple. The diversity and specificity of each of the ex-colonies confirm that the thin homogenizing layer of colonial society more or less concealed ambiguities, subtle resistances, apparent subjugations, syncretism, various hybridities, always imperfect assimilations, interpretative conflicts, mutual incomprehension and contaminations, appropriations of the opposing discourse and unconscious transformations of one's own discourse: in short, an always-problematic contact zone (as defined by Pratt) in which the identities of the colonized and the colonizers were being forged, modified and made more complex; all of which was due to the bi- or pluri-cultural dialogue, always asymmetrical and often dysphoric, which, whether they wanted to or not, the different groups had to maintain with each other.

That is irrelevant due to the overly-generalized tendency to consider that "acculturation" only goes one way, as if North and South American "Western culture" had simply been a transplant, graft or "appendage" of European culture, which had remained "intact" since its advent. What really happens when a society imposes its political, military, economic and, therefore, cultural domination on another is that "in this encounter, the conqueror himself is also transformed, since in order to assert himself he must certainly take into account the concrete society he sees before him and adapt to it" (Ansion 48). It's not for nothing that Mary Louise Pratt defines transculturation—once this notion, like in fact the notion of "dialogue," is freed from any idealization—as a phenomenon characteristic of contact zones (6–7). From there it follows that, alongside but so far from scholarly literature written in Quechua—whose main function was none other than the evangelization (that is, the acculturation) of the Indigenous masses—in the viceroyalty of Peru we find the "permanence of the arts, such as theatre or choreographed folkloric plays, and orality in the creation and transmission of a Quechua tradition" (Glave 476); and not only the permanence of what is one's own, but also the reworking of what is foreign according to one's own cultural models. That is what happened, for example, with the Eucharistic plays, which flooded the streets and plazas of the

Andes during the festivities of the Corpus Christi and which, with time, "were assimilated by *Qosqan* [and other] folklore, turning this theatrical expression into a Hispano-Quechua hybrid" (Avendaño 1: 145).

Indigenous Cultural Practices since Independence

With the independence movement, Quechua progressively began to lose ground since the *criollo* ruling classes on the coast no longer needed to use Quechua to interact socially with the Andean people. This new internal colonialism, established with the creation of Spanish-American states, enabled the new elites to draw up modern national plans based on those of France and England, or the recently-formed United States, in which any element regarded as non-European was immediately marginalized.

This situation began to change toward the end of the nineteenth century, when an ever-growing *mestizo* population began to access economic and political centres of power (Rama 1982: 141–42). Indigenism was the medium they used to spread their *"mestizo"* conception of society.

I will not go into a detailed description of the various indigenist discursive practices. I will, however, point out that, despite their ideological differences which were, on occasion, extreme (from the defence of North American-style capitalistic progress to "Inca" socialism), all forms of Indigenism arise—as is dictated by paternalism—through Indian-authorized spokesmen who advocate Indian "integration" into national society by way of acculturation. Rama refers to this phenomenon as "Indigenism of Mesticism" (1982: 152).

The ideologeme of *mestizaje* conveyed through Indigenism, and which became hegemonic towards the 1950s, triumphs, at least on the surface, where *criollo* Americanism fails: in the assertion of a specific identity, which is considered essential for the construction of different nationalisms, including Latin Americanism (see Chiampi 18). Since then, there have been numerous Latin American texts in which

> se representa a la nación como un espacio abigarrado en el que se yuxtaponen tiempos diferentes y culturas diferentes. Esto da lugar a un ... gesto reivindicativo de revalorización del *pasado*, especialmente *el pasado* de culturas no alfabetizadas en el momento mismo de la modernización. (Franco 414; my emphasis)

> (the nation is represented as a colourful space in which different times and cultures are juxtaposed. This leaves space for a ... gesture of protest for the revaluation of the *past*, especially the *past* of illiterate cultures in the very moment of modernization.)

The problem here is that this gesture does not manage to re-evaluate the *present* of these same cultures. What is more, the appropriation of certain *past* Indigenous cultural traits (or traits considered as such) occurs only once these features have passed through a Western filter (that provided by the Spanish language and by scientific disciplines dedicated to the "translation" of otherness such as anthropology and ethnic history (Lienhard 1987, 560). To borrow a metaphor used in the philosophy of language, the (pseudo-) native elements "integrated" into *mestizo* discourse are *mentioned*, but never *used*. They are noticed, displaced temporally, and converted into things of the past, into something different, strange, foreign: *other*. As Mariátegui pointed out in the 1920s (275), "indigenist" is not synonymous with "Indigenous." Quite the opposite.

Arguedas and *dualismo*

As such, writing which explicitly advocates continental heterogeneity (through generalized *mestizaje* and transculturation) can only exist if it emphasizes that the homogenization of this diversity works to the detriment of internal otherness, languages and cultures which are judged once again as "things of the past." In this way, the dialectic of antimonies endures what has come to be called *dualismo*, according to which Peru consists of two worlds that are completely alien in relation to each other. Any attempt at simple contact without mixing is destined to fail. Indigenists and hispanists alike have, each from their own "world," fuelled this *topos*, which in turn has sustained their sometimes extreme polemic positions.

The problem with *dualismo* is that while showing on an explicit textual level the dynamism and vitality of the group for which the enunciator establishes himself as spokesperson, it presupposes the immutability of *all* the elements that make up its discursive universe. It is only from this radical negation of transformations that we can conceive of two pure worlds, free from all outside contact.

Is Arguedas merely situating himself on the side of the Indigenous person, as has been claimed by a number of commentators of his work? The wisest analysts of his oeuvre refuse to classify his last works as being purely and simply indigenist, the growing problematization of *dualismo* being one of the most conclusive pieces of evidence that he does not conform to this ultimately Manichaean discursive practice. Thus, for example, *Todas las sangres*, the novel that precedes *The Foxes*, does not entirely escape the fundamental aporia of this practice. Now, some of the "anomalies"—such as non-conformity with regards to *dualismo*—indicate that it is a badly-greased wheel that squeaks and grinds, but turns all the same: that makes it possible for the now hegemonic *mestizo*-Hispanic dialectic of antimonies to run.

At this point, Arguedas' fundamental contribution comes into play. As I have pointed out elsewhere, "The 'market of social identities' established by *dualismo* cannot satisfy Arguedas, since his personal experience contradicts the cognitive adaptation of this discourse" (Giménez Micó 1994: 6). Arguedas' unstable position (Hispanized by his social status but Quechuized by professional and biographical circumstances as well as, most of all, by life choices) does not allow him to fit into either of the two spaces offered by the ruling dialectic of antimonies, nor does it facilitate the finding of a new space which would supersede the other two. Arguedas' way of *taking position*, uncertain and hesitant, is, paradoxically, to not take a clear position at all. Or, perhaps it is better expressed by his demonstration, precisely through his indeterminacy, of the limits of *dualismo*.

Todas las sangres cannot be reduced to any doctrine, be it indigenist or hispanist. It is true that the novel conveys the ideologeme of cultural mixing and transculturation, but it is less about defending any specific thesis than about laying bare any form of *dualismo*. *Todas las sangres* does not "know" what the Peruvian nation is, but at least it "knows" what it is not. This kind of inverse knowledge can be easily verbalized, as an eminent specialist on Indigenism, Eugenio Chang-Rodríguez, does fifteen years later: "Peru is not a dichotomy, antinomical nor two-sided by nature" (392). And the Peruvian critic affirms that "it is a many-sided country, with a large variety of components. The Indian is but one part of a multicoloured whole that is at once multicultural and multilingual" (392).

I am not sure that *Todas las sangres* could back up that last assertion. Of course, the novel problematizes *dualismo*, but that does not mean it is exactly out-of-date. Even if *dualismo* has been forced to show certain of its failings, it remains practically the only universe to which *Todas las sangres* can refer. It is as if the novel knew that Peru was much richer than *dualismo* would have it believe, without necessarily succeeding in showing this multiplicity except in some very fragmentary and confused way. For its part, *The Foxes* will only increase this confusion which is, in the final analysis, a confusion of identities.

Now, would not the "identity of confusion" (Giménez-Micó 1994: 40) be the only way to *truly* express this multiplicity of which the "many-sided," the "diverse," the "heterogeneous," the "multicultural," and so on, are only pale reflections, vain attempts to escape the dialectic of antimonies? As Deleuze and Parnet point out,

> a multiplicity is not defined by the number of its terms. We can always add a 3rd to 2, a 4th to 3, etc., we do not escape dualism in this way, since the elements of any set whatever can be related to a succession of choices which are themselves binary. (34)

The critical discourse of Chang-Rodríguez against *dualismo* (his anti-*dualismo*), coherent and univocal, is thus vested with another dualism—with another dichotomy—which, to be specific, could be classified according to the following schematization:

TRUE: Peru = multiform, multicultural, etc.
vs
FALSE: Peru = a dichotomy, antinomical and two-sided by nature

This should not be understood as a refutation of Chang-Rodríguez's argument, which I in fact agree with, but more as an example of the subjection of language—specifically, the language of criticism—to the dialectic of antimonies. Like it or not, "we must pass through [*passer par*] dualisms because they are in language, it's not a question of getting rid of them, but we must fight against language, invent stammering" (Deleuze and Parnet 34).

A critic must be aware that resorting to the dialectic of antimonies is inevitable, but should not stop at that. Nothing stops them from trying to work out a literary text where this "fight against language," this "stammering," this "confused" language occurs. It seems to me that *The Foxes* easily lends itself to experience, all the more so since the "stammering" implemented in this text, far from being a clumsiness attributable to a lack of linguistic control or a simple stylistic device, is symptomatic—doubtless in a much more radical way than in *Todas las sangres*—of the dislocation of identity peculiar to the contemporary world, as well as its consequences; this "transformation born of new and unexpected combinations" so dear to Salman Rushdie (30), one of the authors who has best thematized contemporary hybridity.

Arguedas and the Question of Language

The Foxes reflects on a problem of language, that is, of culture, ideology, and identity, which Arguedas has confronted throughout his oeuvre. This is indeed characterized by the fact that, while being (or seeming to be) written in the legitimate language (so-called standard Spanish), this language is "corrupted" from a traditional linguistic point of view.

But language is never a perfect code that works in a homogeneous community and whose only function is communication. Ultimately, "language is not neutral, not informative. Language is not made to be believed but to be obeyed" (Deleuze and Parnet 22). There is a comparison to be made between the instrument of social control we call the dialectic of antimonies and one of its main parts: the legitimate language—specifically, Spanish. This language has constituted a key obstacle for Arguedas since the beginning of his literary career, as the author himself reflected around the 1930s:

> If we speak in *pure Spanish*, we say nothing of the landscape nor of our inner world; because the *mestizo* has not yet mastered the Spanish language and made it his own, and Kechwa is still his legitimate means of expression. But if we write in Kechwa, we make narrow literature that is condemned to oblivion. (Escobar 76)

This reflection is symptomatic of the double constraint that Arguedas must overcome: his oeuvre must be readable, but this requires the use of the legitimate language. Now, Arguedas is convinced that this practice brings about "the mark of all the errors, discriminations, dominations and destructions that, through the intervention of language, were—and are still being—carried out" (Gómez-Moriana 12). Since Peruvian Spanish is a deterritorialized language as well as a machine to deterritorialize other languages, Arguedas' minor literature finds itself at an impasse similar to that of Kafka and the rest of the Czech Jews in Vienna at the turn of the century: that of living "between three impossibilities . . . : the impossibility to not write, the impossibility to write in German [read "in Spanish"] and the impossibility to write otherwise" (Kafka 395).

We understand why Arguedas could not have written his literary works in "pure Spanish." In a sense, they are written in Spanish *and* they are not written in Spanish, since Quechua (and, to a lesser degree, Aymara) always makes itself felt, either as a more or less stealthy presence or as a trace of its absence.

Let me explain. The awkwardness of Arguedas' idiolect, though it is sometimes apparent through words, phrasings and some Quechua syntactical structures (a sign of the presence of this language), transcends them, permeating Arguedas' entire oeuvre: as well as the real signs of the dominated language, there are also numerous simulated traces that constitute as many signs of its absence. In order to properly understand this double issue of the "presence-absence of the dominated language," we must take into account the fact that the people of "down below" whom Arguedas' oeuvre addresses do not, for the mostpart, know Quechua. That is why the investment of this language in Arguedas' texts, whether syntactical, lexical or otherwise, is merely incidental; what matters is to "be bilingual even in a single language" (Deleuze and Parnet 4).

In the works preceding *The Foxes*, this minor use of the major language is accomplished through a "fiction" that Peruvian linguist Alberto Escobar describes as follows:

> La ficción que resuelve el dilema consiste en hacer que el indio quechuahablante se produzca fluidamente *como si* lo hiciera en su lengua materna, y que el lector lo lea *como si* la comprendiera. Esta mecánica supone dos cuestiones: *a*. el lector sabe que él no domina ni conoce el quechua; y *b*. sabe así mismo (*sic*) que el actor indio no tiene control suficiente del castellano y que aparece como si estuviera hablando en quechua... El castellano es lo presente y el quechua la lengua copresente. (72)

> (The fiction that resolves the dilemma consists of having the Quechua-speaking Indian express himself fluently *as if* he were speaking in his mother tongue, and making the reader read *as if* she understood his language. This mechanism implies two things: *a*. the reader knows that she does speak or know Quechua; and *b*. she also knows that the Indian actor does not have sufficient control over the Spanish language and gives the impression of speaking in Quechua... Spanish is the present and Quechua the co-present language.)

The most conventional way of creating this fiction is obviously to add an explanatory comment from the narrator, like "he said in Quechua," "he affirmed in perfect Spanish," and so on. It is well and truly a realistic "fiction," since it presupposes that, even if the Andean "world" is presented by the narrator himself as being radically different (*ma non troppo*) from the world the reader knows, this world's language can be translated with no problem. The narrator can thus transmit information and voices from the other world, since any language, including Quechua, is presupposed to be outside the real, simple form that serves to express a content that itself is presupposed to be homogeneous.[2] In this way, Arguedas successfully appropriates the legitimate language in order to "update the Quechua message" (Escobar 72), and Spanish thus undergoes a double movement of deterritorialization as an instrument of oppression and of reterritorialization as a new means of expression for the whole community.[3] It could not have been otherwise, given what Arguedas had planned in his youth: to build, through literature, a strong living link, capable of being universalized, between the great, walled-in nation and the generous, humane side of the oppressors (Arguedas 1990, 269).

Todas las sangres, as well as Arguedas' earlier texts, advocates reterritorialization as the only solution to the problem of identity for Peruvians, be they "from up above" or "from down below." Regardless of our writer's temperament and experience, this project of global reterritorialization was made possible through the existence, in the Latin American sociodiscursive universe, of the ideologeme of cultural mixing and of transculturation.

The Foxes and the Tower of Babel

This characteristic trait of Arguedas' oeuvre before *The Foxes* no longer works for his posthumous novel. That is why the minor use of the major language is only accentuated in *The Fox from Up Above and the Fox from Down Below*. Now, its reterritorializing mechanism is out of order since there is no longer a homogeneous vision of the contemporary reality of Chimbote, much less a coherent outline of its future. Everything is fragmentary, more or less comprehensible, irreducible to any kind of preconceived schematization. Both the referent and the old system of references seem to dissolve, which pushes the text toward a disinvestment in the mimetic indigenist system of representation. For its part, the language appears more or less dispossessed of its capacity for communication. Arguedas' minor literature, like Kafka's, seems henceforth to "move toward its extremities or its limits" (Deleuze and Guattari 1975: 23).

The destruction of a good portion of the realist conventions and the progressive dispossession of the communicative power of language (a "language" which is, strictly speaking, neither Spanish nor Quechua) do not at all mean that *The Foxes* has given up understanding and transmitting "what's happening in Chimbote and in the world" (Arguedas 1990: 83). These highly deterritorializing phenomena only confirm that Arguedas' posthumous novel is trying to rid itself of any pre-established constraints, which would consequently be inappropriate for this new reality, which might prevent it from completing this undertaking. The text seems to be saying: the reality of Chimbote is no longer realistic, the language no longer successfully represents the world; or, in any case, *this* world of Chimbote and the rest of the Peruvian coastal cities deterritorialized by the civilized capitalist machine. Deleuze and Guattari showed the immense deterritorializing power of the civilized capitalist machine, using *Capital* to support their argument (1972: 263–85). For his part, Lyotard relates this power to the so-called realist mode of representation:

But capitalism in itself has such a capacity to derealise [sic] familiar objects, social roles and institutions that so called [sic] "realist" representations can no longer evoke reality except through nostalgia or derision—as an occasion for suffering rather than satisfaction. (14)

The capitalist derealization becomes even more evident when we look into the speech of the *Serrano* characters, these *Cholos* that have abandoned their mother tongue while mastering only a few dozen or hundred Spanish words: "Now you take me little brother, beautiful Spanish he talks; when he was a little kid he escaped to Chimbote; now he doesn't wanna talk Quechua . . . Beautiful Spanish he talks; looks down on his sick market-pedlar brother nowadays" (*The Foxes* 144).

Here we have a very significant difference between the Indigenous peoples of indigenist accounts, oppressed in their own territory but proud to conserve and display their signs of collective identity, starting with the Quechua language, and the *Cholos* of Chimbote, speaking Spanish because they are eager to be reterritorialized: "to be like them" . . . but are paradoxically betrayed as being *Serranos* through their skewed language:

> Yu . . . criollo, carajo . . . ¿Quién serrano, ahura?, hablando se acercó a uno de los automóviles de plaza.
> —Oye, chofir—le dijo—a me casa, carajo. Hasta me casa.
> —¿Adónde vas, jefe?
> —¿Acero, barrio Acero? Pescador lancha zambo Mendieta, yo.
> —Barriada dirás, serrano—le corrigió el chofer.
> . . .
> —¿Conoces zambo Mendieta?—preguntó al chofer.
> —Sí "conoces." Es contra, recoge serranos brutos. (*The Foxes* 42)

> (Me *criollo* . . . from the coast, goddamnit . . . Who highlander now? still talking [with a high Andes accent] he went up to one of the cars in the lot.
> —Hey, driver—he said—To me house, damnit. As far as me house.
> —Where you goin,' boss?
> —Acero, Acero suburb? Fisherman *zambo* Mendieta trawler, me.
> —Acero slum you must be sayin,' highlander—the taxi driver corrected him.
> . . .
> —Ya knows *zambo* Mendieta?—he asked the taxi driver [using the familiar form of "you"].
> —Yeah, 'ya knows.' He does things the other way around; he picks up dumb highlanders.)

This dialogue is very telling of the fact that diglossia is the linguistic externalization of a social conflict that is much more complex than the unequal relationship between two languages—or two varieties—of the same language. Asto, a *cholo*, is a fisherman from Chimbote who certainly earns much more money than the *criollo* taxi driver, but this does not prevent the driver from speaking to him in a condescending manner. The driver's Spanish respects the norms, whereas Asto's Spanish is full of Quechuisms: the use of *i* instead of *e* (in the Quechua linguistic system, there is no distinction between these two vowels), the lack of articles and prepositions (Quechua is an inflected language), uncertainty as to the person in verb conjugation . . . The driver's last statement, "[your boss] picks up dumb highlanders," delegitimizes Asto's last attempt to dignify his social position.

The narrator's language, on the other hand, is not as neutral, or standard, and therefore *criollo*, as it seems: "still talking [with a high Andes accent] he went up to one of the cars in the lot" (*hablando se acercó . . .*). The bizarre use of the gerund gives away his distance from the norm and his proximity to an "irregular," minor, reality of the language, permeated with Quechua. The mise-en-scène of this sociolinguistic issue, as well as the position taken by the narrator, indicates that *The Foxes* also addresses one of Deleuze and Guattari's main concerns regarding minor literature:

> Combien de gens aujourd'hui vivent dans une langue qui n'est pas la leur? Ou bien ne connaissent même plus la leur, ou pas encore, et connaissent mal la langue majeure dont ils sont forcés de se servir? Problème des immigrés, et surtout de leurs enfants. Problème des minorités. Problème d'une littérature mineure. (1975: 19)

> (How many people today live in a language that is not their own? Or no longer, or not yet, even know their own and know poorly the major language that they are forced to serve? This is the problem of immigrants, and especially of their children, the problem of minorities, the problem of a minor literature.)

Arguedas' text often comes back to the double aspect of exclusion and self-hatred so characteristic of the *serranos* that have migrated toward the coast. The treatment of the sociolinguistic point of view might appear "normal" for a reader that is not well acquainted with Indigenism since it is within language conflicts that this problem is posed in the most transparent and indeed vicious way. Thus, this worrying subject—because it is symptomatic of the deterritorialization of the Indigenous person—was until then taboo or marginal in Indigenism in general and in Arguedas' literary oeuvre in particular. Didn't he declare in 1950 that it would be "false and horrendous to present Indians speaking in the Spanish of Quechua servants that have become used to the city" (Arguedas 1950, 71)? But now, it seems to me, the falsity would consist in "translating" the way of speaking of these *Cholos* into a stylized, more or less Quechuized Spanish that would be nonetheless legitimate because it would be comprehensible to the Hispanic reader—a realist process that Alberto Escobar has suitably qualified as "fiction."

This deterritorializing usage of the language and of the indigenist thematic material can only irritate those who, having opted for symbolic reterritorialization, however fantastical it may be, prefer to idealize the "authentic" indigenous person—or, better yet, "Andean man," who will "stay home" and will express himself very correctly in "his own language." The indigenist, who needs the "pure" Indigenous person just as the criminal lawyer needs the criminal or the firefighter needs the pyromaniac, loves the person who has preserved his "intimate, mythic connection with his threatened universe," that is he who, unlike Arguedas, has been able to turn away from deterritorialization:

> In Arguedas' three most important novels, we can see a growing, unconscious profusion of the degradation of his threatened universe; a disintegration of the intimate—mythic—connections that establish and maintain coherence in this universe ... The process of frustrating decline culminates with *The Foxes*, in Chimbote, this premonitory symbol of the devastation, dismantling and degradation of Peruvian society ... Chimbote, where we can see the fall, the decline of a community in moral and economic bankruptcy in which dignity rescinds ... There where time loses its bearings and language becomes Babelian—loses the essential meaning of communication. (Bareiro Saguier xvii)

Degradation, disintegration, decline, devastation, dismantling, fall, moral and economic bankruptcy, loss of the sense of communication ... All of these terms, once rid of their moralizing layer, come back to the same basic meaning: deterritorialization. With regards to deterritorialization and also to language, *The Foxes* is no stranger to Kafka's approach. If in Kafka "the situation of the German language in Prague—a withered vocabulary, an incorrect syntax—contribute to" the at-once creative and deterritorializing usage of the language (Deleuze and Guattari 1975: 22), the same goes for coastal Spanish, "Babelian," "multiform," "corrupted," in a constant process of transculturation presented in the Peruvian novel. It is a sometimes quasi-incomprehensible language for a Hispanic audience that does not know Quechua—that is, for the majority of Arguedas' readers, including professional readers of his work.

Part of the criticism, whether indigenist of hispanist, has been distress about this "language [that is] becoming more and more Babelian." It is disappointment at the loss of the stylistic quality of the texts that precede *The Foxes*, that is, the good old days when Arguedas was still able to "translate" the Quechua of his Indigenous characters into a Spanish that was a little strange, to be sure, but was so poetic . . . and, mostly, so easy to understand . . . .

> En esta Torre de Babel el lenguaje incomunica a las gentes. La mayor parte de ellas adolece de un habla tan dialectizada que entorpece la comunicación y divide al individuo, pues lo que dice es incapaz de expresar lo que siente y piensa . . . Se trata de un mundo afásico; su humanidad padece una perturbación lingüística cuyas causas son tanto psíquicas como sociales . . . Más verdadero es el lenguaje inventado de *Yawar Fiesta* o de *Los ríos profundos* que el de *El zorro de arriba y el zorro de abajo*, porque éste carece de elaboración artística, que es lo que da realidad a la literatura. (Vargas Llosa 1980: 25)

> (In this Tower of Babel, language isolates peoples. Most of them speak such extreme dialects that they hinder communication and divide the individual, since the words are incapable of expressing what the person is thinking or feeling . . . It is a mute world; its population suffers from a linguistic disturbance whose causes are both psychic and social . . . What is more real is the invented language in *Yawar Fiesta* or in *Los ríos profundos* than that in *The Foxes*, because this last lacks artistic creativity, which is what makes literature real.)

In his last novel, Arguedas opts for the Tower of Babel. In fact, he opts for making material for literary creation out of the non-standard Spanish of the *cholos*, the Blacks, the *zambos*, the *injertos*, the illiterate *criollos* from the coast, the *yankees* who were part of religious missionaries, the Asians who had been in Peru for generations, of the new European immigrants: in short, of all the groups that abound around Chimbote.[4]

The days of realist legitimizing fictions have gone, to make room for real illegitimate testimonies. It is worth pointing out here that the dialogues and monologues in Arguedas' novel are modeled on interviews by the author of mostly *cholo* subjects. These interviews were to be part of an ethnological project that, like the novel, was left unfinished—who knows, one could even speculate on the possibility that Peru's former president Alejandro Toledo (2001-2006) or one of his family members or friends might have been one of these subjects. The specific formal traits of these testimonies (incorrect lexical and syntactic usages, Quechuisms and/or Aymarisms of any kind), as well as their numerous marks of enunciation (deictics, gestures, stuttering, incoherence) are expressed as faithfully as possible in the novel.[5]

The late 1960s boom in testimonial practices in the Latin American sociocultural environment partially explains Arguedas' change in attitude toward the sociolect of *serrano* immigrants. Now testimonial discourse, even when intended to be respectful of the specific ways of speaking of its subjects, always subordinates these ways of speaking to their immediate sociopolitical "message," that is, to what is referred to in linguistics as the plane of content— that is why the overall perspective of testimonials is mainly that of the so-called "mediator," at the cost of the informant's culture of origin, which is in general non-Western. In Arguedas' novel, on the other hand, what counts is the form, even if it means what is said is meaningless; that is, the very significant phenomenon of the loss, lack or impossibility of conveying meaning.

Minor literature, as we know, is the people's concern (Kafka cited in Deleuze and Guattari 1986, 18). But it is far from being calculated; it is the affair of a people that no longer exist or do not exist yet: a people that do not exist *here and now* because we do not let them exercise their enunciative function.

Arguedas ends up killing himself, unable to complete *The Foxes*; an extreme solution to eclipse the figure of the author, to the advantage of the collective organization of enunciation that could create the hybrid conditions of possibility of the new community.[6]

Conclusion: Babel and Contemporary *Chicha* Culture

Is *El Cholo* Toledo's former presidency of Peru symptomatic of the fact that this new multiracial, multilinguistic and multicultural community-in-training has ended up emerging on the Peruvian sociodiscursive scene? Such a conclusion would be hasty at the least. It is true that the Peruvian Constitution has, for over a decade, recognized the multicultural (though not the plurinational) nature of the country's population, and that Quechua has been considered an official language for three decades. It is estimated that Indigenous people who speak the vernacular make up close to twenty five percent of the total population (about six million inhabitants). Of these, close to half a million speak Aymara, approximately five million speak Quechua and roughly three or four hundred thousand speak one of the forty one languages spoken in the Peruvian Amazon (López and Küper). This, however, does not necessarily imply that there is a greater appreciation for or use of the Indigenous languages, particularly not in Lima and other coastal urban zones. Although it would be an exaggeration to talk about the extinction of Quechua in urban centres, the language is becoming restricted to the family environment and to intraethnic contact, and is progressively being abandoned by generations born in urban centres—in this sense, according to the gossip, first lady Eliane Karp, a Belgian anthropologist, was more fluent in Quechua and knows more about Andean cosmogony than President Toledo. It is also true that migrants from different areas of the Andes communicate with each other in Spanish due to the lack of a standard variety of Quechua: there are at least eight dialectal varieties of the language and, although a "standard" academic Quechua exists, it is not generalized in daily use.

Do the current circumstances, then, paradoxically favour the linguistic and cultural unification of the country around Spanish more efficiently than did the national unicultural and unilingual project of the Republic in the nineteenth and twentieth centuries? Not necessarily. In fact, the current *criollo* elites are despairingly observing the "cholification" of Lima, and even the relatively new phenomenon of the emergence of what they call—often with a mix of repulsion and contempt—"Chicha culture." In 1996, Mario Vargas Llosa was already sounding the alarm against that "strange hybrid in which a sensibility, an idiosyncrasy, some tastes and even some aesthetic values . . . that caught on like fire in the slums of *serrano* emigrants correspond to the rudimentary Spanish or *criollized* slang that is used for communication" (331–32). Is this a display of the "vulgarity," "bad taste" and "inauthenticity" of the masses, as is assumed by the associates of a "lettered city" that is crumbling before their eyes? Of course. Chicha culture is an "informal" culture (in this it only follows the "informality" of the great majority of the Peruvian social body) whose best linguistic vehicle is a Babelian Spanish that ignores the rules and exasperates purists; a Spanish that is very different from the Spanish used in *The Foxes* but which, in a way, had already been foreshadowed in Arguedas' entire oeuvre and, in particular, in his posthumous novel. This "impure" language of communication is but one of the signs that in Lima as, to a lesser extent, in other coastal cities of Peru, various elements related to Andean culture have become fully accepted—though in an uncertain and unstable manner—through their combination with cultural elements that have arisen in other latitudes; a new transculturating process that has been taking place as a logical effect of the "popular overflow" mentioned at the beginning of this article; an "overflow" that, in Peru, has neither reached the political levels nor the grade of legitimacy of the Indigenous minorities of other Andean countries like Bolivia or Ecuador, but in any case—and this is what I want to point out here—signs the death warrant of a *criollo* Nation-State project that, worthy inheritor of the empire that preceded it, obliterated the great majority of its population.

Notes

1. This, as well as any other citation whose reference is in a language other than English, has been translated by Kate Alvo.
2. In his now classic work, Philippe Hamon enumerates the main presuppositions of realist discourse: "1. The world is *rich*, diverse, luxuriant, discontinuous, etc.; 2. I can *transmit information* about this world; 3. language can *copy* reality; 4. language is *second* with respect to reality (it can express reality, but cannot create it . . .); 7. my reader must believe in the *truth* of my information about the world; etc." (422).
3. To properly understand this reterritorialization of Spanish for the Indigenous communities, it is necessary to take into account the fact that knowledge of the Spanish language was traditionally denied to Indigenous Americans. "Ownership and language defined the ruling class . . . . The use of this language brought about a social hierarchy, provided proof of pre-eminence and built a wall to defend against hostile and, mostly, inferior surroundings" (Rama 1984: 46). The reterritorializing mechanism started by Arguedas' literary texts is particularly evident in *Todas las sangres*; see Giménez Micó 1994: 31–32.
4. "Black men, *zambos*, Chinese Indians, drunks, insolent or frightened cholos, skinny Chinese, old men as well as little" (*The Foxes* 43–44). The "Corral" is a grungy brothel, whose motif mirrors life in Chimbote.
5. Martin Lienhard includes the transcriptions of two of these interviews as an appendix in his 1981 book. "We can point out that the stuttering of transcription does not put across the expressivity of the discourses, which are syntactically deficient but which carry voiced inflections that fill that verbal "void" . . . . Arguedas had to invent, from the language of these and other men, literary oral discourses that would compensate verbally for the loss of the gestural dimension inherent to authentic oral discourse" (Lienhard 1981: 193).
6. "When a statement is produced by . . . an artistic singularity, it occurs necessarily as a function of a national, political, and social community, even if the objective conditions of this community are not yet given to the moment except in literary enunciation" (Deleuze and Guattari 1986: 83–84).

Works Cited

Aínsa, Fernando. "The Antinomies of Latin American Discourses of Identity and Their Fictional Representation." *Latin American Identity and Constructions of Difference*. Ed. A. Chanady. Minneapolis and London: University of Minnesota Press, 1994.

Ansion, Jean-Marie. *Démons des Andes: la pensée mythique dans une région des Andes péruviennes (Ayacucho)*. Louvain-la-Neuve: Université Catholique de Louvain, 1984.

Arguedas, José María. *The Fox from Up Above and the Fox from Down Below.* Ed. Julio Ortega. Trans. Frances Horning Barraclough. Critical edition. Pittsburgh: University of Pittsburgh Press, 2000.

———. *El zorro de arriba y el zorro de abajo.* Ed. Eve-Marie Fell. Critical edition. Madrid: Consejo Superior de Investigaciones Científicas de España, 1990.

———. *Todas las sangres.* Buenos Aires: Losada, 1964.

———. "La novela y el problema de la expresión literaria en el Perú." *Mar del Sur* 9, 1950.

Avendaño, Ángel. *Historia de la literatura del Qosqo. Del tiempo mítico al siglo XX.* 3 vols. Qosqo: Municipalidad del Qosqo, 1993.

Bareiro Saguier, Rubén. "José María Arguedas o la palabra herida." *El zorro de arriba y el zorro de abajo.* Ed. Eve-Marie Fell. Critical edition. Madrid: Consejo Superior de Investigaciones Científicas de España, 1990.

Burga, Manuel. *Nacimiento de una utopía: muerte y resurrección de los incas.* Lima: Instituto de Apoyo Agrario, 1988.

Cerrón Palomino, Rodolfo. *El quechua: una mirada de conjunto.* Lima: Centro de Investigación de Lingüística Aplicada, 1980.

Chang-Rodríguez, Eugenio. "El indigenismo peruano y Mariátegui." *Revista Iberoamericana* 127 (1984): 367–93.

Chiampi, Irlemar. *José Lezama Lima. A espressão americana.* São Paulo: Brasiliense, 1988.

Deleuze, Gilles, and Félix Guattari. *Capitalisme et schizophrénie. L'anti-Œdipe.* Paris: Minuit, 1972.

———. *Kafka. Pour une littérature mineure.* Paris: Minuit, 1975.

———. *Kafka: Toward a Minor Literature.* Trans. Dana Polan. Minneapolis: University of Minnesota Press, 1986.

Deleuze, Gilles, and Claire Parnet. *Dialogues.* Trans. Hugh Tomlinson and Barbara Habberjam. New York: Columbia University Press, 1987.

———. *Dialogues.* Paris: Flammarion, 1977.

Escobar, Alberto. *Arguedas o la utopía de la lengua.* Lima: Instituto de Estudios Peruanos, 1984.

Flores Galindo, Alberto. *Buscando un Inca. Identidad y utopía en los Andes.* Lima: Instituto de Apoyo Agrario, 1987.

Franco, Jean. "Cultura y crisis." *Nueva Revista de Filología Hispánica* XXXV. 2, 1987.

Giménez Micó, José Antonio. "Caliban in Aztlan: From the Emergence of Chicano Discourse to the Plural Constitution of New Solidarities." *National Identities and Sociopolitical Changes in Latin America.* Ed. A. Gómez-Moriana and M. F. Durán-Cogan. *Hispanic Issues* 23. New York and London: Routledge, 2001. 320–51.

———. *L'irruption des "autres." Analyse de trois fronts discursifs d'identité et de résistance: chicano, antillais et andin péruvien.* Montréal: Balzac-Le Griot, 2000.

———. *Todas las sangres de José María Arguedas. Ética y estética del mestizaje y de la transculturación*. Montréal: Service des publications G.R.A.L. de l'Université de Montréal, 1994.

Glave, Luis Miguel. "Grito de pueblos silenciados. Intermediarios lingüísticos y culturales entre dos mundos: historia y mentalidades." *Allpanchis* XXII, 1990. 435–513.

Gómez-Moriana, Antonio. "Christophe Colomb et l'*invention* de l'«Indien»." *L'"Indien," instance discursive*. Ed. A. Gómez-Moriana and D. Trottier. Actes du Colloque de Montréal (Université de Montréal, mai 1991). Candiac: Balzac, 1993. 9–31.

Hamon, Philippe. "Un discours contraint." *Poétique* 16 (1973): 119–81.

Kafka, Franz. *Correspondance*. Paris: Gallimard, 1965.

Lienhard, Martin. *Cultura popular andina y forma novelesca*. Lima: Tarea Latinoamericana, 1981.

———. "Etnoficción ladina en el área maya." *Nueva Revista de Filología Hispánica* XXV. 2 (1987): 38–52.

———. *La voz y su huella. Escritura y conflicto étnico-cultural en América Latina 1492–1988*. Lima: Horizonte, 1992.

López, Luis Enrique, and Wolfgang Küper. "La educación intercultural bilingüe en América Latina: balance y perspectivas." *Revista Iberoamericana de Educación* 20, 1999. <www.campus-oei.org/revista/rie20a02.htm>

Lyotard, Jean-François. *Le postmoderne expliqué aux enfants*. Paris: Galilée, 1988.

———. *The Postmodern Explained to Children: Correspondence, 1982–1985*. Trans. Don Barry et al. Minneapolis: University of Minnesota Press, 1993.

Mariátegui, José Carlos. *Siete ensayos de interpretación de la realidad peruana*. Barcelona: Crítica Grijalbo, 1976.

Matos Mar, José. *Desborde popular y crisis del estado: veinte años después*. Lima: Fondo Editorial del Congreso del Perú, 2004.

———. *Desborde popular y crisis del estado: el nuevo rostro del Perú en la decada de 1980*. Lima: Instituto de Estudios Peruanos, 1984.

Pratt, Mary Louise. *Imperial Eyes. Travel Writing and Transculturation*. London/New York: Routledge, 1992.

Rama, Ángel. *La ciudad letrada*. Hanover: Ediciones del Norte, 1984.

———. *Transculturación narrativa en América Latina*. México: Siglo XXI, 1982.

Rostworowski, María. "Las macroetnias en el ámbito andino." *Allpanchis* XXII (1990): 3–28.

Rushdie, Salman. *Patries imaginaires*. Paris: Christian Bourgois, 1991.

Torero, Alfredo. *El quechua y la historia social andina*. La Habana: Editorial de Ciencias Sociales, 1980.

Vargas Llosa, Mario. *José María Arguedas y las ficciones del indigenismo. La Utopía arcaica*. México: Tierra Firme, 1996.

———. "Literatura y suicidio: el caso Arguedas." *Revista Iberoamericana* XLVI, 110–11 (1980): 3–29.

◆ 6

Nuyorican Poetry, Tactics for Local Resistance

Susan M. Campbell

> "If one does not expect a revolution
> to transform the laws of history,
> how is it possible to foil here and now
> the social hierarchization?"
> —Michel de Certeau

Poet Tato Laviera inherits a legacy of local poetic resistance from the Civil Rights-inspired Nuyorican tradition. The purpose of this article is to illustrate how Laviera's poetry functions as a contestatory but non-revolutionary art form in the decade of the 1980s. His poetry is particularly apt for this since his work spans that decade while most other Nuyorican poets began in the 1960s and 1970s while Civil Rights movements were at their peak. Laviera's work holds strongly to the ideals of those movements. Laviera's poetry reflects the thematic of Puerto Rican *plena* music through privileging the perspective of marginal people. He writes in Spanish, English and Spanglish refusing to acknowledge any linguistic sanction or bias. He advocates survival tactics for those Puerto Ricans in New York whose task it is to live through their colonial experience. He cheerfully extols the value and power of Africanness in an America that at times pathologizes it.

Tato Laviera publishes his first collection of poetry in 1979, the year before the election of Ronald Reagan comes to symbolize a growing tide of conservatism. The notion of social change shifted in the decade of the 1980s from a Civil Rights-inspired questioning of the social hierarchy toward a notion of personal achievement and responsibility. It is this difference in political circumstance that gives Nuyorican poetry from the 1980s special meaning, a new reading that distinguishes it from other Nuyorican poetry from the 1960s and 1970s. The qualities of marginal voice and oblique, contestatory perspective take on new meaning when faced with the lowered expectations of social movements' potential to create social change in the 1980s. Once the material situation has changed, that is, the Civil Rights movements linked to Nuyorican poetry have disintegrated, how is it most useful to read this poetry? What becomes the new scope and mission of its production and reading? The range of literary criticism dedicated to understanding Nuyorican poetry can provide some answers. Tato Laviera's poetry, which spans the decade of the 1980s, maintains a politically contestatory focus and innovates the Nuyorican genre, providing an opportunity to measure the value and limitations of Marxist and postmodernist critical tendencies for Nuyorican poetry.

The Critical Spectrum

Since the political paradigm shifted in the 1980s and swept aside the leftist movements' power from two decades before, it is surprising that critical thought on Nuyorican poetry from the 1960s to today tends to maintain a Marxist,[1] socially-oriented focus. This continued focus may be due to the fact that much of Nuyorican poetry has maintained its contestatory, anti-hegemonic qualities throughout its existence despite the decline of leftist movements with which it shared its origin. While any critical approach has limitations in its ability to explain a work of literature, socially oriented Marxist literary theory appears appropriate to a genre that, among other things, candidly denounces mainstream media manipulation and the relegation of certain ethnic, class and gender groups to a subordinate social station.

Juan Flores, the foremost scholar of Puerto Rican literature and culture, shares Marxist concerns in his treatment of Nuyorican literature, and continually emphasizes the effect of the colonial relationship between the United States and Puerto Rico in his analyses. For Flores, colonialism, the most important condition effecting Puerto Rican poverty and marginalization, is key to understanding Puerto Rican literature on the island and on the mainland. The social and political bear upon the literary. One important concept that Flores highlights time and again is the dominant culture's pathologization of Puerto Ricans on the mainland. This motif is a way to signal the racist and classist tendencies present in the ideology of mainstream discourse in the U.S. By focusing on the effects of Puerto Rico's colonial status and being alert to mainstream media's manipulative depiction of Puerto Ricans, Flores holds true to an approach to literature that is socially oriented and inspired by Marxist literary criticism.

In discussing language assimilation, Flores assesses the phenomenon in a way that approaches the work of Jesús Martín Barbero, although the two vary greatly in the scope of their assessments of culture. The Nuyorican scholar works from a more Marxist, modernist perspective than Martín Barbero. Flores does not consider the progressive adoption of English among Nuyoricans as a loss of their "real" culture but upholds that the interplay between Spanish and English affords speakers and writers greater communicative possibilities. He maintains that at least to some degree language is a marker of cultural value. He denies that Puerto Ricans will follow other (im)migrant groups who have lost their languages of origin in favor of the exclusive use of English. Thus he assures the reader that this group will be saved from the fate of total effacement of their culture of origin (1993: 165). Flores emphasizes the close relationship between Puerto Ricans and African-Americans that can be found in large urban areas on the U.S. mainland (1993: 183). He exemplifies this by citing the hip-hop style shared between members of the two groups and the Afro-American influences on Nuyorican poetry. In the case of poet, Tato Laviera, the closeness that Flores speaks to makes up a large part of his poetic theme. These assertions are important given the perception and reality of racial tensions between the two groups in the urban mainland context. By emphasizing the groups' affinity, Flores joins other critics who underline Puerto Ricans' and African Americans' potential to work together toward common political goals. Flores pinpoints one of the central uses of Laviera's poetry, which is the pride many Puerto Rican's take in their African heritage.

Flores sees four stages in the Nuyorican experience. The first is, the poverty and disenfranchisement of the present day which are sensationalized by the mainstream media resulting in (self-)destructive behavior and disproportionate recrimination (1993: 187). The second is the nostalgic and idealizing look back toward the island. The third is self-insertion without invitation by the mainstream into the national dimension. The fourth is the selective connection to other ethnic groups in U.S. American[2] society (1993: 186). Each of these stages is reflected in poems by many Nuyorican writers including Tato Laviera, but since Flores described four stages of Nuyorican Literature using the first three of Laviera's books as examples, the development of poetic and political themes in Laviera's work holds a central and archetypical space in academic analysis of Nuyorican poetry. Flores comments that the nostalgic look back to the island is a way to raise social consciousness and each of the other stages signals a political point of view and circumstance in the real world. Flores' concerns about Nuyorican literature are grounded solidly in its relationship with Nuyorican everyday life, social and material inclusion, participation, empowerment or the lack of these within the North American context.

Edna Acosta-Belén is a scholar who recognizes Flores' call to expose colonialism as the chief apparatus of Puerto Rican social disenfranchisement. Acosta-Belén commenced her work on Nuyorican literature and society in the 1970s by focusing on the literature's power to confirm the value of Nuyorican culture in the face of the dominant Anglo-American society. This focus was and remains common among Puerto Rican literature scholars. In 1992 she revisited her earlier work and updated her analyses and perspectives. She reinforced her previous assertions born out of 1960s and 1970s struggles. That is, social struggle on a national level, based on ethnic identification remained a strong form of fighting the inequalities created under modernization. Acosta-Belén's concerns about negative effects of media images on the Nuyorican community place her firmly in the Marxist camp. Unlike most scholars who write about the death of the grand leftist movements, Acosta-Belén refers to the 1960s and 1970s as the apex of a multicultural movement that continues until today. Thus she affirms that these leftist movements have remained vital despite declarations to the contrary by many other scholars. In her 1992 appraisal of the state of Nuyorican literature, Acosta-Belén points out that the movement has taken on two new, prevalent literary focuses, feminism and a pan-Latino perspective to add to the classic concerns of race, class and ethnicity.

Felipe Luciano, a leader of the Puerto Rican Civil Rights activist group, The Young Lords, and member of the Last Poets[3] contributes to this critical spectrum with a solid revolutionary view of the role of Nuyorican poetry. He claimed that a reigning sub-estimation of the value of Puerto Ricanness plagued the community's efforts to improve their conditions. Luciano believed that the mainstream media's depiction of Puerto Ricans as unimportant except in terms of crime and welfare abuse, influenced their self-image, their willingness to participate in their communities and their expectations of the City's responsibilities toward them as New Yorkers. The cultural plane of The Young Lords' tri-part strategy to revolutionize daily life for Puerto Ricans in New York was directed toward the community itself and consisted in an effort to redefine Nuyorican identity in positive terms. The most important purpose of their discourse was not so much to convince the rest of New York of the validity of Puerto Rican culture, as much as to convince themselves. Luciano saw two causes for the sense of worthlessness among Puerto Ricans: a purposeful attempt on the part of politicians to keep Puerto Ricans from knowing their own power and Puerto Ricans' own internalization of and participation in this whitewash.

If the music could speak to "realities" daily life from a Puerto Rican perspective, it could help to raise the consciousness of the listening public and with an increased sense of their own power, they could mobilize to effect real change in their own communities. In this way, salsa music and Nuyorican poetry among other cultural forms were to become part of a social, cultural and political revolution (Marre 1979). Clearly, Luciano valued Nuyorican poetry mainly for its political capital, its counter-hegemonic effects on the Nuyorican community since he envisioned the art as one facet of a social and political struggle. Luciano's comments on the worth of poetry as a part of his envisioned revolution represent the far end of the critical spectrum in terms of social orientation.

While most scholars of Nuyorican literature focus to a certain degree on its value as a consciousness-raising tool, a few cultural critics have taken a postmodernist view on Nuyorican poetry. Arnaldo Cruz-Malavé challenges the Marxist scholarly focus on Nuyorican poetry as a tool for social change. He characterizes this focus as a historical concern past its usefulness in the present day, an erroneous, outdated understanding of ideology that contemporary, postmodernist theory has been able to rectify. He relates the Nuyorican poets' political, aesthetic critique to the Marxist concept of ideology as "false consciousness" and their own notions of authentic experience as the "true self" (48). He exemplifies his point by comparing the work of Pedro Pietri to that of Victor Hernández Cruz who in their early careers concerned themselves with portraying the daily lives of Puerto Ricans in New York City, a common focus among Nuyorican poets. In their work during the 1960s and 1970s, Cruz-Malavé affirms that Pietri calls for the awakening of the Nuyorican true self through describing the degraded living conditions in Puerto Rican enclaves in New York City. While Hernández Cruz describes similar circumstances, Cruz-Malavé claims he does, "not address these social conditions from a privileged vantage point *outside ideology*"[4] (49, emphasis added). Cruz-Malavé claims this recognition that it is impossible to escape ideology (a stance which lies *within ideology*) has come to replace older Marxist notions of false consciousness and the true self. In Hernández–Cruz's work during the 1980s, *By Lingual Wholes* (1982). Cruz-Malavé sees an even greater distancing from the search for utopia through political action to, "an awareness of the utopic as a linguistic construct" (50). Cruz-Malavé lauds the utopic interweaving of Spanish and English as a "centrality" of the Nuyorican experience, which disproves sociological ideas about this group's marginalization. Thus Cruz-Malavé insists on the power of a utopia, which remains within the bounds of the literary text, that is, it remains unconnected to any real-world social struggle. Unlike Flores' mapping of the use of bilingualism, Cruz-Malavé's notion of bilingual utopia does not go outside the text in which it is written. It does not recognize or challenge commonly held positions that to use Spanglish is to be deficient in standard forms of English and Spanish.

Cruz-Malavé's declaration begins to map a non-revolutionary power in Nuyorican poetry. He tells of the shift in dominance from Marxist literary theory to a postmodern theory that does not step outside of ideology or affect the world outside the text. In this paradigm, the text can contradict commonly held notions about the social group it addresses simply by being. It does not need, or perhaps it is not capable of calling the addressed social group to action in the real world. This postmodern approach is appropriate for Victor Hernández Cruz's work but would be quite limited if it were to be applied to the work of Tato Laviera or most other Nuyorican poets. The bulk of this body of poetry is so overtly political and so clearly intentioned toward real-world change that Cruz-Malavé's analyses fail to address it effectively.

While this formalist and postmodern approach to Nuyorican literature remains minoritary among critical tendencies surrounding the genre, another article in this vein merits study since it illustrates the socially oriented bilingualism of Tato Laviera's work in opposition to that of Hernández Cruz. Carmelo Esterrich focuses on the sense of loss in some of Hernández Cruz and Miguel Algarín's poetry. His analysis highlights the post-Freudian concept of incorporation. In the case of Puerto Ricans living on the U.S. mainland, this explains the recurrent allusions to the island as a means of staving off the reality that the homeland is lost to them. Esterrich explains that as Nuyoricans, Hernández Cruz and Algarín write bilingual poetry and employ island themes in their attempt to be reinserted into the homeland that they lack. This very well grounded essay is written in a way that explicitly avoids the political and social context of the poetry. Esterrich recognizes the strong, politically critical message that dominates the poets' works and acknowledges the breadth of critical analysis that is directed at the social conditions of Nuyoricans.[5] The author however opts to analyze those poems that seem to center themselves on an internal loss or lack rather than on an assignment of blame for that loss. One interesting side point that Esterrich raises is that unlike Hernández Cruz and Algarín, Tato Laviera uses bilingualism to wage a struggle. Laviera provides a number of poetic examples of bilingualism used especially to opine on the validity of Nuyorican bilingual speech patterns and on the corresponding hybrid culture of everyday life in Puerto Rican enclaves in New York City as well as elsewhere.

Miguel Algarín himself, this time as a critic rather than as a poet, assesses this shift from a focus on political activism to one on textual utopia and laments it. A thorough reading of Algarín's poetic work and knowledge of his social, political projects, make it clear that his apolitical, bilingual poetry of loss is marginal to his general body of work, which tends toward a strong, antihegemonic message. Unlike Cruz-Malavé, Algarín sees the flow away from the Marxist concept of the true self as a tragedy rather than as a beneficial step toward a genuine understanding of ideology.

In his short article titled "Nuyorican Literature," he briefly narrates the history of the colonial relationship between the United States and Puerto Rico explaining the way the promise of, "bread, land and liberty" (Algarín 89) was illegitimately sold to the working classes of the island. The subsequent realization that these promises were empty led to hopelessness, and subsistence through welfare for many Puerto Ricans who came to New York City. Algarín explains these desperate acts as the, "rituals and habits that are the remnants of an already badly weakened historical consciousness or historical self" (89). Algarín further laments the loss of, "all historical consciousness" (89) and sees that Puerto Ricans living on the mainland are reduced to trying to maintain ontinuity rather than reaching toward the greater goals they had when they first arrived on the U.S. mainland in large numbers in 1948. For Algarín, clear concepts of historical consciousness and the true self are essential for the struggle toward greater goals. Algarín links this sociological diagnosis to Nuyorican literature by prescribing three functions of the Nuyorican aesthetic. Oral self expression, an accord about forming systems of protection and mutual benefit, and the creation of a space exclusively for people to express themselves publicly[6] are the three functions of Nuyorican literature that in Algarín's view can transform the Puerto Rican community (92). This last function, a space for public expression, Algarín is convinced serves as a psychic cure for the ills incurred as colonials in The United States. Algarín's vision of the value of Nuyorican literature lies in its ability to impel people toward activism through precisely the demythification that Cruz-Malavé claims is an illusion.

Across the critical spectrum about Nuyorican poetry, we find two general camps. The first, which includes Flores, Acosta-Belén, Luciano and Algarín, holds on to Marxist prescriptions of the literature to aid in struggles for social and political change. The other, which includes Cruz-Malavé and Esterrich, moves with a 1980s contemporary trend in criticism to a postmodern focus that distances the texts from their political origins. The Marxist approach tends to prescribe Nuyorican poetry as part of a racial identity- and class-based struggle for change on a national level akin to the Civil Rights movement. The vast changes in geo-political and economic realities have perhaps outmoded this tactic. On the other hand, the postmodern criticism that ignores the political imperatives central to the bulk of Nuyorican poetry renders itself irrelevant to describe the fundaments of the genre. Since most Nuyorican poets continue to write toward social change past the collapse of the grand leftist movements of the 1960s and 1970s, a third approach becomes necessary to explain and measure how the poetry works in the global era that dawns in the 1980s.

In fact, a third focus, neither Marxist nor postmodernist, becomes the most apt for Nuyorican literature that keeps its politically contestatory focus into the global era and must negotiate this new plane. What can be quite useful to this debate is Jesús Martín Barbero's important and subtle distinction between a vision of literature that is separate from the real world and literature that engages the world directly. Martín Barbero thus renders from this dichotomy something more complex. Martín Barbero's approach offers a way to see literature that engages in social struggle after the Civil Rights movements have collapsed. He highlights a third option between Marxist analyses that might no longer be applicable to the current global era and postmodernist approaches that sometimes disregard the political, real-world functions of literature.

Martín Barbero cites some Marxist scholars who criticize a cultural approach to real world problems as an evasion of the real world milieu. While he credits this position as sometimes justified, he also affirms that, "something radically different occurs when culture points to new dimensions of social conflict, the formation of new socio-political actors around regional, religious, sexual and generational identities" (Martín Barbero 1993: 209).

Bilingualism in Mass Migration:
Mobility for Survival

Nuyorican bilingualism uses the linguistic structures of English and Spanish in ways that clash with the languages' standard grammatical and lexical rules. As Frances Aparicio (1988) has explained, this bilingualism exists as a protest against the notion that standard linguistic forms are superior. The Nuyorican bilingual voice of protest not only challenges elite prescriptions for the use of language, it also honors a 'privileged' group who can understand the whole text in its double code. On a local level, Laviera's bilingual poems are directed toward the peripheral neighborhoods where Spanglish is spoken and where, in literary or imaginary terms the poems' themes unfold. On a national level, these poems declare the beauty of Spanglish to others who would malign it.

Laviera's poem entitled, *"my graduation speech"*[7] in the *La Carreta Made a U-Turn* compilation mixes English and Spanish as its medium of expression and articulates the dynamics, the confusion, the misunderstandings and cross-cultural disconnects of living within and between both languages and cultures. The audience for this poem must be Spanish/English bilingual to completely understand its meaning. In other words, this poem is not like some bilingual literature that sprinkles foreign words for flavor and in which it is unnecessary to decipher them to know what is being expressed in the text.[8] Juan Flores (1993) claims that Laviera is more eloquent than he could be if he were to use only one language in this poem (175). This eloquence emerges in the form of a double significance, one: an agile linguistic maneuver in that he swings from the margins of one colonial language to another; and two: a political positioning.

After expressing frustration at translating back and forth between languages, he declares, "so it is, spanglish to matao / what I digo" (*so it is mangled Spanish that I speak*) (this and all following translations, mine) (*Carreta* 7). The poetic voice character is the most accomplished in his class delivering the valedictory speech at his U.S. high school's graduation ceremony and yet he admits that he reads neither English nor Spanish very well. The last verse, "¡ay, virgen, yo no sé hablar!" (7) (*Oh Virgin Mary, I don't know how to speak!*) ends the poem in an apparent linguistic breakdown. The brilliance of this seeming failure of communication is the undercurrent of Laviera's social commentary on linguistic/ethnic prejudice. The poem comically flies in the face of English-only discourse within which the English literacy statistics of Hispanic New York State high school graduates are posited as a threat to prospective employers. It is on this level that the poem addresses not only the Spanglish-speaking Nuyorican community but also a broad and generalized national audience. This text points to the bilingual education debate yet provides no answers to the questions posed within that debate. Tato Laviera seems to offer the space of bilingualism as an imaginary refuge for Nuyoricans who are rejected by both English and Spanish language purists.

This bilingual poem does not separate itself from the political and social realities of Puerto Ricans in the U.S. as some critics claim do the bilingual poems of Victor Hernández Cruz. According to Juan Flores in his book *Divided Borders: Essays on Puerto Rican Identity* most Nuyoricans are bilingual. However, language purists who interpret Puerto Ricans' code switching as deficiency in each standard language would criticize them as alingual

(Flores 1993: 164). Flores sees their linguistic patterns as marks of their colonial status since they speak colonial dialects of English and Spanish and thus don't operate under standard linguistic codes of either. In line with de Certeau, García Canclini and Martín Barbero see this type of hybrid usage as a creative way to slide back and forth within the non-committal, commonwealth space that they inhabit using this mobility to their advantage. The difference between how Flores approaches bilingualism and how García Canclini and Martín Barbero do is significant. Flores has an important and provable point that Spanish-English bilinguals are marginalized on the U.S. mainland partially on the basis of their linguistic practices. It is essential to recognize that social systems on the U.S. mainland function to the detriment of non-standard English linguistic groups. This recognition questions the myth of equality that forms part of the notion of the U.S. as a land of opportunity. To name a breach of justice, to recognize the victimization of Puerto Ricans, while important, lacks a productive element that García Canclini and Martín Barbero provide. To include in the analysis that using bilingual speech patterns could be a source of liberation is potentially more productive in that it can lead toward new forms of struggle.

Ironically, Laviera's poem *commonwealth* in the *AmeRícan* collection, which expresses the very ambivalent consciousness mentioned above, is written completely in English. The declaration to ally himself completely to neither the United States nor Puerto Rico allows Laviera to protect himself from the elite judgment of both nations by shifting between them. In a similar vein, Laviera's best-known poem, *AmeRícan* makes manifest the oblique positioning of Nuyoricans with respect to national identity. Here, rather than distancing himself from the U.S. American and/or Puerto Rican nationalities, the poetic voice implies the decision to be fully American and depends on acceptance from mainstream culture.

> and i dream to take the accent from
> the altercation, and be proud to call
> myself american, in the u.s. sense of the
> word, AmeRícan, America! (1988: 95)

Here, the impermanent, fluid and non-committal space is symbolized by Laviera's bilingual trope on his dual national possibilities: American and Puerto Rican superimposed one on the other to form the hybrid, AmeRícan. In the poem, this term is defined in positive, even triumphant style but the last stanza quoted above makes it clear that it would be better if the conditions that make this hybrid term necessary could change and make way for full participation in and acceptance from U.S. American society. Until this happens, the author will remain in-between. In this case, Laviera presents his non-committal status as an unfortunate rather than opportune condition.

The Tactics of Plena Marginality: A View of/from The Arrabal

Laviera's poetry offers the Nuyorican community tactics with which to survive within hostile spaces. Laviera is recognized as the Nuyorican poet who most reaches toward Afro-Puerto Rican subjects and rhythms through his verse. References to the Puerto Rican musical forms, *bomba y plena* abound in his poetry. *Plena's* characteristic lyrics bring an important musical analogy for Laviera's Nuyorican poetry that focuses on life in *Loisaida*[9] and *El Barrio*.[10]

Plena is known as a musical form by and about people living on the margins. This hybrid of African, Spanish and pan-Caribbean influences deals thematically with local life and neighborhood gossip particularly from a working-class point of view. What happens in the neighborhood is of greater importance in *plenas* than what happens downtown. Even in cases where the songs deal with the metropolis, they do so from a marginal perspective.

Laviera's poetry can teach survival tactics to Nuyoricans who live on the margins of New York society. The *plena* quality of his writing denies the supremacy of what is conventionally thought of as the center. The South Bronx, Loisaida and Spanish Harlem are the foci of his action and the bilingual, colonial dialect spoken there is his language.

Within an atmosphere in which the dominant discourse marginalizes Puerto Rican culture in New York, *plena* counters that dynamic by placing the Puerto Rican neighborhood in the thematic focal point. The poem, *social club* from *Mainstream Ethics* is a *plena* poem for two reasons: first much of the content is dedicated to the detailed description of the interior of a marginal space making that space a place of importance and second the poem privileges the opinions and perspectives of the denizens of this marginal space over the mainstream viewpoint.

The five-page poem begins with a detailed description of a Puerto Rican social club in New York City. This is an example of a typical Puerto Rican neighborhood meeting place that helps its members retain a bit of the lost island within their urban, U.S. American surroundings. Roberta Singer calls these "hometown clubs" (140) since they usually bear the name of a town or village from the island. Laviera lists in detail the wall decorations of the room, photos of John F. Kennedy, Robert Kennedy, Marilyn Monroe and a newspaper clipping about the sex scandal among the three, the mayor of Ponce, Puerto Rico next to the Kennedys, Pope John XXIII, a painting of Saint Lazarus bleeding, statues of other Santería images, Martin Luther King's and Roberto Clemente's pictures rest above the pool table (1988: 42). The American flag is described as just a souvenir in this room but a painting of Rafael Cortijo[11] is described as guarded with a string of metal teeth (43) a form of Santería protection. This signals the greater reverence afforded this *plenero* and Afro-Puerto Rican symbol of pride over the U.S. national symbol and also reminds the reader/listener of the Santería beliefs in effect at the social club. Mingling among these decorations are paintings made by a woman who signs "md." Her playfully irreverent, sexually charged works described in the poem point to a sense of humor and humanity. The attention to the details of this marginal club speak to Laviera's attempt to raise this part of society to a level of importance it has not enjoyed as a peripheral "minority" group. The details in the first half of the poem reveal characteristics and values of the club members that are more complex than mainstream depictions of the Puerto Rican community in New York.

In the second half of the poem, Laviera presents the reader/listener with a portrayal of the club members, themselves. The content of the poem shifts from description to dialogue when a social club member mentions that "md" who he calls, *la doctora de fresquerías* (44) (the doctor of cheekiness) was arrested on suspicion of being a terrorist. The members of the social club at first cannot believe that this woman whose sense of ribald humor they appreciate so much would commit violent crimes. For the social club, "md" is human, not reduced to a crime statistic as she might be in the 1980s Anglo-American news context. Later the group muses about the possibility that she really is a revolutionary. They connect what they know of her story to tales of other revolutionaries who went underground and disguised their real work under "totally absurd" covers (45).

The *plena* perspective on this crime story allows for the humanity of the crime suspect, something generally absent in mainstream discourse about ethnic minorities and crime. In kind, the *plena* perspective allows for the elaboration of a connection between "md" and parts of the social club members' history through the Puerto Rican nationalists' tricks to stay out of jail. As marginal in the metropolis, "md" and the social club are a community even if they have never met. The difference is marked in the labels placed on "md." When one club member relates the news story he heard, he echoes the language of mainstream news media, *la arrestaron por ser terrorista* (45) (they arrested her for being a terrorist) but when the group discusses their own opinions about the situation, they use terms like, *ella era 'de la underground'* (45) (she was from the underground) and, *era como los nacionalistas* (45) (she was like the [Puerto Rican] Nationalists) as well as, *quizás había un tema revolucionario dentro de toda esa fresquería* (46) (maybe there was a revolutionary theme under all that cheekiness). *Plena's* local newspaper / gossip theme implies a human link between those who comment and those who are the subjects of those comments.

In the context of a socially oriented, Marxist critical perspective, this human focus on the *arrabal* takes on the significance of a form of cultural survival. Juan Flores describes the sensationalism in mainstream U.S. media of Nuyorican poverty, anger, and exclusion by the dominant culture's media apparatuses. He claims these phenomena result in self-destructive behavior within the Puerto Rican community and in disproportionate recrimination by the judicial structure (1993: 186). Miguel Algarín underlines the need for a psychic cure for Puerto Ricans living on the mainland, a counter-narrative of their own existence. Other scholars cite the cumulative effects of learning dependence as quasi-colonial subjects of the United States. Laviera's poems with a *plena* perspective provide that psychic cure as well as a counter-narrative to the chronicles of Puerto Rican pathology in some U.S. media sources. This offering to the Nuyorican community has the potential to influence a new form of learning not of dependence but of questioning the roles assigned to them in society.

In the context of the post-collapse of Civil Rights movements, the human focus on the *arrabal* comes to serve a purpose that is less revolutionary than the one prescribed by Flores and Algarín. Michel de Certeau outlines the functions of tactics of the poor within a society that they don't expect to change on more than a personal level.

> If one does not expect a revolution to transform the laws of history, how is it possible to foil here and now the social hierarchization, which organizes scientific work on popular cultures and repeats itself in that work? (25)

In his book, *The Practice of Everyday Life* (1984), de Certeau posits two modes of conflict at work in daily life. The powerful employ strategies while the weak make use of tactics. As the weak possess no right to a proper space they must attempt to creatively make use of the space of others in a way different from its intended use. A tactic is a guerrilla or pirate action, "a calculated action determined by the absence of a proper locus" (37) but as De Certeau expressly adds, these tactics are not thought of as means to revolutionary change. De Certeau further describes the tactic as, "a maneuver, 'within the enemy's field of vision . . . and within enemy territory" (37).

De Certeau quite optimistically notes that those who employ tactics enjoy the advantage of invisibility, the proverbial element of surprise hinting that this advantage means the weak can trump the strong who control, "power bound by its very visibility" (36). He does not however imply that David can kill Goliath every time or that these evasive guerrilla tactics are any way to promote tangible, long-term social change. This mapping of the tactical use of an improper place shares some things in common with Jesús Martín Barbero's notion of a cultural expression that points to new routes of resistance. De Certeau's model, however has a less revolutionary scope.

While it is true that some of the works of Tato Laviera analyzed in this article, particularly poems from his first compilation, *La Carreta Made a U-Turn* call the reader/listener to action against mainstream codes, other later, less directly political poems do not constitute a retreat to the realm of de-politicized, aesthetics. Juan Flores in his article "Qué assimilated brother, yo soy asimilao: The Structuring of Puerto Rican Identity" (1985) states that the nostalgia for the island found in much mainland Puerto Rican cultural production works as an apprenticeship in social consciousness.[12] Like much Nuyorican poetry, Laviera's work is rich in idealized, nostalgic images of the Island. Laviera signals specific changes that engage Anglo-American culture with Nuyorican culture—the new definitions of race that can make the U.S. a more harmonious place. This act distinguishes him among Nuyorican poets and makes him an example of Martín Barbero's notion of culture that points to new forms of struggle. Laviera's poetic nostalgia is only a survival tactic, in that it provides a way to thwart mainstream messages but does not point toward potential new forms of struggle. De Certeau's tactic concept is less ambitious than Martín Barbero's notion of culture that points to a new dimension of social conflict. For de Certeau, the tactic does not necessarily lead to a change in societal structure at any future time. His notion of the *perruque* illustrates this.

The quintessential tactic that de Certeau describes, he calls the *perruque*. The name literally means *wig* but describes an action using the materials provided within a system to achieve an end unprescribed by that system. He gives the example of indigenous groups who were forced to convert to Catholicism under Spanish rule.

> Submissive, and even consenting to their subjection, the Indians nevertheless often *made of* the rituals, representations and laws imposed on them something quite different from what their conquerors had in mind; they subverted them not by

rejecting or altering them, but by using them with respect to ends and references
foreign to the system they had no choice but to accept. (de Certeau 1984: xiii)

As a group from an occupied island which moved to a metropolis on the
mainland and continues to travel back and forth, Puerto Ricans live on *tierra
ajena* (foreign land / land belonging to others). Wherever they are, they are
considered outsiders. In this sense, they live out the tactical dynamic de Certeau
describes. The actions they take to survive in the space that belongs to others
must be quick, inventive and ever changing. This is true in raw economic terms
and in terms of the imaginary. It is this imaginary that Laviera tactically feeds.

Definitions of Race: The "One-Drop" Rule and the Myth of the Rainbow People

Much of Laviera's poetry involves racial issues. In some works, he offers an
educational aspect to his treatise on African identity. In other poems, the poet
moves into national debates in the U.S. through criticism of the construction
of racial categories and hierarchies on the U.S. mainland. In this second case
however, Laviera's poetry provides more than a survival tactic à la de Certeau
for Nuyoricans. It points toward a new form of struggle that differs in scope, if
not in theme from other Nuyorican poetry.

In a criticism common of Nuyorican poets, Laviera marks the difference
in the construction of race between Puerto Rico and the U.S. mainland. In his
poem, "negrito" (black boy) he narrates a moment of cultural/racial confusion
on the part of a young Puerto Rican boy who has just arrived in New York City.
His aunt has been living on the U.S. mainland before the boy arrives and, it
can be assumed, has come to understand the binary racial construction there.
She advises him on how to negotiate his new surroundings by warning him
to stay away from blacks, *no te juntes con / los prietos, negrito* (*AmeRícan*,
41) (stay away from dark people, black boy) she warns. It is clear through the
text that the boy, himself is dark-skinned enough to be called *negrito* by his
family and so is likely to be identified by others as black in New York City.
The important issue at stake for the aunt is to maintain a status separate from
African-Americans in New York City. After the child protests to no avail that,
los prietos son negritos (41) (dark people are black) and that, *así no es puerto
rico* (41) (Puerto Rico isn't like this) the Aunt finally advises him to run if he
is approached by 'cocolos'[13] and to be sure to heed her warning. At the end
of the poem, the boy faces New York City and can only feel confusion at this

introduction to the Anglo-American racial paradigm, which separates him, an Afro-Puerto Rican from others of African descent.

The verse, "así no es puerto rico" (41) reminds the informed reader of the tactical racial positioning of Puerto Ricans who have moved to the U.S. mainland. The binary racial categorization of "white" and "non-white" sometimes allows mainland Puerto Ricans to enter a more privileged rank while relegating others to marginalization. Many new immigrants react to this racial hierarchy by emphasizing their Spanish language in order to distance themselves from African-Americans, the longest marginalized group. On the other hand, the verse claims there is a softer racism or a better racial dynamic on the island compared to the rigid categorization on the mainland. Laviera continues his treatise on the U.S. construct of race with the poem, "boricua" (*Puerto Rican*) in the same volume, *AmeRícan*.

In "boricua" Laviera intimates in a provocative way that the Anglo-American construction of race could be made more just by exposure to the Puerto Rican racial paradigm. He points to the mainstream U.S. culture's binary racial assignations, which include a common consideration of mulattos and mestizos as almost undifferentiated, and most importantly racialized as non-white. Laviera claims ownership of an idealized racial harmony in the poem "boricua" and asserts that he and other Puerto Ricans, believe that,

> color is
> generally color-blind
> with us, that's our
> contribution. (16)

If it is true that with Puerto Ricans 'color is generally color-blind,' then Laviera proposes that Puerto Ricans living on the U.S. mainland contribute to the national mainstream culture by enlightening the dominant society to hold more inclusive attitudes about race. Other Nuyorican poets argue that the mere presence of Puerto Ricans on the mainland complicates this binary notion of race, potentially calls for a more nuanced understanding of it and problematizes racial signification in the U.S. Accusations of racism, mistreatment and prejudice are hallmarks of Nuyorican poetry. With this suggestion that the Puerto Rican people could help the United States move toward racial harmony however, Laviera takes a step further than this common Nuyorican positioning.

In this poem, he discusses race not in terms of demythifying the triumphal Anglo-American discourse on melting-pot inclusion or defending the value of Puerto Rican difference but in terms of guidance, "this is our contribution" (16). As an advisor on race, Laviera steps into a space of diplomatic and cultural superiority relative to the U.S. He positions himself as a representative of an island that has purportedly enjoyed racial harmony since the end of slavery and is positioned to aid this troubled nation by imparting his knowledge and experience. In this way, Laviera momentarily twists the empirical rhetoric of responsibility. He aids and guides the "colony," the United States, which under a reverse-imperial paradigm is constructed as needy of rule. Here we see a rhetorical reversal of the Empire/Colony dynamic in which Puerto Rico is positioned to resolve a social dysfunction in the U.S. In the context of both real and rhetorical constructions of race in the U.S., this offer can expose Anglo-American notions about race as the very particular and artificial constructions they are. Laviera's criticism of U.S. binary racial construction and the history of official segregation has the potential to show those living on the mainland that U.S. American conditions of racism are artificially in place. If understood in the context of Puerto Rico however, this statement changes meaning dramatically.

In the poem, "boricua" Laviera evokes the Puerto Rican myth of "the rainbow people." This concept asserts that cultural identification supersedes racial identification (Rodríguez-Morazzani 1996: 158) thereby understating any role racial prejudice plays in the structuring of society on the island. This opens the space for a pointed critique of the U.S. American construction of race and the United States' history of racial violence and official segregation. In the Island context however, this claim of racial harmony undermines positive social change. Since Puerto Rican intellectuals have been comparing the Island's racial history to that of the U.S. over more than 100 years of Anglo-American domination, they have been able to fashion a racially harmonious image of Puerto Rico in juxtaposition with the United States. Since Puerto Rico never experienced the racial violence of lynching, officially sanctioned segregation and Jim Crow laws, Puerto Ricans could afford to believe that racism in Puerto Rico simply did not exist (Jiménez Román 1996: 20).

Miriam Jiménez Román traces the dynamic of official positions on race in Puerto Rico and finds a surprising contradiction in the discourse. One side of the twentieth-century argument is that Puerto Rico is and always was unfettered by racism and united by a Latin-American cultural identity shared by all Puerto Ricans. Simultaneous to this runs the theory that the Island, the whitest in the Caribbean, was progressively becoming whiter over time. This assertion, most famously declared in *Insularismo* by Antonio S. Pedreira was the standard attitude about Puerto Rican racial make-up in this last century. The insistence of whiteness as the dominant feature among Puerto Ricans with the concomitant minimization of African presence on the island seems to obviate an underlying racist attitude in Puerto Rico. Given this history, Tato Laviera's claim of racial harmony falls into a dangerous trap. By claiming racial harmony in juxtaposition to the U.S. climate of racial tension, Laviera fuels this myth among those Nuyoricans who idealize the island.

Laviera even touches the myth of the progressive whitening of Puerto Rico in his triumphal ode to the creative power of Africanness, "the africa in pedro morejón." In the poem, the poetic voice meant to refer to the voice of musician, Morejón speaking to Laviera hails the underlying presence of Africa throughout the Caribbean, in Britain and in the United States. He triumphantly reminds the reader that much of what we experience around the world originated in Africa. It is in this context that the whitening myth occurs.

> two whites can never make a black . . .
> but two blacks, give them
> time . . . can make mulatto . . .
> can make brown . . . can make blends . . .
> and ultimately . . . can make white. (1979: 44)

As is sometimes the case in Laviera's poetry, problematic issues are presented simply as glorious triumphs. Here Laviera posits that blacks have a (pro)creative power that whites do not and that this should afford them greater respect. It would seem that optimism reigns among Laviera's survival tactics as an Afro-Puerto Rican living in New York. He has found a viewpoint from which to decry the awesome creative power of Africa and although that angle is fraught with pitfalls and contradictions, he follows through to the end. Doubtless, Laviera's body of work makes it clear that he is a champion of positive African valuation. It would be a gross misreading of his text to conclude that Laviera espouses the eventual effacement of the black race. Nevertheless the question must be asked, in this poem why is it positive for two blacks to be able to eventually "make white?" The notion of an Africanness that is placed on a continual path toward whiteness betrays not only the racist notion that black is evolutionarily more primitive than white but that this whitening process is desirable. This statement becomes all the more problematic when it is taken into consideration that Puerto Rican intellectual elites such as Luís Muñoz Marín have written treatises on Puerto Rican national identity that espouse this view of continually diminishing blackness, or the progress toward whiteness that the island has achieved.

Conclusion

It is clear that Marxist literary criticism is more appropriate for the analysis of Nuyorican poetry than postmodern criticism because of the political urgency in the poetic texts. Nevertheless, by the 1980s, this poetry has developed and transformed to move away from the concept of revolutionary social change envisioned within the Puerto Rican Civil Rights Movement. This change does not indicate a retreat from political commitment however. Jesús Martín Barbero's analyses hold the key to this poetry that no longer accompanies a Civil Rights struggle yet points toward new ways of waging another struggle. Tato Laviera's poetry as bilingual expression must be recognized as politically and socially relevant to issues of Nuyorican survival in the U.S. mainland. It provides a de Certauian tactic. Likewise does Laviera's focus on plena marginality. His privileging of the perspectives of Nuyoricans provides them a momentary "psychic cure" for their own marginal, colonial status. Laviera's body of poetry as commentary on race brings complex and contradictory ideals to the discussion table. Laviera fulfills Martín Barbero's condition that culture does not have to be separate from the political realm if it points to new ways of waging struggle. While problematically characterizing Puerto Rican culture as having established constructions of racial harmony, Laviera's poetry does indeed challenge the prevailing binary racial constructions in the United States.

Notes

1. I use the term Marxist to refer to a political perspective that focuses on struggle of alienated, marginalized groups to gain access to the rights enjoyed by the mainstream. This struggle is waged on a national level.
2. Flores does not use the term "U.S. American," rather it is a term I have coined to describe mainstream society in the United States which includes some non-Anglo cultures and excludes others.
3. According to Cortés, Falcón and Flores (1976), Luciano's poetry was seen as part of the revolutionary project. Luciano enacts, through the Young Lords Party a revolutionary vision in which culture was to play a role in the consciousness raising of the Puerto Rican community in New York and other parts of the U.S. mainland.
4. In this context Cruz-Malavé uses ideology as the point of view of the dominant culture toward Puerto Ricans. When he writes of their taking a position outside ideology, he refers to the notion that these mainstream messages are false or ideological while the Nuyoricans' messages are true and thus not ideological.

5. Esterrich cites and uses Aparicio's (1988) interpretation of Spanish words within a mainly English text as *conjuros*, ways to connect with one's culture of origin, in this case, that of Puerto Rico. He later posits that her claim that much Puerto Rican literature contains an evocation of an original Puerto Rican essence cannot be substantiated in the poems that he has chosen to present in his essay.
6. The third function of Nuyorican literature Algarín mentions has taken form as the Nuyorican Poets' cafe on 3rd St. and Avenue C in New York.
7. In this article I follow Tato Laviera's scheme of capitalization when quoting his work or referring to his poem titles. Mr. Laviera uses no capital letters for proper names, first letters of words in his titles or first letters of initial words in sentences. He capitalizes letters and at times, whole words for emphasis. His book titles, however use standard English capitalization.
8. This sort of text will have an exoticizing effect for monolingual readers or listeners. For bilinguals, Frances Aparicio's concept of *conjuros* applies (see note 6). For bilinguals, the individual words in one language within a text based in another language can provide a sense of contact with a reality of their place of origin (1988: 149).
9. Loisaida is a term borrowed from the English, "Lower East Side" of New York City into Nuyorican Spanish. The New York City government has officially recognized this neologism and so street signs bearing "Loisaida" can be found there.
10. This directly translates as "the neighborhood" but refers to the Puerto Rican area of East Harlem.
11. Rafael Cortijo, an Afro-Puerto Rican musician of working-class background was a pioneer in popularizing on a national scale the musical forms, bomba y plena during the 1950s and so has become a hero for others who share his background.
12. Flores posits that Nuyoricans facing Anglo-American mass and elite cultures feel a nostalgia for the local, folkloric culture of their island left behind. In this way they begin to think critically about the mass and elite cultures of their mainland home (1993: 189). This view negates the possibility that mass-produced culture can have a liberating function.
13. The term 'Cocolo' normally refers to Puerto Ricans of African decent who hail from the popular classes and who prefer salsa music to rock music. It is of note that this usually pejorative term is not only based on race but also on cultural affiliations. It is often noted that racism in Puerto Rico, while less obvious than on the U.S. mainland, is often masked as criticism of a cultural nature.

Works Cited

Acosta-Belén, Edna. "Beyond Island Boundaries: Ethnicity, Gender and Cultural Revitalization in Nuyorican Literature." *Callaloo* 15. 4 (1992): 979–98.

Algarín, Miguel. "Nuyorican Literature." *MELUS* 8. 2 (1981): 89–92.

Aparicio, Frances. "La Vida Es un Spanglish Disparatero: Bilingualism in Nuyorican Poetry." *European Perspectives on Hispanic Literature of the United States*. Ed. Genvieve Fabre. Houston: Arte Público Press, 1988. 147–60.
Betances, Samuel. "The Prejudice of Having No Prejudice in Puerto Rico: Parts I&II." *TheRican*. (Wint. 1972, Spring 1973): 41–54.
Bost, Suzanne. "Transgressing Borders: Puerto Rican and Latina *Mestizaje*." *MELUS* 25. 2 (Summer 2000): 187–211.
Cortés, Félix, Angel Falcón, and Juan Flores. "The Cultural Expression of Puerto Ricans in New York City: A Theoretical Perspective and Critical Review." *Latin American Perspectives* 3. 3 (1976): 117–50.
Cruz-Malavé, Arnaldo. "Teaching Puerto Rican Authors: Identity and Modernization in Nuyorican Texts." *A.D.E. Bulletin* 91 (Wint 1988): 45–51.
De Certeau, Michel. *The Practice of Everyday Life*. Trans. Steven Rendall. Berkeley: University of California Press, 1984.
Esterrich, Carmelo. "Home and the Ruins of Language: Victor Hernández Cruz and Miguel Algarín's Nuyorican Poetry." *MELUS* 23. 3 (Fall 1998): 43–56.
Flores, Juan. *Divided Borders: Essays on Puerto Rican Identity*. Houston: Arte Público Press, 1981.
———. "Puerto Rican Literature in the United States: Stages and Perspectives." *A.D.E. Bulletin* 91 (Winter 1988): 39–44.
———. Foreword. *Divided Arrival: Narratives of the Puerto Rican Migration 1920–1950*. 2nd ed. Ed. Juan Flores. New York: Centro de Estudios Puertorriqueños, 1998.
———. "Qué assimilated brother, yo soy asimilao: The Structuring of Puerto Rican Identity in the U.S." *The Journal of Ethnic Studies*. Fall 1985. 1–16.
García Canclini, Néstor. *Las culturas populares en el capitalismo*. México: Editorial Nueva Imagen, 1982.
Hernández Cruz, Victor. *By Lingual Wholes*. San Francisco: Momo's Press, 1982.
Jiménez, Román. "Un hombre (negro) del pueblo: José Cemso Barbosa and the Puerto Rican 'Race' Toward Whiteness." *CENTRO* 8 (1996): 8–29.
Laviera, Tato. *Mainstream Ethics (ética corriente)*. Houston: Arte Público Press, 1988.
———. *AmeRícan*. Houston: Arte Público Press, 1985.
———. *La Carreta Made a U-Turn*. 3rd ed. Houston: Arte Público Press, 1984.
———. *Enclave*. Houston: Arte Público Press, 1981.
———. Marre, Jeremy. "Salsa: Latin Pop Music in the Cities." Videotape. Harcourt Films, 1979.
Martín Barbero, Jesús. *Communication Culture and Hegemony: From the Media to Mediation*. Trans. Elizabeth Fox and Robert A. White. London: Sage Press, 1993.
Milagros González, Lydia. "F¬clavos y libertos en Puerto Rico: Una historia reprimida." *Presencia africana en el Caribe*. Coord. Luz María Martínez. México D.F.: Consejo Nacional para la Cultura y las Artes, 1995.
Pedreira, Antonio S. *Insularismo*. San Juan: Biblioteca de Autores Puertorriqueños, 1957.

Rodríguez-Morazzani, Roberto P. "Beyond the Rainbow: Mapping the Discourse on Puerto Ricans and Race." *CENTRO* 8. 1–2 (1996): 150–69.

Salsa: Latin Music of New York and Puerto Rico. Videocassette. Dir. Jeremy Marre. Shanachie Records, Harcourt Films, 1979.

Singer, Roberta L. "Puerto Rican Music in New York City." *New York Folklore* XIV, 3–4 (1988): 139–49.

◆ 7

Latino, Latin American, Spanish American, North American, or All at the Same Time?

Edmundo Paz-Soldán

(Translated by Gerardo Garza and Kenya C. Dworkin y Méndez)

Six years ago, Chilean writer Alberto Fuguet and I published *Se habla español* (Spanish is Spoken Here), an anthology of short stories and chronicles set in the United States. It was Alfaguara's first serious attempt to start publishing specifically for the U.S. market: it also signaled the fact that large Spanish publishing houses were beginning to acknowledge the importance of such markets in the United States. Currently, the U.S. is third behind Spain and Mexico in the number of Spanish-language books sold each year. Large U.S. publishers, such as Harper Collins, which has been going after a piece of this market for quite sometime now through its imprint Rayo, and Random House, have also acknowledged the importance of this market.

Se habla español includes short stories and chronicles by Latin American writers who write in Spanish and Latino writers who write in English. It was an attempt to bridge two literary spaces that for the most part are distinctly separate. Why not have Mexican writer Jorge Volpi in dialogue with Mexican-American writer Ilan Stavans, or Mayra Santos, who is Puerto Rican, with Colombian-American Silvana Paternostro?

Yet, the anthology made very few people happy, which is not unusual. Its only diehard defender was Nicaraguan writer Sergio Ramírez.[1] With that exception, Latin American critics were extremely upset by the number of English words in the texts: some even considered that Latino writers had no place in such an anthology since they had more than enough access to publishing with U.S. presses. Despite the fact that only four of the 36 texts in the anthology were by Latino writers, pieces that were originally written in English but translated and published in Spanish, a number of people questioned whether we might not have made better use of the space by including more Latin American writers.

Some critics outside of Latin America pointed out that perhaps a Bolivian and a Chilean were not the most qualified of people to create such an anthology, because we were not representative of any major Latino group.[2] They also complained that the anthology's subtitle should not have been *Voces latinas en U.S.A.* (Latino Voices in the U.S.A.), because it was confusing; in fact, the vast majority of Latin American writers included in the anthology did not live in the United States. Hence, their perspective on the relationship between nation and continent would be distorted, more tourist-like than anything else. Writers like Mexican Ignacio Padilla had hardly set foot in the U.S., and there were even authors who had not once visited the U.S. Critics Alberto Sandoval and Frances Aparicio remarked: "the dialogue is with Latin America, not with U.S. Latinos" (683).

The truth is that it was a conscious editorial decision to employ the word *latinas* in the subtitle because the term in the original subtitle, "latinoamericanas/latinas," was not impressive (or unambiguous) enough. Furthermore, it was undoubtedly a mistake to accept it given the preponderance of Latin American writers and the fact that the prologue of the book clearly states that the project is "an anthology about the U.S. . . . as seen through the eyes of Latin American writers . . ." (14).[3] Regarding the Sandoval and Aparicio argument, it was not our goal to create an anthology about life in the United States via testimonial-like journalistic chronicles but rather through a more literary perspective. As such, what was of importance to us were the perceptions, concerns, hopes and nightmares the United States evoked, even from a distance, in the way (Latin American) writers wrote about it without even having been there.

In any event, let us just say that as far as all the criticism is concerned, we expected as much. What we did not expect was that some Spanish critics and writers would also be upset. Writer Martín Casariego wrote in his cultural insert in *ABC* that he was surprised to discover that Spanish writers had not been included in the anthology. He suggested that when it came time for the book to be published in Spain, this tactless omission would be rectified. Our defense at that moment was to say that one of our project's goals was to have Latin American authors dialog with Latino writers: Spanish authors, to our knowledge, were neither Latin American nor Latino. Had we initially thought of including them, the project would have been very different.

Six years later, as I retrace my footsteps, I ask myself what it means to be Latino in the United States and why a Spanish writer could not be considered a Latino. After all, when I published the anthology, I did not consider myself Latino, either. I was a Latin-American writer who had lived in the United States for more than ten years and, while I could admire the works of Melville and Faulkner, I still felt a part of the tradition of Borges and Vargas Llosa. Furthermore, I wrote in Spanish and not in English, something I thought was a requirement to be considered a Latino writer. Yet, reviews of *Se habla español* that appeared in the United States referred to me as a Bolivian-American or Latino writer. Perhaps those critics were confused, or, perhaps, they had not seen my Bolivian passport. I did not know.

In creating a genealogy of Spanish writers whose texts are set within a part of a continent that would later become the United States one could begin with "Naufragios," by Alvar Núñez Cabeza de Vaca. In this manner, one could also include contemporary Spanish writers like Javier Marías, Antonio Muñoz Molina, and Ray Loriga. There has always been a Spanish literary interest in narrating the U.S. landscape. No one would ever question that these writers are Spanish. Yet, what does one do with Spanish immigrant writers in the United States, a writer like Felipe Alfau, for example, who arrived in the United States when he was fourteen years old, wrote all his works in English, and was the recipient of one of the country's most prestigious book awards—the National Book Award? He is clearly a U.S. writer. Could Alfau also be considered a Latino writer?

In her article "Latina or Americaniard?" (which was very influential on my own position about Spaniards in the United States and their relationship with Latino identity), critic Debra Castillo points out that Latinos who engage in an essentialist discourse about identity have difficulty including Spaniards in the same category. Indeed, the Spaniard is part of the Latino cultural identity but this identity is also defined by a "strictly continental" concept: Latinos are immigrants or the descendants of immigrants from the Caribbean or Latin American countries (3). Thus, immigrants of Spanish descent would belong to the European immigrant group. Yet, as Castillo has stated, "the discourse of race and ethnicity in the United States is used in such a way that the dominant society tends to include immigrants of Spanish origin and their families in a different ethnic group, that is, the Latino identity, which very often rejects them" (3).

If one considers Latino identity in the United States not from an essentialist position but rather from a multiple and more fluid perspective of identity, one might see that these Spanish immigrants share many similarities with their European counterparts, but they could also be considered Latinos. Spanish immigrant writers like Barcelona native María-Dolores Boixodós and Valencian-born Concha Alborg not only write in the manner of other "new Latino" writers, in Spanish or English, or in a combination of the two, but have also explicitly stated that their experience in the United States is more in tune with the Latino experience than with the experience of European immigrants.

Regarding the concept of "new Latinos," Castillo defines them in her article "The New Latinos" as first-generation Latinos who were not born in the United States. Their influx is constant and has profoundly changed the cultural map of the United States over the past few years. Even if Mexican, Cuban, and Puerto Rican immigrants continue to predominate, the arrival of large numbers of Colombians, Venezuelans and Ecuadorians as a result of the recession that affected the whole continent after the second half of the 1990s, these latter groups have greatly diversified our understanding of "Latino" in the United States. One important characteristic of these immigrants is that because they have not yet become too attached to their new country, many of them write in Spanish. Some publish through small presses in the United States; whereas, others disseminate their work in their countries of origin. Even though it is accepted, in a reductionist way, that a national literature is defined by a homogeneous language, it is actually clear that "all national traditions are pluralistic rather than singular" (Gunn [quoted in Castillo 456]). Therefore, if when referring to Spain we can no longer speak of only one literature but rather of literatures, because we must also include those under that umbrella written in Catalan, Basque, or Galician, which have been slowly emerging and finally receiving recognition, we might also consider that although it is still expected that literature in the United States be written in English it might be necessary to start to think about the literature of the U.S., a country of immigrants, as the sum of all its literatures. Isaac Bashevis Singer is considered a classic U.S. writer, yet all of his work is written in Yiddish. In the same manner, one of the literatures of the United States is being written in Spanish.

Indeed, writers have been writing in Spanish for a long time in the United States. Different projects have attempted to present a genealogy showing a continuity of texts that connect the past with the present. The most ambitious project, perhaps, is the "Recovering the U.S. Hispanic Literary Heritage," in which a group of professors and academics from the United States, Cuba, Mexico, and Puerto Rico have collaborated for more than ten years. This project has already documented the publication, in Spanish, of more than eighteen thousand works and nearly two thousand newspapers by Latinos from Spanish colonial times to 1960. The project still has a long way to go: *En otra voz*, an anthology published in 2002 by Arte Público Press, with Nicolás Kanellos as general editor, is a good example of such an enterprise. The anthology's objective is clear: to correct the mistaken idea "that the Hispanic literature in the United States is a new and young one, and that it has come about mainly with the Hispanic generations born or raised in the United States after the World War II, bilingual and bicultural generations that, notwithstanding their bilingualism, have preferred to express themselves in English" (xi).

Kanellos and his group of co-editors, Dworkin, Fernández, Gonzales-Berry, Lugo-Ortiz and Tatum, and the general coordinator, Alejandra Balestra, are all encompassing, all-inclusive, perhaps too much so. Works written before the creation of the United States were included (e.g., one finds Alvar Núñez Cabeza de Vaca) as well as canonical Latin American writers such as José Martí and Mariano Azuela. While it is true that José Martí wrote his best chronicles in New York and that Azuela wrote his classic novel *Los de abajo* (The Underdogs) in the United States and published his first edition in El Paso, does this sufficiently justify the inclusion of both authors as part of the Hispanic cultural tradition in the United States and, hence, part of the U.S. literary tradition? Could Alvar Núñez Cabeza de Vaca be considered a U.S. author? I am not sure. Even though a good number of the works by Peruvian writer Alfredo Bryce Echenique were written in France, that is not reason enough for considering it part of French literature. There must be more compelling reasons than the work having been written in a particular country for it to be considered part of the literary tradition of that country.

Kanellos ventures to say: "the Hispanic literature of the United States is of a transnational nature that emerges and remains intimately connected to the crossing of political, geographical, linguistic, cultural and racial borders" (li) and that for this reason one should understand that several of these writers produce their work with their feet planted in more than one tradition; they dialog with both Latin American and U.S. literature (some of these writers, one could add, also dialog with the Spanish tradition). Despite these concerns, the inclusion of these writers in the "Recovering the U.S. Hispanic Literary Heritage" project is important because it helps us reconsider a very complex undertaking—the creation of a Latino canon. Writers such as Alvar Núñez Cabeza de Vaca, Martí, and Azuela complicate any attempt to create a precise genealogy, to permanently situate their texts, once and for all, in a fixed, entrenched place.

One could debate the inclusion of other writers—Reinaldo Arenas, Luisa

Valenzuela, Isaac Goldemberg—but not the overwhelming evidence presented in the anthology *En otra voz.* Spanish-language literature in the United States is a fundamental part of U.S. literature. It is not about just a few texts that might be exceptions to the rule. It is about a solid corpus, in terms of both quantity and quality. Notwithstanding, when one talks about Latino authors today, the names that come to mind are of writers who write only in English: Sandra Cisneros, Julia Alvarez, Esmeralda Santiago, and Oscar Hijuelos. It is time to include names of authors who because they write in Spanish are broadening the concept of what it means to be a Latino writer in the United States and, in that way, expanding the parameters of U.S. literature, too.

Some critics, even those who consider themselves open-minded, pluralistic, capable of thinking about the Latino identity as a "hybrid, alternative subjectivity," are unwilling to accept this Spanish-language literature, this broadening of categories. Alberto Sandoval and Frances Aparicio are good examples. In "Cultural Hybridities: Literature and Culture in the United States," the prologue to their special edition of an issue of *Revista Iberoamericana,* they are concerned by Debra Castillo's attempt to rethink the field of literature and give Spanish-language literature by Latinos a space within it: "Our concern is that the literature of these recent immigrants or the literature of Latin American writers whose works are translated into English, may displace or silence the literature of U.S. Latinos" (687). Sandoval and Aparicio's protectionist response to this attempt on the part of a latinoamericanist critic (Castillo) to invade the sacred space of Latino Studies causes them to take a position that is as absurd as it is impossible to defend. Almost anyone with even a limited knowledge of the context knows how difficult it has been to have Spanish be symbolically recognized as an important language in the United States. Yet, in a tendentious way, in their argument Spanish ends up carrying more weight than English does in the United States. The "new Latinos" analyzed by Debra Castillo in *Redreaming America: Toward a Bilingual American Culture,* writers such as the Peruvian Eduardo González Viaña, supposedly as well known in the United States as Junot Diaz and Sandra Cisneros, find themselves in a privileged position: "A comparison between the "new Latinos" and Latinos in the United States has to begin with the issue of privilege that comes about by having a national Latin American identity and having the Spanish language as a dominant language" (687).

As an aside, the "new Latino" Eduardo González Viaña has lived in the U.S. nearly twenty years. He is so "privileged," thanks to his national identity that his name is hardly known and his books hardly read in Spanish departments across the United States. He will never appear, as Junot Diaz did, on the cover of *Newsweek* magazine: he will never be invited, as Sandra Cisneros was, to give talks at English departments or Latino Studies programs. In fact, the problem here is neither with Junot nor Cisneros; what these two have achieved for Latino culture and Latino literature is commendable. The problem lies with critics like Sandoval and Aparicio, two people who are supposedly so identified with the margins, so moving and politically correct when defending . . . "silenced, exploited, oppressed and marginalized subjects" (669), who make, with disquieting ease, the same mistakes they attribute almost effortlessly to other critics and writers of diverse origins (Stavans, Moraña, de la Campa, Castillo, Fuguet, and so on): exclusion, marginalization, denial of visibility. It is not enough to talk about postmodern theories with regard to the "multiple discursive position" of the Latino subject, or the fact that the Latino subject is "always in the process of change" (672). Paraphrasing Huidobro— 'Oh, the author of this article is a "new Latino" who dialogs more with things Latin American!' It is not a question of talking about the rose but about helping it bloom in the poem.

A Spanish Woman in The United States: The Case of Concha Alborg

What is the Spanish government's language policy regarding the United States? In an interview published in the *Wall Street Journal*, former Spanish Prime Minister José María Aznar, asserted: "I want Hispanics in the United States to know that they have common European roots and a heritage that can be as solid as the Anglo Saxon one."[4] The Spanish language, whose expansion in the United States is of great interest to Spain's cultural, economic and political institutions, is a fundamental part of the 'roots and heritage' to which the controversial former minister alludes. Linguist José del Valle affirms that Spain is very much interested in becoming an important "cultural referent" for Latinos in the United States for political as well as economic and cultural reasons. It has not become one yet, though, and an important factor for this policy to be successful is a rejection of traditional Spanish linguistic nationalism (del Valle 8). Yet, Spanish scholars continue to have problems comfortably accepting the Spanish that is written and spoken in the United States, a language that is in continuous dialogue with English and undergoing constant hybridization. Some see U.S. Spanish and, worse yet, Spanglish, as bastard languages. In fact, there are even those who consider them as languages whose linguistic evolution cannot be legitimately traced.

As an example, I would like cite the case of one of these "new Latina" writers, Concha Alborg, who was born in Valencia and has lived in the United States since her adolescence.[5] There are several reasons for my interest in Alborg's texts: her explicit attempt to build bridges with the Latino world; her particular use of Spanish in certain texts and English in others; and, the dual focus with which she approaches Spanish and U.S. cultural concepts. There is nearly no single moment in her work in which the tensions amongst her multiple identities, those related to her country of origin and those having to do with her adopted country, are not present. Spanish, English, Spanglish, and, yes, Valencian, too, coexist in a somewhat uncomfortable manner in her work. As such, her writing is a challenge to anyone who still thinks in a linear, simplistic manner about the relationship between a country's literature and a homogeneous language. Concha Alborg can be defined in many ways, all of them correct: she is a Valencian, Spanish, and U.S. writer. She is also a Latina writer, which is the definition I am currently interested in exploring.

The first thing that one notices about *Beyond Jet Lag,* Alborg's book published by a small publishing house in New Jersey, in December 2000, is that out of its twenty short stories, ten are written in English while the other ten are in Spanish. Thus, from its inception, the book assumes there is a bilingual reader with complete fluency in both languages. This is not akin to the practice of some Latino writers, who write in one of two languages, preferably English, and sprinkling it with words and exchanges in the other language, a style to which we have grown accustomed. In her prologue, Concha Alborg justifies her decision stating that she is not doing it because she speaks two languages but rather because she lives "between two cultures . . . [and] some of the relationships and events take place in one language while others take place in the other" (8). She suggests that another possibility for her book would have been to produce a bilingual edition, in which the same short story could appear side by side in English and Spanish versions. Simply put, her reason for not doing this in a formal way was due to her deep conviction that a translation never does justice to the original. There are concepts that are intricately tied to a language, such as, the one found in the title of her book, *jet lag.* How does one translate that into Spanish—*desajuste de tiempo* (non-adjustment to time)? Or as people in Chile say, *mareo de tierra* (land sickness)? Alborg, with a foot in each culture, needs to write some short stories in English and others in Spanish, and there is no way to simplify this back-and-forth phenomenon that many immigrants experience between their country of origin and their adopted one: "hopefully, the experience of reading in two languages will reflect, perhaps, the experience of living between two cultures" (9). Clearly, those who do not read in two languages will not be able to see that experience reflected. That is one of the risks of such a project.

In the prologue, Concha Alborg reflects on her split identity, too. Her second book of short stories, *Una noche en casa* (An evening at home), published in 1995, reveals important differences from her first one. Her first book dealt with the experiences of a Spanish woman who lived a "transplanted" life in the United States, and who nostalgically remembered her childhood in Valencia and her adolescence in Madrid. That woman was already living in the United States but the "home" mentioned in the title was still Spain. Along those same lines, the woman who appears in the second book, the short story collection, no longer lives a "transplanted" life in the United States. She feels a part of her new country and has a point of view closer to that of someone from the United States and not Spain. In a way, the title makes reference to this: *Más allá del jet-lag* (Beyond jetlag) as it signifies that the trip has been concluded and that the protagonist of Concha Alborg's short stories has already arrived in the United States. Spain continues being an important point of reference for her, but it is no longer 'home': "evenings at home, I spend them here now, in spite of not being my home of origin" (7).

There are other details that make one aware of the fact that Concha Alborg is closer to the United States than to Spain and closer to English than to Spanish. It is no longer a Spanish publisher that publishes her work, as in the case of *Una noche en casa* (*An Evening at Home*). Instead, it is a U.S. one. The title is no longer in Spanish but in English: the same could be said of the introduction. Furthermore, we already know the importance the title and the prologue have in establishing the terms of the debate. It is as if now Spanish existed side by side with English in Alborg's work, but as if the English now had certain precedence over the Spanish. The book's narrative thrust also reveals something about the position of Spanish in the United States, which has been acquiring steadily increasing, symbolic value, due to the demographic growth of the Latino population and their increasing purchasing power. Still, it has yet to achieve the status of English.

Concha Alborg also writes about her Latina identity. She is an "other," according to the response she gave on the United States census questionnaire: "[I am] Latina in some respects, but not from the Hispanic countries more often recognized by a U.S. reader—Cuba, Mexico, Puerto Rico—and yet, [I am] related to them by culture and language" (8). In one of her short stories, the narrator comments on the typical question her family was asked in the United States—"Where are you from?"—to which her family would reply "Spain." The next thing they would hear would be: "Seriously? Great! I love Mexico..." Even if her narrator attempts to clarify that Spain is south of France, in Europe, she does not seem offended by her interlocutor's confusion. Through the years in the United States, she will become more and more identified with immigrants from Hispanic countries. Shared culture and language will help her build bridges with those other countries. Accordingly, the Spanish immigrant's trip to the United States ends when she identifies herself as "Latina in some respects." Deep down inside, all Latinos in the United States are like her, "Latinos in some respects," and in others, something else.

Sometimes there is an essentially untranslatable concept at the root of some of Alborg's short stories. In "The Prom-Mom," for example, the narrator states: "This is one of the stories I have to write in English because how could I explain in Spanish what a "senior prom" is?" (67). An attempt at cultural translation fails: "It is something like those *fiestas de quinceañeras* (fifteenth birthday parties for young women [like sweet sixteen, coming out parties]) in the Puerto Rican culture, a celebration of [a girl's] formal introduction into society, but since we do not have anything similar in Spain, it would not help much either" (67). There is no generic Latino identity here. For Alborg, it is not enough to translate the English-language concept into one for which there is a term in some version of Latin American or Peninsular Spanish: she wants to translate it into Peninsular Spanish, as if to suggest that the constant comparison that she is making is between two cultures, specifically between the U.S. and Spanish cultures. Latino identity is very general and includes and obscures a great diversity of countries and local nuances.

A Personal Testimony

By way of conclusion, I would like to cite my own experience in the United States. I arrived in this country in 1988, two years before the publication of my first book. Eighteen years later, with six novels and three books of short stories under my belt, all of them written entirely in Spanish, sometimes I feel that there are people who are surprised by the fact that I have never felt compelled to write in English, to integrate myself more explicitly into the realm of Latino literature written in English and, moreover, into U.S. literature in general. To tell the truth, my early years in the United States were marked by my fear of cultural upheaval: the force of a U.S. culture that absorbs everything, that appropriates everything and reinvents it through its own codes, forced me to take a defensive stance and protect myself in my own cultural universe. While some of my writer friends from Chile and Argentina freely read the work of U.S. writers of our generation, I spent my time in the United States trying to keep up with new developments in Spanish and Latin American literature. Not only that, I wanted to write in correct, authentically "pure" Spanish, in the worst sense of the word, without any trace that might betray the fact that I was living in the "bowels of the monster."

Of course, this attitude caused me to have a paranoid view of language. In my first book of short stories, *Las máscaras de la nada* (Masks of Nothingness) (1990), I wrote, in one instance, that the character had arrived at a certain place, because it seemed to me that "to arrive" (arribar) was a more literary word than "to get" (to a place) (llegar). A critic, nevertheless, told me that I needed to be careful with my Anglicisms: "arribar" came from "to arrive" and, in that context, I should have simply used, *llegar* (for 'to get to a place'). Could my subconscious be betraying me? I did not think so. At that moment, I should have realized that my struggle was in vain. I was not only dealing with how I was writing but also with the way in which I could be read. I had to accept the influence of English on my work due to the fact I was living in the United States. Even then, it took me a while to accept the inevitable, and do it in a positive manner. Languages and cultures grow; they are stimulated by contact with other languages and cultures. My writing might benefit from continuous close contact with English.

Recently, with my fourth novel, *Sueños digitales* (Digital Dreams) (2000), I began to let loose. There are many Spanish words in it but they are differentiated from the English by italics, to highlight their foreignness: *screensaver, cut, zapping, background* . . . There was a reason: the novel's action takes place at a newspaper and most of those words are part of the everyday language of journalists. They are related to the media, particularly those dealing with film and computers, and while it is true that in Spain there is always an attempt to translate these terms, with varying degrees of success, and "screensaver" becomes *salvapantalla* (screensaver), it is also true that Latin Americans feel more comfortable using "screensaver" than *salvapantalla*.

Starting with my next novel, *La materia del deseo* (The Matter of Desire) (2001), I took more chances: the action in certain chapters takes place in the United States and I tried to have my characters speak U.S. Spanish, interspersing it with a word or phrase in English, fusing concepts as though in Spanglish. Yasemín, a German woman in the Latin American studies program at the University of Madison, says things like: "Les sigue costando entender que una pueda estar interesada en quote unquote Latinoamérica desde el punto de vista conceptual, as a sophisticated intellectual game . . . Mírense ustedes, ¿qué hay de parecido entre un venezolano y un boliviano? Nada, aparte del idioma. Not even soccer" (49) ("It's still hard for them to understand that I could be interested in quote unquote Latin America from a conceptual point of view, as a sophisticated intellectual game . . . Look at yourselves! What are the similarities between a Venezuelan and a Bolivian? Nothing—aside from the language. Not even soccer"). I wanted to recreate the atmosphere in which Spanish develops in the U.S. academic world but it was clear to me that I was writing a novel in Spanish for readers who did not necessarily know English. For that reason, I wrote all the essential information needed to understand the plot or the characters' motives in Spanish. I had no desire to assume that the reader had to have what Debra Castillo calls in *Redreaming America* a "cultural and linguistic doubleness" (13), as is the case with writers such as Giannina Braschi or Concha Alborg. I thought I was being a traditionalist, somewhat conservative—not experimental, in any case. That is why I must confess I was surprised at the virulence with which some critics attacked this aspect of my novel: I was called a snob for having my characters speak in such a way, so I could show that I was fashionable.[6] I felt that in order for those critics to understand what I had tried to achieve, they would have to pay a visit to the world of U.S. academe. It was also clear that such misunderstandings would continue.

Of course, by this time I was ready to accept the misunderstandings. I may live in Spanish, write in Spanish, and breathe Spanish, but I have given up any attempt to achieve artificial and lackluster linguistic purity. Of course, my loss of fear regarding cultural upheaval is also due to the fact that while I was writing and reading in Spanish, I was becoming rooted in the United States. I began to discover that I was actually a member of a U.S. racial minority group and with it acquired a new Latino or U.S. identity, as it were. I still mainly dialog with the Latin American literary tradition but my personal contemporary canon also includes Latino authors such as Daniel Alarcón, Francisco Goldman and Silvana Paternostro. Juan Bruce-Novoa has asked a key question: "At what point can an immigrant Mexican writer be considered a Chicano?" (147).[7] One does not know with certainty. I suspect this is a very individualistic process, one in which one immigrant may take six months, another ten years, and yet another never become one. I suppose it all depends on his or her degree of attachment to the local Latino culture, to the everyday debate about the important things that affect Latinos from diverse classes and races in the United States. A Mexican can live most of his life in Chicago but continue to write in Spanish, engaging in dialogue with Mexican culture while turning his back on the complex issue of Latinos in the United States. A Peruvian can arrive in Los Angeles and six months later feel viscerally Latino (this does not mean he feels assimilated or has cut ties with Peru). Perhaps, how one is defined by others is not as important as how one defines one's self, if one feels part of a culture, of a tradition.

Of course, identity is not a game in which something can be added only in exchange for losing something else. After almost ten years of living in the United States, I began to feel a part of the United States, without that meaning that I had set aside my Bolivian or Latin American or Spanish American identity. I consider myself part of the great Spanish literary tradition and believe my challenge—a challenge faced by many others like me, e.g., Santiago Vaquera, who was born in the United States but writes his literature in Spanish[8]—is to become part of the Latino and U.S. literary traditions without having to give up writing in Spanish. It is a great challenge—one that must be met. We must work to broaden the understanding of what it is to have a Latino identity; include Spaniards who live in the United States as part of that identity; expand the concept of what is understood as Latino literature; give more visibility to those who are writing it in Spanish; and finally, broaden the concept of literature in the United States. Someday, those who study Spanish and Spanish-language literature of the United States will no longer only study them as part of the curriculum of foreign language departments. Spanish can be many things in the United States but it has not been "foreign" for a long time. It lives in many places and one of them is the United States, despite the concern of some.

Notes

1. In "La lengua mojada," *Opinión* journal (Managua, Nicaragua), January 4, 2001.
2. In "McOndo y otros mitos," Diana Palaverish is surprised to find that a Bolivian, who has lived in the United States for only a few years, and a Chilean, who is a 'gringophile' and whose native tongue is English, as he states, proudly, on his Web page, can both come to the United States and 'discover' the Latino voices in this country." When that anthology was published, I had lived in the United States for twelve years.
3. Another section of the prologue states: "one of the anthology's premises' consisted in "searching, though comedies or dramas, adventures or thrillers, for the Latin Americans lost/trapped/seduced in the depths of the United States" (17).
4. José del Valle mentioned this in a question and answer session of an informal talk given at the Cornell University, November 21, 2003.
5. This is also highlighted in a yet unpublished article on Alborg by Debra Castillo.
6. An example: Peruvian critic Javier Agreda wrote: "As regards the language, too, we detect a less rigorous and more conceding attitude. If until now Paz Soldán had avoided using regionalisms and Anglicisms in his books, here he not only employs colloquial expressions from his country; there are also real abuses of the language and even paragraphs entirely in English. [It is a] strange combination that attempts to be in tune with the language presently spoken by Latin American young people."
7. Sandoval and Aparicio also ask themselves this question, although they do not give a

specific answer to it. They do accept that "this complicates debates on definitions of what it means to be Latino and Latinohood (latinidad)" (684).
8. Vaquera is a virtually unpublished author. We included one of his stories, "Esperando en el Lost and Found" in *Se habla español*. The difficulties he has had in publishing his works with U.S. as well as Mexican publishers demonstrates that the prospects for Latino writers who write in Spanish are not always easy. Their "natural" (native) publishing houses, the U.S. ones, would prefer not to have to deal with the extra cost of translating them into English, and the Mexican publishers are not used to Vaquera's Spanish, which in some cases turns out to be a form of Spanglish.

Works Cited

Agreda, Javier. "La materia del deseo." Críticas sobre Edmundo Paz Soldán; La materia del deseo, September 13, 2005. <http://es.geocities.com/agreda5/Literatura/pazsoldan.html#3>.
Alborg, Concha. *Beyond Jet-Lag: Other Stories*. New Jersey: Nuevo Espacio, 2000.
———. *Una noche en casa*. Madrid: Huerga and Fierro, 1995.
Bruce-Novoa, Juan. "Chicano Literary Space." *Retrospace: Collected Essays on Chicano Literature*. Houston: Arte Público Press, 1990.
Castillo, Debra. *Redreaming America: Towards a Bilingual American Culture*. Albany: SUNY Press, 2005.
———. "Los 'nuevos' latinos y la globalización de los estudios literarios." *Más allá de la ciudad letrada: Crónicas y espacios urbanos*. Ed. Boris Muñoz y Silvia Spitta. Pittsburgh: Instituto Internacional de Literatura Iberoamericana, 2003. 439–59.
———. "Latina or Americaniard?" Unpublished document.
Del Valle, José. "Spanish Language Policy and the Logic of Post-Nationalism." Informal talk at Cornell University, November 21, 2003.
Kanellos, Nicolás, Kenya C. Dworkin y Méndez et al., eds. *En otra voz: Antología de la literatura hispana de los Estados Unidos*. Houston: Arte Público Press, 2002.
Palaverish, Diana. "McOndo y otros mitos." <www.literaturas.com/McondoyotrosmitosOPINIONjunio23.htm>.
Paz Soldán, Edmundo, and Alberto Fuguet, eds. *Se habla español: Voces latinas en USA*. Miami: Alfaguara, 2000.
Paz Soldán, Edmundo. *La materia del deseo*. Miami: Alfaguara, 2001.
———. *Sueños digitales*. La Paz: Alfaguara, 2000.
———. *Las máscaras de la nada*. Cochabamba: Los amigos del libro, 1990.
Sandoval, Alberto and Frances Aparicio. "Hibridismos culturales: La literatura y cultura de los latinos en los Estados Unidos." *Revista Iberoamericana*, LXXI. 212 (July-September 2005): 665–97.

Part III
Spanish in the Era of Multiculturalism and Globalization

◆ 8

Language Imperialism and the Spread of Global Spanish[1]

Clare Mar-Molinero

Introduction

This essay will explore the spread of Spanish as a global language in the contemporary world, examining the extent to which it maintains a role as a linguistic colonizer in the way it manifestly did in earlier centuries and in particular during the height of the Spanish Empire (e.g., Lodares, this volume). In order to do this, it will be necessary to establish whether Spanish is indeed a 'global' language and to explore the nature of its current global spread in the context of language and globalization, about which there is a growing volume of theoretical literature (Cameron 2000; Crystal 1997; Gardt and Huppauf 2004; Graddol 1997; *Journal of Sociolinguistics* 2003; Maurais & Morris 2003; Wright 2004). The long-established importance of the relationship between language and national identity will continue to be significant, albeit in the way in which this now jostles with supranational, global identities. For this reason, national language policies are still relevant and influential. In the Spanish-speaking world, various national governments have shown an interest in promoting and/or protecting Spanish; the three meetings of the *Congreso de la Lengua Española* (Spanish Language Conference) held in Zacatecas (1997), Valladolid (2001) and Rosario (2004) serve to underline the concerns and determinations of the elites of this linguistic community to further the status of Spanish. Particularly prominent in these activities is the Spanish government and, in the final part of this essay, therefore, I will concentrate on discussing the work of one of the agents of Spain's language policies, the Instituto Cervantes. Such top-down management of language might be described as a form of (conscious or unconscious) linguistic imperialism (Phillipson 1992); the results of what Hamel (2003a) has called 'language armies.' Regarding the spread of English and its global dominance, many processes besides those that could be described as overtly imperialist can be identified; for Spanish, the link with deliberate language spread policies does indeed suggest deliberate efforts to impose and dominate.

Language and Globalization

Globalization today frames much of our understanding of world systems and our social, political, and cultural inter-connections. Within the growing volume of literature on globalization, there are clear differences and disputes as to the nature and outcomes of the phenomenon (Wright 2004). It is, however, especially associated with new relationships that are being formed globally, often cutting across traditional borders, particularly national ones. Modern electronic technology has dramatically enhanced the communications that underpin these relationships. However, Blommaert stresses that the fact that we are envisaging interactions on such a wide geographical level should not lead us to believe there is total uniformity about globalization processes (612). As these processes cross boundaries and connect at transnational levels, there are tensions between both the national and the transnational reactions to global trends. Blommaert argues that "the system is marked by both the existence of separate spaces (for example, states) and deep inter-connectiveness of the different spaces, often, precisely, through the existence of worldwide elites" (612). Blommaert goes on to state that "Globalization implies that developments at the 'top' or the core of the world system have a wide variety of effects at the 'bottom' or the periphery of that system" (612).

It is precisely such a hierarchy that suggests to me that the world's inter-connectiveness is best understood in terms of power and dominance, reminiscent indeed of empires and imperialism. Moreover, globalization has brought with it a role for 'global' languages, crossing borders and taking over in domains where previously local languages were used. This, in turn, has seen an expansion in the role of world languages and a decrease, and even death, of a multitude of smaller, more local languages (Crystal 2000; Mühlhäusler 1996). This is a postmodern kind of imperialism where the agents of imperialism are no longer only armies and national governments, but, for instance, multinational companies, transnational culture and leisure organizations, global media corporations, or international political elites. Furthermore, by using an imperialist theoretical framework to understand these phenomena, we can explore more readily who it is that controls and acts in these processes. Hamel (2003a), in particular, has argued strongly that the ability to identify the agent of language change and language spread is often lost when analyzing political, cultural and linguistic processes from the globalization perspective alone. He argues that theories of globalization tend to lose sight of the actor or agent in the process. He writes that, with globalization

> new impersonalised tertiary bonds, mediated by technologies and corporations, increasingly determine our lives . . . New de-territorialised "third cultures" such as fashion or the new international management culture, are emerging with their own discourses and language usages. (Hamel 2003a: 7)

He refers to

> the increasing dominance, restrictions and global control over a growing number of domains in our lives, while at the same time the actors and sources behind the scenes appear more and more diluted. (2003a: 7)

Hamel urges a reinterpretation of current global linguistic change from the linguistic imperialism perspective in order to identify the actors and agents of language spread and to understand the power dominance within this.

In his pioneering (and much criticized) book on this concept, Phillipson argues that Linguistic Imperialism is a "subset of linguicism" which in turn he defines as "ideologies, structures and practices which are used to legitimate, effectuate and reproduce an unequal division of power and resources (both material and immaterial) between groups which are defined on the basis of language" (Phillipson 47). Even as Phillipson is criticized for explaining the spread and creation of 'world' English as being *solely* the product of linguistic imperialism and linguicism (i.e., Brutt-Griffler 2002; Spolsky 2004), his contribution to a theory of language spread and language hierarchies is useful and frequently applicable. The link between language spread, imposition and dominance and the political and economic dominance imposed by colonial and neo-colonial powers also highlights how this has been, above all, a European and Western-led process.

A key factor in modern linguistic imperialism is the provision of (foreign and/or second) language teaching and learning of the world language in question. This in turn raises questions surrounding what form of the language should be used and taught—the Standard Language question—and also what cultural values are reflected in the language curriculum. To discuss these issues in a contemporary situation, I will turn to the case of Spanish, first setting this in context by outlining its current spread around the world. Much of the historical spread of Spanish was clearly the result of imperialism and colonization. Although I will argue that such dominance and imposition continues in many spheres of Spanish language policies today, I acknowledge that we can also observe grassroots movements and 'bottom-up' processes that also affect the current spread of Spanish, in particular amongst Latinos in the United States. However, the latter will not be discussed in this essay.

The Spanish-Speaking Community Today

The spread of Spanish today has been affected by many of the forces of globalization both in terms of quantity—how many people speak Spanish—and in terms of the nature of its use—who speaks Spanish and for what purposes?

Estimates as to how many people speak Spanish inevitably vary, reflecting the unreliability of many language censuses. I am, however, fully aware of the need to treat statistics reporting numbers of speakers of languages with caution given the potential ambiguities and uncertainties that such censuses may contain, arising from, for example, the nature of the questions asked, by whom, in what language and where.[2] Self-reporting can hide very different attitudes and behavior, from the desire to hide ethnic origins to a wish to exaggerate linguistic competence. Categories such as 'mother tongue,' 'language' and even 'speaking a language' can contain a wide variation resulting in significant differences in the totals produced. The Summer Institute of Linguists' *Ethnologue* publication is a generally respected source for linguistic data, where the number of 417 million speakers of Spanish across the world is currently reported (SIL 2005),[3] placing it amongst the most widely spoken languages, after English and Chinese. All the principal Spanish-speaking states border on other Spanish-speaking states with the exception of Spain (as well as Equatorial Guinea and the Philippines where speakers of Spanish have been reduced significantly). This has been important in terms of language spread and in maintaining the presence of the language.

However, the size of the population alone is not enough to determine the influence and global role of a language. We need to ask who these speakers are and distinguish between very different categories. For example, if we follow Kachru's (1985) well-known concept of 'concentric circles' we can examine the Spanish-speaking community to see what proportion are mother tongue speakers, what proportion are second language speakers, and how many foreign language speakers.[4] Kachru refers to an 'inner' circle (mother tongue or first language speakers), an 'outer' circle (second language speakers) and an 'expanding' circle who are those learning the language as a foreign language.

The majority of Spanish speakers fall within Kachru's 'inner' circle of mother tongue speakers. Albeit the category 'mother tongue' is a very contested term, we can accept that a majority of those who live in Spain and in nearly all the twenty Latin American countries where Spanish is the official language, as well as a part of the Spanish-speaking community in the U.S., acquire Spanish as their first language. This proportion is lower or even a slight minority in one or two Latin American countries where there is a strong presence of other indigenous languages, such as in Paraguay and Bolivia. In these countries, as with much of Latin America and parts of Spain, there are linguistic minority groups who nonetheless will learn Spanish very early in their lives (probably when they go to school) and speak it to a high competence level. This latter category of Spanish speakers, such as many Catalans and Guarani speakers, fits Kachru's 'outer' circle. Together these two groups make up for a very high percentage of the speech community referred to as Spanish speakers.

However, there also exists a growing community of the third 'expanding circle' of Spanish speakers. Included in this group are those who learn Spanish as a foreign language as part of their education curriculum or, in adult life, for purposes such as business, leisure, and international communication. This latter group is particularly significant when assessing the level of the global role of Spanish as they represent those with a perceived need, motivation, and desire to learn Spanish voluntarily and enthusiastically. They are influenced by the need to understand Spanish because it is used in some or all of the domains that are discussed next. It is precisely the presence of Spanish in a range of prestigious public domains that indicate its growing status as a global, not simply international, language. Use and recognition of Spanish in political, economic, cultural, educational, and scientific spheres of life all represent ways in which the 'expanding circle' grows.

'Global' Spanish[5]

Twenty-one countries recognize Spanish as their official or national language, and Spanish is an official language in many international bodies, such as the United Nations and its offshoots (i.e., UNESCO), as well as the European Union. The political and economic kudos of these Spanish-speaking countries, however, varies from the buoyant economy of Spain, to the expanding markets of, say, Chile, Mexico and some of the *Mercosur*[6] countries, to the very poor and weak economies of countries like the Dominican Republic or Guatemala with notably high levels of illiteracy. In terms of economic power, we should also be aware of the growing influence of Spanish speakers in the U.S.

In the context of global languages and processes of globalization, it is essential to note how widely used (or not) Spanish is on the Internet. Marcos Marín reports that the Spanish share of the linguistic output on the Internet is only five percent, and that this is in fifth place after English (far ahead of any other language), Japanese, German, and Chinese. However, he highlights the fact that Spanish language search engines do exist such as Spanish versions of the widely-available general search engines, and academic lists in Spanish (325). More importantly, however, the trend towards languages other than English on the Internet appears to be on the increase, and, particularly in response to the rise in e-commerce. Given its use by such developed countries as Spain and the U.S., Spanish is likely to be a beneficiary of this trend.

Spanish is also the language of the education systems of all the countries where it is the official language, and it is widely taught elsewhere as a foreign language, particularly in the U.S. where it is the first foreign language (Instituto Cervantes 2000). Increasingly Spanish is offered both in secondary curricula across the world, most notably in the Far East (Japan), Australia, Europe, and, notably, Brazil, although in almost all of these places, it is the second foreign language after English. It is also increasingly evident as a popular language in continuing and adult education classes.

The Instituto Cervantes' Centro Virtual *El español en el mundo* (*2000*) provides some interesting and revealing data about the level of use and language learning of Spanish in various countries. Brazil is considered a particularly significant site for the growth of Spanish, a view shared by other contemporary commentators (e.g., Del Valle and Gabriel-Stheeman 2002). The reasons given for this increase in the demand for learning Spanish as a foreign language, which the *Anuario* describes as 'de bonanza, de auge y de prestigio' (prosperity, peak, and prestige) (Instituto Cervantes, 2000), are political (the emergence of the Southern Latin American 'Common Market' *Mercosur*), economic (as well as Mercosur, the expanding investment by Spanish companies in Brazil) and cultural (the boom in Hispanic culture worldwide in recent years).

Cultural production in Spanish is another area where the language's profile can be and is being raised, both through the activities of such organizations as the Instituto Cervantes, and, more recently, with the current popularity of Latin music and bands. Tourism to Spanish-speaking regions, on the one hand and, once again, the U.S. Latino community on the other, are expanding global interaction with the Spanish language. This so-called boom in Hispanic culture also includes both book and record publishing. It is also important to note the sudden popularity in both America and Europe of Latin-style bands and pop groups (Buena Vista Social Club, Ricky Martin, Jennifer López, Cristina Aguilera, Shakira, Enrique Iglesias, and so on) and in salsa dance classes and club evenings. While the pop stars themselves do not all sing in Spanish, the positive attitudes that their connection with a Spanish-speaking world brings about an increased interest in and a desire to learn Spanish amongst the tourists and leisure seekers of the developed world. Publishing in Spanish is also on an upward trend, reflecting the provision of Spanish teaching on the one hand, and an increase in the literacy rate across the Spanish-speaking world on the other, as well as a genuine increase in the popularity of reading in Spanish (Carreira 2002).

Spanish and Globalization

Such high profile use and demand for Spanish certainly exposes the language to many processes of globalization. Coupland (2003) suggests that there are four key processes to take into account when analyzing language in a global era; these include: *interdependence, the compression of time and space, disembedding,* and *commodification.*

Taking these in turn, we can see that the spread of Spanish means that the global *interdependence* of Spanish-speaking communities to one another and to other parts of the world system has a significant impact on the language itself. The Spanish-speaking world shares media and cultural production, in particular those available through fast technological forms of communication such as television, film, recorded music, and the Internet. Collectively, this language community responds to new linguistic needs and creates or borrows new words and terms. The second process identified by Coupland, the *compression across time and space,* experienced by this large population of Spanish speakers is part of the same phenomenon with electronic communication making the geographical distances insignificant.

There is no doubt, too, that the Spanish language is increasingly seen as a *commodity* as will be seen, for example, in the Instituto Cervantes' packaging of it on behalf of the Spanish government. Hüppauf argues in a discussion about the success of English and the perceived decline in popularity of German that "the global language (i.e., English) is highly attractive and successful in seducing people the world over . . . It is the idiom of hopes and promises . . . of consumption and unrestricted movement" (17). This kind of popularity and 'seduction' is increasingly recognized by the guardians and the promoters of Spanish who are currently selling their product to a world-wide public whose attraction to Spanish is characterized, for instance, by a craze for Latino music, dance and fashion, by mass tourism to Spanish-speaking destinations, as well as by the recognition of the existence of growing Spanish-language economic markets in Spain, Latin America, and the U.S.

The concept of *disembedding* referred to by Coupland (and following the well-known work of Giddens 1995a, 1995b) is evident in, for example, the transfer of culturally specific speech items originated in one Spanish speech community to another and their consequent adaptation or re-embedding. Coupland (468) cites Giddens (1991: 18) in explaining this concept as "the 'lifting out' of social relations from their local contexts and their rearticulation across indefinite tracts of time-space." In the case of Spanish, the twin effects of this are hybridity, on the one hand, and homogeneity, on the other. That is to say that Spanish created to address international or global audiences (for example, in films, the media, the Internet) is characterized both by a tendency to bring together various regional or national varieties (often those considered non-standard, and frequently also peppered with anglicisms) or the opposite effect of aspiring to an exaggerated neutral form of the language bereft of any regional or national traces. Neither form is owned by a speech community. It is not the Spanish of Spain or the Spanish of Mexico or the Spanish of Argentina exclusively. Such disembedding leads to alarm and a sense of protection from those who see their role as guarding the pure standard form of Spanish. These are above all (but not exclusively) those who support Castilian Spanish from central Spain as the model for the language.

In their attempts to respond to such features of globalization affecting Spanish, these same guardians, such as the Spanish Government, the Spanish

Royal Language Academy (*Real Academia de la Lengua española*, RAE), Spanish media outlets, academics, and educationalists, seek to promote and extend the role and status of Spanish and to define the nature of the language. Insofar as the relationship between language and national identity has always been a significant and often contentious one throughout the history of Spanish nation-building (Mar-Molinero 2000), this defence is also to some extent a rearguard action against the forces of globalization in a world where the nation-state is losing its centrality. Furthermore, it is an example, too, of the desire of many Western European nations to maintain control of their linguistic and political hegemony across the world. Globalization, thus, is seen as potentially the cause of a perceived threat to the dominance and control by former imperialist powers. However, paradoxically, these same elite language protectors also recognize that globalization can serve to further and retain the linguistic dominance of global languages if the process of commodification is successfully harnessed.

Spain's Global Language Planning: The Imposition of a Norm

In the final section of this essay, I would like to examine how then this deliberate global spread of Spanish is being realized by focusing on the teaching of Spanish as an international language (and through that the transmission of Spanish language culture), and how this raises questions about concepts of standard language. Lippi-Green, amongst others, has identified the link between language standardization and cultural dominant groups as Standard Language Ideology which she defines as "a bias towards an abstract, idealized, homogeneous spoken language which is imposed and maintained by dominant bloc institutions and which names as its model the written language, but which is drawn primarily from the spoken language of the upper middle class" (54). In the case of much of the international Spanish promoted by the Spanish government across the world, we might also add that it is drawn too from the educated variety of Castilian Spanish from central Spain.

Today, Spanish continues to spread by the intergenerational transmission of the language amongst Spanish-speaking communities, including those created by recent migration (such as in the U.S. and parts of Northern Europe). However, it has also spread through effective and popular teaching of Spanish as a foreign language in many parts of the world. The demand displayed for learning Spanish is based on a series of reasons mentioned previously including those overtly promoted by the Spanish government as part of its aim to strengthen and enhance a pan-Hispanic community across the world. As already argued, part of this is the desire to strengthen Spain's sense of its own national identity in a world of increasing supranational identities, and it is also a desire to consolidate a power bloc which might claim to compete with the overwhelming march of global English. The Spanish language learning/teaching industry, *español como lengua extranjera* (ELE) (Spanish as a Foreign Language) is thus a flourishing and expanding one. It is considerably smaller in scale, but nonetheless resembles in many ways the enormous English as a foreign language/English language teaching (EFL/ELT) industry.

A significant agent in this delivery of Spanish language learning is the Instituto Cervantes, which has been modelled to a great extent on the UK's British Council. I will, therefore, in this section highlight some of the characteristics of the Instituto Cervantes and particularly of its language teaching program. First, I will give some background information about the Instituto Cervantes as well as provide extracts from some of its key documents, before discussing how far we can identify an ideological agenda underpinning this organization—either consciously or unconsciously.

The Instituto Cervantes

Since its beginnings in 1991, the Instituto Cervantes has expanded the number of its centers across the world dramatically. Besides those in existence in Spain, there are now centers in Europe, North America, Brazil, Africa, the Middle East, and Asia. Today, there are some forty Instituto Cervantes centers around the world. On the Instituto's website its purpose is described as the following:[7]

> El Instituto Cervantes es la institución pública creada por España en 1991 para la promoción y la enseñanza de la lengua española y para la difusión de la cultura española e hispanoamericana. (www.cervantes.es)

> (The Instituto Cervantes is the public institution created by Spain in 1991 for the promotion and teaching of the Spanish language and for the diffusion of Spanish and Hispanoamerican culture.)

'Spain' in this context includes a host of significant and influential people and groups, given that the Instituto is to be overseen by a *Patronato* (governing body) which nominally includes the King and the Spanish President on its board, as well as representatives from the world of culture and letters in Spain and in Latin America (for example, from the Royal Academy, Latin American language academies, universities and other institutions). Moreover, and significantly, its *Consejo de Administración* (management body) which approves the general plans and projects of the Instituto consists of representatives from the ministries of Foreign Affairs, Education, Culture and Sport, Treasury, and Home Affairs, as well as from the *Patronato* itself. A clear commitment and interest in the shape and direction of the Instituto and its activities are manifested by such a high-profile membership. Therefore, even though the broad mission and aims of the Instituto are likely to be shared across the political spectrum in Spain, the policies and philosophy of the Spanish government of the day can be expected to be reflected in its work.

The website declares the Instituto's aims and objectives as:

Objetivos y funciones:
- Organizar cursos generales y especiales de lengua española.
- Acreditar mediante certificados y diplomas los conocimientos adquiridos por los alumnos y organizar los exámenes de los Diplomas Oficiales de Español como Lengua Extranjera (D.E.L.E.).
- Actualizar los métodos de enseñanza y la formación del profesorado.
- Apoyar la labor de los hispanistas.
- Participar en programas de difusión de la lengua española.
- Realizar actividades de difusión cultural, en colaboración con otros organismos españoles e hispanoamericanos y con entidades de los países anfitriones.
- Poner a disposición del público bibliotecas provistas de los medios tecnológicos más avanzados. (www.cervantes.es)

(To organize general and specialized Spanish language courses; To accredit by means of certificates and diplomas the knowledge acquired by its students and to organize the examinations of its Official Diploma of Spanish as a Second Language (D.E.L.E.); To ensure up-to-date teaching and teacher training methods; To support the work of Hispanists; To participate in programs to promote the Spanish language; To provide cultural activities in collaboration with other Spanish and Hispanoamerican organizations and groups from the host nations; To provide public libraries equipped with the most up-to-date technological resources.)

Clearly the teaching of Spanish is seen as the Instituto's most important role and activity. Since its creation, the Instituto has translated this priority into the provision of language classes, teacher development, and examination venues throughout its many centers. It has developed its own foreign language teaching/learning methodology and established an on-line Spanish language learning environment (AVE, *Aula Virtual de Español*). It has also worked with Spain's national radio and television to deliver Spanish language courses. With its publications, on-line bibliographies, library holdings, and the hosting of major conferences on the state of the Spanish language, the Instituto aims to provide vast coverage of the needs of learners of Spanish as a Foreign Language (ELE).

In order to give coherence and direction to its language curriculum, as it claims on its website, the Instituto Cervantes has developed a 'curricular plan' to serve as a blueprint for its courses across the many centers. The features characterizing this plan represent the Instituto's pedagogical philosophy and methods. These are described in the following list:

- Es un plan abierto, ya que parte de una serie de propuestas de carácter general que deben adaptarse a las circunstancias concretas del entorno social, cultural y educativo de cada centro y a las características propias de cada grupo de alumnos.
- Es un plan centrado en el alumno, que considera fundamental el diálogo entre el profesor y los alumnos sobre los objetivos, los contenidos e incluso la metodología de la enseñanza.
- Es un plan integrado, en la medida en que los distintos componentes curriculares—objetivos, contenidos, metodología y evaluación—actúan de forma simultánea y no sucesiva.
- Es un plan ecléctico en la selección de las informaciones que ofrece y en el planteamiento de las propuestas de actuación.
- Es un plan flexible, dado que, a partir de las líneas generales de actuación que el propio plan establece, cada centro organiza la distribución de los cursos y la oferta de horarios en función de las necesidades de su alumnado.
- Es un plan homogéneo, en la medida en que establece para los distintos centros unos mismos objetivos generales, distribuidos en los cuatro niveles—inicial, intermedio, avanzado y superior—en los que se organiza la enseñanza. (www.cervantes.es)

(It is an open plan, given that it works from a series of general assumptions which should be adapted to the concrete circumstances of the social, cultural and educational environment of each center and to the particular characteristics of each group of students;
It is a student-centered plan which considers as fundamental the dialogues between teacher and student over objectives, content and even the teaching methods;

It is an integrated plan insofar as the different curricular components—objectives, content, methodology and evaluation—operate in a simultaneous and non-sequential way;
It is an eclectic plan in the choice of information it offers and in its implemantation;
It is a flexible plan, given that working from the general lines of implementation that the plan establishes, each center organizes the spread of courses and the type of timetable according to the needs of the students;
It is a homogeneous plan in the way in which it establishes for different centers the same general objectives, distributed over the four levels—beginners, intermediate, advanced and higher—into which the teaching is organized.)

The plan is thus described, on the Instituto Cervantes website, as student-centered, adaptable, flexible and at the same time homogeneous in its ultimate aims. However, of particular interest to this chapter, are certain underlying principles concerning the *model* of language to be used by the Instituto and its centers when delivering Spanish language learning. To discover this we can note the criteria given for the materials and courses available on the on-line website, the *Aula Virtual de Español* (Spanish Virtual Room), or AVE. Here we find an important statement concerning the choice of linguistic varieties to be used:

La variedad principal del AVE y norma del corpus que se propone al alumno como modelo de lengua para su reproducción es el español peninsular central. (. . .) se optó por el español peninsular central por no estar en interacción con otras lenguas y tener menos elementos diferenciadores con respecto a la lengua común. (. . .) La selección de esta variedad como principal está fundamentada en que el español peninsular central tiene suficiente importancia demográfica y proyección hacia el conjunto de la comunidad hispanohablante a través de manifestaciones culturales y medios de comunicación. (www.cervantes.es)

(The principal variety of the AVE and the corpus's norms which are presented to the students as a model of language for them to copy is central peninsular Spanish. [. . .] [C]entral peninsular Spanish was chosen because it is not in contact with other languages and has the fewest differentiating characteristics as regards the shared language. [. . .] The selection of this as the principal variety is based on the fact that central peninsular Spanish has sufficient demographic importance and status amongst the Spanish-speaking community through media and cultural expressions.)

Furthermore we are told:

> [...] el español general o estándar recoge los rasgos comunes y compartidos por sus variedades. [...] Las variedades secundarias están presentes en el AVE a través de la presentación y comentario de sus rasgos y/o de la actuación de sus hablantes. (www.cervantes.es)
> ([...] General or standard Spanish brings together the common features shared by all its varieties [...] The secondary varieties are present in the AVE through presenting and commenting on their features and/or through their use by their speakers.)

This particular position regarding language varieties taken by the Instituto Cervantes through its AVE materials suggests a very clear ideological position vis-à-vis a perception of standard Spanish. The standard form is conceived by the Instituto and promoted through its language courses and resources as being that of not only Spanish from Spain, but also that of central Spain, uncontaminated, it claims, by such influences as other regional languages or dialects and accents. Moreover, the use of the term 'secondary' to refer to the varieties that are different from the 'central peninsula' one, implicitly or explicitly implies a position of inferiority. It is claimed that this central variety has a certain demographic importance, which is an extraordinary claim. The current population of all of Spain is some forty million, of whom the 'central peninsula' variety speakers are only a part. Given that the figures for global Spanish speakers, on the other hand, are estimated at over four hundred million, the claim, it would seem, is based rather on a perception of this variety's importance through its 'media and cultural expressions.' This further underpins the ideologically framed interpretations of the position of the peninsular Spanish variety.

By 'cultural expressions' we understand the Instituto to refer to those practices, activities and output that the AVE stress form an important part of the sociocultural content of their materials. Their website claims that

> El conocimiento de la cultura de los países de habla hispana constituye uno de los objetivos básicos del AVE. Los contenidos socioculturales de los cursos ofrecen una imagen real de la sociedad y de la cultura hispanas en toda su variedad y riqueza a través de materiales de distinta procedencia: prensa, literatura, cine, música. (www.cervantes.es)
>
> (Knowledge of the culture of Spanish-speaking countries constitutes one of the main objectives of the AVE. The sociocultural content of the courses offers a

true image of Hispanic culture and society in all its variety and richness through materials from diverse sources: press, literature, cinema, music.)

However, the question must be asked as to what a 'true image' is and who decides it. The selection, interpretation, and presentation of this Hispanic diversity is inevitably a subjective one, and one based therefore on the ideology, beliefs and agenda of those who guide the policy and the decisions of the Instituto Cervantes, identified previously as being at the heart of the Spanish Government. Significantly, the Spanish President said in his speech to the 2005 annual meeting of the *Patronato* (and published in the Institute's in-house magazine *Cervantes,* enero-febrero, 2005) "La lengua no es sólo palabras, sino un fiel reflejo de nuestra concepción del mundo, y en ella se recoge nuestra historia" ("Language is not only words, but a faithful reflection of our conception of the world, and in it we incorporate our history").

It is not just the nature of the cultural content of the materials used in language courses or of the selection of the quintessential Castilian central peninsular linguistic variety that suggest that the ideological baggage of the Instituto Cervantes reflects a worldview of *Hispanidad* as having its center in Madrid. The mission of the Instituto to promote 'widespread cultural activities,' albeit in collaboration with "Spanish and Hispanoamerican organizations," has meant that its centers across the world are highly proactive in introducing cultural events, lectures, film showings, book launchings, and so on, all of which celebrate a particular Hispanic worldview, one which is not necessarily only Spanish (from Spain) yet is nonetheless seen as coming from a privileged position which has been awarded by European and Western guardians of Hispanic culture.

Conclusion

The Instituto Cervantes does not claim to *deliberately* impose the Castilian language in its peninsular form with an elite Eurocentric set of cultural practices on all the learners in its language courses and visitors to its centers in order to relegate other Spanish varieties and non-peninsular culture to a secondary position. In fact, it is eager to insist that the Instituto represents the wide diverse Spanish-speaking population accurately and in good faith. Moreover, it does from time to time seek to promote activities that highlight the languages and cultures of the non-Castilian communities in Spain. However, it does, consciously or unconsciously, operate from the premise that Spanish originated with the Spaniards. Insofar as the Spanish language is a symbol of Spanish nationhood, any fragmentation into transnational or global configurations is a threat to Spanish national identity. The Spanish Government and the Instituto Cervantes understand the importance and strength of the high numbers of the global Spanish-speaking community and wish to foster a sense of a shared community. However, as with all those who seek to create an empire, they aim to do this from a position of leadership and, moreover, from a position of economic gain, as Spain recognizes the profitability of the linguistic product that is the Spanish language today.

Notes

1. Parts of this chapter have appeared elsewhere in an expanded form in Mar-Molinero, 2004, and Mar-Molinero, 2006.
2. A recent and relevant example of the controversy that can surround census gathering has emerged as a result of disputes over the accuracy and bias of the recent U.S. 2000 census and the figures this reports regarding the Hispanic sector of the population (e.g., 'Unos 200,000 niños no fueron contados en el Censo' *La Tribuna Hispana*, December 10, 2002). A very interesting general commentary on the problems of the 2000 U.S. census is given in Crawford, J. (2002) 'Making Sense of Census 2000.' See also Leeman (2004).
3. The Ethnologue (2005) reports a possible 322,200,000 to 358,000,000 First language users. It believes that with second language (L2) users included this would be four hundred and seventeen million, although an exact definition of first language (L1) or L2 speakers is not given. The figures incorporate data reported by the World Almanac.
4. For a fuller analysis of these questions see Moreno Fernández and Otero, 1998.
5. For a fuller discussion of the use of Spanish world-wide, see Mar-Molinero, 2004.
6   For a detailed discussion of the Mercosur bloc and the situation of language there, including the role of Brazil and of Portuguese, see Hamel, 2003b.
7. All translations from the original Spanish are mine.

Works Cited

Blommaert, Jan. "Commentary: A Sociolinguistics of Globalisation." *Journal of Sociolinguistics* 7. 4 (2003): 607-24.
Brutt-Griffler, Janina. *World English: a Study of its Development*. Clevedon, et al: Multilingual Matters, 2002.
Cameron, Deborah. *Good to Talk: Living and Working in a Communication Culture*. London: Sage, 2000.
Carreira, María. "The Media, Marketing, Critical Mass, and other Mechanisms of Linguistic Maintenance." *Southwest Journal of Linguistics*, 21. 2 (2002): 37-54.
Coupland, Nikolas. "Introduction: Sociolinguistics and Globalisation." *Journal of Sociolinguistics* 7. 4 (2003): 465-73.
Crawford, James. "Making Sense of Census 2000." 2002. <www.asu.edu/educ/epsl/LPRU/features/article5.htm>.
Crystal, David. *Language Death*. Cambridge: Cambridge University Press, 2000.
———. *English as a Global Language*. Cambridge: Cambridge University Press, 1997.
Del Valle, José, and Luis Gabriel-Stheeman, eds. *The Battle over Spanish between 1800 and 2000: Language Ideologies and Hispanic Intellectuals*. London/New York: Routledge, 2002.
Gardt, Andreas, and Bernd Huppauf, eds. *Globalization and the Future of German*. Berlin/New York: Mouton de Gruyter, 2004.
Giddens, Anthony. *Consequences of Modernity*. Stanford: Stanford University Press, 1995a.
———. *Beyond Left and Right: The Future of Radical Politics*. Stanford: Stanford University Press, 1995b.
———. *Modernity and Self-Identity: Self and Society in the Late Modern Age*. Cambridge: Polity, 1991.
Graddol, David. *The Future of English*. London: British Council, 1997.
Hamel, Rainer Enrique. *The Development of Language Empires*. Universidad Autónoma Metropolitana, México, D.F. (unpublished working paper), 2003a.
———. "Regional Blocs as a Barrier against English Hegemony: the Language Policy of Mercosur in South America." *Globalizing Languages*. Ed. Jacques Maurais and Michael Morris. Cambridge: Cambridge University Press, 2003b.
Hüppauf, Bernd. "Globalization: Threats and Opportunities." *Globalization and the Future of German*. Ed. Andreas Gardt and Bernd Huppauf. Berlin/New York: Mouton de Gruyter, 2004. 3-25.
Instituto Cervantes. *El español en el mundo. Anuario 2000*. Centro Virtual Cervantes. <http://cvc.cervantes.es/obref/anuario/>.
Journal of Sociolinguistics. Sociolinguistics and Globalization 7. 4, November 2003.
Kachru, Braj. "Standards, Codification and Sociolinguistic Realism: the English Language in the Outer Circle." *English in the World: Teaching and Learning the Language*

and Literatures. Ed. R. Quirk, et al. Cambridge: Cambridge University Press, 1985. 11–30.

Leeman, Jennifer. "Racializing Language: A History of Linguistic Ideologies in the U.S. census." *Journal of Language and Politics,* 3. 3 (2004): 507–34.

Lippi-Green, Rosina. *English with an Accent: Language, Ideology and Discrimination in the United States.* London/New York: Routledge, 1997.

Marcos Marín, Francisco. "La lengua española en internet." *El español en el mundo. Anuario 2000.* Instituto Cervantes. Madrid: Instituto Cervantes/Plaza Janés, 2000. 299–359.

Mar-Molinero, Clare. "The European Linguistic Legacy in a Global Era: Linguistic Imperialism, Spanish and the Instituto Cervantes." *Language Ideologies, Policies and Practice: Language and the Future of Europe.* Ed. Clare Mar-Molinero and P. Stevenson. Basingstoke/New York: Palgrave Macmillan, 2006. 76-91.

———. "Spanish as a World language: Language and Identity in a Global Era." *Spanish in Context* 1. 1 (2004): 3–20.

———. *The Politics of Language in the Spanish-Speaking World.* London/New York: Routledge, 2000.

Maurais, Jacques, and Michael Morris, eds. *Languages in a Globalising World.* Cambridge: Cambridge University Press, 2003.

Moreno Fernández, Francisco, and Jaime Otero. "Demografía de la lengua española." *El español en el mundo. Anuario 1998.* Instituto Cervantes. Madrid: Instituto Cervantes/Arcolibros, 1998. 59–87.

Mühlhäusler, Peter. *Linguistic Ecology: Language Change and Linguistic Imperialism in the Pacific Region.* London/New York: Routledge, 1996.

Phillipson, Robert. *Linguistic Imperialism.* Oxford: Oxford University Press, 1992.

SIL. *Ethnologue.* Summer Institute of Linguists, 15th edition, 2005. <www.ethnologue.com>.

Spolsky, Bernard. *Language Policy.* Cambridge: Cambridge University Press, 2004.

Wright, Sue. *Language Policy and Language Planning.* Basingstoke/New York: Palgrave, 2004.

◆ 9

Signs of Empire in Mexican Graphic Narrative: A Research Agenda

Bruce Campbell

U.S. cultural policy in the Americas is articulated with greatest force and consistency through commercial criteria and the capitalist market, a cultural diffusion of "consumer styles" and upper middle class habits at the service of the geo-political interests of the nation-state. Indeed, neo-liberalism and its individualist *habitus* comprise a hegemonic cultural language of Empire that extends even to those precincts of regional social life where English does not. A critical examination of recent Mexican graphic narrative production illustrates how U.S. modernizing norms circulate among popular sectors, and how these norms are positioned in relation to Mexican national identity.

Mexican comics are a useful object for the study of the cultural politics of Empire. Graphic narrative (including the cheaply-produced *historieta* form, glossier comic book series and more artful graphic novels) is extensively consumed in Mexico, and is considered one of the country's strongest culture industries of the twentieth century. The cultural currency of graphic narrative in Mexico is also a reflection of the relatively weak role of traditional literature as a national cultural institution in a country where a majority of the population is semi-literate. The presentation in Mexican comics of neo-liberal discourse and U.S.–style consumerism is strongly indicative of the role of visual culture in bridging the gap between elite discourse on globalization, which circulates most prominently in English among elites in the Americas, and the experience of popular sectors.

It bears noting, however, that the assertion of U.S. cultural hegemony through market-led globalization in recent years has not been documented or analyzed in the media of popular culture in the same manner as the critical dissection of U.S. cultural imperialism a generation ago. During this earlier period, anti-imperialist cultural critique took up a position alongside, or within, discourses of cultural nationalism, including dependency theory, national liberation movements, and even official national projects, such as the Popular Unity government in Chile. Perhaps the most well-known example of this kind of critical position-taking is *How to Read Donald Duck* (Para leer al Pato Donald), co-authored by Armand Mattelart and Ariel Dorfman in 1971, which demonstrated the diffusion of imperialist ideology in Latin America through the mass distribution of the adventures of Disney's comic strip duck. This critical approach, reprised in Dorfman's *The Empire's Old Clothes* (1983), was directed at exposing how the importation by developing nations of U.S. behavioral models and their consumption in popular cultural form "clashed head-on with the immediate needs of their consumers."[1] The nation and the national, grounded in the concept of popular sovereignty, were the stakes of anti-imperialist cultural analysis during this period.

Meanwhile, much subsequent movement away from the Dorfman and Mattelart model has been marked by a globalist cosmopolitanism. Ilan Stavans, for example, writing in the "Foreword" to his *Latino USA: A Cartoon History* (2000) and with reference to the Dorfman and Mattelart book, dismisses as "nonsense" any link between the comics industry and U.S. imperialism: "Our global culture is not about exclusion and isolation, but about cosmopolitanism, which, etymologically, derives from the Greek terms 'cosmos' and 'polis,' a planetary city."[2] In this view, globalization and a globalist ecumenism would remain the frame of reference for the politics of cultural criticism, for the political meaning of the production, distribution and consumption of popular culture, despite the evidently still heavy hand of national interests and values in determining the shape of the global in the Americas.

Critical analysis of a national experience of globalization as mediated through a popular narrative genre allows us to recognize the extension of U.S. cultural and ideological influence, and also to discern the limits of such influence. But, in view of the frequent emphasis on globalism in treatments of popular culture, before turning to an examination of Mexican graphic narrative specifically, it is important first to trace—beginning with official U.S. discourse—the continued relevance of nation and Empire as points of reference for the cultural dimensions of globalization. The discussion will then turn to the analysis of four distinct representations of globalization in graphic narrative in order to outline the operative poles of cultural conflict in the Mexican genre.

The examples considered are "Maldita Ambición" (Damned Ambition, 2001), an issue of the *Libro Semanal* series published by Novedades Editores, which enjoys the largest circulation of any magazine in Mexico with a weekly distribution of eight hundred thousand copies[3]; *Operación Bolívar* by Edgar Clement, a "comic de autor," or independent author's comic, published in installments in the magazine Gallito Comics, and later as a graphic novel in 1999, with a distribution of a thousand copies; "Carrera por la vida" (Race for Life, 2004), an issue of *Las Aventuras del Dr. Simi*, a series published by Farmacias de Similares, a Mexican generic drugs pharmacy chain, with a monthly distribution of one hundred thousand copies; and "Guía del migrante mexicano," an illustrated guide published by the Mexican government in 2004 to educate migrants about the U.S.-Mexico border, with an initial print run of 1.5 million copies. These are, to be certain, anecdotal samples drawn from a broad and complex cultural field, but have been selected as suggestive of some of the more salient ways in which globalization and the U.S. cultural model are positioned in relation to competing concepts of the nation in Mexican popular culture.

Empire Strikes Back

The complexity of globalization's cultural dimensions has been summed up usefully, if somewhat statically, by Arjun Appadurai's spatial nomenclature for the overlapping, shifting contours of global cultural production: mediascapes, ethnoscapes, ideoscapes, technoscapes, and financescapes. Appadurai's terminology frames global culture flows in the manner of a landscape painting, but more as perspective than as procedure—more as cultural environment than as cultural politics. What is left out of Appadurai's perspective is the manner in which globalization itself is often the *object* of cultural representations, where competing discourses seek to organize the view onto the features of the global landscape, efforts that often respond to and deploy national cultural media and materials, constructing meaning and identities through the conjugation of national and other differences in the mediated environment. Extending Appadurai's visual-spatial constructions, one is inclined to call this form of politics "culturescaping."

Without discounting completely the moralizing framework offered up by Samuel Huntington to U.S. policy elites, the ethical guidelines (and hence the cultural parameters) of U.S. policy in Latin America continue to be neoliberal ones. In order to confirm the predominance of commercial ethics over the so-called "civilizational," it is sufficient to note that beginning in 1995 the U.S. Department of State put into practice an extension of section 2202 of the "Omnibus Trade and Competitiveness Act" of 1988, requiring that U.S. embassies collaborate in an annual evaluation of the legal, economic, cultural, and political conditions for private foreign investment in all countries with which the U.S. maintains diplomatic relations. It is important to note that these "Country Commercial Guides" were modeled on the annual "Country Human Rights Reports" instituted by the Carter administration in the late 1970s.

If we observe closely the application of commercial criteria in U.S. discourse on Latin America—in this case a discrete overlapping of ideoscapes and financescapes—it is possible to appreciate the manner in which national interest fuses with neoliberal doctrine in official U.S. culturescaping. The following selections of text come from the "Country Commercial Guide: Mexico," for fiscal year 2001:[4]

> [The North American Free Trade Agreement] has been a net boost to all three economies and, in its undeniable role in spurring competitiveness, institutional reform, worker rights, and environmental stewardship, has served as a positive force for change in Mexico in areas beyond trade. (2)

> While Mexicans are a diverse and independent people, U.S. standards, business practices, and consumer styles are embraced in Mexico. (3)

> The upper middle class represents about 18 percent of the population and is characterized by university educated people, who serve as professionals or company managers, who own homes and cars, have capacity to buy a wide range of household appliances, and occasionally travel internationally. (3)

> In two decades, Mexico has been transformed from one of the most protectionist economies, with a large role for government, to one of the most liberalized. (10)

The discourse of the commercial guide emphasizes the agency of the market, the privatization of public goods, and the extra-commercial benefits of trade liberalization—all characteristic ingredients of neo-liberal discourse. One can also observe several significant points of contact with the emergent Huntington doctrine—in particular the importance of shared cultural values and attitudes, and, even more tellingly, the articulation of U.S. norms as the dominant axis of the international relationship. Although unnamed, culture is posited as a strategic element, a la Huntington, despite the fact that, according to analysts of the accord, the North American Free Trade Agreement contains very little relative to cultural issues or production.[5] When Samuel Huntington comments that the success of NAFTA depends on "the convergence already underway between Mexican, U.S. and Canadian culture," he does not elaborate on the prime mover of such a convergence.[6] Official U.S. discourse suggests that the primary mechanism is the market itself, "serving as a positive force for change in Mexico in areas beyond trade."

Later issues of the Country Commercial Guide for Mexico (i.e., those of the George W. Bush administration) eliminated references to the embracing of U.S. norms in Mexico and placed greater emphasis on problematic differences, such as a slower pace of decision-making ("the concept of time is flexible in Mexico") and the Fox administration's stalled pro-business reform agenda. Other significant changes include more detailed and targeted, strategic information for investors, all within the same transnational frame of NAFTA ("the most outstanding feature of the bilateral relationship").[7] The readership of these commercial reports is global, facilitated by the availability of the texts as Portable Document Format files on the Internet (The Canadian government also posts them). If the sector-by-sector analysis of obstacles and opportunities in the Mexican commercial environment reads like a transnational political agenda for Mexico, that is likely an effect of the culturescaping implicit to the text's official function. The imperial moment of economic globalization is legible in the organized view onto the nation, a studiously constructed perspective on the insufficiency of "mexicanness" vis-à-vis transnational capital and official U.S. cultural norms.

Despite the evident operation of this perspective on the global cultural and political landscape, many of the discussions that orbited around the concept of "globalization" during the 1990s tended to elide nationalist accenting of cultural politics and critique. This elision of the national marked a range of discursive positions, from globalist triumphalism to calls for a transnational cultural politics responsive to global movements of capital, labor, information and symbolic goods. Néstor García Canclini's emphasis on cultural hybridization and Arjun Appadurai's "postnational" ethics sought to counterbalance the tendencies toward cultural homogeneity and "Americanization" promoted by capitalist globalization.[8] At the same time, these critical discourses sought leverage against the recrudescence of nationalist fundamentalisms in response to globalizing trends.

In an important sense, however, it was the principle of popular sovereignty that faded under the bright lights of globalization. By 2000, Michael Hardt and Antonio Negri would posit "Empire" as a post-national condition, as an ideological and institutional frame-up of the entire globe by a transnational juridical sensibility now unmoored from its historical origins in the national poles of the world system. Hardt and Negri's counterweight to official Empire was to be the multitude, an oceanic conception of the popular unbounded by the nation-state. Not surprisingly, the principal resonance for this argument outside the academy could be found among anti-globalization activists whose resistance to "globalization from above" sought an alternative discourse on globalization[9] capable of uniting and catalyzing an otherwise implausibly fractious aggregate of multi- and transnational grassroots alliances.

The Hardt and Negri argument was challenged initially by a questioning of its scientificity (the positing of such sweeping agency for ideation raised many doubts, most prominently about the relationship between the authors' analysis and basic Marxist insights regarding material conditions).[10] But, in the final analysis, the greatest challenge to the Hardt and Negri thesis came in the form of the U.S.-authored global War on Terror, which countermanded most globalist prophecies, and shoved anti-globalization activism to the margins of public debate everywhere. The ideological fundamentalism on which U.S. imperialist doctrine is now predicated (a la Samuel Huntington's "clash of civilizations" hypothesis) has had the effect of restoring "nation" as a central category of "Empire." Importantly, in Latin America, this restoration has coincided with a growing antipathy for the so-called "Washington consensus" on neo-liberal economic policy, and a revalorizing of national identity and popular sovereignty under pressure from broad-based, often extra-official, social movements.[11]

Neo-liberal cosmopolitanism is not, in fact, nation-free. (As suggested by the language of the Country Commercial Guides, which are only available in English despite their use value, in theory, for a post-national commercial order, it could be observed that neo-liberalism posits a nationless subject everywhere except at home). Insofar as the modernization hypothesis (i.e., that market-led cultural diffusion generates the U.S.-style individualism, consumer rationality and capitalist ethos necessary for the one true modernity) continues to be the primary axis of institutionalized globalization, cultural analysis must continue to dissect cultural discourses in order to trace the signs of Empire in the management and diffusion of meaning, particularly at the popular level where the cultural reproduction of the nation remains rooted to a significant degree.

There are, of course, a number of important criticisms of the Dorfman and Mattelart model. Chief among these is the authors' binary construction of

Empire/Nation, assuming a unified and authentic national identity opposed to a coherent and invasive imperial culture.[12] The coherence and unity of both categories are complicated by the decentering effects of globalizing processes over the past two decades, resulting in more complex North/South power relations. For example, García Canclini notes that the ongoing global processes of hybridization include not only U.S. cultural influences in Latin America, but a simultaneous and dramatic "Latinization" of U.S. culture and society, as well as the "Neohispanoamericanization" of Latin America, i.e., "the expanding ownership of publishing houses, airlines, banks and telecommunications by Spanish companies."[13] Nonetheless, despite the fading away of national liberation projects in the post-Cold War era, what remains of the earlier conditions to which Dorfman and Mattelart responded is cultural diffusion as a site of ideological contest.

This, after all, is the key insight motivating the Dorfman and Mattelart model, the historic contribution to cultural analysis of critiques of modernization theory prior to the emergence of the globalization problematic and "the end of history": the recognition of the market not as abstraction but in practice, as the arena of distribution not only of wealth but of cultural goods and meaning, and thus as a locus of North/South power differentials and struggles. Whereas the Dorfman and Mattelart model presumed the application of state power to the problem of neo-colonialist cultural diffusion, in Mexico, the country where comic book production and consumption has been most intense in Latin America, the state has mainly concerned itself with controlling the perceived moral effects of graphic narratives[14] but otherwise ignores the implications for national identity of the market for D.C. Comics, Marvel and other U.S. companies.

Although precise data are difficult to come by, it has been calculated that production levels for the Mexican historieta reached more than seventy million per month by the early 1980s,[15] and despite the erosion of circulation provoked by the prolonged economic crisis beginning at that time, twenty years later production remained at more than seven million per month.[16] Consumption of the historieta represents the lion's share of the national literary diet—a source of considerable concern for book publishers in Mexico,[17] while at the same time a crucial source of revenue for Mexican enterprises such as Novedades Editores, which until recently had subsidized its less lucrative daily newspapers with the historietas that it publishes.

These economic data correspond to a significant presence for comics in the Mexican public sphere. The popularity of historietas is in evidence on public buses and on metro trains, in public parks and in the constant recycling of used copies in the informal street markets. Engagements with Mexican popular culture in this context frequently have taken up the Mexican comic book as a touchstone for combining critical evaluation of popular media with the deployment of these media as channels of critical discourse. The work of Rius (Eduardo del Río), for example, operates as meta-discourse in relation to both Mexican popular graphics traditions and nationally-relevant cultural discourses. Julio Cortázar's hybrid graphics novella *Fantomas contra los Vampiros Multinacionales* (1976) presented the world-historical relevance of the Russell Tribunal alongside a critique of the individualism and fatalism built in to superhero comics, even in the case of a nationally-produced series such as the Mexican Fantomas. The novels of Paco Ignacio Taibo II often deliberately draw upon a recognizable comic book aesthetic in treating national political issues and institutional conditions, as with *Máscara Azteca y el Doctor Niebla* (1996). Political cartoonist El Fisgón (Rafael Barajas) has published widely, including a cartoon narrative critically detailing for the Mexican comics reader the realities of globalization in *Cómo sobrevivir al neo-liberalismo sin dejar de ser mexicano* (How to Survive Neoliberalism and Still Be Mexican) (1996). In practice, in other words, over the past generation the nationalist left has not ceded the nation's market as a contested space, and instead has experimented with comics and graphic narrative forms as important elements of a nationally-specific popular aesthetic.

The Mexican left does not compete solely or directly with the U.S. comics industry, arguably responding instead to the broad weight of the national cultural field. There is a range of political positions legible in the Mexican cultural field with respect to nation, globalization and the popular. Comic book characters and the graphic narrative format constitute an important public "language," employed increasingly by a range of Mexican actors to reach a mass audience. Within this field of cultural production the U.S. cultural model appears in different guises in representations of globalization directed at the middle, working, and lower middle classes in Mexico.

Los neo-liberales también lloran

"Maldita Ambición," published in June of 2001, is typical of the Libro Semanal series in the manner in which it combines the print format of the historieta with the melodramatic narrative arc of a television soap opera. Employing standardized frames—most of these rectangular and of half-page size—and schematically realist and monochrome drawing, this graphic novel narrates in

146 pages the story of Alba Rojas, a young Mexican woman with ambitions of overcoming her poor, working class origins. As with the entire Libro Semanal series, the narrative aims to reinforce a moral, in this case against selfishness and self-promotion. Nevertheless, in the end the object of moral criticism turns out not to be self-interest as a market value, but female ambition as a threat to traditional gender roles.[18]

At the beginning of the narrative Alba receives her executive secretary's degree and is recognized as "the best student of the group." But when her mother congratulates her for now being able to earn a salary, get married and have children, Alba responds saying "I'm not going to do what other women do." This conflict, between Alba's individualist ambition and the family values of her working class cultural environment, structures the entire plot. Eventually she does marry, to Efrén, a young man of upper-class birth who manages a small garment factory in the neighborhood. However, Alba grows frustrated with Efrén because, despite his financial success, he is satisfied with an upper-middle-class life. Alba wants more, and so she leaves Efrén to travel to New York with a famous Mexican financier, thinking she will marry him and thus realize her evidently limitless ambitions. At the end of the story, when the couple returns to Mexico, instead of attaining her goal as wife and business partner of an international businessman, the financier leaves her in the airport after offering her money for her time—effectively marking her as a prostitute.

The frame for this portrait of ambition is the neoliberal model of globalization. At the same time that individualist self-interest is presented as the motor for the generation of wealth and modernization, the external signs of modernization appear as mobility, technology and an expansion of the private sphere. Repeatedly, the action of the historieta takes place in transit, either in automobile or airplane, culminating in a round-trip voyage to New York. Although ambition is the central theme, this psychological force is only treated critically with reference to the actions of Alba; neither Efrén nor the famous businessman receive critical attention for their own efforts to enrich themselves. Ambition, as it turns out, fits quite well within the logic of the market—it only deserves critique when it complicates stable family roles and relationships. In "Maldita Ambición," globalization—present in the transnational mobility of the business elite and the centrality of commerce for the "good life"—is a logical extension of local entrepreneurial activity.

If the reigning image of globalization presented in U.S. culturescaping is framed by a promise of cultural transformations, in "Maldita Ambición" such promises are experienced within the private sphere instead of the public sphere. Within the scenery of private interests and easy movement of people and capital, commerce eclipses labor. With the exception of a lone image of smiling garment workers in Efrén's maquiladora, the human body appears almost exclusively as consumer, whether this be in the tianguis (open air market), the bar, the hotel or the airplane.

The contextualizing operations of the historieta impose certain limits on the unstated utopianism of neoliberal discourse, an effect discernible in the national cultural elements exhibited in the plot and the semiotics of the comic. The actions and moral judgment of the characters are situated amid traditional gender roles and recognizable national sites and spaces such as the Ciudad Satélite suburb, tourist hotels and the urban tianguis. Nonetheless, while historically modernization discourse competed publicly with socialist and nationalist development models which posited a practical relationship between popular social sectors and the progress of the nation, in the historieta modernization is privatized, carried out as an individual project for which the explicit collective context is the family, not the nation or social class. Official U.S. discourse on globalization is reproduced in "Maldita Ambición," reinforcing the classic modernizing values of a fictionally expansive middle class that includes both the tianguis and the wealthy suburbs of Ciudad Satélite, Alba's poor family and the transnational entrepreneur. The conflicts that emerge are interpersonal ones, not political ones in a national sense. The de-politicization of modernization is so complete in "Maldita Ambición" that the problematic of transnationalization is counter-balanced only by traditionalist popular sentiment denatured of national value—the non-commercial values of the private sphere embodied in the family. The potential for a critical social evaluation of self-interest and social exploitation attendant to the neo-liberal model of globalization is deflected by censure of female ambition, on the one hand, and contained by the alibi of *machismo* (the only social sin of the Mexican financier) on the other.

Adventures in Hyperreality

The deployment of the comic book narrative in the Mexican public sphere for specific political ends has become commonplace. In the last presidential elections in Mexico, for example, the candidate for the Partido de Acción Nacional, Vicente Fox, campaigned with the symbolic support of "Kalimán, el hombre increíble," a popular Mexican superhero since the 1970s. In 2002, the Fox administration published an historieta titled *El cambio en México ya nadie lo para* (Change in Mexico Can't be Stopped) in order to defend and promote the executive's political agenda. In 2004, Mexico City mayor and leading presidential candidate for the left-of-center Partido de la Revolución Democrática Andrés Manuel López Obrador printed two million copies of an historieta titled *Las fuerzas oscuras contra Andrés Manuel López Obrador* (The Dark Forces Against Andrés Manuel López Obrador), confronting a right-wing plot against his political future. The Sindicato Mexicano de Electricistas (Union of Mexican Electrical Workers) has distributed eight hundred thousand copies of a comic, *Que no nos roben la luz* (Don't Let Them Steal Our Light), arguing against the Fox administration's plans for privatization of the energy sector.

Among this array of politically customized comics narratives, *Las aventuras del Dr. Simi* represents an intriguing recent addition. Presenting to the Mexican public the philanthropic exploits of "Dr. Simi," the avuncular mustachioed mascot for the pharmaceutical chain Farmacias de Similares and synonym for Victor González Torres, the company's founder, owner and managing director, the comic book fuses the marketing function of an advertising campaign with the personalized public relations maneuvering of a political campaign. González Torres has opened some 3,000 pharmacies in Mexico (with additional outlets in Guatemala, Brazil and Argentina), providing low-cost generic drugs and basic medical treatment to Mexicans who cannot afford brand name pharmaceuticals and adequate health care. He has announced his candidacy for the 2006 presidential elections, primarily as an antagonist to López Obrador. His public discourse generally combines attacks on the mayor of Mexico City, rejection of "populist" politics, allegations of corruption and incompetence leveled against the Instituto Mexicano de Seguro Social (the government health care system), and promotion of the private sector as an answer to the country's problems. His political agenda, which he calls "moderate socialism," is backed by the "Grupo por un país mejor," an alliance of his pharmacy chain and philanthropic organizations founded by him.

"Carrera por la vida" opens with the unassuming Dr. Simi reading a biography of Mahatma Gandhi and explaining to his pet dog the principle of non-violence. What follows are two storylines, each describing Dr. Simi's involvement in life-saving good deeds, transporting to the hospital first a motorcycle accident victim, then an impoverished boy found unconscious in the Baja desert. His vital intervention is not an individual project, however, but involves the concerted action of the Simi Team (Equipo Simi). Under the paternal supervision of the good doctor, the Simi Team includes three Mexican women with prominent public profiles: actress Marifer Murillo; soap opera star Luz Elena González; and race car driver Elizabeth Wayas. Through the actions and attitudes of these characters, the comic narrative projects what might be called a corporate corporativism, a hierarchized and paternalistic bundling of multiple subjects under one authority, mirroring the historic political corporativism of Mexico's Partido Revolucionario Institucional but with a personalized, private-sector variant. Instead of the Party, the organizing principle and protagonist vis-à-vis the social body is the Company, personified by Dr. Simi, an enlightened and fatherly authority figure, a kind of soft *caudillo*.

The team represents the globalist promise of modernity in a number of ways. Whether by car (driven expertly by Elizabeth Wayas) or by corporate jet, the team moves with speed and facility from one place to the next, within a narrative that emphasizes the importance of transportation technology in collapsing space as an obstacle. The virtues of the proper social order expressed by the Simi Team show a clear affinity for those values articulated in the U.S. Department of State *Country Commercial Guide*, including repeated mention of the value of punctuality and efficiency. Luz Elena, who is studying Japanese, declares "Since I've been with [the team] I've had more and more desire to learn." In a discussion about the conservation of natural resources and the environment, the women decide that "If things are done well and in an orderly fashion, there's no problem." The only reference to the historical specificity of Mexico in the comic deals with the history of the port city of La Paz in Baja state, which Dr. Simi identifies with the history of globalization pre-dating the formation of the Mexican nation (see Figure 1). In the frame immediately following Dr. Simi's mini-lecture, Elizabeth Wayas celebrates the city's status as a duty-free port where, "One can buy a lot of imported items at a very good price."

Figure 1. Dr. Simi and the Simi Chicas celebrate punctuality, consumerism and globalization on board the Simi jet. *Courtesy of Farmacias de Similares, S.A. de C.V.*

Allusions to non-violence, environmentalism and equality for women imbue the teamwork with an aura of progress, but these values are subordinated to the machismo of the Doctor's relationship with the group of younger, attractive women, and by the greater emphasis on technology and consumption in the story. Within this arrangement, one finds the popular dimension of the nation relegated to a minor and abstract supporting role in constructing a collective, modernizing agency embodied by the corporate team. Dr. Simi's pet dog, Simidog, who communicates telepathically with the team members and perseverates constantly about his desire to eat, serves as a metaphorical reminder of the presence of the subaltern—a class equivalent, subject to instruction by his corporate master on the proper use of language and the immorality of violence.

This marginalization of the popular is reinforced by the hyperrealism of the comic book's format, which supplements cartoon renderings of real people with photographs of them. This is true even in the case of the goofy-looking Dr. Simi character, who makes a real-world appearance in the photo-documentary insert in the comic of a Farmacias de Similares publicity event inaugurating ten new pharmacies in Argentina. The fatherly doctor appears in photographs alongside Mayan activist Rigoberta Menchú, an advocate of the generic drugs distributor in Guatemala, and the corporate owner Víctor González Torres. Curiously, the impoverished boy rescued from certain death in the Baja desert has no photographic counterpart, no empirical datum reinforcing or demonstrating the national realities of which he is a part. In fact, although the reader of the comic will reasonably conclude that the child is laying near death in the desert because of a failed effort to cross the treacherous U.S.-Mexico border, Dr. Simi offers no insight as to who the boy is or what he was doing in such a desolate place. Reality on this point (i.e., Mexico's concrete experience with globalization) is glossed over, while the strategically placed portrait photos of the celebrity women on the cover, and in the publicity insert with the full color photo display of the Farmacias de Similares public relations event, refer the comic book reader to the "real" presence of the main characters in the nation's commercialized public sphere. This hyperrealist presence in the comic narrative—the ersatz reality of television and mass entertainment culture—is the grounding for the (globalization-friendly) nation and its peculiar political authority in the comic book.

Invasion of the Body Snatchers

In contrast, *Operación Bolívar* is marked by critical nuance and tends to politicize key elements and processes of globalization. Its title, for example, carries strong Pan-Latin American associations (the reference to nineteenth century independence fighter Simón Bolívar) at the same time that it recalls military counter-insurgency operations in the region (i.e., Operación Cóndor in the southern cone under the U.S.-backed dictatorships of the 1970s and 1980s, Operación Bolívar in Colombia more recently). Unlike the soap-operaesque style of "Maldita Ambición" or the blithe globalism of "Dr. Simi," *Operación* displays a dark and de-mystifying aesthetic. The optic of the graphic novel reflects creatively some of the hybrid visual languages generated by mass cultural production—combining visual elements from Catholicism (the forms and juxtapositions of the illuminated manuscript); advertising discourse; the Mexican tradition of graphic art (including the *grabado* of José Guadalupe Posada); film (a photographic realism and an amplifying of the standard narrative frame of the comic); comic art itself (interspersing distinct drawing styles in order to visualize non-optic senses); and the history of "high" art (recycling details of Picasso's "Guernica," the anatomical drawings of Leonardo da Vinci and Francisco Goya's oil paintings).

The action of *Operación Bolívar* takes place in a fictional country, "Angelópolis," where pre-modern and hyper-modern cultural materials are syncretized—colonial churches alongside skyscrapers, indigenous traditions adjacent advanced technology. The narrative departs from a premise at once mystical and bloody: there are angels, and there are angel hunters who historically have had the ability, inherited through indigenous ancestry, of killing angels. The hunt for the mythical beings follows an economic logic, because angelic body parts possess an array of instrumental values. For this reason, transnational corporations and the CIA are also interested in the angels, hoping to monopolize this supernatural resource in order to strengthen their own technological development and the national security apparatus of the U.S. In this way, in *Operación Bolívar* globalization also appears as the operative context of the narrative.

However, while in "Maldita Ambición" globalization extends spatially and ethically from local entrepreneurial activities, in *Operación Bolívar*, globalization intervenes conflictually in the local traffic in goods. That is, the representation of globalization includes conflict between transnational and local actors. This is not, however, the most critical point that distinguishes *Operación* from "Maldita Ambición." Even more important is the representation of

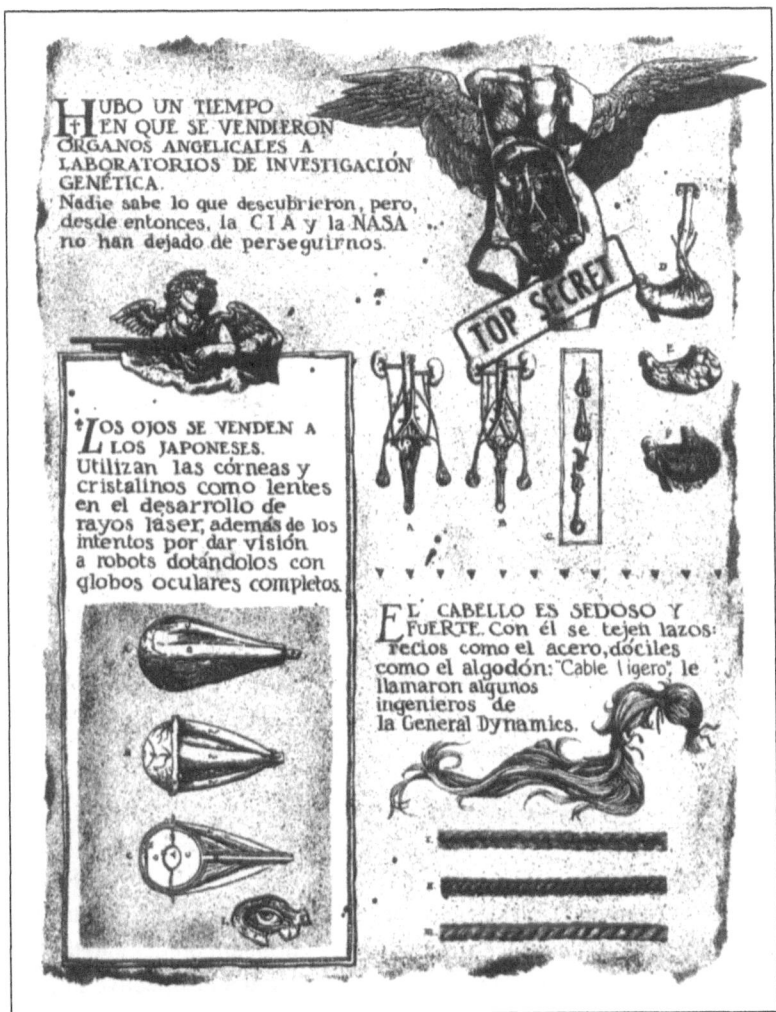

Figure 2. Commodity production is a bloody business in Operación Bolívar. *Courtesy of Edgar Clement.*

commerce, an activity presented once again at the center of the experience of globalization. In *Operación*, wealth and modernity are associated with technology and movement, but they are generated through violence. The body, whether of angel or human, is presented as an object caught up in a machinery of physical repression and bloody extraction of surplus value (see Figure 2).

The merchandise of capitalism, target of espionage and dispute on the global stage, carries with it a history of death, torture and domination.

Significantly, these outlines of a "true history" of the commodity are presented to the reader in *Operación Bolívar* from a national perspective, despite the fantastical location of the action. A variety of visual and narrative cues suggest the Mexican context: one of the more violent characters is Román, described as "un policía judicial," a police force vilified in the Mexican popular imagination for widespread allegations of human rights abuses; the comic deploys images of indigenous campesino heritage immersed in urban modernization; and in several frames the front pages of the national newspapers *Reforma* and *La Jornada* appear as a narrative support, an obvious reference to the Mexican public sphere. The climax of the novel is reached when angels are lured to their death at Tlatelolco, site of the 1968 Mexico City massacre of student protesters by Mexican troops. Globalization is thus situated in the graphic novel within the problem of national modernity. But the reader will not find repeated here any optimistic visualizing of globalization as the royal road to modernization. On the contrary, violence and social domination, albeit hidden from everyday public view, are the obscure truth behind the political and economic orders. In the end, the angels are gunned down by an assemblage of Mexican judicial police, U.S. mercenaries and drug dealers with technical support from the Pentagon and Drug Enforcement Agency.

Amazing but True! Mexico Invades the U.S.

In December 2004, the Secretaría de Relaciones Exteriores (Foreign Ministry) of Mexico published and distributed 1.5 million copies of a survival guide for those Mexican migrants seeking to cross Mexico's northern border into the U.S. Consisting of 34 pages of straight-forward advice to the prospective migrant, the "Guía del migrante mexicano" (Guide for The Mexican Migrant) provoked outrage among certain sectors of the U.S. elite, including denunciations by right-wing activists and politicians in U.S. border states, and even claims that the guide represented an "act of war." In fact, the guide simply offers practical advice to migrants regarding the treacherous overland border crossing, tips on avoiding undue attention from authorities on the U.S. side of the border, and information about their rights and how to contact the nearest Mexican consulate. Although its discursive function is technical and descriptive instead of narratological, the didactic text of the guide is supplemented with comic book-style depictions of migrants, the border and the institutions that manage the international line.

The visual discourse of the guide is indicative of a bureaucratic effort to intervene in the informality that haunts institutionalized globalization. The strategy for distribution of the guide centered on two related markets: the transnational market for cheap labor in the U.S., which draws disproportionately from a handful of Mexican states (Oaxaca, Jalisco, Michoacán, Zacatecas and Puebla); and the transnational market for cultural goods like the *Libro Semana* and other historieta series, which can be found as far north as Minnesota in the U.S., passing from reader to reader often without any exchange of value beyond the initial purchase. The targeted labor market determined the geographic scope of diffusion of the guide, with two thirds of the first print run circulating in the states of origin for most Mexican migrants, with additional copies distributed to Mexicans already living on the U.S. side in New Jersey, Atlanta and Dallas. The guide is also available via the Internet. The cultural market corresponding to potential Mexican wage-laborers determined the aesthetic form and semiotics of the guide, which was circulated as a supplement/insert in the *Libro Semanal* and *Libro Vaquero* series published by Novedades Editores. These two series are the most widely circulated publications of Novedades Editores, and enjoy a wider readership than any other magazine in Mexico.

Figure 3. Muscular, anglicized migrants cross the Río Bravo in the Mexican government's "Guide for the Mexican Migrant." <www.sre.gob.mx/tramites/guiamigrante/>.

The graphics of the guide are formally indistinguishable from the representational aesthetics of the *Libro Semanal* or *Libro Vaquero*. The male migrants depicted wading across the Rio Bravo possess the same heroically muscled physique as many of the male protagonists of the *Libro series* (see Figure 3).

Female migrants' bodies boast sexualized physical features, such as ample, rounded buttocks and accentuated cleavage. But this historieta standard for the physical rendering of a character has more than just an aesthetic effect on the representation of the migrant. Skin color is blanched out, leaving no recognizable racial characteristics of mestizaje or of indigenous heritage other than dark hair and eyes. Only the migrants' physical relationship to the border clearly marks their socio-economic class position in Mexico (or in the U.S.), or acknowledges the unofficial realities of official globalization.

The migrant of the guide is an abstraction, devoid of any visual anecdote or texture suggestive of specific regional origin, stripped of any discernible motivation for making the crossing in the first place. The guide addresses itself on the first page to the *connacional* (co-national) who has made the "difficult decision to seek new labor opportunities outside your country." These migrants are not identifiable as indigenous Mexicans making the trek into the U.S. economy from as far south as Chiapas because the poorly capitalized agricultural niche into which they were born in Mexico can no longer sustain a community. Nor are they urban working class Mexicans who move back and forth across the U.S.-Mexico border as required by the ebb and flow of the labor market, and steady downward pressure on real wages in Mexico. In fact, *lo popular* and hence in any significant sense *lo mexicano*, has been artfully expunged from the bodies and belongings of these Mexicans except for the transnational signifiers of the backward baseball cap, tennis shoes and blue jeans. National identity is thereby reduced to the moment of mutual recognition between citizen and consulate, a moment presented in the front page graphics under the symbolic authority of the Mexican tricolor. The only moment in the text where an unambiguous identification of the Mexican migrant with national popular culture and experience might be perceived is precisely at the moment of its suppression: the migrant is informed that it is unwise to draw attention on the U.S. side of the border by playing loud music or participating in parties.

The abstract character of the migrant in this text is the image of a bureaucratic glossing of the national condition—analogous to Dr. Simi's mass cultural glossing—and marks clearly the political distance between the neo-liberal state and the national-popular discourse that characterized the revolutionary nationalist state in the 1920s and 1930s. The visual language of the historieta form possesses little more than a phatic discursive function, opening a communicative channel between the state and popular sectors regarding the experience and practice of the latter in the context of neoliberal globalization. Equally on display, in the communicative content of the guide, is the extremely attenuated agency of the state with respect to shaping, directing or responding to popular experiences of globalizing forces.

Conclusion

Although not a fully representative sample, these graphic narratives are indicative of the contested profile of globalization in the popular cultural medium. As evidenced by the Guía del migrante mexicano and Las Aventuras del Dr. Simi, political and economic elites in Mexico are attentive to the cultural languages of the popular sectors when articulating the relationship between nation and globalization. In recent years, this kind of culturescaping is evident on the part of a range of economic, cultural, and political actors in Mexico, as the state, civil society, and the private sector organize competing vantages onto the relationship between Mexico and the global economic order. The texts represent varied constructions of the nation in relation to the U.S. model of globalization, and therein signal several points of tension or contradiction between the two poles of reference.

Despite their use of a popular cultural medium, the "Guía," Dr. Simi and "Maldita" all demonstrate how both private sector globalist discourse and official Mexican representation of globalization conspicuously absent or attenuate popular experience in their communicative content. The Dr. Simi narrative perhaps most faithfully reproduces the U.S. model, suppressing social class and popular experience in favor of figments of the mass cultural market, and elevating the social role of the individual capitalist to that of enlightened father figure. But even so, the individualist fantasy is contained by an implicit political corporativism that contradicts the individualist appeal of neo-liberal discourse. While "Maldita Ambición" embraces neoliberalism, it does so with a selective appeal to popular sensibilities, contextualizing its private melodrama in the spaces of the urban working and middle classes. It proposes an entrepreneurial vision of popular experience, but the moral of the story sets a gendered limit to the promises of globalization by counterbalancing the transnational pull of the market with a traditionalist family morality. Although "Maldita" addresses popular experience and Dr. Simi banishes it in favor of an affinity between the corporation and the mass cultural sensibilities promoted by commercial culture, both narratives color the global with a patriarchal politics.

The implicit neo-liberalism of the "Guía" poses more of an obvious contradiction for the logic of Empire with its vision of a state-assisted transnational labor market. The politically-limited, bureaucratic construct of nation nonetheless crosses the border alongside the Mexican national, and is thus perceived by some of the strongest U.S. proponents of market liberalization as a threat to the integrity of the imperial center.

In the contrasting views on globalization in these graphic narratives one can discern, even within the neo-liberal "consensus" of U.S. hegemony, the cultural politics of globalization in action. But it is in the stark contrasts of *Operación Bolívar* that the stakes of this politics are thrown into clearest relief. In *Operación* the nation bears a close resemblance to the "deep Mexico" identified by Guillermo Bonfil Batalla,[19] an unofficial nation dating to the ruptures of the Conquest, a fusion of indigenous and popular cultures obscured by officialdom and preyed upon by the forces of modernization. *Operación* designs an unofficial view of the global order that foregrounds simultaneously the violence of globalization and the tendency of the institutional order (corporations and states) to obscure that violence.

Significantly, the critical discourse of Clement's work arises from social conditions of production not easily identifiable with either the state-published "Guía" or with the private sector comics industry. When he authored *Operación*, Clement was a member of the Taller del Perro (Dog's Workshop), a visual arts collective organized around the task of renovating national traditions in the comics genre. The Taller was a latter day representative of a phenomenon of the Mexican cultural field emergent in the 1970s, a decade known among art historians as "the decade of the groups," because of a turn toward collaborative cultural production and direct engagement with national political issues in the arts. Important segments of Mexico's current cultural production continue to be marked by this earlier political history: arts collectives aimed at articulating "high" artistic production with popular culture, working through a close identification with those social sectors engaged in struggle for political independence from the corruption and conservativism of the Mexican state.

This distinctive feature of Clement's project underscores a defining feature of the globalist positions articulated in the other comics. Viewed against the contrast of *Operación*, the strategic absences and exclusions of the other narratives become much more obvious. Not only are national realities tendentiously glossed and de-politicized, but the nation itself is divested of labor and social organization. It is not only the figure of the popular that is diminished, but that of civil society. Importantly, these lacunae are implicated in the reshaping of Mexico's political economy under pressure from the processes of globalization—i.e., propagation of neo-liberal doctrine regarding national economic controls; expansion of the reach, efficacy and speed of communicational and transport technologies; segmentation and trans-nationalization of networks of production, publicity and distribution of goods—resulting in abandonment of the import-substitution policies that historically subtended the national-popular in official discourse and cultural production. In this new national scenario, what remains of the corporativist political model has been re-tooled in order to contain and marginalize opposition to the transferal of wealth from the public to the private sector. The effect has been an intensified struggle over symbolic and cultural patrimony, and the emergence of social and political organizations aimed at carving out a sphere of semi-autonomy from official controls, the most famous case being the Zapatista movement.

Elements of a semi-autonomous civil society have grown both more combative and increasingly marginal to the institutional and cultural instruments of official representation. Institutional assaults on activist networks opposing neo-liberal policy have included efforts at pro-business labor law reform, continued isolation of the Zapatista movement, the closing of bank accounts channeling international solidarity monies to Chiapas, the undermining of proposed indigenous autonomy, and legalistic maneuvering to foreclose on the presidential candidacy of Mexico City mayor López Obrador. At the same time, unionists have increasingly rejected official control of organized labor amid declining union density and privatization of key sectors such as the railway system, telecommunications, and mining. Ongoing privatization has fractured official unionism, and resulted in the formation in 2002 of the Union, Campesino, Social, Indigenous and Popular Front, a promising alliance against neo-liberal policy representing organized labor and campesino, indigenous and middle class organizations.[20]

These social relations are so marginal for neo-liberal discourse and economic policy that the U.S. Country Commercial Guide for Mexico mentions under the heading "civil society" only national business associations. And yet national civil societal networks also trace the possibility of rescuing the stakes of cultural politics from the commercial cultural model dominant in the Americas. After all, the question of the character of the nation cannot be reduced to the polarities of state versus market agency, as with neo-liberal discourse, but is a matter in dispute among the multiple agencies of civil society. And here, it seems, one can turn back to the texts at hand and make out the aesthetic form of this question, and perceive the broader outlines of a critical research agenda. Consigned to oblivion by the culturescaping of the imperial model of globalization, by the neoliberal state and by the private sector, the figures of civil society—network of social relations exceeding the grasp of the purely commercial or the strictly governmental—reappears in the unofficial imagination as a fleeting, fantastical, angelic promise cohabiting the global landscape, despite concerted efforts to effect its disappearance.

Notes

1. Ariel Dorfman, *The Empire's Old Clothes*, New York: Pantheon Books, 1983, p. 4. For a later adaptation of this model to a retrospective analysis of U.S. imperialist perspective on Southeast Asia in the context of the U.S.-Vietnam War, see David Kunzle, "Dispossession by Ducks: The Imperialist Treasure Hunt in Southeast Asia," *Art Journal*, Summer 1990, 159–66.
2. Ilan Stavans, *Latino USA: A Cartoon History*, New York: Basic Books, 2000, xi.
3. Medios Publicitarios Mexicanos, *Tarifas y Datos de Medios Impresos*, edición número 169, February 2001.
4. United States Department of State, *Country Commercial Guide: Mexico*, Fiscal Year 2001.
5. Silvio R. Waisbord, "The Ties that Still Bind: Media and National Cultures in Latin America," *Canadian Journal of Communication*, 23: 1998, 381–401.
6. Samuel P. Huntington, "The Clash of Civilizations?" *Foreign Affairs*, Summer 1993, 27.
7. United States Department of State, *Doing Business in Mexico: A Country Commercial Guide for U.S. Investors*, Fiscal Year 2004.
8. Néstor García Canclini, *Hybrid Cultures*, Minneapolis: University of Minnesota Press, 1995; and Arjun Appadurai, *Modernity at Large*, Minneapolis: University of Minnesota Press, 1996.
9. For an important version of an oppositional "globalization from below" see Jeremy Brecher and Tim Costello, *Global Village or Global Pillage*, Boston: South End Press, 1994.
10. For a sustained critique of the Hardt and Negri thesis, see Timothy Brennan, "The Empire's New Clothes," *Critical Inquiry*, Winter 2003, 337–67.
11. The official turn away from U.S.-led economic policy has spread dramatically in recent years beyond Venezuela's emphasis on national sovereignty under Chávez. This shift is driven in part by elite hostility to the hard-line unilateralism of the Bush administration. But popular movements have played an important role in disciplining national elites who follow U.S. direction too closely. In Argentina, Bolivia and Ecuador, mass mobilizations have unseated numerous presidents in recent years. In Uruguay, voters approved a referendum prohibiting further privatization of water services.
12. For a critical view of the argument of *How to Read Donald Duck*, see Martin Barker, *Comics: Ideology, Power and the Critics*, Manchester: University of Manchester, 1989.

13. Néstor García Canclini, "Hybrid Cultures in Globalized Times," *Hybrid Cultures*, Minneapolis: University of Minnesota Press, 2005.
14. Anne Rubenstein, *Bad Language and Naked Ladies, and Other Threats to the Nation*, Durham: Duke University Press, 1998.
15. Harold E. Hinds and Charles Tatum, *Not Just for Children: the Mexican Comic Book in the Late 1960s and 1970s*, Westport: Greenwood Press, 1992.
16. See the *Encuesta Industrial Mensual* published since 1994 by the Mexican government's Instituto Nacional de Estadística, Geografía e Informática.
17. Sealtiel Alatriste, "Elevar el índice de lectura en México significaría emprender estrategias de capacitación efectivas," *Líderes Mexicanos*, December 1, 1995.
18. The *Libro*'s formulaic, gendered morality is its distinctive "brand" in the Mexican comics industry. Laura Bolaños Cadena, creator of the series and author of many of its storylines, defended the honor of the publication in a 2003 letter to the editors of *La Jornada*, which had published a brief study of the historieta form and degrading attitudes toward women: "The Libro Semanal does not deal with violent themes, and certainly does not degrade women. Most of its audience is female and its success is based on the defense of women and the criticism of machismo." *La Jornada*, February 6, 2003.
19. Guillermo Bonfil Batalla, *Mexico profundo: una civilización negada*, Mexico City: Grijalbo, 1989.
20. See Dan La Botz, "Mexico's Labor Movement in Transition," *Monthly Review*, June 2005.

Works Cited

Alatriste, Sealtiel. "Elevar el índice de lectura en México significaría emprender estrategias de capacitación efectivas." *Líderes Mexicanos*, December 1, 1995.
Appadurai, Arjun. *Modernity at Large*. Minneapolis: University of Minnesota Press, 1996.
Barker, Martin. *Comics: Ideology, Power and the Critics*. Manchester: University of Manchester, 1989.
Bonfil Batalla, Guillermo. *Mexico profundo: una civilización negada*. Mexico City: Grijalbo, 1989.
Brecher, Jeremy and Tim Costello. *Global Village or Global Pillage*. Boston: South End Press, 1994.
Brennan, Timothy. "The Empire's New Clothes." *Critical Inquiry*, Winter 2003. 337–67.
Clement, Edgar. *Operación Bolívar*. Mexico City: FONCA, 1999.
Dorfman, Ariel. *The Empire's Old Clothes*. New York: Pantheon Books, 1983.
———. and Armand Mattelart. *How to Read Donald Duck: Imperialist Ideology in the Disney Comic*. New York: International General, 1984.

Farmacias de Similares. "Carrera por la vida." *Las aventuras del Dr. Simi*, Number 34, December 2004.
García Canclini, Néstor. "Introduction: Hybrid Cultures in Globalized Times." *Hybrid Cultures*. Minneapolis: University of Minnesota Press, 2005.
———. *Hybrid Cultures*. Minneapolis: University of Minnesota Press, 1995.
Hardt, Michael and Antonio Negri. *Empire*. Cambridge: Harvard University Press, 2000.
Hinds, Harold E. and Charles Tatum. *Not Just for Children: the Mexican Comic Book in the Late 1960s and 1970s*. Westport: Greenwood Press, 1992.
Huntington, Samuel P. "The Clash of Civilizations?" *Foreign Affairs*, Summer 1993. 22–49.
La Botz, Dan. "Mexico's Labor Movement in Transition." *Monthly Review*, June 2005. <www.monthlyreview.org/june2005.htm>.
Medios Publicitarios Mexicanos. *Tarifas y Datos de Medios Impresos*. Edición número 169, February 2001.
Novedades Editores. "Maldita Ambición." *El Libro Semanal*. México City: June 21 2001.
Rubenstein, Anne. *Bad Language and Naked Ladies, and Other Threats to the Nation*. Durham: Duke University Press, 1998.
Secretaría de Relaciones Exteriores de Mexico. *Guía del migrante mexicano*. November 2004.
Stavans, Ilan. *Latino USA: A Cartoon History*. New York: Basic Books, 2000.
United States Department of State. *Doing Business in Mexico: A Country Commercial Guide for U.S. Investors*. Fiscal Year 2004.
———. *Country Commercial Guide: Mexico*. Fiscal Year 2001.
Waisbord, Silvio. "The Ties that Still Bind: Media and National Cultures in Latin America." *Canadian Journal of Communication* 23 (1998): 381–401.

◆ 10

Spanish, English, or Spanglish?
Truth and Consequences of U.S. Latino Bilingualism

John M. Lipski

Introduction

When referring to racial and ethnic minorities in the United States, a number of words and expressions once used frequently and insensitively have fallen out of favor and are now shunned in favor of more accurate designations. Words once openly spoken in reference to African Americans, Jews, Italians, Asians, Native Americans, Latinos, and those with mental and physical disabilities, and found in radio and television programs, popular literature, films and public discourse in general are now socially and politically unacceptable. One particular subset of these terms refers to individuals or groups that result from racial or ethnic mixture, generally included in ersatz cover terms such as *half-breed*. Of the racial/ethnic terms that have survived the enhanced focus on civil rights and social conscience, only one refers simultaneously to language use and—by inference rather than by direct indication—to specific ethnic groups: *Spanglish*. An obvious blend of *English* and *Spanish* this word has become the less transparent *espanglish* in the Spanish-speaking world. Although *Spanglish* has at times been used to refer to a wide variety of phenomena (see Lipski 2004 for a representative survey), in the vast majority of instances *Spanglish* targets the language usage of Latinos born in or residing in the United

States. In a few instances, *Spanglish* is a strictly neutral term, and some U.S. Latino political and social activists have even adopted *Spanglish* as a positive affirmation of ethnolinguistic identity. In the usual circumstances, however, *Spanglish* is used derogatorily, to marginalize U.S. Latino speakers and to create the impression—not supported by objective research—that varieties of Spanish used in or transplanted to the United States become so hopelessly entangled with English as to constitute a "third language" substantially different from Spanish and English. This "third language" in turn is seen as gradually displacing Spanish in the United States, thereby placing U.S. Latino speakers at a disadvantage vis-à-vis their compatriots in other countries, and ultimately resulting in the deterioration of the Spanish language.

Within the United States, the designation *Spanglish* is most commonly used by non-Latinos (or by Latinos who are openly critical of non-standard language usage), in reference to the speech patterns of resident Latino communities. The most frequent targets are the nation's two oldest Hispanophone communities, those of Mexican and Puerto Rican origin. In the southwestern United States, *Tex-Mex* is often used (by non-Latinos) as a synonym of *Spanglish*, as is *pocho* among Mexican-Americans. *Spanglish* is occasionally used to refer to Cuban-Americans and increasingly to resident Dominicans; rarely if ever does one hear *Spanglish* used in conjunction with expatriates from Spain or Southern Cone nations perceived as "white," thus suggesting an element of racism coupled with the xenophobia that deplores any sort of linguistic and cultural hybridity.

Despite the lack of empirical evidence, the view that *Spanglish* constitutes a specific type of language is widespread; one can find dictionaries, grammar sketches, greeting cards, t-shirts, bumper stickers, and an enormous number of editorial comments and references in popular culture, all suggesting that *Spanglish* has a life of its own.[1] One common thread that runs through most accounts of *Spanglish* is the idea that Latinos in the United States and perhaps in Puerto Rico and border areas of Mexico speak this "language" rather than "real" Spanish. Since upwards of fifty million speakers are at stake, the matter is definitely of more than passing interest. The ambivalence and ambiguity that shrouds all things *Spanglish* is nowhere better illustrated than in definitions found in two of the most widely used and presumably authoritative dictionaries of the English language. The *American Heritage Dictionary* (1666) gives the generic and neutral definition "Spanish characterized by numerous borrowings from English." On the other hand, the prestigious and etymologically well-researched *Oxford English Dictionary* (v. XVI, 105) defines *Spanglish* as "A type of Spanish contaminated by English words and forms of expression, spoken in Latin America." Thus, from the outset, we are confronted with the ever-shifting and potentially insidious manipulation of hybrid terms designed to undermine the credibility and human capital of internally colonized groups.

In Search of the Origins of *Spanglish*

A transparent linguistic blend such as *Spanglish* is likely to arise spontaneously whenever contacts between English and Spanish are under discussion, and therefore to assign the creation of this term to a single individual or event is unrealistic. *Spanglish* takes its place among a plethora of language-contact blends, including *Taglish* (Tagalog-English in the Philippines), *Hinglish* (Hindi-English in India), *franglais* (mixture of French and English), *portuñol/ portunhol* (Portuguese-Spanish), *guarañol* (Guaraní-Spanish), and many others. Despite the unlikelihood that *Spanglish* has a unique parentage, the *Oxford English Dictionary* places the first known written attestation of this word—in Spanish rather than in English—in a setting that represents the quintessence of conflicting linguistic attitudes: Puerto Rico. The ambiguous status of Puerto Rico—at once a Spanish-speaking Latin American nation and a colony of the world's most powerful English-speaking society—has provoked a level of concern about the purity of the Spanish language and an ambivalence towards the English language unmatched in the Spanish-speaking world. The number of popularizing works that purport to describe and decry the "contamination" of Puerto Rican Spanish by English is enormous; serious linguistic studies are much fewer, but a pair of prominent monographs have kept the debate alive. The Spanish linguist Germán de Granda (1972), who resided briefly in Puerto Rico, described the *transculturación* of Puerto Rican Spanish in terms that would do credit to the spread of an epidemic. Granda is by no means a purist; his studies of Afro-Hispanic creole languages and the languages of Equatorial Guinea are legendary, as is his work with Paraguayan and Andean varieties, all based on rigorous fieldwork and a deep sense of appreciation and respect for the communities in which he lived. Granda's perspective on Puerto Rican Spanish can therefore not be summarily dismissed as an elitist neocolonial diatribe, although few scholars of Puerto Rican sociolinguistics would agree with his portrayal. The exiled Cuban linguist Paulino Pérez Sala (1973), a professor at a Puerto Rican university, spoke of the *interferencia lingüística del inglés* in Puerto Rican Spanish. Such interference no doubt occurs, especially under the avalanche of English-language advertising, technical language, and school discourse, but many of Pérez Sala's examples are typical of English-dominant bilinguals, and not of the Spanish-dominant population of the island.[2]

The term *Spanglish* (*espanglish* in Spanish) appears to have been coined by the Puerto Rican journalist Salvador Tío (1954), in a newspaper column first published in 1952. Tío—who certainly considers himself the inventor of this word (an opinion largely shared by others in Latin America)—was concerned about what he felt to be the deterioration of Spanish in Puerto Rico under the onslaught of English words, and waged a campaign of polemical and satirical articles over more than half a century. Tío (1954: 60) stated his position unashamedly: "No creo ni en el latín ni en el bilingüismo. El latín es una lengua muerta. El bilingüismo, dos lenguas muertas" (I don't believe either in Latin or in bilingualism. Latin is a dead language, bilingualism, two dead languages). Many of Tío's examples are legitimate borrowings from English— some in unassimilated form—that are found in modern Puerto Rican speech. Most refer to consumer products marketed in the United States or to aspects of popular youth culture, but Tío felt that Puerto Rican Spanish could suffer a far worse fate than simply absorbing foreign borrowings—which, after all, had been occurring in Spanish for more than a thousand years. Evidently not understanding that creole languages are formed under conditions far different from the bilingual borrowing found in Puerto Rico, he examined Papiamentu, an Afro-Iberian creole language spoken mainly in Aruba and Curaçao and concluded that it was a degenerate form of Spanish. He warned that the same fate could befall Puerto Rican Spanish (Tío 1992: 91): "Si en ese estado de postración cayó el español de Curazao y Aruba, también podría ocurrir algo similar en Puerto Rico si no se extrema el rigor para evitarlo. Puede tardar más tiempo por muchas razones pero si le ha ocurrido a otras lenguas en todos los continentes no hay razón para creer que somos indemnes al daño" (Tío 1992: 25) (If the Spanish of Curaçao and Aruba could sink to such depths, something similar could occur in Puerto Rico if stiff measures are not taken to avoid it. This could take longer for various reasons, but if it has happened to other languages in every continent there is no reason to believe that we are exempt from this danger). Tío's early article also contained humorous "Spanglish" words of his own invention, which were not used at the time and have not been used since, thereby creating some confusion between legitimate examples of language contact and sarcastic parodies. Although Tío had lived in New York City, and therefore had experienced first-hand true bilingual contact phenomena, he accepted uncritically others' parodies of Spanish-English interaction: "[el español] se pudre en la frontera nuevo-mejicana donde, como dice H. L.

Mencken en su obra *The American Language*, dos nuevo-mejicanos se saludan con esta joya de la burundanga lingüística: '¡Hola amigo! ¿Cómo le how do you dea?' 'Voy very welldiando, gracias'" (Tío 1992: 91) (Spanish is rotting on the New Mexican border [*sic*] where as H. L. Mencken says in *The American Language*, two New Mexicans greet each other with this gem of linguistic nonsense . . .). This example, from Mencken (1962: 650–51), does not actually come from the latter author, whose other observations on Spanish in the United States and its influence on English are in general well-documented and factually accurate. Rather, Mencken quotes (uncritically, it appears) a "recent explorer" (McKinstry 1930: 336), whose concern for linguistic accuracy was highly questionable. McKinstry wrote during a time when Mexican-bashing was an acceptable literary pass-time, and although his witty anecdotes about his linguistic experiences on the U.S.-Mexican border suggest that he actually spoke Spanish, his factual account of borrowed Anglicisms stands in stark contrast to his mocking account of the language skills of Mexicans living near the border:

> While the Mexican of the border appropriates the words of his neighbor in a truly wholesale manner, there is neither hope no danger that he will ever become English-speaking. It is only the bare words that are adopted. They are woven ingeniously into a fabric of grammar and pronunciation which remains forever Mexican. Although every other word your Nogales or Juárez peon uses may be English, he could not, to save his sombrero, put them together into a sentence intelligible to an American, that is, beyond such simple household phrases as *all right* and *goddam* [. . .] This mongrel jargon of the border is naturally shocking to the ears of the well-bred Mexican of the interior.

By uncritically quoting this crude parody together with legitimate examples of borrowing and calquing, Tío (and Mencken) contributed to the false impression of a "mongrel" language teetering on the brink of total unintelligibility.

Despite his affirmation of concern about the status of Spanish in Puerto Rico—and by extension in other areas where English threatens to overwhelm it—Tío offers his own version of *Spanglish,* a travesty of bilingual behavior that sets the stage for later debates on *Spanglish*. As an example, Tío creates new verbs based on whimsical convergences between Spanish and English:

> Tree—árbol. To climb—trepar. To climb a tree—treepar un árbol. ¿Por qué no formar una palabra que exprese en ambos idiomas el mismo sentimientos? Para nosotros que somos bilingües la cosa es clara. Se acuña una palabra nueva y se atacuña bien. Y ha nacido un nuevo idioma [. . .] *Treepar*. He aquí una palabra

llena de movimiento. Es una especie de taquigrafía lingüística cuya única dificultad consiste en que es más rápida que el pensamiento. Es una palabra que puede expresar, en dos idiomas a un tiempo, no ya dos palabras, dos oraciones completas. Y lo grande de esta idea, lo original, es que se pueden conjugar a un tiempo, no dos verbos, sino dos pensamientos completos en dos lenguas distintas. La lengua queda recogida en el verbo, y paradoja, se acaba la verborrea [. . .] Para decir "Me subí a un árbol" (I climbed a tree), basta decir: *treepé*. (1954: 64)

(Why not form a word that expresses the same feeling in both languages? For us bilinguals it's clear. You coin a new word and "rub it in." And so a new language is born [. . .] *Treepar*. Here's a word full of movement. It's a kind of linguistic shorthand whose only problem is that it is faster than thought. It's a word that can express in two languages at the same time not just two words, but two complete sentences. And the best part, the most original, is that one can conjugate at the same time not two verbs but two complete thoughts in two different languages. The language is contained in the verb, and, paradoxically, verbage is eliminated [. . .] To say "I climbed a tree" it's enough to say *treepé*.)

Tío continues in this fashion, creating other neologisms via similar leaps of logic; for example:

Rocking chair—sillón. De ahí formamos el sustantivo: *rollón* y el verbo: *rollar* (to rock—mecerse) [. . .] y para decir: "I get up from the rocking-chair" (Yo me levanto del sillón), basta decir: "Yo me desenrollo." (1954: 64–65)

(From this we form the noun *rollón* and the verb *rollar* [. . .] and to say "I get up from the rocking-chair" one just says "I unroll.")

Tío then offers some lexical neologisms, for example from *piscina/swimming pool* come *pipool, polina, swicina;* from *mattress/colchón/colchoneta* come *machón/machoneta*; the mixture of *pull* and *influencia* gives *opulencia*, an so on. Tío—perhaps inspired by McKinstry's grotesque parody—then illustrates what a dialogue in such *Spanglish* might sound like:

¿Espiblas Espanglish? —Yi, Minor. (1954: 65)

Yi is a blend of *yes* and *sí*; *espiblar* combines *speak* and *hablar*, and *Minor* is derived from *Mister* and *Señor*. Tío then echoes the affirmation that "anyone" can speak *Spanglish* by just making things up as one goes along. This xenophobic diatribe is frequently voiced in reference to creole languages such as Papiamentu, Lesser Antilles French Creole (known locally as *patois*), Philippine Creole Spanish (known as *Chabacano*), and so on i.e., that by simply "mixing together" two or more languages in a polyglossic free-for-all a new language is instantly created. For Tío:

> Éste es un idioma que se aprende en tres lecciones. El resto lo pueden hacer ustedes por su cuenta. Por su cuenta y riesgo [. . .] Esta lengua que surge del choque de dos culturas es la única solución al problema de las Américas. No nos entenderemos mientras no hablemos el mismo idioma [. . .] Hay que crear una nueva lengua que no se preste a engaños. Por ahora sólo está en teoría, la teoría del "espanglish," la teoría para acabar con el bilingüismo en nombre del bilingüismo. (1954: 65)

(This is a language that can be learned in three lessons. You can do the rest on your own. On your own and at your own risk [. . .] this language that arises from the clash of two cultures is the only solution to the problem of the Americas. We will never understand one another as long as we don't speak the same language [. . .] we must create a new language that can't be tampered with. For now this language only exists in theory, the "Spanglish" theory, the theory that will get rid of bilingualism in the name of bilingualism.)

Although Tío offers this wry "if you can't beat 'em, join 'em" pseudo-solution to language and culture clash, his bitter refutation of English comes through clearly. Tío's many remarks about *Spanglish*—scattered across several articles and four decades—present an ambiguous picture. On the one hand, Tío shared with many other Puerto Rican intellectuals of the time the fear that United States cultural imperialism and the crushing weight of English would eventually displace a language that had landed with Columbus and had survived unaltered until only a few decades previously. After all, Tío could remember the English-only schools that arrived with the American occupation of Puerto Rico, and his first comments on *Spanglish* were written just after Puerto Rico had finally wrested from the United States government the right to elect its own governor and congress. By the middle of the twentieth century, world-wide Spanish already contained numerous well-integrated Anglicisms, and Puerto Ricans used even more, including those that had entered via the American school system, consumer advertising, American businesses located in Puerto Rico, and by the increasing tide of Puerto Ricans who emigrated to the mainland to work and returned with new English expressions. All these Anglicisms were either assimilated unaltered—except for the basic phonetic adaptations— (words like *welfare, teacher, míster* and *miss*) or were morphologically adapted to Spanish patterns (*leak* > *liquiar*, *spell* > *espeliar*). False cognates might become true cognates in a language-contact environment (whence *aplicar* could mean "to apply for a job" and *registrar* "to register for a class"), the use of the gerund or progressive verb tenses might be more frequent than in monolingual Spanish (e.g., *le estamos enviando el paquete mañana* instead of *le enviamos/ enviaremos* [. . .]), and occasional idiomatic expressions from English might be calqued into Spanish—on the mainland but seldom on the island except among returning *nuyoricans* (e.g. *llamar para atrás* "to call back").[3] Nowhere did one find—in Puerto Rico or elsewhere among Spanish speakers in contact with English—bizarre linguistic chimeras like *treepar*, *rollón*, *pipool*, or *machoneta*. Tío had clearly never heard such items, nor was there any danger of his ever doing so. He deftly avoided any discussion of true language-contact phenomena, which have enriched Spanish for at least thirteen centuries, in favor of creating a xenoglossic straw man emblazoned with the epithet *Spanglish*, with which to bludgeon those who might not share his abhorrence of Spanish-English bilingualism. Tío, like McKinstry and scores of nameless commentators before and since, deliberately invented pseudo-bilingual monstrosities into order to denigrate legitimate bilingual speech communities individually and collectively. For McKinstry the prime motivation was racist supremacy: Mexicans were regarded as inferior to Anglo-Americans, hence incapable of adequately acquiring English but all too capable of losing their grip on their own native language once confronted—even at a distance and separated by a national border—with the English language juggernaut. Tío may well have harbored racist sentiments against Anglo-Americans—and his scorn for the Afro-American language Papiamentu provides a possible bit of evidence—but his harshest broadsides are directed at his fellow citizens for their failure to embrace monolinguism, for Tío a primordial virtue. Tío foreshadows a viewpoint that would later be taken up in the continental United States by expatriate intellectuals like Roberto González Echeverría (to be discussed next), namely that even educated Latinos willingly allow their language to be overrun by English in the mistaken view that this increases their upward social mobility.

Other Viewpoints and Definitions

Even within Puerto Rico, not all regard *Spanglish* with animosity. Nash offers a somewhat different definition and set of observations on "Spanglish" in Puerto Rico:

In the metropolitan areas of Puerto Rico, where Newyorricans play an influential role in the economic life of the island, there has arisen a hybrid variety of language, often given the slightly derogatory label of Spanglish, which coexists with less mixed forms of standard English and standard Spanish and has at least one of the characteristics of an autonomous language: a substantial number of native speakers. The emerging language retains the phonological, morphological, and syntactic structure of Puerto Rican Spanish.... Spanglish as defined here is neither language containing grammatical errors due to interference nor intentionally mixed language. (1970: 223–25)

Most of Nash's examples represent the sort of lexical borrowing found in all bilingual contact situations.

In a recent survey of attitudes and inquiries about Spanish in the United States, Fairclough (2003: 187) defines *Spanglish* as simply "la mezcla del inglés y del español" (the mixture of English and Spanish). Odón Betanzos Palacios, president of the North American Academy of the Spanish Language is of the opinion that

> El *espanglish* y el *engliñol* han sido y son dos problemas normales en comunidades donde conviven los de lengua española y los estadounidenses, comunidades en las que sus hablantes son monolingües y tienen necesidad de comunicarse. El de lengua española ha recogido palabras del inglés, de las que entiende su significado y, sencillamente, las españoliza; igualmente hará con las formas verbales y así, en su variedad de injertos, se aproximará a la comunicación con el de la otra lengua... el *espanglish* es, sólo, medio de comunicación temporal... Creo que [los que promueven la enseñanza del spanglish] no se han percatado del enorme error que cometen al querer hacer de amplitudes y querer enseñar una jerga de comunidades que ni siquiera podrán entender otras comunidades de sus cercanías. (2001: 2)

> (*Spanglish* and *Engliñol* have been and continue to be two normal problems in communities where Spanish speakers and Americans live together. The Spanish speaker has taken those English words whose meaning is understood and, simply, has Hispanized them; the same is done with verbal forms and with such hybrids, some approximation to communication in the other language will be achieved ... *Spanglish* is only a temporary means of communication... I believe that those who promote the teaching of *Spanglish* are not aware of the huge mistake in teaching this jargon that cannot even be understood in neighboring communities.)

Adopting an anti-imperialistic stance and considering *Spanglish* to consist primarily of the use of Anglicisms by Spanish speakers, the distinguished literary critic Roberto González-Echeverría laments the negative implications of *Spanglish*:

> El spanglish, la lengua compuesta de español e inglés que salió de la calle y se introdujo en los programas de entrevistas y las campañas de publicidad, plantea un grave peligro a la cultura hispánica y al progreso de los hispanos dentro de la corriente mayoritaria norteamericana. Aquellos que lo toleran e incluso lo promueven como una mezcla inocua no se dan cuenta de que esta no es una relación basada en la igualdad. El spanglish es una invasión del español por el inglés. La triste realidad es que el spanglish es básicamente la lengua de los hispanos pobres, muchos de los cuales son casi analfabetos en cualquiera de los dos idiomas. Incorporan palabras y construcciones inglesas a su habla de todos los días porque carecen del vocabulario y la educación en español para adaptarse a la cambiante cultura que los rodea. Los hispanos educados que hacen otro tanto tienen una motivación diferente: algunos se avergüenzan de su origen e intentan parecerse al resto usando palabras inglesas y traduciendo directamente las expresiones idiomáticas inglesas. Hacerlo, piensan, es reclamar la calidad de miembro de la corriente mayoritaria. Políticamente, sin embargo, el spanglish es una capitulación; indica marginalización, no liberación. (1)

> (Spanglish, the language made up of Spanish and English off the streets and introduced into talk shows and advertising campaigns represents a grave danger for Latino culture and the progress of Latinos in mainstream America. Those who tolerate and even promote [spanglish] as a harmless mixture don't realize that this is not a relationship of equality. The sad truth is that spanglish is basically the language of poor Latinos, many of whom are illiterate in both languages. They incoporate English words and constructions into their daily speech because they lack the vocabulary and training in Spanish to adapt to the culture that surrounds them. Educated Latinos who use this language have other motives: some are ashamed of their origins and try to blend in with everyone else by using English words and literally translating English idioms. They think that this will make them part of the mainstream. Politically, however, Spanglish represents a capitulation; it stands for marginalization, not liberation.)

This condemnation of *Spanglish* as a manifestation of defeat and submissiveness by Hispanic communities in the United Status recalls Odón Betanzos Palacios' lament (Betanzos Palacios, n.d.), when he speaks of "el problema de algunos hispanos en Estados Unidos, de los que no han podido ni tenido la oportunidad de aprender ninguna de las dos lenguas (español e inglés)" (the problem of some Hispanics in the United States, who have not had the opportunity to learn either of the languages [Spanish or English]). In another commentary on *Spanglish*, the Spaniard Joaquim Ibarz offers the following observation, which clearly confuses regional and social dialects, youth slang, and language contact phenomena:

> Hablar medio en español, medio en inglés, no es tan descabellado si se piensa en la mezcla de las culturas, las migraciones y todas las circunstancias que han hecho que estos dos idiomas puedan combinar ... La lengua resultante del mestizaje entre español y el inglés, conocida como 'spanglish,' es hablada por más de 25 millones de personas a ambos lados de la frontera entre México y Estados Unidos, zona en la que residen cerca de 40 millones de latinos. La mayoría utiliza formas diferentes de este dialecto, que cambia según el país de origen de quién lo utiliza, como el cubonics de Miami, el nuyorrican de los puertorriqueños de Manhattan y el caló pachuco de San Antonio. (2002: 3)

> (Speaking half in Spanish, half in English, isn't so crazy if we think about cultural mixture, migrations, and other circumstances that have brought these two languages together ... the language resulting from the mixture of Spanish and English, known as 'spanglish,' is spoken by more than 25 million people on both sides of the U.S.-Mexican border, an area in which some 40 million Latinos live. Most use some variety of this dialect, which varies according to the country of origins, like Cubonics in Miami, Nuyorican for Puerto Ricans in Manhattan and Pachuco caló of San Antonio.)

Another Spaniard, Xosé Castro gives a similar appraisal:

> El espanglish tiene una lógica forma de ser y un origen explicable y comprensible. Su función es claramente comunicadora, pero sólo puede darse cuando existe una carencia de vocabulario en alguna de las dos partes que forman un diálogo. Cuando existe alguna duda o algo que obstaculice la comprensión, se echa mano de la versión inglesa, idioma que ambos interlocutores comprenden, y la comunicación, por fin, se completa ... la marginalidad del espanglish ... excluye al hispano que no entiende inglés, y al angloparlante que no entiende español. Se restringe, por tanto, a una reducida comunidad de hablantes. (1996: 3)

> (Spanglish has its own logic and a logically explained origin. It serves a clear communicative function, but it can only occur when one of the dialog partners lacks a vocabulary item. When in doubt, to eliminate any obstacle to communication, one reverts to the English version, understood by both interlocutors, and communication takes place ... the marginal status of spanglish ... excludes Latinos who don't understand English and English speakers who don't understand Spanish. It is therefore restricted to small speech communities. We must acknowledge that New

York Spanglish has little to do with its Los Angeles counterpart. Therefore we are not speaking of a single language but rather of a group of dialects as varied as the speech communities it represents.)

For the Cuban linguists Valdés Bernal and Gregori Tornada (2001: 5), *Spanglish* is in essence a phenomenon peculiar to Puerto Ricans living in New York, but these linguists (unable to travel to Miami to observe the situation first hand) assert that "el *spanglish* queda para los puertorriqueños en sus barrios neoyorquinos. Sin embargo esto ya es historia, y el spanglish, como era de esperar, ha hecho su aparición en Miami entre la nueva generación de los cubanoamericanos—los yacas—quienes se 'divierten' hablando esta variedad de lengua 'en parte español anglosajonizado, en parte inglés hispanizado, y en parte giros sintácticos, que usan niños y adultos, a veces casi sin darse cuenta'" (Spanglish was for Puerto Ricans in their New York neighborhoods. But this is now history, and spanglish, as might be expected, has made an appearance in Miami among the new generation of Cuban-Americans—yacas—who "mess around" speaking this dialect "part Anglicized Spanish, part Hispanized English, and part syntactic combinations used unconsciously by children and adults). Most of the cited examples include code-switching, but in some cases the results of language erosion among increasingly English-dominant bilinguals is taken as an indicator of *Spanglish* (for example the use of the familiar pronoun *tú* in conjunction with deferential address forms such as *señor alcalde* 'honorable mayor').

Many professional educators have viewed terms like *Spanglish* with alarm. Milán specifically recommended that researchers and educators [in New York City] refrain from using the term "Spanglish" and use instead neutral designations such as "New York City Spanish" (202–203). Acosta-Belén observed that "Speakers of the non-defined mixture of Spanish and/or English are judged as 'different,' or 'sloppy' speakers of Spanish and/or English, and are often labeled verbally deprived, alingual, or deficient bilinguals because supposedly they do not have the ability to speak either English or Spanish well" (151). On the other hand the linguist and Latina activist Zentella (1997: 82) has demonstrated that younger Puerto Ricans in New York and other cities of the Northeastern United States are beginning to adopt the word "Spanglish" with pride, to refer explicitly to code-switching: ". . . more NYPR's are referring to "Spanglish" as a positive way of identifying their switching." She concludes that "Contrary to the attitude of those who label Puerto Rican code switching 'Spanglish' in the belief that a chaotic mixture is being invented, English-Spanish switching is a creative style of bilingual communication that accomplishes important cultural and conversational work" (112–13). Zentella's proposed grammar of "Spanglish" is in reality a compilation of grammatical and pragmatic constraints on code-switching.

Latino Activism and the New *Spanglish*

The evolving social and political identity of the U.S. Latino communities and the upsurge in dialog between intellectuals and activists has resulted in a rebirth of the notion of *Spanglish* in new guises. Just as *Chicano* has vastly different connotations and implications than this word had in Mexico and the southwestern United States a few decades ago, so has *Spanglish* been deliberately claimed as linguistic and cultural patrimony, albeit with no single unifying thread. To illustrate the range of ideas and viewpoints encompassed by "neo-*spanglish*," the writings of two well-known protagonists will be examined. Ed Morales takes a politically-grounded stance, linking *Spanglish* with the notion that:

> Latinos are a mixed-race people . . . there is a need for a way to say something more about this idea than the word "Latino" expresses. So for the moment, let's consider a new term for the discussion of what this aspect of Latino means—let us consider Spanglish. Why Spanglish? There is no better metaphor for what a mixed-race culture means than a hybrid language, an informal code; the same sort of linguistic construction that defines different classes in a society can also come to define something outside it, a social construction with different rules. Spanglish is what we speak, but it is also who we Latinos are, and how we act, and how we perceive the world. It's also a way to avoid the sectarian nature of other labels that describe our condition, terms like Nuyorican, Chicano, Cuban American, Dominicanyork. It is an immediate declaration that translation is definition, that movement is status quo. (2002: 3)

While acknowledging that many observers—particularly from other Spanish-speaking nations—regard Spanglish as "Spanish under siege from an external invader" (5), Morales goes on to celebrate the emerging Latino language as an affirmation of resistance and the construction of a powerful new identity. The remainder of his work deals with manifestations of the Spanish-English interface in literature, popular culture, and political discourse, and represents the most eloquent manifesto of *Spanglish* as an originally derogatory term that is being co-opted by its former victims as a badge of pride and courage.

A very different perspective comes from the self-declared admirer and promoter of *Spanglish* Ilan Stavans, an expatriate Mexican writer now teaching in Massachusetts, whose prolific popular writings on *Spanglish* and purported specimens of this "language" have made him a lightning rod for polemic as well as a widely-cited source among international scholars unfamiliar with the reality of Spanish-English bilingualism in the United States. Rather than applying *Spanglish* to an already existent discourse mode or sociolinguistic register (as done, for example, by Ed Morales or by the New York Puerto Ricans cited by Zentella 1997), Stavans invents his own mixture of Spanish and English, loosely modeled after true intrasentential code-switching typical of U.S. Latino communities. Stavans initially defines *Spanglish* innocuously as "The verbal encounter between Anglo and Hispano civilizations" (2003: 6). His anecdotal accounts of learning *Spanglish* upon arriving in New York City from Mexico reveal an often less than affectionate reaction: "But to keep up with these publications [Spanish-language newspapers in New York City in the 1980s] was also to invite your tongue for a bumpy ride. The grammar and syntax used in them was never fully 'normal,' e.g., it replicated, often unconsciously, English-language patterns. It was obvious that its authors and editors were *americanos* with *a lo* connection to *la lengua de* Borges" (Stavans 2003: 2).

While perhaps initially offended by varieties of Spanish that seemed exotic to one coming from Mexico and by the frequent code-switching, loan translations and assimilated Anglicisms characteristic of these typical bilingual environment, Stavans came to profess a deep admiration for code-switched discourse, which for him forms the essence of *Spanglish*. Stavans appears to regard all code-switching as a deliberate act of creativity, whereas most linguists who have studied code-switching—in a wide variety of language-contact environments throughout the world—analyze spontaneous code-switching in spoken language as a loosely monitored speech mode circumscribed by basic syntactic restrictions but largely below the level of conscious awareness. Only in written language, particularly in creative literature, is deliberate manipulation of code-switching to achieve specific aesthetic goals a viable option. Beginning in the 1970s, the use of code-switching in U.S. Latino literature has become increasingly common, first in poetry and eventually in narrative texts as well. Such writers as Alurista, Tato Laviera, Roberto Fernández, and Rolando Hinojosa have fine-tuned the language of U.S. Latino communities to create a striking "third language" in their innovative literary texts. Even in their most creative flights of fancy, these writers almost always adhere to the syntactic and pragmatic rules that govern spontaneously-produced bilingual speech. The most general restriction on mixing languages within the same sentence is that no grammatical rule in either language be violated, and in particular that the point of transition be "smooth" in the sense that the material from the second language is in some way as likely a combination as a continuation in the first language. Fluent code-switching may therefore produce combinations in which, e.g., a switch occurs between article and noun, between a complementizer and a subordinate clause, between a conjunction and one of the conjuncts, and so on.[4] Spontaneous code-switches not accompanied by hesitations, pauses, or interruptions, are normally unacceptable in the following circumstances: 1) between a pronominal subject and a predicate; 2) between a pronominal clitic and the verb; 3) between a sentence-initial interrogative word and the remainder of the sentence; 4) between an auxiliary verb (especially *haber*) and the main verb; and 5) adverbs of negation are normally in the same language as the verbs they modify. The restrictions reflect the general need to maintain the grammatical rules of each language, following the linear order both in English and in Spanish, and to retain easily identifiable chunks of discourse.

Although surrounded by bilingual discourse since arriving in the United States, Stavans reports on a particularly apocryphal experience that revealed the creative potential of written code-switching. During an early teaching assignment, some Latino students frustrated with the treatment of Latinos by the American "system" expressed their alienation by rendering the Pledge of Allegiance, the United States Constitution and the Declaration of Independence into a humorous but obviously non-authentic mixture of languages:

(a) Yo plegio alianza a la bandera de los Unaited Esteits de America . . .

(I pledge allegiance to the flag of the United States of America.)

(b) Nosotros joldeamos que estas truths son self-evidentes, que todos los hombres son creados equally, que están endawdeados por su Creador con certain derechos unalienables, que entre these están la vida, la libertad, y la persura de la felicidad.

(We hold these truths to be self-evident, that all men are created equal, that they are endowed by their Creator with certain inalienable Rights, that among these are Life, Liberty, and the pursuit of Happiness.)

(c) We la gente de los Unaited Esteits, pa' formar una unión más perfecta, establisheamos la justicia, aseguramos tranquilidá doméstica, provideamos pa' la defensa común, promovemos el welfér, y aseguramos el blessin de la libertad de nosotros mismos y nuestra posterity, ordenando y establisheando esta Constitución de los Unaited Esteits de América.

(We the people of the United States, in order to form a more perfect union, establish justice, insure domestic tranquility, provide for the common defense, promote the general welfare and secure the blessings of liberty to ourselves and our posterity, do ordain and establish this Constitution for the United States of America.) (Stavans 2003: 15)

Although these cynical parodies do not violate any major grammatical restrictions on language mixing, they contain unlikely Anglicisms (*joldeamos, endawdeados, establisheamos*) and an admixture of colloquial speech forms (*pa'* for *para, tranquildá* for *tranquilidad*) that clash with the solemn and formulaic language of these iconic texts. For Stavans, these parodies constituted "an exercise in ingenuity ... show[ing] astuteness, a stunning capacity to adapt, and an imaginative aspect ... that refuses to accept anything as foreign." He was inspired to try his hand at similar "recasting" of classic literary texts, with the following results:

(a) Sudenmente fuera del air estéril y drowsy, el lair de los esclavos Como un lightning Europa dió un paso pa'lante ... (Walt Whitman, *Leaves of grass*)

(b) You no sabe de mí sin you leer un book by the nombre of *The Aventuras of Tom Sawyer*, pero eso ain't no matter (Mark Twain, *Adventure of Huckleberry Finn*)

(c) La tierra was ours antes que nosotros were de la tierra. It was nuestra tierra más de cien años pa'tras (Robert Frost, "The gift outright") (16)

Like his students' parodies, Stavans' imitations combine improbable Anglicisms (*sudenmente*) and rapid-speech forms (*pa'lante, pa'tras*). In addition, there are violations of basic code-switching restrictions, e.g., between pronominal subject and verb (*sin you leer, you no sabe*) as well as inappropriate combinations in Spanish (*sabe de mí*). The linguistic differences between Stavans' bilingual texts and those of his students underscore the fact that fluent code-switching forms part of the basic competence of native bilingual speakers and is not easily acquired among second-language learners.

Stavans' early attempts at creating a literary *Spanglish* were largely unknown until he revealed them in his 2003 book, but the end result of his linguistic manipulations have made Stavans and his definition of *Spanglish* a much-quoted commodity among intellectuals in other Spanish-speaking countries who decry the state of Spanish in the United States. In a tour de force which thanks to the World Wide Web has reached untold thousands of readers,

Stavans has offered a purported "translation" of the first chapter of *Don Quijote* into *Spanglish*:

> In un placete de La Mancha of which nombre no quiero remembrearme, vivía, not so long ago, uno de esos gentlemen who always tienen una lanza in the rack, una buckler antigua, a skinny caballo y un grayhound para el chase. A cazuela with más beef than mutón, carne choppeada para la dinner, un omelet pa los sábados, lentil pa los viernes, y algún pigeon como delicacy especial pa los domingos, consumían tres cuarters de su income. El resto lo employaba en una coat de broadcloth y en soketes de velvetín pa los holidays, with sus slippers pa combinar, while los otros días de la semana él cut a figura de los más finos cloths. Livin with él eran una housekeeper en sus forties, una sobrina not yet twenty y un ladino del field y la marketa que le saddleaba el caballo al gentleman y wieldeaba un hookete pa podear. El gentleman andaba por allí por los fifty. Era de complexión robusta pero un poco fresco en los bones y una cara leaneada y gaunteada. La gente sabía that él era un early riser y que gustaba mucho huntear. La gente say que su apellido was Quijada or Quesada—hay diferencia de opinión entre aquellos que han escrito sobre el sujeto—but acordando with las muchas conjecturas se entiende que era really Quejada. But all this no tiene mucha importancia pa nuestro cuento, providiendo que al cuentarlo no nos separemos pa nada de las verdá. (2002: 5–6)

This text contains numerous syntactic violations of code-switching, together with phonetically unlikely combinations (e.g. *saddleaba*), and hints of popular or uneducated Spanish (e.g., *pa* < *para* 'for,' *verdá* < *verdad* 'truth') which implicitly reinforce the notion that only uneducated people speak *Spanglish*. That Stavans' *Quijote* is not simply a foreigner's innocent attempt to mimic authentic bilingual speech is amply demonstrated by his considerable proficiency in producing realistic code-switched language in his expository prose writings (e.g., Stavans 2000, 2003). Regardless of Stavans' motivations, his *Quijote* rendition has been widely cited—always disapprovingly—as "evidence" of the deplorable state of Spanish in the United States.

Spanglish: Who Needs It?

The bibliography of empirical research on varieties of Spanish in the United States is vast and continually growing, and all results converge on a single conclusion: there is no "third language" or cohesive *Spanglish* to be found anywhere in this country, nor can extrapolation from contemporary language contact environments project such a language in the foreseeable future. Each

Latino speech community retains the major dialect features of the countries of origin, together with the inevitable dialect leveling in urban areas where several regional varieties of Spanish are in daily contact. In the aggregate, Spanish speakers living in the United States use more Anglicisms than their monolingual counterparts in other Spanish-speaking countries; these include loan translations, false and partial cognates, and assimilated borrowings. However in no cases are basic grammatical principles of Spanish violated among fluent speakers of Spanish, although patterns of usage may vary. Only among second- and third-generation English-dominant speakers is it possible to find combinations that would be grammatically unacceptable in fully fluent Spanish. This, however, is not *Spanglish* but rather the natural consequence of the LANGUAGE SHIFT > LANGUAGE LOSS trajectory typical of most immigrant speech communities.[5] The implicit failure to distinguish between fluent bilinguals and semi-fluent heritage language speakers is partially responsible for misleading statements about the prevalence of *Spanglish* among U.S. Latino communities.

What is the future of *Spanglish*? Will it continue to be the whipping-boy for purists and xenophobes or will it emerge into the sunshine as the positive affirmation of U.S. Latino identity? To address these questions within an academic essay is to engage in mere speculation, but some factual points may be brought to bear. First, despite the enormous bibliography of empirical research on U.S. varieties of Spanish, spanning nearly a century of scholarship and nearly every Spanish-speaking community residing within the United States, little of this knowledge has penetrated elementary and secondary education, the mass media, the entertainment industry, or the diplomatic service. Although there is greater reluctance to employ offensive terms in public discourse, popular notions about the language of U.S. Latinos differ little from those in vogue more than half a century ago. At the university level matters are much more salutary; courses on U.S. Latino culture and literature and Spanish language courses designed for native and heritage language speakers are encouraging portents, but seldom does this enlightenment penetrate the "town vs. gown" barrier. It is therefore difficult to envision an eventual widespread acceptance of *Spanglish* as a proud affirmation of ethnolinguistic identity. In the history of U.S. sociocultural discourse, no term has risen from bigotry to splendor. It is true that within Mexico *chicano* has often been used as a negative stereotype for Mexican-Americans, but the word itself is simply a retention of the archaic pronunciation of *mexicano*. No racial or ethnic slur has been transformed into a favorable epithet across wide sectors of American society.[6] Items like *African-American, physically challenged, Asian, Native American, domestic partner,* and the like are modern usages that bear no resemblance to the host of ugly tags once found in common parlance. If *Ebonics* survives unscathed—and this is very much up for grabs—it will be at least in part due to its lack of similarity to any of the popular or academic terms previously used to designate these language varieties.

Urgently needed is a greater public awareness of the reality of U.S. Latino language, and if *Spanglish* is allowed to creep into the (re)education of the American public, I fear for any remediation. *Spanglish* is as out of place in promoting Latino language and culture as are *crazy, lunatic, crackpot, nut case* in mental health care, or *bum, slob, misfit, loser* in social work. From the perspective of a linguist who has spent more than three decades studying the Spanish language in its U.S. setting, *Spanglish* will always be a signpost on the wrong road, a road whose many way-stations range from misunderstanding to intolerance. The expression *el que habla dos lenguas vale por dos* (the person who speaks two languages is worth twice as much) does not admit qualifiers, and neither should our acceptance of the nation's largest bilingual community.

Notes

1. *Spanglish* has even made its way into children's literature, for example, in a humorously didactic novel by Montes (2003) in which a Puerto Rican girl is teased by her English-only classmates. The cover blurb sets the stage:

   Maritza Gabriela Morales Mercado (Gabí for short) has big *problemas*. Her worst enemy, Johnny Wiley, is driving her crazy . . . Gabí is so mad she can't even talk straight. Her English words keep getting jumbled up with her Spanish words. Now she's speaking a crazy mix of both, and no one knows what she's saying! Will Gabí ever make sense again? Or will she be tongue-tied forever?

   The book provides a touching lesson in cultural sensitivity and a few examples of realistic code-switching, although the idea that bilingual speakers 'jumble up' their languages when they become angry is unlikely to score any points in the bilingual education arena.

2. Similar viewpoints have been expressed by the journalists Lloréns (1971) and Varo (1971). See Lipski (1975, 1976) for a different viewpoint.
3. For a discussion of *patrás* and similar phenomena, see Lipski (1985b, 1987), Otheguy (1993).
4. The literature on the syntactic constraints which govern code-switching is vast and

still growing. Summaries of relevant theories and approaches are found in Lipski (1982, 1985a) and Toribio (2001a, 2001b).
5. See the examples in Bills (1989, 1997), Bills et al. (1995, 2000), Lipski (1985c, 1992, 1993, 1996a, 1996b), Silva-Corvalán (1994).
6. It is true that *nigga* has positive attributes in African-American hip-hop culture, but this term is not freely available for use by non-members of this community and is rejected by more conservative African-Americans. *Queer* has become accepted in academic circles (to wit queer studies, queer theory), but "on the street" it retains the traditional locker-room flavor.

Works Cited

Acosta-Belén, E. "Spanglish: a Case of Languages in Contact." *New Directions in Second Language Learning, Teaching and Bilingual Education*. Ed. Marina Burt and Helen Dulay. Washington, DC: TESOL, 1975. 151–58.

Betanzos Palacios, Odón. El "espanglish" y sus accidentes. <www.elcastellano.org/espangl.html>.

———. "El español en Estados Unidos: problemas y logros." Presented at the II International Congress on the Spanish Language, Valladolid, Spain, October, 2001.

Bills, Garland. "Language Shift, Linguistic Variation, and Teaching Spanish to Native Speakers in the United States." *La enseñanza del español a hispanohablantes: praxis y teoría*. Ed. M. Cecilia Colombi and Francisco X. Alarcón. Boston and New York: Houghton Mifflin, 1997. 262–82.

———. "The U.S. Census of 1980 and Spanish in the Southwest." *International Journal of the Sociology of Language* 79 (1989): 11–28.

Bills, Garland, Eduardo Hernández Chávez, and Alan Hudson. "Spanish Home Language Use and English Proficiency as Differential Measures of Language Maintenance and Shift." *Southwest Journal of Linguistics* 19 (2000): 11–27.

———. "The Geography of Language Shift: Distance from the Mexican Border and Spanish Language Claiming in the Southwestern United States." *International Journal of the Sociology of Language* 114 (1995): 9–27.

Castro, Xosé. "El espanglish en Internet y en la computación/informática." Presented at the Congreso sobre Internet organized by Novell, Madrid, Spain. June 12–14, 1996.

Fairclough, Marta. "El (denominado) *Spanglish* en los Estados Unidos." *Revista Internacional de Lingüística Iberoamericana (RILI)* 1 (2003): 185–204.

González-Echeverría, Roberto. "Hablar spanglish es devaluar el español." Translation in *Clarín* of an article originally appearing in the *New York Times*. March 28, 1997. <www.clarin.com.diario/1997/04/05/@spangli.htm>.

Granda, Germán de. *Transculturación e interferencia lingüística en el Puerto Rico contemporáneo*. Río Piedras: Editorial Edil, 1972.

Ibarz, Joaquim. "In un placete de La Mancha." *El Espectador* (Bogotá), 3 de julio de 2002 [Internet version].
Lipski, John. "La lengua española en los Estados Unidos: avanza a la vez que retrocede." *Revista Española de Lingüística* 33 (2004): 231–60.
———. "Patterns of Pronominal Evolution in Cuban-American Bilinguals." *Spanish in Contact: Issues in Bilingualism*. Ed. Ana Roca and John B. Jensen. Somerville, MA: Cascadilla Press, 1996a. 159–86.
———. "Los dialectos vestigiales del español en los Estados Unidos: estado de la cuestión." *Signo y Seña* 6 (1996b): 459–89.
———. "Creoloid Phenomena in the Spanish of Transitional Bilinguals." *Spanish in the United States: linguistic contact and diversity*. Ed. Ana Roca and John Lipski. Berlín: Mouton de Gruyter, 1993. 155–82.
———. "Language—Varieties of Spanish Spoken, English Usage among Hispanics, Spanish in Business, the Media and Other Social Environments, Bilingualism and Code-switching." *The Hispanic-American almanac*. Ed. Nicolás Kanellos. Detroit: Gale Research Inc, 1992. 209–27.
———. "The Construction *pa(ra) atrás* among Spanish-English Bilinguals: Parallel Structures and Universal Patterns." *Ibero Americana* 28/29 (1987): 87–96.
———. *Linguistic Aspects of Spanish-English Language Switching*. Tempe: Arizona State University, Center for Latin American Studies, 1985a.
———. "The Construction *pa(ra) atrás* in Bilingual Spanish-English Communities. *Revista/Review Interamericana* 15 (1985b): 91–102.
———. "Creole Spanish and Vestigial Spanish: Evolutionary Parallels." *Linguistics* 23 (1985c): 963–84.
———. "Spanish-English Language Switching in Speech and Literature: Theories and Models." *Bilingual Review* 9 (1982): 191–212.
———. "Structural Linguistics and Bilingual Interference." *Bilingual Review/Revista Bilingüe* 3 (1976): 229–37.
———. "The Language Battle in Puerto Rico." *Revista Interamericana* 5 (1975): 346–54.
Lloréns, Washington. *El habla popular de Puerto Rico*. Río Piedras: Editorial Edil, 2nd ed, 1971.
McKinstry, H. E. "The American Language in Mexico." *American Mercury* 19(75), March 1930, 336–38.
Mencken, H. L. *The American Language*. New York: Alfred A. Knopf, 4th edition, 1962.
Milán, William. "Spanish in the Inner City: Puerto Rican Speakers in New York." *Bilingual Education for Hispanic Students in the United States*. Ed. Joshua A. Fishman, and Gary D. Keller. New York: Columbia University, Teacher's College, 1982. 191–206.
Montes, Marisa. *Get Ready for Gabí! A Crazy Mixed-up Spanglish day*. New York: Scholastic Press, 2003.
Morales, Ed. *Living in Spanglish: The Search for Latino Identity in America*. New York: St. Martin's Press, 2002.

Nash, Rose. "Englañol: More Language Contact in Puerto Rico." *American Speech* 46 (1971): 106–22.

———. "Spanglish: Language Contact in Puerto Rico." *American Speech* 45 (1970): 223–33.

Otheguy, Ricardo. "A Reconsideration of the Notion of Loan Translation in the Analysis of U.S. Spanish." *Spanish in the United States: Linguistic Contact and Diversity*. Ed. Ana Roca, and John Lipski. Berlin: Mouton de Gruyter, 1993. 21–45.

Pérez Sala, Paulino. *Interferencia lingüística del inglés en el español hablado en Puerto Rico*. Hato Rey: Inter American University Press, 1973.

Silva-Corvalán, Carmen. *Language Contact and Change: Spanish in Los Angeles*. Oxford: Clarendon Press, 1994.

Stavans, Ilan. *Spanglish: The Making of a New American Language*. New York: Harper-Collins, 2003.

———. "Translation of the *Quijote* into 'spanglish.'" *La Vanguardia* (Barcelona) July 3, 2002. 5–6.

———. *Spanglish para millones*. Madrid: Colección Apuntes de Casa de América, 2000.

Tío, Salvador. *Lengua mayor: ensayos sobre el español de aquí y de allá*. Madrid: Editorial Plaza Mayor, 1992.

———. *Teoría del espanglish. A fuego lento, cien columnas de humor y una cornisa*. Rio Piedras: University of Puerto Rico, 1954. 60–65.

Toribio, Almeida Jacqueline. "Accessing Billingual Code-switching Competence." *International Journal of Bilingualism* 5 (2001a): 403–36.

———. "On the Emergence of Bilingual Code-mixing Competence." *Bilingualism, Language and Cognition* 4 (2001b): 3–31.

Valdés Bernal, Sergio, and Nuria Gregori Torada. "Identidad, uso y actitudes lingüísticas de la comunidad cubana en Miami." *Unidad y diversidad, programa informativo sobre la lengua castellana* 4 de abril de 2001.

Varo, Carlos. *Consideraciones antropológicas y políticas en torno a la enseñanza del "spanglish" en Nueva York*. Río Piedras: Ediciones Librrería Internacional, 1971.

Zentella, Ana Celia. *Growing Up Bilingual: Puerto Rican Children in New York*. Malden, Massachusetts: Blackwell, 1997.

◆ 11

Language and Empire: A Conversation with Ilan Stavans

Ilan Stavans and Verónica Albin

In 2002, Ilan Stavans caused an international uproar with the publication—in the Barcelona newspaper *La Vanguardia*—of his translation into Spanglish of Part I, Chapter 1 of Miguel de Cervantes's *Don Quixote of La Mancha*. A scrutiny of the debate that ensued revealed the opposing sides: the foes, linguistic purists and prescriptivists who believe Spanglish heralds the ruin of the Spanish language in the United States; and the endorsers, who trust that the sizable Latino minority north of the Rio Grande is a new *mestizo* civilization in the making. Among the former were those who accused Stavans of being an *agent provocateur* who stepped beyond his own scholarly boundaries, and posited that a philologist should explore the transformations a language undergoes in history without attempting to accelerate those changes; and the latter proffered accolades for his bridging the gap between knowledge and action. For both camps, Stavans became a symbol. Yet for those who had followed his intellectual journey, the uproar was but one more endeavor in Stavans's wide-ranging activities as a daring man of letters.

The *San Francisco Chronicle* once described Stavans as a twenty-first century Octavio Paz, approaching Hispanic culture as a vortex where a wide array of historical, social, economic, and religious forces coincide. Indeed, Stavans, the Lewis-Sebring Professor in Latin American and Latino Culture and the Five-College Fortieth Anniversary Professor at Amherst College, is a veritable cultural compass and barometer. Stavans most certainly belongs to an intellectual elite, but he refuses to play the Ivory Tower game and relishes getting his hands dirty. If his erudition defies boundaries, so does his generosity. His mastery of language and his ability to write with seemingly effortless simplicity allow him to engage a wide audience in intellectual dialogue.

The child of immigrants in Mexico who hail from Catherine the Great's Pale of Settlement, Stavans spent his formative years in a Bundist school where instruction was imparted in Yiddish. Learning Hebrew at Temple and Spanish in the neighborhood, Stavans also studied English, and later the other Romance languages that also piqued his interest. In 1985, he left Mexico for the United States. Because of his multi-faceted cultural background, his experience as a child of immigrants and as an immigrant himself, his commentaries on language and culture are always incisive.

Equally comfortable and intellectually engaged at a library carrel reading Spinoza as on a bench in the *tianguis* reading *Memín Pinguín* while devouring *unos buenos tacos*, Stavans can readily quote not only from history, literature, or Scripture, but also from comic strips, soaps, and other types of popular culture. In the following conversation, which took place on August 15–19, 2005, he explores the tension between language and politics in the Americas. A few months earlier he had published *Dictionary Days: A Defining Passion* (Graywolf), where he had paid tribute to Samuel Johnson and the makers of the *Oxford English Dictionary* and also presented lexicography as a tool of Empire. My objective was to encourage him to discuss the work of other lexicographers and grammarians, particularly Antonio de Nebrija and Andrés Bello, and to further explore the power of language and the legacy of colonialism on this side of the Atlantic. Objectives are great, but the truth is that when talking to Stavans you never know where his intellect will take you. Here, then, is Ilan Stavans on language and empire . . . and more.

Verónica Albin: Are words neutral?
Ilan Stavans: Language obviously isn't an empty bank of conventionally-accepted sounds and graphs. It is infused with history. Each of the words at our disposal has undergone a series of permutations. A word's etymology only points to its roots. The permutations enable us to peel away the layers of meaning accumulated through time. Take "Bible," for instance: a designation we use for the sacred Jewish and Christian scriptures consisting of the Old and New Testaments. It comes from the Greek "βιβλία," that is, "the books."

Upon being exposed to it, an Extraterrestrial wouldn't appreciate the accrued meanings. How did a classical term—not Aramaic, not Hebrew, not even Latin—become the most influential term in the world?

VA: Most people use language mechanically, though. They have no interest in linguistics.
IS: How is a bone marrow transplant performed? What does a microchip do? Knowledge is always the property of a small elite.

VA: You've been quite a controversial figure in the study of language. Are you a linguist by training?
IS: No, but neither were Antonio de Nebrija nor Andrés Bello. Being an amateur allows for enormous freedom.

VA: In what sense?
IS: One doesn't need to pay homage to the rigid parameters of an established discipline.

VA: Have your studies in the history of language turned you into a linguist, though?
IS: I prefer the word "philologist." Like the word "humanist," it has unfortunately gone out of use; in American English, at least. But it is closer in spirit to the approach I believe one needs to take to understand language.

VA: How would you describe that approach?
IS: An all-encompassing one. If language is history, one needs to use whatever tool is available to appreciate it: sociology, philosophy, science, anthropology, religion, lexicography, politics, literature . . .

VA: What does a philologist do?
IS: Philology is the study of language in all its possibilities. In other words, the study of culture.

VA: You've been accused of mixing yourself in your field of study.
IS: Could it be otherwise? Language is *us*.

VA: But should a philologist studying an emerging way of communication also translate a work of literature into it, as you did in rendering the first chapter of *Don Quixote of La Mancha* into Spanglish?

IS: It is a mistake to hide behind the coldness of the scientific method. The scientist tackles a phenomenon from the outside, uncommittedly. How could that succeed when language is everything—our speech, our dreams, our ideology, the food we eat, the fashions we embrace, etc.? A philologist cannot look at language from a distance. He needs to get his hands dirty. His explorations are forms of advocacy.

VA: Does it bother you to be the target of animosity? The reaction to your reflections on Spanglish has generated a world-wide debate.
IS: Not in the least.

VA: Your books are engaging, learned, and enormously readable. They are released by major publishing houses and targeted to a large audience.
IS: Academics love to build self-enclosed turfs through obscure, obstructing jargon. It's nonsense. Ludwig Wittgenstein said it best in 1922, in his *Tractatus Logico-Philosophicus*: "What can be said at all can be said clearly; and whereof one cannot speak thereof one must be silent." By the way, I believe silence should also be an area of study for linguists. It is an essential aspect of communication.

VA: You have explored silence in many of your works.
IS: It is a topic that intrigues me. Isaac Babel rebelled against the Man of Steel by ceasing to write. In 1934 he told the Congress of Soviet writers: "I have invented a new genre—the genre of silence." Furthermore, in a story I just finished set in Belgium, I argue that that country engaged in a silence that turned it into an accomplice of National Socialism and that that silence proved devastating to Belgian Jewry. Shakespeare, by the way, was also intrigued by it. In *Henry VI, Part 2*, Act III, Scene ii, Suffolk says:

> Would curses kill, as doth the mandrake's groan.
> I would invent as bitter-searching terms,
> As curst, as harsh, and horrible to hear,
> Delivere'd strongly through my fixed teeth,
> With full as many signs of deadly hate,
> As lean-faced envy in her loathsome cave:
> My tongue should stumble in mine earnest words

And Edward Gibbon worried about it as well. So, what does the *OED* have to say about silence? "The fact of abstaining or forbearing from speech or utterance (sometimes with reference to a particular matter)" and "the state or condition resulting from this." And then it states: "muteness, reticence, taciturnity." It also suggests that silence is repressed speech, that it is the cause of a compulsion to cease speaking on a particular occasion, and finally, that silence is proof that an argument has been overcome.

As I mentioned in my essay "The Impossible," included in *Dictionary Days*, it still isn't clear to me, existentially, what silence is. Is it stillness? Is it absence? Stillness is an attribute of being. Absence, on the other hand, is the disappearance of being. Like most people, in my youth I loved sound—all kinds of sounds: speech, music, the noises heard in a sports arena . . . I love silence now: silence from my children's sighs and shrieks, my students debating a certain topic, a symphony by Brahms. As adulthood has settled in, I've become more attracted to silence. Silence is quietness. But at different stages in life it acquires distinctive connotations.

Every word at our disposal has its own double: a non-word. Every dictionary that has ever produced a catalogue of words available to a particular group of people also creates its counterpart, a lexicon of unavailable words, words that are not possible, cannot be uttered, words that cannot exist or come into being.

VA: Is this lexicon of impossible words a dictionary of silence?
IS: Wouldn't it be fitting to seek the definition of silence and, yes, come across a vacuum, an empty page? But I'm not the first to consider this. In my essay "Pride and Prejudice," I gave that credit to Alex Debeljak who compiled a Slovenian dictionary of silence.

VA: You've also perfected the genre of the interview . . . *Dominical*, the Sunday supplement of *El Mundo* in Spain, called you *"un comunicador nato"* (a natural communicator). Do you have any idea how many media Q&A you've done in radio, TV, and newspapers?
IS: Several dozen, perhaps over a hundred.

VA: I gather you've been thinking about language since childhood. When did you begin studying it in a more systematic way?
IS: The moment I emigrated to the United States in 1985, I became fascinated with the topic of translation. About a decade later, I embarked on an exploration of the twists and turns of Spanglish. This led me to do sustained readings in linguistics, religion, and politics. I became interested

in the development of Spanish, English, French, Portuguese, and German as self-sufficient tongues and in their vicissitudes through time. How to explain their life cycles? To what extent did conquest and colonization change these languages? Lexicons became an obsession. What role do dictionaries play in their maturity? In regards to the transition from *castellano* to *español* to the Spanish spoken in the Americas, the work of Amado and Dámaso Alonso, Arturo Capdevila, Ramón Menéndez Pidal, Raimundo Lida, Ángel Rosenblatt, Fernando Ortíz, Fernando Lázaro Carreter, Rafael Lapesa, and Antonio Alatorre was invaluable. In retrospect, I see what I've done as simply connecting the dots.

VA: Is Spanglish a language in formation?
IS: It has been moving from the purely oral to the written realm. There are novels, poems, stories, essays available in it already. These include Ana Lydia Vega's "Pollito Chicken," Giannina Braschi's *Yo-Yo Boing*, María Eugenia Morales's "T'was the Night," Felipe Alfau's *Chronos*, Cecilio García-Camarillo's *Talking to the Río Grande*, and Suzanne G. Chávez-Silverman's *Killer Crónicas*, as well as the music of Juan Luis Guerra, Café Tacuba, and Cypress Hill. People are looking into a standard orthographic spelling, even for a systematic syntax. But Spanglish is also something else: a state of mind. It allows us an opportunity to appreciate the creation of a new minority culture in the United States. As the discovery of new galaxies allowed astronomers to better understand the secrets of our universe.

VA: Yet Spanglish has often been seen as a bastardization of the language of Castile, an inferior mode of communication, a 'restricted' code of the impoverished classes. You have brought this construct under attack, remarking on its richness.
IS: Why shouldn't the zest and improvisational drive of Spanglish-speakers be applauded? Who establishes the parameters of richness and poverty in language? When I come across a fluent Spanglish-speaker, I'm in awe at the versatility of the language. It seems not to know any barriers.

VA: In your introductory essay in *Spanglish: The Making of a New American Language*, which includes your explorations on the hybrid tongue (you refer to it as "*la jerga loca*"), a lexicon of approximately six thousand terms, and your translation of *Don Quixote*, you mention that academicians are allergic to it. They itch and scratch and dismiss it as a nuisance.
IS: Academics are eager to defend against all odds the security of their

tenured positions. They also pride themselves as educated. For them to get involved with the lower strata is a waste of time, a nuisance. More than once I've come across a linguist whose research involved exposure to a Spanglish-speaker. What does he do? He registers in a comfortable hotel. Once a day he spends a couple of hours in *La Losaida*, as the Lower East Side is known among Spanglish-speakers, then dines at an elegant restaurant. He shapes his paper in the isolation of his office in an Ivory Tower institution.

VA: Octavio Paz claimed: "Spanglish is neither good nor bad. It's abominable."
IS: Paz was utterly blind to the reality of Latino culture in the United States. The first chapter of *The Labyrinth of Solitude* is nothing short of embarrassing. It is ironic that so enlightened an intellectual should be so blind to a crucial aspect of *la mexicanidad*. Paz isn't the only antagonist, though. The list of Latin American intellectuals who have gone on record against it is long. In fact, during the *III Congreso Internacional de la Lengua Española*, celebrated in Rosario, Argentina, in 2004, whose theme was linguistic identity and globalization, José Saramago, Nobel Laureate from Portugal—a non Spanish-speaking country—stated that he hated Spanglish because it threatened to dilute the language of Cervantes into a broth that is fifty percent English and fifty percent Spanish. Saramago's equation is wrong, of course: Spanglish is never a fifty-fifty brew. In any case, I'm not surprised.

VA: Why?
IS: There is a sense in Latin America, and it obviously reaches as far as Portugal, that nothing good or worthwhile will come out of Hispanic culture in the United States.

VA: Is this due to the construct of *rascuachismo*?
IS: *Rascuachismo* is an esthetic of the dispossessed; it suits Spanglish to the dot. If Saramago and others who embrace a Marxist ideology paid closer attention to its social origins, they would embrace it wholeheartedly.

VA: Have you discussed this with Saramago?
IS: When we met in Boston, we talked politics of another sort. He had just spent time in Ramallah and he compared the Israeli army to the Nazis.

VA: Is there an agenda on your part in endorsing Spanglish?
IS: What kind of agenda?

VA: By subverting the academicians' opinion of Spanglish being nothing more than a *jerga rascuache*, by transforming it from an unacceptable mode of speech to one that is hip, and interesting, and valuable, and worth studying you're also pushing for a reconsideration of Latino identity in general, right?
IS: Sure. There is nothing wrong with Spanglish. It is a legitimate form of speech. English is the only ticket to success in the United States. Every Latino needs to be fluent in it. But not at the expense of Spanglish. Why can't the two—or better, the three, for Spanish forms the triptych—coexist?

VA: Doesn't this benefit you?
IS: How so? To be honest, there are days when I tire of talking about Spanglish—not *in* Spanglish but *about* it. But then I recognize my role as agitator, with which I'm comfortable. Don Francisco, the host of the Univisión variety show *Sábado Gigante*, once introduced me as "the destroyer of the Spanish language." He, needless to say, meant it as a joke, for he and his audience are fluent in it. Imagine what would happen if a single individual had, at the tip of his fingers, the power to unravel an entire language!

VA: Some have also described you in *The New York Times* as an assimilationist, even branded you as an "Uncle Tom."
IS: *El Tío Tom* . . . I'm not making myself clear to them. Actually, I embrace the opposite principle: resistance through language. I often think of Jean Anouilh's version of Sophocles's *Antigone*, staged in Paris in 1944. His mission wasn't to stage a Greek tragedy as much as it was to incite his countrymen to rebel against the Nazi usurpers.

VA: Should Latinos actively rebel against Americans, then?
IS: Rebellion is most successful when it is subtle.

VA: What does your friend Richard Rodríguez, author of *Hunger of Memory*, think of Spanglish?
IS: I don't think it sparks his mind. He's mostly interested in miscegenation.

VA: *Tu wat extent can an Espanish orthografy bi uzd tu reprizent Inglish*?
IS: This movement is sheer folly. Although it was born in England in the 1950s when Mont Follik, a professor of comparative philology at the University of Manchester in his capacity as a Labour MP promoted a Spanish-based spelling system he had devised in the 1930s, it is currently kept alive by

a bunch of *gringos* who argue that since the English language has an almost inscrutable orthography, and who posit that since a number of states in the Union will soon follow the route of California and Texas—i.e., they will have a white minority and a multiethnic majority—propose teaching English to all—Latinos and Anglos—using the phonetic spelling of Spanglish. This emphatically leads to the threat of the browning of America, which makes Conservatives go wild.

VA: Was your translation of *Don Quixote* into Spanglish a one-time shot? Have you continued the endeavor?
IS: Part I of Cervantes's novel is almost finished.

VA: When do you expect to publish it?
IS: Not until the entire manuscript is done.

VA: If Spanglish is still in formation, without its own syntax, what are your morphological parameters?
IS: I tackle the issue in a *nota bene* in *Spanglish*. In seeking to reflect the polyphonic and polymorphic nature of the tongue, I used elements from Nuyorrican, Dominicanis, Cubonics, Chicano Spanglish, and other varieties. Mine is a middle-ground.

VA: The effort is . . . well, Quixotic. Are you also hoping to update the lexicon?
IS: Since the book appeared in 2003, I've been accumulating more entries. I have close to 2,000 already. My intention is to one day create an Internet lexicon.

VA: Ah, that Palm Pilot vademecum you've talked about, where one might envision rapid access to the latest meaning of a word. The Internet is certainly a much more flexible medium than the printed word.
IS: It is also more democratic. I'd like to invite Spanglish-speakers to offer fresh terms.

VA: It could be maddening . . .
IS: Every entry in *Spanglish* was rigorously checked. At least three occurrences needed to be recorded. And the spelling, when possible, was standardized by means of discussion with colleagues. The same approach would need to be taken in the Internet version.

VA: Do you ever get down to analyzing morphologically a single sentence?
IS: In the classroom, I frequently zoom in and out of grammatical patterns, scrutinizing morphological and syntactical structures.

VA: You've been primarily concerned with Spanish in the United States. In the article "Giving Spanish Its Due," published in *The Chronicle of Higher Education*, about the responsibility of Spanish departments to teach undergraduates using an interdisciplinary approach, you wonder: "Is Spanish a foreign language in the United States?"
IS: It is the most often-taught language on American campuses after English, often superseding in the amount of students the combined enrollment totals for French, Russian, German, Italian, Greek, Latin, and Hebrew. This isn't a quantitative issue but a historical one. Spanish is a fixture in the Southwestern territories of what is the United States today since the colonial period. It might have been eclipsed in certain periods but it never lost its gravitas. And the demographic explosion of Latinos makes it the nation's "official second language."

VA: You've also referred to "*el español en América*" not as a unity but as a plurality.
IS: The astonishing complexity of the Latino minority can't be ignored. Before the Treaty of Guadalupe Hidalgo, signed in 1848 at the end of the Mexican-American War, the Spanish spoken by Iberian explorers, missionaries, and *adelantados* metamorphosed into the type used in northern Mexico. But there were self-sufficient exceptions: *el español novomexicano*, for instance; the idiosyncratic form used by Californios, some Chileans, others Mexican; and so on. At the close of the nineteenth century and the early decades of the twentieth, that type was dramatically enriched by exiled communities such as Cubans in Key West and Puerto Rican *tabaqueros* in New York. Over time, Dominican, Colombian, Ecuadorian, and Salvadorian vernaculars, to name just some, were added to the stew. Within each of these national subgroups, there are also lexical variants. The result is a delightfully aromatic *pozole*. What kind of Spanish is used by Don Francisco? Is it the same heard on Spanish-language national radio? Yes, nowhere in the globe (and perhaps at no other time in human history) has the language of Antonio de Nebrija been at a more decisive crossroads.

VA: Reporters in particular see this crossroads as perilous. Is Spanish in danger in the United States?

IS: News of its demise go back at least to the Spanish-American War of 1898. For instance, Rubén Darío, the Nicaraguan *modernista*, believed el *inglés* would ultimately take over. Here is his *"Los cisnes"* of 1905:

> ¿Seremos entregados a los bárbaros fieros?
> ¿Tantos millones de hombres hablaremos inglés?
> ¿Ya no hay nobles hidalgos ni bravos caballeros?
> ¿Callaremos ahora para llorar después?

I quote from Greg Simon's and Steven F. White's version:

> Are we to be overrun by the cruel barbarian?
> Is it our fate that millions of us will speak in English?
> Are there no fierce shining knights, no valiant noblemen?
> Shall we keep our silence now, to weep later in anguish?

Also in 1905, Darío wrote a poem shortly after making a comparison between the Anglo and Hispanic Americas. It is called "To Roosevelt." Again, Greg Simon's and Steven F. White's version:

> But our own America, which had plenty of poets
> even from the ancient times of Netzahualcóyotl,
> and which retained the footprints from the feet of Great Bacchus,
> and, over the course of time, learned the Panic alphabet:
> it sought advice from the stars, and knew of Atlantis,
> whose name was a legacy, resonating in Plato.
> Even from the most remote moments in its boundless life,
> it has lived by light and fire, by fragrances and by love:
> America of the great Moctezuma and the Inca,
> America redolent of Christopher Columbus,
> Catholic America and Spanish America,
> the place where once long ago the noble Cuauhtémoc said,
> "I'm not on a bed of roses!" Yes, that America,
> trembling from its hurricanes and surviving on its Love...
> It lives with you, with your Saxon eyes and barbaric souls.
> And dreams. And loves, and vibrates; it's the daughter of the Sun.
> Be careful. Spanish America is alive and well.

VA: So, should we worry?
IS: Like any living organism, languages go through a life cycle: they are born out of necessity, spread as a result of invasion and colonial enterprise,

undergo a series of mutations, and die when their speakers no longer have use for them. Spanish in the United States will last as long as it needs to—not a second more. Other immigrant languages have faced a similar destiny.

VA: Is Spanish an immigrant language?
IS: Yes and no. In so far as it was brought by newcomers from the Caribbean Basin, Latin America, and Spain, it certainly is. Ironically, to some extent it is also an aboriginal language in that prior to the Declaration of Independence in 1776, it was already in use in what is today the United States, from the Southwest to the Commonwealth of Puerto Rico.

VA: In the forward to *Growing Up Latino: Memoirs and Stories*, you talk about the difference between *ser* and *estar*.
IS: I echo Borges: "*El español es facilísimo.*" But I might add that it suffers from severe limitations, for instance, its reluctance to compound words. The nuances of "to be" in Spanish, on the other hand, are exquisite. Other languages are poorer on this front: Italian makes the same distinction in that it has *essere* and *stare*, but doesn't exploit the nuances quite as richly as Spanish does; French is limited to *être* (etymologically related to *estar*), which, interestingly, is conjugated in some grammatical persons like "*ser*" ("*Je suis un bouffon,*" "*nous sommes tant aimés,*" "*ils sont enfin libres.*"); Hebrew disregards the complication; as for Russian, it is even dryer, for it has no auxiliary verbs whatsoever: no "ser" and no "estar." Russians say "I professor" or "I doctor," but Russian does have an infinitive meaning ("to be a professor") that makes use of the instrumental case for declensions: profesorom, doktorom. Mario Benedetti, the ideologically-engaged Uruguayan author, once wrote a poem about the dichotomy and how English-language users are imprisoned in a single form of the verb 'to be.' The poem, anti-American in tone, is called "*Ser y estar*":

> Oh marine
> oh boy
> una de tus dificultades consiste en que no sabes
> distinguir el ser del estar
> para ti todo es to be
>
> así que probemos a aclarar las cosas

por ejemplo
una mujer es buena
cuando entona desafinadamente los salmos
y cada dos años cambia el refrigerador
y envía mensualmente su perro al analista
y sólo enfrenta el sexo los sábados de noche

en cambio una mujer está buena
cuando la miras y pones los perplejos ojos en blanco
y la imaginas y la imaginas
y hasta crees que tomando un martini te vendrá el coraje
pero ni así
por ejemplo
un hombre es listo
cuando obtiene millones por teléfono
y evade la conciencia y los impuestos
y abre una buena póliza de seguros
a cobrar cuando llegue a sus setenta
y sea el momento de viajar en excursión a capri y a parís
y consiga violar a la gioconda en pleno louvre
con la vertiginosa polaroid

en cambio
un hombre está listo
cuando ustedes
oh marine
oh boy
aparecen en el horizonte
para inyectarle democracia.

Not long ago I came across an English translation by Charles D. Hatfield. Or should I say reinvention? After all, how else would one convey in Shakespeare's tongue the dichotomy between *ser* and *estar*. Hatfield calls it "Being and Seeming":

Oh marine
oh boy
part of your problem is that you don't know the difference
between "being" and "seeming"
to you everything just "is"

now let me explain

for example
a woman "is" good
when she sings the psalms out of tune
and gets a new refrigerator every two years
and sends her dog to an analyst every month
and only deals with sex on saturday nights

on the other hand, a woman "seems" good (at least to me)
when you gaze at her and your puzzled eyes go blank
and you dream of her dream of her dream of her
and you think a martini will give you the courage when not even that'll do it
for example
a man "is" done
when he earns millions over the phone
and evades taxes and his conscience
and buys into a good retirement plan
to cash in when he turns seventy
and it's time to fly to capri and paris
where he gets to rape the gioconda right in the louvre
with his speedy polaroid

on the other hand,
a man "seems" done (done-for, that is)
when you boys
oh marine
oh boy
appear on the horizon
to give him a dose of democracy

VA: Do all languages have the same blueprint?

IS: Think of the nineteenth-century Romantic concoction introduced by Polish oculist and linguist Ludwik Lejzer Zamenhof: *Esperanto*. Although it was taught throughout the world, Esperanto never quite achieved the international recognition its inventor hoped for it. This is because artificial languages have their own metabolism; they aren't connected to the principal engine behind the communication effort. Let us not forget that language is the pull of a common memory based on tradition, literature, and national pride. Language is love of country. Languages are born out of necessity; they emerge when a group needs to distinguish itself, at the verbal level, from its surroundings. The need isn't enough, actually. The historical circumstances must be ripe. How did Old English evolve? What kind of break did a work like Geoffrey Chaucer's *Canterbury Tales* create? Think of the development of Hittite, Phoenician, Babylonian, and Persian.

VA: Why did some perish and others survive?
IS: Languages are "exposed to the elements," so-to-speak. They are at the mercy of historical forces.

VA: How about the death of a language?
IS: When there is no longer a necessity for it, a language disappears. That is the pattern of Hittite, Babylonian, and Phoenician. They also fossilize, like Aramaic and Latin. And at times they also die abrupt deaths. Yiddish, for instance, almost vanished by 1945 in Auschwitz and other concentration camps under Adolf Hitler's war machine. Another example of a language that faced death by edict is Spañolit, *aka* Ladino, when in 1492 the Jews who spoke it were expelled from Spain by Isabella. Yiddish has managed to stay alive (albeit barely) thanks to the diligent work of people like Aaron Lansky, founder of the National Yiddish Book Center in Amherst, and Spañolit is hanging on fragile spiderwebs thanks to Dr. Emese bain-Medgyesi, director of the *Europees Bureau voor Taalminderheden* (European Bureau for Lesser Used Languages) in Brussels, to Haïm Vidal Sephiha, founder of the *Vidas Largas Association* in Paris, and Aaron Koen, director of *La Autoridad Nasionala del Ladino* in Israel. But when language death is concerned, we must not forget the attempts of the Generalísimo Francisco Franco to eradicate Gallego, Aragonés, Euzkera, Catalán, Valenciano, Mallorquín ... Tyranny, famine, expulsion, and massacres have a terrible effect on language. When reading about the bloodbath in Rwanda and Burundi, for instance, I cannot help but wonder if the Hutu and Tutsi tongues, with their common base in the Bantu branch of the Niger-Congo family, are likely to survive.

VA: And Spanish?
IS: The fall of the last Moorish stronghold, Boabdil's Granada, and the consolidation of the Spanish Empire at the hands of the Catholic Monarchs Ferdinand and Isabella, brought forth a unified national spirit. It coalesced under a single banner: one state, one religion, one language. It also recognized Spanish as the de facto official language. From his *cátedra* at the University of Salamanca, Antonio de Nebrija, who once was Bishop of Ávila, is the

spokesperson for the cause. "Language," he said in his prologue to the *Gramática castellana*, published in the *annus mirabilis* of Spanish history, "has always been the perfect instrument of empire." He added: "After Your Highness takes under her yoke many barbarian towns and nations with strange tongues, and with the conquering of them, they will need to receive the laws that the conqueror puts on the conquered and with those, our language." At the time Sebastián de Covarrubias's *Tesoro de la lengua española o castellana* is released, under the aegis of the Holy Office of the Inquisition, in 1611—in between part I and II of *Don Quixote*—he is ambivalent, even in the title, between the terms I mentioned before: "*castellano*" and "*español*." Which one to use? The ambivalence remains palpable today.

VA: You've mentioned Nebrija and Bello. *ABC* in Madrid once described you as "our modern Nebrija."
IS: As a Renaissance man, Antonio Martínez de Cala y Jarava, born in Lebrija (Seville) and known to the world as Antonio de Nebrija, was a true humanist. He believed in language as a springboard (the "*scienza nuova*" is the denotation given by Gianbattista Vico) for the birth of a new man and a way to understand the universe as a whole. I would have loved to meet him. He was versed in Greek and Latin, the languages of erudition of his day and age. In addition to grammar, he was also committed to the study of theology, rhetoric, jurisprudence, history, medicine, and cosmogony. He believed Spanish to be "*obra de la providencia*."

VA: How about Andrés Bello?
IS: The Venezuelan Bello was a polymath of the first order. His mind moved in several directions at once: linguistics, poetry, jurisprudence, history . . . He founded the Universidad de Chile and was its chancellor from 1843 to 1865. His reflections on Spanish are incisive. He published lucid studies in lexicography and proposed as series of emendations to Spanish-American orthography, most of which were rejected. His overall quest was to preserve the language as "*medio providencial de comunicación*" of the people in the Americas so that "*la confusión de idiomas, dialectos y jerigonzas, el caos babilónico de la Edad Media*" could be avoided. To achieve his objective, he wrote the *Gramática de la lengua castellana destinada al uso de los americanos*. Pedro Henríquez Ureña thought highly of it. Almost four hundred years after Nebrija, he still understood Spanish to come from above, a gift from the Almighty.

VA: In a much-quoted essay, "Translation and Identity," you discuss the indigenous languages in the Americas. What kind of verbal landscape was there prior to 1492?
IS: Spain was in the midst of its misnomered Golden Age, *el siglo de oro*, when Christopher Columbus arrived in San Salvador. The admiral sent a couple of his captains, Rodrigo de Escobedo and Rodrigo Sánchez de Segovia, with instructions to keep an eye out as they and others took possession of the island. About the indigenous peoples, the Genoese admiral wrote in his diary: "They must be good servants, and intelligent, for I can see that they quickly repeat everything said to them. I believe they would readily become Christians; it appeared to me that they have no religion." Indeed, the Spanish language arrived *con fuerza* with the *conquistadores*. The type of unsophisticated adventurer-cum-knight interested in making the voyage was from Extremadura. The exception, for there is always one, was Hernán Cortés, who, although an Extremeño, had studied law and his *Cartas de Relación* show a clear and sophisticated mind. But let me answer your question from the subaltern's perspective. In the Americas, around two hundred distinguishable codes of communication were in use, from from Aymara to Zapotec. In Mexico alone the linguistic variety was simply breathtaking. A list of aboriginal tongues includes Yumano, Chinanteco from Quiotepec, Chinanteco from Palantla, Chinanteco from Lataní, Matlazincano, Zapoteco from Ixtlán, Mixteco, Amuzgo, Popoloca, Tepehua, Chol, Chontal from Tabasco, Tzeltal, Tzotzil, Tojolabal, Jacalteco, Kanjoba, Pima, Papago, Yaqui, Cora, Huichol, Náhuatl, Purépecha, and Kikapu, to mention a few. The Iberian newcomers weren't interested in linguistic lushness, though. Their mission was to conquer and colonize. To accomplish their task, they brandished the sword and the cross. At first sight, the former might appear more powerful; in the long run, the latter probably had a longer-lasting impact.

VA: Through *catequismo*?
IS: *Catequismo* is a euphemism for spiritual and intellectual subjugation. It is the rationale behind the enterprise of *mestizaje*, i.e., the transculturation that resulted from the superimposition of Catholicism over the idolatrous religions of the pre-Columbian world. In retrospect, it can be argued that syncretism as a strategy is at the heart of the Hispanic-American experience. It is also what characterizes the vicissitudes of Spanish in the United States. The capacity to absorb from the environment, to recycle that absorption while mixing it with our ancestral views is a signature of our culture. Some describe this as the sign of colonialism. But colonialism isn't altogether negative; it offers resources to cope with hybrid times like ours.

VA: On the other hand, endorsing the native (though not always the nativist) viewpoint has been fashionable in Latin America.
IS: Think of Augusto Roa Bastos, José María Arguedas, Humberto Ak'abal, María Sabina, Rigoberta Menchú . . . And prior to them, Sor Juana Inés de la Cruz, *la Décima Musa*, who spoke of the magic and wisdom of the native peoples of Mexico.

> *¿Qué mágicas infusiones*
> *de los indios herbolarios*
> *de mi patria, entre mis letras*
> *el hechizo derramaron?*

In Margaret Sayers Peden's translation:

> What are those magical infusions
> of the herbalist Indians
> of my land, that spread their spell
> through all the letters from my pen?

In Sor Juana's century, just as in ours, the Indian population has traditionally remained *ninguneada*. The English equivalent is "ignored" but "*ningunear*," an enchanting *mexicanismo*, is more idiosyncratic. Among the scholars of Indian literature is one I admire profusely and whose reputation in the United States is null: Fr. Ángel María Garibay. A priest and a *rara avis* in Mexican scholarship, Garibay is unjustly unknown in the United States, especially among Latinos. Dead in 1967 at the age of seventy-five, his erudition was of the highest order. Although he was a Hebraist and a translator of Greek and Latin classics, his major contribution is to be found in his interest in pre-Columbian languages and literatures. He specialized in Náhuatl and focused on the oeuvre of Fray Bernardino de Sahagún, the primary source of Aztec civilization. The contemporary thinker that most resembles him is his student, the remarkable Miguel León Portilla, author of the popular *The Vision of the Vanquished*. Garibay was brave, a quality frequently missing in intellectuals. For instance, he left us renditions of pre-Columbian erotica, such as this:

> *Yo te vine a dar placer, florida vulva mía*
> *paladarcito inferior mío.*
> *Tengo gran deseo del Rey Axayacatito.*
> *Mira por favor mis cantaritos floridos,*

Mira por favor mis cantaritos floridos:
¡son mis pechos!

Again, Sayers Peden's translation:

> I came to you to give delight, my flower vulva,
> my beckoning pleasure palate.
> I feel great desire for King Axayacatito.
> Look, please, upon my brimming flower pitchers.
> Look, please, upon my brimming flower pitchers.
> They are my breasts!

VA: Why is "Spanish Golden Age" a misnomer?
IS: Have you ever read José Vasconcelos's *Breve historia de México*? It is built on a triptych of fallacies: it isn't brief, nor is it a history; and it's not about Mexico, really. The same ought to be said about *el siglo de oro español*: it lasted longer than a century; gold was an excuse for merciless abuses of power; and it wasn't only about Spain and its citizens, but about a vast continent across the Atlantic sacked by the voraciousness of the Iberian enterprise. A golden age for whom? Not for the dwellers in the colonies; not for women, children, the ill, and the unschooled; and certainly not for the Jews and Muslims on Spanish soil. The year 1492 brought an end to *La Reconquista*. It also invited Spain to use language as an instrument of colonization. It isn't unlike the use by the United States today of the media to accomplish the task. Rock, blues, jazz, Hollywood movies, fashion, fast food are all badges of empire. Likewise, Spanish was the conduit that allowed the Iberian Peninsula to force itself on the native population.

VA: In the essay "Translation and Identity" you discuss translation as a *modus vivendi* in Spain and the Americas in the fifteenth century.
IS: Prior to the Expulsion Edict of 1492, urban centers like Toledo were emblems of cohabitation, *La Convivencia*. In the twelfth century, Toledo was home to the *Escuela de Traductores* (established by King Alfonso X, known as "the Wise"), to which Judá ben Moses Hacohen, a doctor in charge of revising the *Tablas Alfonsinas* as well as translating *El libro conplido en los iudizios de las estrellas*, was affiliated. The *Escuela* also counted among its affiliates Ali Aben Rabel, also known as 'don Abraham,' a personal physician to King Alfonso X, who translated Ibn Heithan; Isak ibn Sid, who compiled

Los libros del saber de astronomía del Rey Alonso in Spanish; and Judá
Mosca, who translated *Lapidario* by Aegidius de Thebaldis. In Granada
today a statue in honor of Yehuda ibn Tibón, perhaps the most distinguished
translator of the *Escuela*, stands proud. Spain has always been a cradle of
languages and dialects. In addition, by the sixteenth century the educated crust
of society was also fluent in Greek and Latin, and some had access to Aramaic
and Hebrew. Overall, the period is known for its baroque inclinations.
Borges described its style as verging on caricature. It certainly is one that
emphasizes *las apariencias*, i.e., not reality but the expression of reality. The
Spanish saying *"las apariencias engañan"* dates back to those times. Think of
Nebrija's *Gramática* along with the *Comentarios reales* by the Inca Garcilaso,
the *comedias* by Lope de Vega and *Las soledades* by Luis de Góngora. And,
of course, Baltasar Gracián's *Criticón*. Language was perceived as a veil.
Translations, on the other hand, were tributes to the masters: Francisco de
Quevedo pays homage to Torcuato Tasso by rewriting him. And Cervantes
imagined his novel *Don Quixote* to be a loose translation from an Arabic
manuscript by one Cide Hamete Benengeli.

VA: Earlier in the conversation you mentioned the *Bible*. You've analyzed its
various Spanish translations used in the New World, from colonial times to the
present.

IS: The topic is perfect to understand the intricate relationship between
translation and empire. An edict from the Holy Office of the Inquisition
issued in Toledo in 1551 forbade the translation of the *Bible* into Spanish and
other vernaculars. But demography sooner or later sets the pattern of culture.
The first translation was actually commissioned by Alfonso X in 1260; it is
known as the *Biblia Alfonsina* or *Española*. It is a paraphrase of the *Vulgata*.
There are also the *Biblia de Alba*, preserved in the Biblioteca del Duque de
Alba. And the *Biblia* of Alfonso V, translated from the Hebrew and Latin.
The famous *Biblia* of Ferrara, Italy, appeared in 1553 translated from the
Hebrew by two Portuguese Jews: Duarte Pinel (*aka* Abraham Usque) and
Gerónimo de Vargas (Yom Tov Atias). In the latter, the syntax is strange; still,
it is the principal source of dissemination of the Christian faith in the New
World. There is also the so-called *Biblia del Oso* of 1569 and the rendition
by Cipriano de Valera (1602). In other words, in spite of the edict, Spanish
versions were made available. Furthermore, the history of those versions is an
exercise in selective misreading: sexual scenes disappear, pagan references are
attenuated, and the Jewishness of the text is made to justify the advent of Jesus
Christ. Take the example of the *Biblia de Alba*. Don Luis de Guzmán, Grand

Master of the Order of Calatrava, commissioned it. He sought '*vna biblia en rromançe, glosada e ystoriada*,' a *Bible* to be translated into *Romance*. Its purpose, Guzmán claimed, would be to make available the Holy Scripture in the language of the uncultured masses. The edition was to have explanations, annotations, commentary, and illustrations. Who did de Guzmán commission it to? A rabbi by the name of Moses Arragel. In a long and tortured letter, the rabbi adamantly refused the commission, raising all sorts of objections. It was precisely the letter, fifteen chapters-worth of explanation, which convinced de Guzmán that Arragel was the right man for the job. Skeptics argue that the rabbi's complaint was in fact an astute demonstration of his competence. In any case, Arragel refused the offer once, then agreed to the task. His translation was done in 1433 from the original Hebrew and Aramaic. It was funded by Pope John II. In his introduction (drafted after he completed the job), Arragel claims he is not about to criticize Christian beliefs, nor praise Jewish ones. Yet he makes a record of the egregious incisions done to the text in the past. For instance, he writes: "Since I have done no more than relate or record [*memorar*], everyone is left free to believe, dispute [*disputar*] and defend their law as much as they can." But the rabbi did not shy away from pointing out 'mistakes' in his commentaries, such as the one proffered after the translation of *Exodus* 1:5: "*Seventy souls*. In Hebrew there are no more [than this]; but in the translation of St. Jerome there are 'seventy-five'; and it is the same in the *Actus Apostolorum*, chapter seven; and Nicolau de Lira says that the law mentions the number twice, once saying seventy, and the next seventy five; but in the Hebrew there are only seventy in both instances." The reprints of the *Biblia de Alba* often left out Arragel's commentary. His own identity as a Jew was eclipsed. This sequence of abuses is proof that translation and manipulation have gone hand in hand.

VA: Let's explore more the crossroads of language and colonialism.
IS: As empires sally forth, their languages undergo contamination. To be exposed to other cultures is to lend and borrow. Imperial languages become mechanisms of control. But they are also transformed from the inside. Again, let's focus on Spanish. Its adventures on this side of the Atlantic Ocean might be seen as an attempt to breach the national borders, to explore other landscapes. But those explorations result in a weakening of the central linguistic core. To put it in other words, they expose the language to different influences. And those influences eventually shape its course. The Spanish of the Americas has indeed acquired its own characters, each modeled after a different natural and human climate. The variety of the River Plate is

unique, as is the one from Lima. Then there are the vernaculars Lunfardo and Cocoliche from Argentina (mainly from Buenos Aires) that incorporate Italian words; and there are creoles like Opita, Valluno, and Rolo from Colombia. These are comparable to Cockney, Joual, Gaunersprach, Giria, Bargoens, Balibalán, Germanía, Hiant-Chang, and Gergo, among others.

VA: Is Lunfardo like Spanglish?
IS: To some extent. Borges was quite interested in Lunfardo. In fact, everything about the Argentine language fascinated him. Along with José Edmundo Clemente, he published a slim volume in 1968, *El lenguaje de Buenos Aires*, which includes his essays *"El idioma de los argentinos," "Las alarmas del doctor Américo Castro,"* and a curious meditation, *"Las inscripciones en los carros,"* on the aphorisms found painted on Argentine vehicles. About Lunfardo Borges said: ". . . *es jerigonza ocultadiza de los ladrones. El lunfardo es un vocabulario gremial como tantos otros; es la tecnología de la furca y de la ganzúa"* (it is the enigmatic slang of thieves. Lunfardo is an occupationally-specific language, just like any other: it is the technology of muggers and picklocks). In other words, the language of crime and prostitution. The author of "The Aleph" argued that authentic Argentine poetry was to be found in the lyrics of *tangos* and *milongas*. But Lunfardo is the language of cant born in Argentina in the second half of the nineteenth century. It is defined by class. Spanglish is more multitudinous. It goes beyond a particular social group. It isn't a mere vocabulary of displeasure and aggression.

VA: You've accused the *Real Academia Española* (RAE) of maintaining a tight fist on the speakers of Spanish. You've also criticized the *Diccionario de la Lengua Española* (DRAE) as an instrument of repression.
IS: The RAE is stuck in the past. Gabriel García Márquez, also one of its critics, once lost count of the time it takes for a word coined in Quito, Ecuador, to make it to the DRAE. Its members believe their eighteenth-century institution is responsible for safeguarding the Spanish language. Safeguarding it from what? Their motto is *"Limpia, fija y da esplendor,"* which—and I'm not the first to suggest it—sounds like a detergent commercial. There are approximately forty million people in Spain. The total number of Spanish-language speakers in the world is estimated at four hundred million. In Mexico alone there are over one hundred million. And the number of Latinos in the United States is over forty million. Why should

Spain remain the central command? Shouldn't a less centralized, more
democratic approach to the language of Cervantes and Nebrija, with that of
Sor Juana, Darío, and Borges be devised? The affiliates of the *RAE* never act
as independent units. They are extremities of the one in Madrid.

VA: An empire always refuses to look at its colonies as equals.
IS: Instead, it sees its own efforts at educating the colonials—*los bárbaros*—
as philanthropic. Lately I've been reading about the paternalistic attitude
of the British toward India. For instance, in 1835, Thomas Babington
Macaulay—later known as Lord Macaulay—addressed the question of what
type of culture should the population of India be exposed to under British rule.
Should the natives learn science in English? Today his response sounds like an
endorsement of Conservativism. It reminds me of Saul Bellow's statement, in
an Op-Ed piece published in *The New York Times* in 1988, at the height of the
culture wars, in which he asked: "Who is the Tolstoy of the Zulus? The Proust
of the Papuans?" Similarly, Lord Macaulay argued: "All parties seem to be
agreed on one point, that the dialects commonly spoken among the natives
of this part of India, contain neither literary nor scientific information, and
are, moreover, so poor and rude that, until they are enriched from some other
quarter, it will not be easy to translate any valuable work into them. It seems
to be admitted on all sides, that the intellectual improvement of those classes
of the people who have the means of pursuing higher studies can at present
be effected only by means of some language not vernacular amongst them.
What then shall that language be? One-half of the Committee maintains that
it should be the English. The other half strongly recommends the Arabic and
Sanskrit. The whole question seems to me to be, which language is the best
worth knowing?"

VA: I assume Lord Macaulay chose English.
IS: He was an honest man. "I have no knowledge of either Sanskrit or
Arabic," he said. Lord Macaulay then goes on to justify the superiority of
European civilization. "I have done what I could to form a correct estimate
of their value," he added. "I have read translations of the most celebrated
Arabic and Sanskrit works. I have conversed both here and at home with men
distinguished by their proficiency in the Eastern tongues. I am quite ready
to take the Oriental learning at the valuation of the Orientalists themselves.
I have never found one among them who could deny that a single shelf of
a good European library was worth the whole native literature of India and

Arabia. The intrinsic superiority of the Western literature is, indeed, fully admitted by those members of the Committee who support the Oriental plan of education." Finally, Lord Macaulay stated: "It will hardly be disputed, I suppose, that the department of literature in which the Eastern writers stand highest is poetry. And I certainly never met with any Orientalist who ventured to maintain that the Arabic and Sanskrit poetry could be compared to that of the great European nations. But when we pass from works of imagination to works in which facts are recorded, and general principles investigated, the superiority of the Europeans becomes absolutely immeasurable. It is, I believe, no exaggeration to say, that all the historical information which has been collected from all the books written in the Sanskrit language is less valuable than what may be found in the most paltry abridgements used at preparatory schools in England. In every branch of physical or moral philosophy, the relative position of the two nations is nearly the same."

VA: I like his use of the word "relative."
IS: Lord Macaulay could be described as a relativist, even though his ideas are absolutist.

VA: In sum, you don't see empire as evil, do you?
IS: Empire is a synonym of progress. To be against it is to fall into an idealistic trap. There have always been, and will always be, colonizers and colonized. In linguistic terms, they push language to change. English is often described as the *lingua franca* of today. Yet as it reaches beyond its boundaries, it is undergoing dramatic transformations, giving room to spin-offs like Spanglish. It isn't improbable that one day these spin-offs will become imperial themselves. It is part of the same cycle.

Works Cited

Borges, Jorge Luis, and José E. Clemente. *El lenguaje de los argentinos*. Buenos Aires: Emecé, 1968.
Calzada Pérez, María. *Apropos of Ideology: Translation Studies on Ideology—Ideologies in Translation Studies*. Manchester, UK: St. Jerome Publishing, 2003.
Darío, Rubén. *Selected Writings*. Ed. Ilan Stavans. Trans. Andrew Hurley, Greg Simon, and Steven F. White. New York and London: Penguin Classics, 2005.
Delisle, Jean, and J. Wordsworth, eds. *Translators Through History*. Amsterdam: John Benjamins Publishing, 1995.

Hatfield, Charles D. *Little Stones at My Window: Poems by Mario Benedetti.* Willimantic, CT: Curbstone Press, 2003.

Hermans, Theo. *Crosscultural Transgressions: Research Models in Translation Studies II, Historical and Ideological Issues.* Manchester, UK: St. Jerome Publishing, 2002.

Katan, David. *Translating Cultures: An Introduction for Translators, Interpreters and Mediators.* Manchester, UK: St. Jerome, 2004.

La Cruz, Sor Juana Inés de. *Poems, Protest, and a Dream.* Trans. Margaret Sayers Peden. New York and London: Penguin Classics, 1997.

Paz, Octavio. *Sor Juana, or The Traps of Faith.* Trans. Margaret Sayers Peden. Cambridge, Mass.: Harvard University Press, 1988.

Pym, Anthony. *Negotiating the Frontier: Translators and Intercultures in Hispanic History.* Manchester, UK: St. Jerome Publishing, 2000.

———. *Method in Translation History.* Manchester, UK: St. Jerome Publishing, 1998.

Sokol, Neal. *Ilan Stavans: Eight Conversations.* Madison: University of Wisconsin Press, 2004.

Stavans, Ilan. "Giving Spanish Its Due." *The Chronicle of Higher Education* (July 29), 2005.

———. "*La imaginación restaurada.*" *El español en el mundo. Anuario Cervantes.* Madrid: Círculo de Lectores, Instituto Cervantes, Plaza and Janés, 2004.

———. *Spanglish: The Making of a New American Language.* New York: HarperCollins, 2003.

———. *The Essential Ilan Stavans.* New York: Routledge, 2000.

———. with Harold Augenbraum. *Growing Up Latino: Memoirs and Stories.* Boston: Houghton Mifflin, 1994.

Venuti, Lawrence. *The Scandals of Translation: Towards an Ethics of Difference.* New York: Routledge, 1998.

———. *The Translator's Invisibility: A History of Translation.* New York: Routledge, 1995.

◆   Afterword:
     Spanish among Empires

Luis Martín-Estudillo and Nicholas Spadaccini

In Tommaso Campanella's oeuvre one can perceive some of the contradictions inherent to empires and the significance that languages have for their hegemonic impulses. As the prophetic participant in a failed 1599 Calabrian revolt against Spanish colonial rule, Campanella had to feign madness in order to avoid the death penalty. After enduring brutal torture, he spent twenty-seven years in a Neapolitan prison, a time he used to write a vast amount of literature which included philosophical and political works, among them *Monarchia di Spagna* (Spain's Monarchy), a text which supported the idea of a universal monarchy under the king of Spain. Given Campanella's antecedents, one can imagine that the Dominican friar wrote the *Monarchia* less out of admiration for the Spanish crown than out of respect for its power and its potential for defeating the formidable threat posed by the Turk. At the same time a victim and an apologist of the Spanish empire, an advocate of political change and a theocratic conservative, Campanella embodied the paradoxes of the baroque moment. Moreover, the importance attributed by him to the role of language in the imperial scheme was also characteristic of his time:

> Empires, Campanella argued, subject as are all the parts of God's universe to triadic distinction, are founded upon three things: language, wealth, and the sword. These,

in their turn, are instruments of *prudentia and fortuna*. "Language," he wrote, "is the instrument of religion, of prudence, that is, of the goods of the soul. The sword is the instrument of the body and of fortune, while wealth has only the status of a secondary instrument of the body." Of the three, by far the most important was language, something that, he claimed, the Spaniards "understood by instinct." (Pagden 55)

It may not have been "instinct," but rather a long tradition of linking political interests to linguistic policies, an option that Nebrija had famously synthesized in his *Gramática*—as we have been reminded throughout this volume—following a commonplace dictum imported from Italy through Aragon (Alvar in Elliott 27). Interestingly, Campanella not only defended the instrumental importance of the master's language for imperialistic purposes, but also urged in pragmatic fashion the teaching of Arabic instead of Greek and Hebrew as a way of combating the infidels, "thus reviving not simply the interests of Raymond Lull and the Council of Vienne but, more immediately, current Iberian educational practices all too inadequately applied" (Headley 216).

Campanella's observations, made in the intersection of his commitment towards, and resistance to, Spanish Hapsburg rule, are by no means unique. The instrumental and symbolic role of languages in the rise and sustenance of empires had been a topic of discussion at least since Virgil's Rome, and it has regained momentous status in present-day debates on this general topic. Thus, Michael Hardt and Antonio Negri, who understand "Empire" as "a new form of sovereignty [. . .] that governs the world" (xi), have emphasized the dependence that this novel type of post-national imperialism has on informational, and therefore, communicative, exchanges. Hardt and Negri argue that this "decentered and deterritorializing apparatus of rule" (xii) "takes form when language and communication, or really when immaterial labor and cooperation, become the dominant productive force [. . .] The superstructure is put to work, and the universe we live in is a universe of productive linguistic networks. The lines of production and those of representation cross and mix in the same linguistic and productive realm" (385). Language then is not only seen as a symbolic element framing relations and shaping worldviews, but also as an essential constituent of the new, post-industrial economies. Nevertheless, one might notice that nation-states are still strong actors on the global scene so that the concept of nation might still be deemed to be necessary as an important category linked to empire (see also Bruce Campbell in this volume).

The significance of global linguistic networks has facilitated what some have viewed as a neo-imperialist expansion of Spanish-based companies in

Latin America. Taking advantage of the secular financial, cultural, and linguistic relationships between the former metropolis and the American republics, an entrepreneurial group of "new conquistadors" (as they have been called by critics: see Estefanía; Arce 103; del Valle 159) such as Telefónica, BBVA or Repsol-YPF have penetrated the region without bothering to mute the neocolonialist overtones of their rhetoric. These enterprises have elicited nationalistic reactions in the former colonies, such as those evidenced in Argentina during its last financial and political crisis, which President Kirchner partly blamed on foreign investors, protesting the *conquistadors'* control over some essential public services (Arce 99–103). Other reactions have been occasionally associated with movements defending the rights of indigenous groups which have been marginalized culturally and economically for centuries by the local, Spanish-speaking elites and which now see global competition as a window of opportunity to fight for social justice, as has been the recent case in Evo Morales's Bolivia (Lewis) and the nationalization of its natural gas fields.

In the case of Spain, the most recent American expansion has contributed to the explosive growth of its economy within the broader context of the European Union. In some ways, Spain's development can be related to that of Ireland (the other Western European country which has undergone major development during the last few years) in that both nations have benefited greatly from belonging to major cultural and linguistic areas, an important advantage when exploiting financially those vast networks of "immaterial labor and cooperation," to use Hardt and Negri's expression. The impact of these global economic developments on the Spanish language is obviously not restricted to Spain. It is worth mentioning that Brazilian authorities have expressed great interest in the teaching of Spanish in all of that nation's schools, mainly with an eye towards the consolidation of Brazil's strong position in the economy of South America (especially since the creation of Mercosur in 1991). Meanwhile, a growing number of U.S. college students see Spanish as an important tool for professional success in this country.

What stands out from these facts is a growing awareness of the relevance that linguistic and cultural affinities hold for the latest developments of capitalism. This has focused increased attention on the economic dimension of certain symbolic practices whose material impact was previously disregarded. Thus, a recent estimate of the economic importance of Spanish language-related services in Spain is said to be in the order of 15 percent of GDP, and 9.4 percent of the world's GDP when they are added to those of Latin America and the U.S. (Lodares 60).

But there are a number of less tangible, although equally important, factors that play a role in the equation language/empire in a globalized world. Tensions arise when groups displaced by the forces of the globalized economy begin to organize through the construction of networks of symbolic kinship which may seem threatening to other groups. As we have seen in the U.S. during the Spring of 2006 with the case of thousands of galvanized Hispanics, the humanitarian demands of undocumented immigrants generate anxieties in the mainstream population especially when those demands are codified in (or around) a language other than the dominant one; i.e., when the manifest use of Spanish is performed as a cohesive element that does not hide difference at the same time that it emphasizes a will of belonging to a national community. This kind of tension was made particularly patent with the April 2006 release of "Nuestro Himno," a Spanish version of "The Star-Spangled Banner" which originated passionate discussions that found an echo even at the White House:

> Asked at a news briefing in the Rose Garden [. . .] whether he believed the anthem would have the same value in Spanish as it did in English, Mr. Bush said flatly, "No, I don't." (Rutenberg)

Opponents perceived the translated anthem as a sign of "cultural balkanization," while supporters defended it as a way of helping Spanish speakers to "fully understand the character of 'The Star-Spangled Banner,' the American flag and the ideals of freedom that they represent" (music producer Adam Kidron as quoted by Rutenberg). It is a matter of fact, however, that the notion of Spanish as a "foreign" language in the U.S. can prove rather misleading, since it has been spoken by inhabitants of certain parts of the country (especially the Southwest) since well before their incorporation to or annexation by the Union.

Although statistically speaking it would be easy to attribute minority status to Spanish within the U.S., it is interesting to notice that such is not always the case. In fact, there have been voices within North American Hispanism that have denounced the hegemonic status of Spanish in this academic field, arguing that the overwhelming presence of Spanish (and of topics directly associated with this language) in classrooms and in research areas tends to silence "other" enriching cultures and traditions which are also minoritary in their respective countries. The idea seems to be that where Spanish predominates, there is less recognition of "minorized" languages. This kind of criticism has great value as it helps us to constantly rethink what we do as intellectuals and how we do it, contributing to an awareness of practices which run the risk of becoming totalizing enterprises.

Yet, one cannot escape from certain practical realities, as is the case with the study of Spanish at U.S. universities (where the majority of students take Spanish for pragmatic reasons) or with the mere size of the cultural production in this language in contrast with that of others such as, for example, Quechua, Nahuatl, Basque, or Galician, or even other "major" languages such as French, German, or Italian (Spadaccini 313). Moreover, such position tends to ignore the fact that in some (not all, but also not minor) sectors of the U.S. academy, Spanish is perceived as having less symbolic weight than English in the criticism of Hispanic cultures and literatures.

The essays in this volume of *Hispanic Issues* seem to show how various approaches and theoretical models used to discuss (or even program) the connections between language and empire must ultimately be seen in conjunction with the practices of specific communities with varying degrees of agency, whether from above or from below. Language and empire are concepts whose articulation requires an understanding of a multiplicity of related issues, which range from a discussion of specific languages—in this particular case, Spanish and its relation to other languages in Spain, Latin America, and the U.S.—specific time frames—from the period of conquest and colonization of the Americas to independence and nation-building, to a present time characterized by constant tensions between the nation-state and globalizing forces—and different ways of imagining and confronting the complex relationships between them.

Juan R. Lodares argues in this volume that within the Spanish Empire there was an acceptance of a multiplicity of languages and that it is misleading to equate imperial and linguistic hegemony. He also points out that, ironically, Spanish spread precisely "when imperial power waned" and trade with the ports of America was liberalized toward the end of the eighteenth century. Lodares also argues, convincingly, that the spread of the Catholic faith was "antithetical to linguistic unification" (13)—a point, one might add, that was to be reemphasized by Vatican II with its stress on the use of the vernacular to propagate the message of Christ. The early Spanish State did not have a linguistic policy per se; rather, it had multiple linguistic strategies depending on specific interests and contexts. In the case of indigenous languages, their most zealous proponents were in fact religious orders, among them Franciscans, Dominicans, Augustinians, and Jesuits, who were also relying on the authority of the papal bull *Sublimis Deus* (1537). However, there was a noticeable change in the reality of these linguistic practices over time, due mainly to market pressures (from which the Church was not free), the diminishing influence of the indigenists, and the overall dynamics that regulate people's uses of languages according to their needs. Such is the case with Spanish, which has become a *lingua franca* in certain contexts marked by a plurality of languages. One might mention, for instance, the case of Latin American countries where different indigenous languages are spoken in addition to Spanish, or Spain, where speakers of Galician, Basque and Catalan switch to Spanish in discussing matters of mutual concern. In the end, these issues cannot be dealt with simply along theoretical lines, but must be weighed against the practical interactions that occur in everyday negotiations, which are usually guided by principles of economy of language.

Fernando Ordóñez explores the linguistic policies at the borders of the Spanish empire, arguing that Jesuits' approach to evangelization—which included a resettlement (*reducciones*) program—was a "utopian representation" of the "Christian empire." The Jesuits instructed their Amerindian flock in a language called *Guaraní jesuítico*, which they created from a language of the Tupi-Guarani linguistic family. This language was to persist even after the Jesuits' expulsion in 1767. The Guarani of the settlements were given a new language and a new voice, but no real agency. For a while at least, they received more humane treatment, even if that meant destroying their previous way of life in order to save them both physically and spiritually in accordance with the principles of the Christian faith. Despite these attempts, which involved, among other things, the imposition of a language, the experiment was eventually unsuccessful because it could not survive the destructive logic of the empire as imposed from its center.

Juan C. Godenzzi reviews the general linguistic situation during the colonial period along three fundamental lines: Spanish hegemony, the use and expansion of Quechua for purposes of evangelization and administrative control, and the difficult subsistence of numerous other languages, many of which were eventually to disappear (52). His essay focuses on a "social and historical revision of the Andean linguistic formation" in order to ultimately discuss the relationship between language and empire for purposes of seeing how language functions both as a tool of domination and as an instrument of resistance. In discussing imperial languages as instruments of decolonization, Godenzzi focuses on Quechua as a "Pan-Andean symbol of 'indigenous authenticity,'" despite the fact that it came to some indigenous peoples through imperial expansion. Godenzzi's larger point is that the power of languages goes beyond "the time and space of empires" and relies instead on human needs to communicate (62). Thus, despite ever-changing policies dictated from above, it is the need of certain social groups struggling to find their own physical and symbolic spaces which matters most.

José Antonio Giménez Micó connects Arguedas' posthumous novel *El zorro de arriba y el zorro de abajo* and its use of a "corrupted" language with current polemics regarding Peruvian identity. Giménez Micó argues that despite a growing official recognition of cultural and linguistic diversity in the Andean nation during the last few decades, there persists resistance from certain groups to the emergence of "Chicha culture," one shaped by the encounter of Andean migrants to the coastal cities of Peru who express themselves through a "Babelian" Spanish which does not follow the normative standard (113). This is said to have been anticipated by Arguedas in the approach to deterritorialization which vertebrates his novel and illustrates a complex social conflict which goes beyond "the unequal relationships between two languages—or two varieties of the same language" (109).

Edmundo Paz-Soldán questions the boundaries associated with the category of "Latino/a" especially if it excludes expatriate writers from Spanish-speaking countries who work in the U.S. He advocates a broader, more flexible, understanding of that concept to include individuals with a problematic position within the U.S. literary system. Such is the case with Spanish-born authors (he mentions Concha Alborg) who write in both Spanish and English but whose labeling as Latino/a has found resistance from critics with a more rigid approach to that category. At the same time, Paz-Soldán argues against identifying a national literature with a dominant language, most especially in a country of immigrants such as the U.S where several linguistic and literary traditions have historically flourished. (On this and related topics, see also Shumway).

John M. Lipski reviews the polemics surrounding Spanglish, showing how, to varying degrees, its initial negative assessment in intellectual circles has persisted until this day, even if there has been increased interest among certain intellectuals and political activists to view it in a more positive light. Lipski's own position is that "there is no 'third language' or cohesive Spanglish to be found anywhere in this country" (213), pointing to differences in each Latino speech community, for each "retains the major dialect features of the countries of origin, together with the inevitable dialect leveling in urban areas where several regional varieties of Spanish are in daily contact" (214). For Lipski, "Spanglish will always be a signpost on the wrong road, a road whose many way-stations range from misunderstanding to intolerance" (215).

Clare Mar-Molinero explores the role of Spanish as a "linguistic colonizer" taking into account the relationship between language and identity, the relevance of national language policies, and the role of particular agents such as Spain's Instituto Cervantes. Following Blommaert, Mar-Molinero argues that "the world's interconnectiveness is best understood in terms of power and dominance, reminiscent indeed of empires and imperialism" (156). In the discussion of agency in connection with the question of empire and imperialism, there is an acknowledgement of the role of organizations that go beyond state entities to include multinational corporations, especially those related to global media and leisure, as well as "international political elites" (157).

Turning to the case of Spain's language policies, particularly as related to the work of the Instituto Cervantes, Mar-Molinero seems to be focusing on "top-down" policies while acknowledging, at the same time, that they are not always effective within certain contexts. Other concepts used in her essay include Kachru's notion of concentric circles to better dissect the Spanish-speaking community today, and Coupland's ideas regarding processes of interdependence, the compression of time and space, commodification, and disembedding to analyze the status of Spanish in the global era. The latter notion is particularly useful as it offers an explanatory model for the emergence of an international variety of Spanish, which oscillates between certain homogenizing tendencies and a propensity toward hybridity.

Mar-Molinero's assessment of the work of the Instituto Cervantes is quite accurate. Yet, one might ask if the Instituto's mission could realistically go beyond the symbolic and practical acknowledgement of the various linguistic realities of Spain and other Spanish-speaking nations and communities. One could imagine the reaction of certain organizations associated with other languages within plurilingual communities if the Instituto sought to enter their spheres of influence in order to "appropriate" their symbolic productions. Of course, the Instituto, by definition, is a conservative organization funded by the Spanish central government whose goals are both cultural and economic, and whose agency, in practical terms, might be said to be somewhat limited. In other words, who, in the Latino communities of the U.S., or among other groups which have an instrumental approach to Spanish as it serves their communicative needs in complex contexts, really cares about the Instituto Cervantes and its expressed (or implicit) agendas?

On the issue of agency in connection with the topic of Spanish and imperialism, Ilan Stavans also seems to give undue weight to the Spanish Royal Academy of Language (RAE) and its *Dictionary* as repressive entities. One wonders how effectively repressive is an institution whose members are usually elderly scholars and writers with no executive power beyond the walls of the Academy. While it is true that the RAE would be horrified by certain uses of the language both within and outside Spain, in the end its influence is limited to the symbolic realm, where it is, at best, modest. While Stavans's defense of

Spanglish as "a state of mind," and as "a legitimate form of speech" which also offers "an opportunity to appreciate the creation of a new minority culture in the United States" (224), is quite suggestive, one could well argue, along with Lipski (in this volume), that the plethora of Latino speech communities in the U.S. resists the notion of a unified language, no matter how attractive the latter might be from a creative point of view. Certainly, considering the provenance of Latinos from so many different cultural and linguistic backgrounds and their exposure to different experiences in their daily lives in various parts of the U.S. (from Los Angeles' City Hall to Spanish Harlem in New York to the neighborhoods of Chicago or Atlanta or the towns of the Upper Midwest), it is difficult to reduce their diversity to a single, unitary form of speech.

Identity issues associated with immigration and bilingualism are explored by Susan Campbell as she analyzes the work of Nuyorican poet Tato Laviera as a contestatory discourse which privileges marginality and Africanness within the conservative context of the Reagan era. According to Campbell, Laviera's work has a "*plena* quality" (*plena* being a popular Puerto Rican music form) which "denies the supremacy of what is conventionally thought of as the center" (127), even if his denunciation of social inequality and racism does not encompass alternatives.

Issues of immigration, bilingualism, and national identity are also dealt with by Thomas Harrington, who reflects on the work and life of the Majorcan polygraph Joan/Juan Torrendell to examine the possibilities for a reconsideration of peripheral Iberian nationalist discourses toward the end of the nineteenth and the beginning of the twentieth centuries (1890–1920). Those discourses tended to "imitate, and install as normative, the monistic logic of Castilianism . . . at the expense of the long-standing history of co-existence and co-operation between them" (70), something which was duplicated to some extent by the national movements of the Southern Cone. Torrendell's work in the multi-cultural environment of Buenos Aires and Montevideo, as well as in the Balearic Islands and Catalonia, advocated for a more flexible understanding of national identity issues and the need to establish "respectful dialogue between disparate cultural options" (87).

Bruce Campbell studies the cultural politics of empire through an analysis of recent Mexican graphic narratives and argues for going beyond the well-known position of Armand Matterlart and Ariel Dorfman in *How to Read Donald Duck* (1971), with its reliance on a binary construction of empire/nation, following the assumption of an invasive imperialist culture and a unified national identity. Some thirty-five years after the above-mentioned study, empire and nation are now "points of reference for the cultural dimension of globalization" (175). North-South power relations cannot be seen as unidirectional (as García Canclini and others have shown) if one thinks of U.S. influences in Latin America and the growing latinization of U.S. culture and society. Moreover, during the last twenty years there has been an increasing expansion of economic ties between Spain and Latin America, a relationship that is by no means unidirectional, as the substantial economic presence of Spanish multinationals in Latin America is matched by an ever-greater presence of Latin American immigration to Spain.

In the *historietas* analyzed by Bruce Campbell, there emerge contrasting views of modernization "even within the neo-liberal consensus of U.S. hegemony" (192). Thus, the reader will not always find "optimistic visualizing of globalization as the royal road to modernization" (188), as can be seen in *Operación Bolívar*, in which the nation bears a resemblance to what anthropologist Guillermo Bonfil Batalla identified as an unofficial 'deep Mexico,' "a nation dating to the ruptures of the conquest, a fusion of indigenous and popular cultures obscured by officialdom and preyed upon by the forces of modernization" (192).

From the discussions undertaken in this volume, there emerges a realization that paying close attention to the contexts where Spanish is spoken might well be the key to an understanding of the different, and sometimes contradictory, roles that the language of Cervantes, Sor Juana, and *Operación Bolívar* has played across the centuries in a world that could now be described as a global semiosphere. At the same time, one might also keep in mind that while contexts impact upon meanings, they are far from being "natural" realities, insofar as they are shaped by a complex set of forces, each with its own specific interests. Furthermore, contexts can be conceptualized—and thus constructed—from a number of intellectual positions.

The processes resulting from the currently prevalent framework of planetary interconnectedness experienced a decisive impulse with the introduction of Spanish to the Americas (including the U.S.), where it was to come in contact with other languages within a variety of social, economic, and cultural realities. Today Spanish might be viewed from a double (and often overlapping) perspective: as both a central and a marginal communicative instrument which, within the tensions of globalization, can be said to enjoy a privileged standpoint, one from which speakers can negotiate their position on the global scene and scholars can observe the different phenomena that are forging brave new networks.

Works Cited

Arce, Alberto. "Las inversiones españolas en Argentina." *Política Exterior* XVIII. 101 (september-october 2004): 97–106.
Elliott, John H. *Lengua e imperio en la España de Felipe IV*. Salamanca: Ediciones Universidad de Salamanca, 1994.
Estefanía, Joaquín. "Ambiciones globales de las multiespañolas." *El País*, April 30, 2006.
Hardt, Michael, and Antonio Negri. *Empire*. Cambridge, Mass.: Harvard University Press, 2000.
Headley, John M. *Tommaso Campanella and the Transformation of the World*. Princeton, N.J.: Princeton University Press, 1997.
Lewis, Tom. "Hope and Challenge in Bolivia: Will Evo Morales End Neoliberalism?" *International Socialist Review* 46, March-April 2006.
Lodares, José Ramón. "La batalla de las lenguas en la Unión Europea." *Revista de Occidente* 278–279 (julio-agosto 2004): 51–78.
Pagden, Anthony. *Spanish Imperialism and the Political Imagination: Studies in European and Spanish-American Social and Political Theory 1513–1830*. New Haven and London: Yale University Press, 1990.
Rutenberg, Jim. "Bush Enters Anthem Fight On Language." *New York Times*, April 29, 2006.
Shumway, Nicholas. "Hispanism in an Imperfect Past and an Uncertain Present." *Ideologies of Hispanism*. Ed. Mabel Moraña. Hispanic Issues 30. Nashville: Vanderbilt University Press, 2005. 284–99.
Spadaccini, Nicholas. "Afterword." *Ideologies of Hispanism*. Ed. Mabel Moraña. *Hispanic Issues* 30. Nashville: Vanderbilt University Press, 2005. 311–20.
Valle, José del. "Spanish, Spain, and the Hispanic Community." *Interpreting Spanish Colonialism: Empires, Nations, and Legends*. Ed. Christopher Schmidt-Nowara and John M. Nieto-Phillips. Albuquerque: University of New Mexico Press, 2005. 139–61.

◆ Contributors

Verónica Albin is Senior Lecturer of Spanish and Translation at Rice University. She is the author of a book-long interview with Ilan Stavans called *Love and Language* (Yale University Press), forthcoming in 2007.

Bruce Campbell is Associate Professor of Spanish and Latino/Latin American Studies at the College of St. Benedict/St. John's University in Collegeville, Minnesota. He is the author of *Mexican Murals in Times of Crisis* (University of Arizona, 2003). His work on art, popular culture and cultural politics in the Americas has appeared most recently in the *Journal of Latin American Cultural Studies* and *XCP: Journal of Cross Cultural Poetics*. He is currently working on two book projects treating ideological conflict arising from economic globalization, one centered on Nicaraguan newspaper poetry and national identity, and the other examining Mexican graphic narrative. He is editor for the online translation project "Southern Voices" of americas.org, a publication of the Resource Center of the Americas.

Susan M. Campbell is an adjunct faculty member at the University of Milan, Bicocca. Her doctoral dissertation, *Nuyorican Resistance: Fame and Anonymity from Civil Rights Collapse to the Global Era* centers on the way Civil Rights inspired music and poetry functioned after the political movement declined. She has also published articles on salsa music as a neo-Baroque genre. She is currently working on an article tentatively titled "Carmen Boullosa's La otra mano de Lepanto," a "Partisan Truth" about the Mexican novelist's intertextual relationship with Miguel de Cervantes.

Kenya C. Dworkin y Méndez is Associate Professor of Hispanic Studies at Carnegie Mellon University, where she has taught Latin American and Latino Studies since 1993. Her research interests include Cuban, Cuban American, Latin American, U.S. Latino and Sephardic historical, theater, literary and cultural studies. Dworkin is co-editor of *Herencia: The Anthology of Hispanic Literature in the United States* (Oxford 2001) and *En otra voz: Antología de la literatura hispana de los Estados Unidos* (Arte Público 2002), *Recovering the U.S. Hispanic Literary Heritage Project. Volume V,* and has published numerous book chapters and articles on Tampa cigarworker theater, and Cuban and Latin American literature. She is also currently researching Sephardic-Latino identities in the U.S. and is the coeditor of *Latin American Jewish Studies.*

Nelsy Echávez-Solano is an Assistant Professor of Spanish at the College of Saint Benedict/Saint John's University in Collegeville, Minnesota. Her research interest include the implementation, facilitation, and evaluation of technology-enhanced language learning in foreign language classes; the role of error correction in language learning; the use of Spanish Creoles in contemporary Latin America, Caribbean Spanish, Latin American theater, and Latino theater in the United States. She is the author of *Computer Use in the Language Classroom* (2005), and is an Associate editor of Hispanic Issues.

José Antonio Giménez Micó is Associate Professor of Spanish and Latin American Studies at Concordia University (Montreal, Canada). He also holds the titles of Adjunct Professor at the University of Calgary (Canada) and *Professeur Associé* at the Université Laval (Quebec City, Canada). He is the author of *L'irruption des "autres"* (Montreal, Balzac/Le Griot, 2000). He has also written articles in English, French and Spanish on Latin American, Caribbean, Spanish and French literatures, as well as on semiotics, hermeneutics, and cultural studies. His current research, "Les conflits des imaginaires au Pérou et leur représentation dans des textes littéraires et non-littéraires," is his individual contribution to the international research group GRIPAL (*Groupe de recherche sur les imaginaires politiques en Amérique latine*). Giménez Micó is the president of the Canadian Association of Hispanists.

Juan C. Godenzzi is Associate Professor of Hispanic Linguistics at the University of Montreal, Canada. His books and essays center on language and Andean culture, Spanish in contact with Amerindian languages, and Bilingual Intercultural Education. Presently, his research examines the Spanish spoken in Lima, focusing on sociolinguistic variation, language contact and identity reconfigurations of Andean immigrants.

Thomas Harrington is Associate Professor of Contemporary Iberian Culture at Trinity College in Hartford, Connecticut. The primary focus of his research in recent years has been on the dynamics of "cultural commerce" (the strategically inspired transfer of cultural goods from one national cultural system to another) within early twentieth century Spain and Portugal as well as between the Iberian nations and the countries of the Caribbean and the Southern Cone. He has also published studies on Galician thought, Catalan cinema and ideas, the journalistic enterprises of José Ortega y Gasset, the history and function of Hispanism in North America and the development of Spanish Cultural Studies.

John M. Lipski is Professor of Spanish and Linguistics at the Pennsylvania State University. His research interests include Spanish phonology, Spanish and Portuguese dialectology and language variation, the linguistic aspects of bilingualism, and the African contribution to Spanish and Portuguese. Combining theoretical linguistics with empirical data he has done fieldwork on every continent and virtually everywhere that Spanish is spoken. He is the author of numerous articles and ten books, including *A history of Afro-Hispanic language: five centuries and five continents,* and *Latin American Spanish* (translated into Spanish and Japanese). He is the editor of *Hispanic Linguistics* and of a linguistics monograph series for Georgetown University Press.

Juan R. Lodares, 1959–2005. Spanish linguist and Professor of Spanish at the Autonomous University of Madrid. He is the author of numerous works about Spanish in a historical, political, and cultural context. Among his most noted publications are: *El paraíso políglota* (Taurus, 2000), which was a finalist for the Premio Nacional de Ensayo 2000, *Gente de Cervantes* (Taurus, 2001) and *Lengua y patria* (Taurus, 2002). He also frequently published in the mainstream Spanish media.

Clare Mar-Molinero holds a Ph.D. from the University of Southampton and is Reader in Spanish and Head of Modern Languages at the University of Southampton where she was also founding Director of the Centre for Transnational Studies. She teaches and has published widely on language policies and on global Spanish. Her publications include *The Politics of Language in the Spanish-speaking World* (Routledge, 2000), co-edited with Angel Smith *Nationalism and the Nation in the Iberian Peninsula* (Berg, 1996), and, co-edited with Patrick Stevenson, *Language Ideologies, Policies and Practices: Language and the Future of Europe* (Palgrave Macmillan, 2005). She has co-edited with Miranda Stewart *Globalisation, Language and the Spanish-Speaking World* (Palgrave Macmillan, forthcoming) where she develops her current interests in language and globalization. She is chair of the recently-formed International Association for the Study of Spanish in Society (SiS).

Luis Martín-Estudillo is Assistant Professor of Spanish and Cultural Studies at the University of Iowa. He has published several articles on Spanish literature and cultural history in American and European journals and is co-author of the book *Libertad y límites. El Barroco hispánico* and co-editor of *Hispanic Baroques: Reading Cultures in Context*. His research interests include the relationships between early modern and contemporary aesthetics and epistemologies. He is co-director of *Ex Libris, Revista de Poesía*.

Fernando Ordóñez is Graduate Instructor at the University of Minnesota, where he specializes in early modern Spain and colonial Latin America. He has taught in Uruguay and has held research fellowships in Italy. He is co-author of *Estudios socio-religiosos en el Uruguay* and has participated in many research projects dealing with social and cultural issues in Spain and Latin America. He is the former executive director of the OBSUR social science research center in Montevideo, Uruguay.

Edmundo Paz-Soldán is Associate Professor of Hispanic Languages and Literatures at Cornell University. He has published a book on the indigenista writer Alcides Arguedas, and has edited a book with Debra Castillo on Latin American Literature and Mass Media. He has also written articles on Bioy Casares, Huidobro, and contemporary authors such as Alberto Fuguet and Rodrigo Fresán. He has published six novels and three books of short stories, translated to several languages. He is the winner of the Juan Rulfo award for the novel, and the Bolivian National Book Award.

Nicholas Spadaccini is Professor of Spanish and Comparative Literature at the University of Minnesota. He has published books, editions, and collective volumes, with an emphasis on early modern Spain and Latin America. His most recent studies include *Libertad y límites. El Barroco hispánico* (co-autored) and *Hispanic Baroques: Reading Cultures in Context* (co-edited). He is currently completing a book on Cervantes and the culture of crisis of baroque Spain. He is editor-in-chief of the Hispanic Issues series.

Ilan Stavans is Lewis-Sebring Professor in Latin American and Latino Culture and Five-College 40th Anniversary Professor at Amherst College. His books include *The Hispanic Condition* (1995), *The Riddle of Cantinflas* (1998), *On Borrowed Words* (2001), *Spanglish* (2003), and *Dictionary Days* (2005). He is the editor of the four-volume Encyclopedia Latina (Scholastic), the three-volume *Isaac Bashevis Singer: Collected Stories* (Library of America), as well as *The Poetry of Pablo Neruda* (Farrar, Straus and Giroux), and *Lengua Fresca* (Houghton Mifflin). The recipient of numerous awards, including a Guggenheim fellowship and Chileans Presidential Medal, he is the host of the syndicated PBS show Conversations with Ilan Stavans.

◆ Index

Compiled by Eric Dickey

Aben Rabel, Ali, 237
Academia Argentina de Letras, 85
Academia Mayor de la Lengua Quechua, 55
Acosta, Father José de, 20, 24, 50
Acosta-Belén, Edna, 120, 123, 208
Agreda, Javier, 151n6
Aguilar, Father Plácido de, 18
Aguilera, Cristina, 161
Aguirre, José Antonio, 87
Aínsa, Fernando, 98
Ak'abal, Humberto, 236
Alarcón, Daniel, 150
Alatorre, Antonio, 224
Alborg, Concha, 142, 146–48, 150, 151n5, 251
Alcover, Joan, 79, 92n33
Aldrete, Bernardo de, 4, 7, 12, 13
Alfau, Felipe, 141, 224
Algarín, Miguel, 122, 123, 129
Almanac dels noucentistes, 82
Almirall, Valentí, 78
La Almudaina, 75, 77, 79, 80, 83, 91
Alomar, Gabriel, 76, 78, 79, 84, 86, 87
Alomar, Joan, 86
Alonso, Dámaso, 224
Alvarez, Julia, 144
Alvear, Manuel, 86

Alvo, Kate, 114n1
Amaru, Tupac, 54
Amengual, Bartomeu, 76, 80
The American Revolution, xx; as creation of English as *de facto* common language, xx, xxiv
Amerindian languages, 3, 21, 22, 24, 27, 28, 30
Amorim, Enrique, 83
Andean region, 98, 101, 106, 113; as linguistic formation, 48, 49, 51, 52, 55–58, 60, 61, 98, 250, 251
Anouilh, Jean, 226
Anqasa Amin or *Puerta de la Fe*, 13; in relation to the Koran and the Gosphels, 13
El año literario, 91n27
Aparicio, Frances, 124, 136n5, 136n8, 140, 144, 145, 151n7
Appadurai, Arjun, 175, 177, 194n8
Aquinas, St. Thomas, 14
Arandía, Pedro Manuel de, 29
Araújo, Orestes, 90n16
Arbol fructuoso, 18
Ardao, Arturo, 75
Arenas, Reinaldo, 143
Arguedas, José María, 98, 102–7, 109–13, 114n3, 114n5, 236, 251
Armesto, Fernández, 33

Arragel, Moses, 239
Atlántida, 83, 84, 91n28
Augustinians, 24, 38, 249
Aula Virtual Español (AVE), 166–68
Avila, Francisco de, 54
Ayala, Baltasar, 7
Azaña, Manuel, 87
Aznar, José María, 145
Aztec Empire, 35, 236
Azuela, Mariano, 143

Babel, Isaac, 222
Bain-Medgyesi, Emese, 233
Balestra, Alejandra, 143
Barajas, Rafael (El Fisgón), 180
Barca, Calderón de la, 19
Barker, Martin, 194n12
Barrenechea, Porras, 53
Barrios, Eduardo, 74
Barros, Juan de, 12
Bashevis Singer, Isaac, 142
Basque language, 15, 19, 20, 24
Batlle i Carreó, José, 90n16
Batlle i Grau, Lorenzo, 90n16
Batlle y Ordóñez, 73, 74, 82
Bautista Álvarez de Toledo, Juan, 4, 27, 30
Bello, Andrés, 220, 221, 234
Bellow, Saul, 241
La Ben plantada, 82
Benedetti, Mario, 230
Betanzos, Fray Domingo de, 24
Betanzos Palacios, Odón, 205, 206
Beyond Jet Lag, 146
Bianchi, Alfredo, 85, 92n35
Bilingual Intercultural Education (BIE), 61, 62n4
Bilingualism, xxii, xxiii, 122, 126, 253; and bilingual education, xxiii, 125
Bioy Casares, Adolfo, 85

Blanco, José María, 30
Blandengue, 73, 74, 84, 90n17
Blanes Viale, Pedro, 90n16
Blommaert, Jan, 156, 251
Boixodós, María Dolores, 142
Bolaños Cadena, Laura, 195n18
Bolívar, Simón, 186
Bonaparte, Napoleon, 6
Bonet Castellana, Antonio, 90n16
Bonfil Batalla, Guillermo, 192, 195n19, 254
Borges, Jorge Luis, 83, 141, 210, 230, 238, 240, 241
Borrás, Enric, 79
Boundary Treaty, xxviiin6
Braschi, Giannina, 150, 224
Brecher, Jeremy, 194n9
Brennan, Timothy, 194n10
Breve historia de México, 237
British Empire, xiii–xvi, xix, xxi, xxviiin3
Bruce-Novoa, Juan, 150
Buades Crespí, Joan 73, 90n15
Buena Vista Social Club, 161
Buigas, Cayetano, 90n16
Bunge, Carlos Octavio, 84
Burgos, Fausto, 84
Bush, George W., 177
Butrón, José, 16
Buxareo, Felix, 90n16

Cabello Balboa, Miguel, 50
Cabeza de Vaca, Alvar Núñez, 141, 143
Cabrera de Córdoba, Luis, 7
Cacique, 37, 42, 55
Calça, Francesc, 11
Calvet, Louis-Jean, 60
El cambio en México ya nadie lo para, 182
Cambó, Francesc, 82, 87, 92n35

Campanella, Tommaso, 245, 246
Campbell, Bruce, xxiii, 246, 253, 254
Campbell, Susan, xvi, 253
Canterbury Tales, 233
Capdevila, Arturo, 224
Caras y Caretas, 83
Cardona de, Hernando, 10
Caro Baroja, Julio, 19
Carrau, Juan, 90n16
La Carreta Made a U-Turn, 130
Carrió Trujillano, Bartomeu, 91n21
Casariego, Martín, 140
Casas, Fray Bartolomé de las, 23
Casas, Ramón, 76
Castells, Manuel, xiii; and "network society," xiv, xv
Castillejo, Cristóbal de, 12
Castilla, Father Gregorio de, 18
Castillo, Debra, 141, 142, 144, 150, 151n5
Castillo, Diego del, 16
Castrillo, Alonso de, 7
Castro, Xosé, 207
La Cataluña, 80–82, 87, 92n34
Catecismo y Sermones, 44
Certeau, Michel de, 126, 129–31, 135
Cervantes, Miguel de, 4, 219, 225, 227, 239, 241, 254
Chang-Rodríguez, Eugenio, 103, 104
Charchoaga de, Juan, 8
Chaucer, Geoffrey, 233
Chávez, Hugo, 194n11
Chávez-Silverman, Suzanne G., 224
Cholo, 97, 108–11; and Alejandro Toledo, 97, 112
Chornos, 224
Cibils, Jaime, 90n16
Cisneros, Sandra, 144, 145
La ciudad, 80, 81
Claramunt, Tomás, 90n16
Clarín y su ensayo, 76

Clement, Edgar, 175, 192
Clemente, Roberto, 128
Clemente, José Edmundo, 240
Colloquis de la insigne ciutat de Tortosa, 9
Colomer, M.A., 86
Colonialism *see also* colony, xv, xvi, xxvii, 48, 100, 101, 118, 120, 158, 220, 228, 235, 239, 242, 250; and imperialism, xv
Colony *see also* colonialism, xv, 60, 133
Columbus, Christopher, 35, 36, 53, 203, 235
Comentarios Reales, 238
Cómo sobrevivir al neo-liberalism sin dejar de ser mexicano, 180
Compte i Riqué, Enriqueta, 90n16
Condori Mamani, Gregorio, 58
Congreso de la Lengua Española, 155
III Congreso Internacional de la Lengua Española, 225
Conquista Espiritual del Paraguay, 39
Corpus Christi, 101; as Eucharistic celebration, 100
El Correo de Cataluña, 83
Cortázar, Julio, 180
Cortés, Félix, 135n3
Cortés, Hernán, 235
Cortijo, Rafael, 128, 136n11
Costa I Llobera, Miquel, 79
Costello, Tim, 194n9
Cotacachi, Mercedes, 61
Council of the Indies, 19
Council of Lima, 20
Council of Mexico, 23
Council of Trent, 15, 53
Council of Vienne, 246
Coupland, Nikolas, 161, 162, 252

Covarrubias, Sebastián de, 234
Crawford, James, 170n2
Criollo, xx, 25, 26, 30, 98, 101, 109, 111, 113
Criticón, 238
Cruz, Sor Juana Inés de la, 236, 241, 254
Cruz-Malavé, Arnaldo, 121–23, 135n4
Cuban War of Independence, xxi, 73; and rise of American dominance, xxi
Currita Albornoz, 76

Da Vinci, Leonardo, 186
Darío, Rubén, 229, 241
De Procuranda Indorum Salute, 20
Debeljak, Alex, 223
La Décima Musa, 236
Declaration of Independence, 230
Deleuze, Gilles, 104, 107, 109
Despuig, Cristobal, 9
Diario de Barcelona, 79
Díaz de Saavedra, Hernán, 40
Díaz de Solís, Juan, 38
Diccionario de la Lengua Española (DRAE), 240, 252
Dictionary Days: A Defining Passion, 220, 223
Diet of Works, 33
Dietrich, Wolf, 41
Dijk, Jan van, xiii
Dirección General de Instrucción Pública, 73
Doctrinero, 37
Dominicans, 24, 36, 38, 249
Don Quijote de la Mancha, 238
Donadíos, 33
Dorfman, Ariel, 174, 178, 179, 194n1, 253
D'Ors, Eugeni, 80, 82, 84, 89n10

Dou, Ignacio, 11
Dualismo, 102–4; and *Todas las sangres*, 103
Dreyfus Affair, 77
Dworkin y Méndez, Kenya C., 152

Echenique, Alfredo Bryce, 143
Editorial Tor, 84
Eisenstadt, Shmuel Noah, xii
Els dos esperits, 79
Els Encarrilats, 78, 79
Empire, xi–xiv, 4, 33, 49, 62, 133, 156, 173, 174, 178, 179, 192, 220, 237–39, 241, 242, 245, 246, 248–50, 252, 253; as English language, xi, xiii, xv, xvi, xix–xxi, xxiii, xxvii, xxviiin2, 10, 119, 121, 122, 124–26, 139–42, 144–50, 152n8, 156–58, 160, 162, 164, 173, 174, 198–201, 203–11, 214, 224–28, 230, 231, 233, 236, 241, 242, 249, 251; as epistemic crises, xi; as identity construction, xvi; as product of modernity, xii; as social formation, xii; as Spanish language, xi–xiii, xvi–xxvii, xxviin2, 4–11, 14, 16–19, 22, 24, 26–30, 32, 34–36, 43, 44, 48, 51, 52, 55, 56, 58–62, 63n4, 98, 99, 102, 105–11, 113, 114n3, 117, 119, 121, 122, 124–26, 132, 139–51, 152n8, 155, 156, 158–66, 168–70, 198–201, 203–11, 213, 214, 219, 224–26, 228, 230, 233–35, 237–40, 247–52, 254; in the creation of national identities, xii, 179; and the role of language, xvii–xix, xxiv, xxv, 245, 246
The Empire's Old Clothes, 174, 194n1
En otra voz, 143, 14

Enbaqom, 13
Encomienda, 36, 38, 39, 45n2
Entre Franco y Perón: Memoria e identidad del exilio republicano español en Argentina, 89n7
Erasmus, (Desiderius) of Rotterdam, 24
Escalante, Carmen, 58, 63n7
Escalas, Fèlix, 76, 78
Escobar, Alberto, 106, 110
Escobedo, Rodrigo de, 235
Esterrich, Carmelo, 122, 123, 136n5
Esteve, Josep, 10
Eurocentrism, xiv
European Union, 247

Fairclough, Marta, 205
Falcón, Angel, 135n3
Fantomas contra los Vampiros Multinacionales, 180
Fariña, Sara, 76
Faulkner, William, 141
Fernández Moreno Alfonsina Storni, Baldomero, 85
Ferreira, Eduardo, 73, 74, 90n13
Ferrer Barceló, Jaume, 73
Fígaro, 78
Figuerola, Laureano, 5
Fiol de Perera, Alejandro, 90n16
Flores, Juan, 118–20, 122, 123, 125, 126, 129, 130, 135n2, 135n3, 136n12
Fongivell, Antonio, 90n16
Fox, Vicente, 177, 182
Francesc Rossell, Joan, 10
Franciscans, 24, 25, 38, 249
Franco, Francisco, 233
Franco, Jean, 70
Fuentelapeña, Fray Antonio de, 23
Fuguet, Alberto, 139
Fujimori, Alberto, 97

Gadsen Parchase, xxviiin6
Galvez, Manuel, 84, 91n28
Gandhi, Mahatma, 183
Ganivet, Ángel, 85
García, Father Diego, 16
García-Camarillo, Cecilio, 224
García Canclini, Nestor, 126, 177, 179, 194n8, 195n13, 254
García Márquez, Gabriel, 240
Gracilaso, Inca, 238
Garibay, Ángel María, 236
General Law of Education, 55
Gervasio Artigas, José, 90n17
Gibbon, Edward, 222
Giddens, Anthony, 162
Giménez Micó, José, xxi, 114n3, 251
Giralt, Pedro, 90n16
Giró, Francisco, 90n16
Giusti, Roberto, 85, 92n35
Globalization, xi, xiii, xxiv–xxvi, xxvii, xxviin1, 155–57, 162, 163, 173–75, 177–82, 184–93, 225, 247, 249, 254; as cultural representation, 174, 175; as economy, xii, 247, 248; as national identity, 155, 163, 170; in relation to language, xi, xii, 155–58, 160, 161, 163, 246, 252
Godenzzi, Juan Carlos, xxi, 250
Goldemberg, Isaac, 144
Goldman, Francisco, 150
Gómez Andrín, Juan, 9
Gómez, Fernando, 45
Gómez de la Serna, Ramón, 83
Góngora, Luis de, 238
González, Luz Elena, 183, 184
González Biaña, Eduardo, 144
González Echeverría, Roberto, 204, 206
González Holguín, Diego, 54
González Torres, Victor, 183, 185

Goya, Francisco, 186
Gracián, Baltsar, 3, 238
Graell, Guillem, 81
Gramática de la Lengua Castellana, xvi–xviii, 6, 34, 53, 234, 238, 246
Granda, Germán de, 199
Greek Empire, xvii
Gregorio Torada, Nuria, 208
Guadalupe Posada, José, 186
Guaraní, xviii, xix, xxiii, 25, 40–45
Guaraní Sermons, 44
Guattari, Félix, 107, 109
Guerra, Juan Luis, 224
Guzmán, Luis de, 238, 239

Hamel, Rainer Enrique, 156, 157, 170n6
Hamon, Philippe, 114n2
Haqqiwa Qarwarupay, Luis, 63n5
Hardt, Michael, xiii–xv, 178, 194n10, 246, 247
Harrington, Thomas, xxi, 88n1, 88n2, 88n3, 91n19, 91n25, 253
Harrison, Regina, 63n8
Hastings, Adrian, 30
Hatfield, Charles D., 231
Haynes, Alberto, 83, 84
Hazm, Ibn, 6
Henríquez Ureña, Pedro, 234
Heredamientos, 33
Hernández Cruz, Victor, 121, 122, 125
Herrero, Sánchez, 37
Hijuelos, Oscar, 144
Hinds, Harold E., 195n15
Hinojosa, Ortiz de, 13
Historia de los Reyes Católicos, 7
Hitler, Adolf, 233
El Hogar, 83
Hornberger, Nancy, 59

How to Read Donald Duck, 174, 194n12, 253
Humboldt, Alexander von, 3, 30
Hunger of Memory, 226
Huntington, Samuel, 176–78, 194n6
Hüppuauf, Bernd, 162

Ibarz, Joaquim, 207
Ibsen, Henrik, 85
La idea imperial de Carlos V, 8
Iglesias, Enrique, 161
Imperialism, xi–xvi, xxi, xxvi, xxvii, 4, 5, 156, 157, 174, 203, 205, 246, 252, 253; as American hegemony, xxi, 174, 178; as epistemic crises, xi; as linguistic heterogeneity, 4; in relation to language, xi, xii, xix, 4, 157, 158, 245, 246
Incan Empire, 35, 48, 50, 52, 53, 55, 56, 58–61, 98
Industrial Revolution, xiii
Instituciones Latinas, 6
Instituto Cervantes, xxiii, 156, 160–62, 164–70, 251, 252
Instituto Popular de Conferencias, 85

Jaume y Bosch, Miguel, 90n16
Jesuits, xviii, 24, 29, 38–40, 42–45, 249, 250; and missions to Paraguay, xviii, xx, 32, 44, 45
Jiménez Román, Miriam, 133
Johnson, Samuel, 220
Juanicó, Francisco, 90n16
Junta de Instrucción Pública, 5

Kachru, Braj, 159, 252
Kafka, Franz, 105, 107, 110
Kanellos, Nicolás, 143
Kapsoli, Wilfredo, 56
Karp, Eliane, 113

Kennedy, John F., 127
Kennedy, Robert, 127
Kidron, Adam, 248
Killer Crónicas, 224
King Jr., Martin Luther, 128
Kipling, Rudyard, 85
Koen, Aaron, 233
Kunzle, David, 194n1

La Botz, Dan, 195n20
The Labyrinth of Solitude, 225
Lansky, Aaron, 233
Lapesa, Rafael, 224
Laviera, Tato, 117–19, 122, 124–35, 136n7, 253; as contestatory poetry, 117, 253; as *plena* music, 117, 127–29; and racial issues, 131–35
Laws of Burgos, 36
Lázaro Carreter, Fernando, 224
El lenguaje de Buenos Aires, 240
Leon, Luis de, 85
León Portilla, Miguel, 236
La ley y el amor, 75
Ley para la Educación Bilingüe Intercultural, 63n4
Ley General de Educación, 63n4
Ley de Preservación y Difusión de las Lenguas Aborígenes, 63n4
Libro Semanal, 175, 180, 181, 189, 190, 195n18
Los libros del saber de astronomía del Rey Alonso, 238
Lida, Raimundo, 224
Lienhard, Martin, 114n5
Lima Council, 53
Lippi-Green, Rosina, 163
Lipski, John, xxv, 215n2, 215n3, 216n4, 216n5, 251, 253
Lira, Nicolau de, 239
Llambí, Francisco, 90n16

Lloréis, Washington, 215n2
Loaysa de, Fray Rodrigo, 20, 21, 25
Loaysa de, García, 7, 8
Lodares, Juan R., xviii, 249
López, Jennifer, 161
López Medel, Tomás, 22
López Obrador, Andrés Manuel, 183, 193
López de Palacios, Juan, 7
López Solís, Luis, 26
Lorenzana, Francisco de, 27
Loriga, Ray, 141
Los de abajo, 143
Louisiana Parchase, xxviiin6
Luciano, Felipe, 120, 121, 123, 135n3
Lull, Raymond, 246
Lunfardo, 239, 240
Lyotard, Jean-François, 107

Macaulay, Thomas Babington (Lord Macaulay), 241, 242
"Maldita Ambición," 180–82, 186, 191; as graphic novel, 180
Malespina, Alejandro, 30
Mannheim, Bruce, 56, 62n1, 62n3, 63n8
Manso, Pedro, 15, 18, 20
Mapamundi, xiv
Mar-Molinero, Clare, xxiii, 170n1, 170n5, 251, 252
Maragall, Joan, 76, 78, 79, 81, 82, 87
Maravall, José Antonio, 34
Marcos Marín, Francisco, 160
Marías, Javier, 141
Marimon, Antoni, 72, 90n11
Martí, José, 143
Martin, Ricky, 161
Martín-Barbero, Jesús, xvi, 119, 124, 126, 130, 135

Martín-Estudillo, Luis, xxvii
Martínez de Cala y Jarava, Antonio, 234 *see also* Antonio de Nebrija
Martínez Estrada, Ezequiel, 83
Marxism, 118–24, 129, 135, 135n1, 178, 225
Más i Pi, Juan, 85
Máscara Azteca y el Doctor Niebla, 180
Las máscaras de la nada, 149
Massò, Magino, 18
La materia del deseo, 149
Matos Mar, José, 98
Mattelart, Armand, 174, 178, 179, 253
McClennen, Sophia, xxiii
McKinstry, H.E., 201, 202, 204
Medina, Francisco de, 12, 13
Melville, Herman, 141
Menchú, Rigoberta, 185, 236
Mencken, H.L., 201
Mendieta, Jerónimo de, 23
Menéndez Pidal, Ramón, 8, 224
Mercedarians, 38
Mestizo, xx, 20, 21, 25, 26, 30, 56, 101, 102, 105, 219, 235
Mexican-American War, xxviiin6, 228
Mexican Cession, xxviiin6
Mexican graphic novel, xxiv, 173–75, 179, 180, 186, 188, 191, 253; as comic art, 182–86, 192; as historieta, 173, 179–83, 189, 190, 195n18, 254; as transnational experience, xxiv
Mignolo, Walter, xxi, xxv, 40
Milán, William, 208
Modernisme (Mallorcan), 76–79
Monarchia di Spagna, 245
Monolingualism, xxvi
Monroe, Marilyn, 127

Montano, Arias, 7
Montes, Marisa, 215n1
Montoya, Rodrigo, 63n7, 63n8
Morales, Ed, 209, 210
Morales, María Eugenia, 224
Moreno Fernández, Francisco, 170n4
Moscoso, Juan Manuel, 54
Motis, Guirao, 91n24
Moya de Contreras, Pedro, 13
Moyano, Claudio, 5
Multilingualism, xxii, 23
El Mundo, 83
Mundo Argentino, 83
Muñoz Marín, Luís, 134
Muñoz Molina, Antonio, 141
Murillo, Marifer, 183

La nacionalitat catalana, 82
Nahuatl, 35, 38, 236, 249
Nash, Rose, 204, 205
Nation-State, 69, 173, 246, 249
Nebrija, Antonio de, xvi–xix, 4, 6, 7, 9, 10, 12–14, 30, 34, 35, 53, 62n2, 220, 221, 228, 233, 234, 238, 241, 246
Negri, Antonio, xiii–xv, 178, 194n10, 246, 247
Nervo, Amado, 85
Nietzsche, Friedrich, 78
North American Free Trade Agreement (NAFTA), 176, 177
Nosotros, 85, 86
Nova Palma, 78
Nuestra América, 84
Nunes, Duarte, 12
Nuyorican poetry, xvi, 117–27, 129–32, 134, 135, 136n6, 136n9, 136n12; as anti-hegemonic, 118; as bilingualism, 124, 125; and Civil Rights movements, 118, 124, 129, 135; as class-based/racial

struggle, 124; as marginalization, 127; and racism, 132

Olaguer Feliu, Antonio, 90n17
Oliver, M.S., 77, 78, 80, 87, 91n22
O'Maoil, Flaithrí, 15
O'Neill, Hugo, 14
Operación Bolívar, 186–88, 192, 254
Ordoñez, Fernando, xviii, 250
L'organ de la collectivitat de Pollença a l'Argentina, 86
Ortiz, Fernando, 224
Ostler, Nicholas, xxviiin4
Otero, Jaime, 170n4
Otheguy, Ricardo, 215n3

Padilla, Davila, 24, 140
Palaverish, Diana, 151n2
Pané, Ramón, 23
Paris de Oddone, M. Blanca, 90n16
Parnet, Claire, 104
Partido Revolucionario Institucional (PRI), 184
Paternostro, Silvana, 139, 150
Paz, Octavio, 219, 225
Paz-Soldán, Edmundo, xxiv, 251
Pedralbes, Adolfo, 90n16
Pedralbes, Joaquim, 90n16
Pedreira, Antonio S., 133
Peña, Father Alonso de la, 24, 26, 27
Pérez Petit, Victor, 74, 75, 84
Pérez Sala, Paulino, 199, 200
Phillipson, Robert, 157
El picaflor, 75
Picasso, Pablo, 186
Pietro, Pedro, 121
Pimpollos relatos, 76
Pinel, Duarte, 238
Pinpin, Tomás, 29
El Poble Català, 78

El político, 3
Poma de Ayala, Guaman, 60
Pons i Pons, Damià, 90n12, 91n18, 91n20
The Popular Overflow, 98
Postcolonialism, xi, xii, xv, xvi, xxii, xxiii, xxvi, xxvii; and colonialism, xv
Postmodernism, xv
Poza, Andrés de, 19
Pratt, Mary Louise, 100
La Prensa, 85
Primo de Rivera, Miguel, 15
El Procés de Montjuic, 77
Puiggros, Ernesto, 90n16

Quechua, xix, xxi, xxiii, 20, 30, 35, 48–60, 62, 63n4, 99–101, 105–13, 249, 250
Quevedo, Francisco de, 238
Quiroga Roberto Arlt, Horacio, 83

Rahola, Federico, 81
Rama, Ángel, xxiii, 101
Ramírez, Sergio, 139
Ramírez de Fuenleal, Sebastián, 24
Reagan, Ronald, 117
Real Academia Española, xxiii, 163, 240, 241
Reconquista, 33, 34, 51, 237
Reducciones, 38, 42–45, 53, 250
Repartimientos, 33
Rescaniere, Ortiz, 59, 63n7
Reyles, Carlos, 75
Ribera-Rovira, Ignasi, 81
Ricard, Paul, 25
Riqué, Benito, 90n16
Rivarola, José Luis, 63n7
Rivera, Lázaro de, 4, 30, 43
Roa Bastos, Augusto, 236
Rodó, José Enrique, 75, 90n16

Rodríguez, Richard, 226
Rohde, Jorge, 84
Roldós y Pons, Jaime, 90n16
Roman Empire, xvii, 6, 7, 12, 33
Rosenblatt, Ángel, 224
Rossell i Rius, Aleix, 90n16
Rousseau, Jean Jacques, 85
Roxlo, Carlos, 90n16
Rubenstein, Anne, 195n14
Rubial, Costa, 91n24
Rucabado, Ramón, 91n26
Ruiz de Montoya, Antonio, 39, 41, 42
Rushdie, Salman, 104
Rusiñol, Santiago, 76, 78

Sabat Ercasty, Carlos, 90n16
Sabina, María, 236
Sahagún, Fray Bernardino de, 236
Salaberría, Santiago de, 28
Salomón, Frank, 63n7
San Martín, Zorilla de, 76
Sánchez de Segovia, Rodrigo, 235
Sandoval, Alberto, 140, 144, 145, 151n7
Santiago, Esmeralda, 144
Santo Tomás, Domingo de, 51, 53
Santos, Mayra, 139
Sants Oliver, Miquel dels, 76, 79, 92n34
Saramango, José, 225
Sayers Peden, Margaret, 236, 237
Schwarzstein, Doris, 89n7
Se habla español, 139, 141, 152n8
Semanario Católico, 72
Sepp, Father, 25
Serrano, José, 44
Shakespeare, William, 85, 222, 231
Shumway, Nicholas, 251
Sid, Isak ibn, 237
Silva-Corvalán, Carmen, 216n5

Simon, Greg, 229
Singer, Roberta, 127
Society of Jesus, 38
Soler, Mariano, 90n16
Solidaritat Catalana, 82
Solórzano, Castillo, 7
Spadaccini, Nicholas, xxvii
Spanglish, xxv, xxvii, 117, 122, 124, 125, 145, 146, 152n8, 197–210, 212–15, 215n1, 219, 221–27, 240, 242, 251, 253; as code-switching, 208–13, 215n1, 215n4; and *Don Quijote*, 213, 219, 221, 224, 227; as *rascuache*, 225, 226
Spanish-American War, 229
Spanish Empire, xiii–xxii, xxvi, xxviiin3, 3–8, 10–14, 21, 24, 25, 29–32, 34, 36–39, 51, 53, 61, 99, 155, 233, 245, 246, 249, 250; as Catholic Church (Orthodoxy), xxvi, 15–18, 20, 21, 25–27, 30, 32, 35, 38, 44, 235; as colonization/conquest of "New World," xii, xiv, xviii, xix, xxvi, xxviii, 35, 36, 39, 51–53, 98, 99, 192, 224, 235, 237; and language education, xx, xxii, 7, 158, 163–69; as linguistic hegemony, xiv, xix, xxvi, 4, 5, 35, 48, 52, 57, 58, 61, 99, 100, 163, 173, 249, 250; as linguistic legislation, 5, 10, 21, 22, 26, 27, 32–34, 37, 42, 44, 53, 55, 56, 155, 156, 249–52; as linguistic unification, 11, 12, 14, 34, 35, 249; as multiplicity of languages, xviii–xx, xxii, xxiii, xxv, 3, 10, 34, 99, 249; and Spanish missionaries, 16, 20, 21, 23–25, 29, 30, 32, 36–38, 42, 44, 45, 54; as spread of Christianity (evangelization), 12–14, 20, 21,

23–27, 29, 32, 35–40, 43, 48, 54, 100, 130, 249, 250; as spread of language (Spanish), xx, xxv, 3–5, 12, 13, 21–23, 28, 30, 32, 36, 37, 40, 43, 48, 53, 55, 99, 100, 155, 157–59, 161, 163, 164, 249; as transculturation, 100, 102, 103, 107, 110, 113, 199, 235; as unification of Spain, xvii, 3, 51
Spanish Inquisition, 17
Spanish Regenerationism, 77
Stavans, Ilán, xxv, 139, 174, 194n2, 210–13, 219, 220, 252
Sublimis Deus, 23
Sueños digitales, 149
Summer Institute of Linguistics, 158
Sunyer I Capdevila, Francisco, 90n16
Synod of Charcas, 27
Taibo, Paco Ignacio, 180
Talking to the Río Grande, 224
Tarapaki Astu, Wikturyanu, 63n7
Tasso, Torcuato, 238
Tatum, Charles, 195n15
Tawantinsuyo, 99
Teixeira, Manuel de, 16
Tesoro de la lengua española o castellana, 234
Thebaldis, Aegidius de, 238
Tibón, Yehuda ibn, 238
Tío, Salvador, 200–204; as inventor of term *Spanglish*, 200
Todas las sangres, 102–4, 107; as reterritorialization, 107, 114n3
Toledo, Alejandro, 97, 98, 111–13; as Incan descendant, 98
Tomo Regio, 27
Torero, Alfredo, 52
Toribio, Almeida, 216n4
Torrendell i Escalas, Joan, 72–87, 90n10, 90n13, 90n17, 91n23, 91n27, 91n28, 91n29, 91n30, 92n31, 92n34, 92n35, 253; and emigration to Uruguay, 73
Torres, Bartolomé, 16
Torres, Fray Tomás de, 24
Torres-García, Joaquin, 89n10, 90n16
Tractatus Logico-Philosophicus, 222
Tratado de Libre Comercio, 28
Treaty of Guadalupe Hidalgo, xxviiin6, 228
Tupac Amaru, Gabriel, 60

La Última Hora, 77
Una noche en casa, 147
Unamuno, Miguel de, 78, 81
La Unión Republicana, 77, 78
Universitas Cristiana, 32, 33

Valderrama, Ricardo, 58, 63n7
Valdés Bernal, Sergio, 208
Valenzuela, Luisa, 144
Valera, Cipriano de, 238
Valle, José del, 145, 151n4
Valtanás, Domingo de, 12, 13
Vaquera, Santiago, 151, 152n8
Vargas, Jerónimo de, 238
Vargas Llosa, Mario, 113, 140
Varo, Carlos, 215n2
Vasconcelos, José, 25, 237
Vázquez de Menchaca, Fernando, 7
Vega, Ana Lydia, 224
Vega, Lope de, 19, 85, 238
Vehils, Rafael, 92n35
Vera, Edgar, 57, 63n6
Vértiz, Pedro, 28
La Veu de Catalunya, 80, 82
La Veu de Mallorca, 78
Victoria, Francisco de, 39
Vida, Francisco, 90n16
Vidal Sephiha, Haïm, 233
Vidiella, Francisco, 90n16
Vigil, Constancio, 83, 84

Villamajó, Julio, 90n16
Villardebó, Teodoro, 90n16
The Vision of the Vanquished, 236
Volpi, Jorge, 139
Voltaire, 85

Waisbord, Silvio R., 194n5
Wallerstein, Immanuel, xiii
War of Independence, 5
Wayas, Elizabeth, 183, 184
Westphalian Peace Treaty, 11
White, Steven F., 229
Wittgenstein, Ludwig, 222

Xirgu, Margarida, 90n16

Yapuguái, Nicolás, 44
Yo-Yo Boing, 224
Yupanqui, Tupac, 50

Zamenhof, Ludwik Lejzer, 232; and *Esperanto*, 232
Zapatista Movement, 193
Zentella, Ana Celia, 208–10
El zorro de arriba y el zorro de abajo, 98, 102, 104, 106, 107, 109–13, 251; as language, culture, ideology, and identity, 104; as "popular overflow," 98
Zumárraga, Fray Juan de, 24, 38, 45n3

VOLUMES IN THE HISPANIC ISSUES SERIES

34 *Spanish and Empire*
   edited by Nelsy Echávez-Solano and Kenya C. Dworkin y Méndez
33 *Generation X Rocks: Contemporary Peninsular Fiction, Film, and Rock Culture*, edited by Christine Henseler and Randolph D. Pope
32 *Reason and Its Others: Italy, Spain, and the New World*
   edited by David Castillo and Massimo Lollini
31 *Hispanic Baroques: Reading Cultures in Context*,
   edited by Nicholas Spadaccini and Luis Martín-Estudillo
30 *Ideologies of Hispanism*, edited by Mabel Moraña
29 *The State of Latino Theater in the United States: Hybridity, Transculturation, and Identity*, edited by Luis A. Ramos-García
28 *Latin America Writes Back. Postmodernity in the Periphery (An Interdisciplinary Perspective)*, edited by Emil Volek
27 *Women's Narrative and Film in Twentieth-Century Spain: A World of Difference(s)*, edited by Ofelia Ferrán and Kathleen M. Glenn
26 *Marriage and Sexuality in Medieval and Early Modern Iberia*,
   edited by Eukene Lacarra Lanz
25 *Pablo Neruda and the U.S. Culture Industry*, edited by Teresa Longo
24 *Iberian Cities*, edited by Joan Ramon Resina
23 *National Identities and Sociopolitical Changes in Latin America*,
   edited by Mercedes F. Durán-Cogan and Antonio Gómez-Moriana
22 *Latin American Literature and Mass Media*,
   edited by Edmundo Paz-Soldán and Debra A. Castillo
21 *Charting Memory: Recalling Medieval Spain*, edited by Stacy N. Beckwith
20 *Culture and the State in Spain: 1550–1850*,
   edited by Tom Lewis and Francisco J. Sánchez
19 *Modernism and its Margins: Reinscribing Cultural Modernity from Spain and Latin America*, edited by Anthony L. Geist and José B. Monleón
18 *A Revisionary History of Portuguese Literature*,
   edited by Miguel Tamen and Helena C. Buescu
17 *Cervantes and his Postmodern Constituencies*,
   edited by Anne Cruz and Carroll B. Johnson
16 *Modes of Representation in Spanish Cinema*,
   edited by Jenaro Talens and Santos Zunzunegui

15 *Framing Latin American Cinema: Contemporary Critical Perspectives*, edited by Ann Marie Stock
14 *Rhetoric and Politics: Baltasar Gracián and the New World Order*, edited by Nicholas Spadaccini and Jenaro Talens
13 *Bodies and Biases: Sexualities in Hispanic Cultures and Literatures*, edited by David W. Foster and Roberto Reis
12 *The Picaresque: Tradition and Displacement*, edited by Giancarlo Maiorino
11 *Critical Practices in Post-Franco Spain*, edited by Silvia L. López, Jenaro Talens, and Dario Villanueva
10 *Latin American Identity and Constructions of Difference*, edited by Amaryll Chanady
9 *Amerindian Images and the Legacy of Columbus*, edited by René Jara and Nicholas Spadaccini
8 *The Politics of Editing*, edited by Nicholas Spadaccini and Jenaro Talens
7 *Culture and Control in Counter-Reformation Spain*, edited by Anne J. Cruz and Mary Elizabeth Perry
6 *Cervantes's Exemplary Novels and the Adventure of Writing*, edited by Michael Nerlich and Nicholas Spadaccini
5 *Ortega y Gasset and the Question of Modernity*, edited by Patrick H. Dust
4 *1492–1992: Re/Discovering Colonial Writing*, edited by René Jara and Nicholas Spadaccini
3 *The Crisis of Institutionalized Literature in Spain*, edited by Wlad Godzich and Nicholas Spadaccini
2 *Autobiography in Early Modern Spain*, edited by Nicholas Spadaccini and Jenaro Talens
1 *The Institutionalization of Literature in Spain*, edited by Wlad Godzich and Nicholas Spadaccini

www.ingramcontent.com/pod-product-compliance
Lightning Source LLC
Chambersburg PA
CBHW030107Q10526
44116CB00005B/141